CIVILIZATION WITHOUT SEXES

WOMEN IN CULTURE AND SOCIETY

A series edited by Catharine R. Stimpson

MARY LOUISE ROBERTS

CIVILIZATION WITHOUT SEXES

RECONSTRUCTING GENDER IN POSTWAR FRANCE, 1917–1927

THE UNIVERSITY OF CHICAGO PRESS
Chicago & London

The University of Chicago Press, Chicago 60637
The University of Chicago Press, Ltd., London
© 1994 by The University of Chicago
All rights reserved. Published 1994
Printed in the United States of America
03 02 01 00 99 98 97 96   5 4 3 2

ISBN (cloth): 0-226-72121-3
ISBN (paper): 0-226-72122-1

Library of Congress Cataloging-in-Publication Data

Roberts, Mary Louise.
    Civilization without sexes : reconstructing gender in Postwar France, 1917–1927 /
Mary Louise Roberts.
        p.   cm. — (Women in culture and society)
    Originally presented as the author's thesis (Ph.D.—Brown University), 1990.
    Includes bibliographical references (p.) and index.
    ISBN 0-226-72121-3. — ISBN 0-226-72122-1 (pbk.)
    1. Sex role—France—History—20th century.   2. Women—France—Social con-
ditions.   3. World War, 1914–1918—Social aspects—France.   4. World War,
1914–1918—Women—France.   I. Title.   II. Series.
HQ1075.5.F8R63   1994
305.3′0944—dc20   93-26899
                                                                              CIP

For Jacqueline Roland

CONTENTS

FOREWORD

In 1917, World War I was in its third year of mud, rats, poison gas, and gangrene. Marshal Henri Pétain, the commander-in-chief of the French forces, was 61 years old. Léon Blum, the French Socialist who was to spend World War II in prison, was 45; Pierre Laval, a leading Nazi collaborator in the World War II government of Pétain at Vichy, was 34. The Lumière brothers, who had invented film technology, were in their 50s; Debussy, the composer, was 55; Marie Curie, the scientist, 50; Matisse, the painter, 48; Colette, the writer, 44. The next generation of French politicians, intellectuals, and artists had reached the age of ripe cannon fodder. Jean Renoir, the film director, was 23; André Breton, the writer, 21. The adults of World War II were children. Jean-Paul Sartre was 12; Claude Lévi-Strauss and Simone de Beauvoir, 9; Simone Weil, 8.

In 1918, a year later, the war had bled itself to an end. Its survivors recognized that civilization had changed irrevocably; for many, catastrophically. Moreover, from 1917 to 1927, France experienced, not only the transformations and dislocations that World War I caused, but a shift to a mass consumer economy. This decade is the subject of Mary Louise Roberts's poised, probing, lucid, compelling cultural history, *Civilization without Sexes: Reconstructing Gender in Postwar France, 1917–1927*.

Roberts's focus on gender serves two purposes. First, she analyzes changes in the French sex/gender system itself. World War I battered the structures, conventions, and images that regulated gender. Trench warfare gutted a masculinized portrait of the virile warrior. Women's performance of "male" jobs in the public labor force smeared a feminized portrait of the homebound lady. Second, Roberts has beautifully read Joan Wallach Scott's influential essay of the 1980s, "Gender: A Useful Category of Historical Analysis." Roberts knows that when a society talks about gender, it is always talking about both gender and *something else again*. This "something else again" includes identity, power, morality, and change itself. For example, jeremiads about new gender roles mask the fear that the moral order is collapsing. Conversely, a celebration of new gender roles debunks such fears. To understand a society's discourse of gender—messy and obsessive as it can be—is to understand a whole society. To grasp its construction of the female and the male is to grasp its hopes and fears, sense of social relations, and ethos—in brief, its "cultural economy." Roberts writes, "gender was central to how change was understood in the postwar decade. . . . Debate concerning gender identity became a primary way to embrace, resist, or reconcile oneself to changes associated with the war."

Like all reliable cultural historians, Roberts uses a wide variety of materials: the media, reports about fashion, school textbooks, social manuals, and government debates. Reading carefully and well, she draws most extensively on popular fiction. She argues that, during World War I, the French simultaneously blurred gender roles in daily life and polarized the cultural representation of women into two images: the good, patriotic mother, who protected the homefront, and the bad, pleasure-seeking wanton, who cavorted on the homefront while men suffered on the battlefront. The wanton's masculine counterpart was the war profiteer, raking in money and living in ease. Like vampires, the bad of both sexes betrayed and sucked the blood of good soldiers.

After World War I, the French constructed three images of women that dominated the quarrel about gender. The first, that of "the modern woman" *(la femme moderne)*, represented change. She was independent and sexually free. Flirting with boyishness as well as with a variety of boys and girls, she had short hair and a flapper's outfit. The second image, that of "the mother" *(la mère)* represented continuity and tradition. If the proper man served the state through sacrificing his body in war, the proper woman served the state through sacrificing her body in birth. Advocates of the mother feared that women, especially bourgeois women, were now choosing to *have* a life rather than to give life. The good mother, in France's cultural logic, was a part of the postwar natalist movement, which expressed "a fundamental ideological linkage between population and national strength." To make matters worse, any weakening of women's desire to mother threatened, not only the state, but veterans eager to prove their postwar virility through fathering a child.

The third image, that of the "single woman" *(la femme seule)*, was an unstable effort to mediate between the modern woman and the mother. She was economically independent but, unlike the modern woman, she was celibate. She might not bear children, but she would be abstinent. Ostensibly, the image of the single woman reflected a demographic fact. The French thought that male deaths in World War I meant there were far more marriageable women than men after the war. However, Roberts points out, the war did not skew the ratio of marriageable women to men that radically. The image of the single woman was also a cultural artifact felt to have the truth of a demographic fact. This image provoked a range of responses, some ludicrous. Doctors, for example, proposed polygamy as a solution to the grievous plight of a woman who had no home and husband. More usefully, the image of the "single woman" also occasioned debates about women's autonomy, status as citizens, and education: the upbringing of their minds, and bodies, and their working competencies.

Perhaps the subtitle, *Reconstructing Gender in Postwar France, 1917–1927,* is too modest for this book, for its last pages widen its perspective. Roberts, who has helped us to see a significant decade of French history anew, concludes by suggesting some of the implications of her study. I largely interpret her in this way. We must engage in constant cultural criticism of our narratives, dramas, and images— from the past and of the present. The more complex and volatile a society, the more complex and volatile its narratives, dramas, and images may be. As a textual garment, they form neither a seamless whole nor a transparent coat over "reality." They instead help to construct realities. The more a society changes, the more jagged, rent, and patched the garment of its texts will become. A changing society also creates a set of defense mechanisms against too traumatic an experience of change. Narratives, dramas, and images are among these mechaniams. A society will indulge in great bursts of nostalgia, longing to return to a past that sober analysis says is irretrievable. If a society cannot have the whole past, it will carry as much as it can on its back as it marches and wanders and wavers along. It will, for example, conjure up an image of home, hearth, and sexual difference. Of this image, it will say, "Everything can change but not this, never this. Here goodness must rest."

Finally, crucially, *Civilization without Sexes* shows us the political danger of one particular group of defenders of a "traditional" image of home, hearth, and sexual difference, a group that has high-profile contemporary descendents. In the France of the 1920s, these defenders wanted an old-style family. They also wanted industry, commerce, and technology to be spiffy, rationalized, up-to-date. The private sphere was to be conservative; the public sphere modern. During World War II, some members of this group gained a terrible power— as participants in the Vichy Government of Pétain.

Catharine R. Stimpson
Rutgers University

ACKNOWLEDGMENTS

GRANTS AND FELLOWSHIPS provided by the Council of European Studies, the Fulbright-Hays Program, the Social Science Research Council including the Roy O'Connor Tocqueville Fund, the National Endowment for the Humanities and Stanford University made the research for this book financially possible. I would like to thank these institutions for their generous research support. I would also like to thank Karen Wilson, Senior Editor at the University of Chicago Press, for her patience, enthusiasm, and unerring skill in bringing this book into the world.

This project would not have been completed without the intellectual and emotional support provided by teachers, colleagues and friends. At Brown, where this study was completed as a dissertation, I would particularly like to thank Mary Gluck for her intellectual inspiration, generosity, and friendship. I would also like to thank, at Brown, Mari Jo Buhle, Burr Litchfield, Tom Gleason, Naomi Lamoureaux, Becky More, and Elizabeth Weed. At Stanford, I am especially grateful to Judy Brown, Estelle Freedman, Aron Rodrigue, Paul Robinson, and Jim Sheehan. The book benefited enormously from their insights and guidance. Keith Baker was kind enough to read the entire manuscript at a decisive point and to give me invaluable advice. Karen Sawislak read draft after draft of most chapters and offered invariably good criticism. Her humor and unflagging support have made the adventure not only possible but fun.

Among my colleagues and friends, I would also like to thank the following for their help and support in the completion of this project: Andrew Aisenberg, Susanna Barrows, Marjorie Beale, Gail Bederman, Philippe Buc, Kathleen Canning, Terry Castle, Josh Cole, Sarah Farmer, Elizabeth Francis, Dan Gordon, Jennifer Jones, Carolyn Kay, Susan Kent, Suzanne Kolm, Cathy Kudlick, Rene Marion, Lynn McFarlan, Louise Newman, Dolores Peters, Tip Ragan, Becky Rogers, Sylvia Schafer, Vanessa Schwartz, David Scobey, Ann-Lou Shapiro, Jay Smith, Mary Steedly, Tyler Stovall, Regina Sweeney, and Glennys Young. In France, I would like to thank Geneviève Acker, Claire-Lise Chevalley, Françoise Monnoyeur, Michelle Perrot, Jean-Luc Pinol, Ann-Marie Sohn, Françoise Thébaud, and the staff at the Bibliothèque Marguerite Durand, who were consistently enthusiastic and helpful.

Lissa McLaughlin has been a constant source of creative inspiration throughout this project, as well as my most faithful friend. She has brought her gifts as a writer to both the translations and the prose of this book. Without her strength and her steadfast support, it would not have been written. I am also deeply grateful to my parents, Emmie and Jim Roberts, who have modeled excellence in all aspects of their lives and who, with my three sisters—Elizabeth, Pam, and Kathie— have given me the gifts of humor, encouragement and love.

Two teachers have been particularly important to the creation of this book. First, my most profound thanks go to Joan Scott, whose work on gender serves as the very premise of my own, and whose passion for French History inspired me to return to graduate school in the first place. Through Joan, I was, to use Dickens' phrase, "recalled to life." She nurtured this project from its inception, carefully and patiently reading proposals and chapters, alternating criticism and encouragement in just the right proportions and at just the right times. She made it possible for me to spend the 1988–89 academic year at the Institute for Advanced Study in Princeton, a year during which I wrote a first draft of five chapters of this book. Most importantly, she has helped me to envision what the life of a woman scholar can mean, that power can be justly and generously used, that intellectual work must be disciplined yet passionate and politically engaged, that teaching is an enabling and affirming activity, that the study of women's history is a project worth our consciences and our sacrifices.

Finally, I want to thank Jacqueline Roland, who has been, by turns, both my teacher and my colleague at The Lincoln School in Providence, R.I. With her spirited renditions of Voltaire and Molière, she inspired in me a life-long love of French literature and culture; I have never passed by the Comédie française without thinking of her. Out of pure generosity and sheer love of the language, she tutored me in French during two summers—once when I was sixteen and once when I was twenty-nine. In profound appreciation for what she has given me and countless other students, I dedicate this book to her.

Introduction

"THIS CIVILIZATION
NO LONGER HAS SEXES"

"ON THE 11TH OF NOVEMBER," a historian has noted, "an era of sheer madness opened up for the French."[1] The 1920s, at least in Paris, have commonly been portrayed as a noisy, raucous caricature of pleasure, in Maurice Sach's words, "a perpetual 14th of July."[2] Dadaists performed their rude outrages, and Josephine Baker, her waist ringed with bananas, dazzled audiences at the Théâtre des Champs-Elysées. Pencil-thin, cigarette-wielding women swayed to the rhythm of jazz bands, and unprecedented quantities of wine were consumed. France, it seemed, was caught in the uncontrollable grip of desire.[3]

How to explain the frenzied hedonism of the postwar years in France? Many of the French understood this postwar "madness" as a response to the trauma of the First World War and the dramatic changes that accompanied it. As the literary critic and writer Elisabeth de Gramont put it in her memoir, "We all wanted to forget the war; while eminent men were discussing its consequences, we were dancing."[4] Postwar hedonism provided an escape from a world where the war was both everywhere and nowhere: everywhere inasmuch as it informed so many of the political, social, and economic issues with which legislators had to grapple, but also nowhere in the sense that some of the most fundamental questions concerning it were often evaded. For the so-called generation of 1914, the war was to have been a great crusade to restore moral values such as discipline, honor, and progress.[5] But with its faceless state machinery and unremitting mechanized slaughter, the war instead collapsed these old ideals.[6] After the armistice, many French men and women decided that what had been achieved seemed very little indeed in relation to the price paid for it. What had the war really accomplished? What had it really meant? Could the fragments of life be picked up and put back together again? Faced with questions like these, many found it easier to ignore the war and its legacy altogether and to insist on the vitality of the moment itself.[7]

The questions that darkened the brilliant surface of postwar French culture emerge in the writings of veterans such as Pierre Drieu la Rochelle. Best known later as a fascist and collaborator, Drieu la Rochelle came of age and fought during the war at Charleroi, Champagne, and Verdun. His novels depicted veterans like himself who returned from the trenches only to sink into a life of drinking and promiscuity—a life mad with pleasure.[8] But Drieu la Rochelle also openly expressed a profound cultural despair concerning the changes brought about by the war: "This civilization no longer has clothes, no longer has churches, no longer has palaces, no longer has theaters, no longer has paintings, no longer has books, no longer has sexes."[9] What Drieu la Rochelle presented here was a no-man's-land in which the artifacts of culture, its very architecture, were rubble, the ruins of a civilization.[10] He produced the image of a denuded culture, one whose pretensions or "clothes" had been stripped away by the reality of war.

Drieu's words marked a profound crisis in Western humanist values, to which the notion of "civilization" was closely bound. Historians would argue that such visions of cultural mortality were not unique to the postwar period, and that writers had expressed this kind of angst since the middle of the previous century.[11] Still Drieu's epitaph for a dead civilization appeared again and again in wartime and postwar literature.[12] His pessimism was considered extreme but also common among men of his generation, for whom the war marked a civilization gone mad.[13] As the literary critic and veteran Benjamin Crémieux remarked in 1931, the war's lesson "was the sudden realization of the instability of this world, and the instability of Western civilization, like any other."[14] The novelist Romain Rolland similarly bade "adieu" to Europe in a 1917 pamphlet entitled *A la civilisation:* "You have lost your way, you are standing in a cemetery. It has become your home."[15] During the postwar decade, Oswald Spengler's well-known work, *The Decline of the West* (1918) popularized the idea of the demise of Western civilization.[16] In another well-known postwar book, *La Possession du monde* (1919), the physician and novelist Georges Duhamel asked,

"What is this civilization of which we are so proud, and that we pretend to impose upon people of other continents? What does it become when its cruelty and danger have been revealed?"[17] In *Civilisation,* which won the Prix Goncourt in 1918, Duhamel expressed bewilderment concerning those "virtues" of Western civilization—technology and scientific progress—that had been turned to destructive ends.[18]

Paul Valéry's 1919 letter to *La Nouvelle revue française* would become the most famous expression of this postwar sense of cultural mortality. "We modern civilizations, we too now know that we are mortal like the others," Valéry began. Ancient civilizations such as Elam and Babylon, he argued, were until recently only "vague names" whose "total ruin" held little meaning. But modern disdain for such dead cultures was no longer possible: European civilization now had to confront its own mortality. "We see now that the abyss of history is big enough for everyone. We feel that a civilization has the same fragility as a life . . . the loveliest things and the most ancient, the most formidable and the best designed, are perishable *by accident.*"[19] Like Duhamel, Valéry believed that the very virtues of Western civilization—"*savoir,*" or scientific knowledge, and *devoir,* or "discipline"—had been "applied to fearful ends" against civilization itself: "Without so many virtues, so many horrors would not have been possible."[20] Valéry ended his letter by envisioning an "intellectual Hamlet" who stands on an immense platform running from Basle to Cologne, from the marshes of the Somme to the plateau of Champagne. Holding the skull of Leonardo, of Leibnitz, of Kant, "who begat Hegel, who begat Marx, who begat ...," this Hamlet stares at millions of European ghosts, and "meditates on the life and death of truths."[21]

The despair voiced by Drieu la Rochelle and Paul Valéry exposes the troubled underside of postwar hedonism. Central to this discourse of cultural pessimism, at least for Drieu la Rochelle, were representations of gender—or the way in which men and women are normatively defined in relation to each other. Drieu la Rochelle ended his lament with the phrase "[This civilization] no longer has sexes." He presented this phrase as a sort of grand finale on a list of the war's casualties. By positioning "no longer has sexes" there, Drieu la Rochelle signaled not only his concern that the boundaries between "male" and "female" had been blurred during the war, but also that the gender boundary was the most fundamental or significant. In addition, Drieu la Rochelle somewhat surprisingly situated "sexes" in the pantheon of civilization's most highly valued cultural achievements, that is, alongside religion, painting, literature, and architecture. In so doing, he implied that the war's radically destructive effects extended beyond mere cultural artifacts into the realm of "nature" or what were perceived as "natural" gender roles. Yet the same phrase could be read as an assertion that gender is a "cultural," not a "natural," phenomenon. It also implied that gender, no less than architecture or literature, was one of the great cultural achievements of French civilization. Drieu la Rochelle used gender to signal a crisis in French culture after the war. The blurring of the boundary between "male" and "female"—a civilization without sexes—served as a primary referent for the ruin of civilization itself.

Besides an elite of writers such as Drieu la Rochelle, social observers, popular novelists, doctors, members of parliament, and journalists all used gender issues to talk about the war's meaning and impact. The decade after the 1918 armistice witnessed an enormous preoccupation with the issues of female identity and woman's proper role. There was a marked increase in attention to these issues in periodical, fictional and political discourse.[22] Included in this literature—what I will call the postwar debate on women—were articles and sociological studies on every aspect of the so-called changing roles of the sexes, as well as surveys on the subject in literary and political journals such as *La Renaissance politique,* and *La Revue bleue.* Gender issues also pervaded the fiction of the period, notably scandalous "best-sellers" such as *La Garçonne* (1922) by Victor Margueritte and *Le Diable au corps* (1923) by Raymond Radiguet. In parliament, discussion over such issues as abortion, maternal care, and women's suffrage consumed enormous amounts of time.[23] Finally, the social and educational reform literature of the period, in particular natalism, vocational guidance, and sexual education, demonstrated an intense concern with changing gender identities.

I propose to examine this debate on women as a set of responses to the war's impact on French culture and society.[24] My general purpose is to explore in two ways the relationship between gender and change during the decade 1917 to 1927. First, I want to show how certain images of female identity—the "modern woman" and "the mother"—provided the French with a compelling, accessible way to discuss the meaning of social and cultural change. Second, I want to demonstrate that the debate on women worked on a literal as well as on a symbolic level. Debating other images of female identity—"the single woman," in particular—helped the French come to terms with changes in the social organization of gender.

The First World War initiated a period of sudden, often traumatic transformation. It accelerated changes that had slowly begun to alter French cultural, social, and economic life in the first decades of the twentieth century.[25] In 1914, the French viewed the world as relatively fixed or stable—capable only of slow, barely perceptible alteration. But by the late years of the war, French men and women expressed shock concerning what seemed to be a sudden and dramatic metamorphosis. In 1917, for example, the senator and prominent lawyer Charles Chenu asked, "On the ruins of an overturned world, a new world is going to rise. Who will be its architects and artisans? How will the immense work be shared? What power will be able to direct their efforts in order to assure harmony and prevent conflict? I do not know. Who can know?"[26] Once a rich nation, France emerged from the war financially ruined, its entire production machine shattered. The war's fighting destroyed whole villages and towns and transformed eight million acres of land into barren desert.[27] The so-called Red Years after the war—including increased strike activity and the founding of the French Communist Party—provoked fears that a worldwide socialist revolution was at hand. Bankruptcy and inflation plagued the middle classes. The franc fell in value by 50 percent within a year and remained chronically unstable throughout the decade.[28] Under these conditions, the "return to normalcy" became both a fierce desire and a frustrated dream.[29]

Historians have studied in great detail the demographic, economic, and social changes that occurred during these years, but they have paid much less attention to how the French actually understood change as it took place—how they represented it in images and in texts, how they embraced and struggled against it, and how they reconciled it with cherished traditions. I shall argue that gender was central to how change was understood in the postwar decade. The discursive obsession with female identity during these years reveals that a wide variety of French men and women made it a privileged site for a larger ideological project: how to come to terms with rapid social and cultural change, and how to articulate a new, more appropriate order of social relationships. Debate concerning gender identity became a primary way to embrace, resist, or reconcile oneself to changes associated with the war. To make sense of these changes, French men and women had to understand them on their own terms. Further, to make these changes comprehensible, they focused on a set of images, issues, and power relationships that were both familiar and compelling. For many French men, it was simpler to think about the dramatic shifts in their

wives's behavior or in women's fashion than it was to seek to understand something as abstract as the fall of the franc or the decline of the
middle class. Because gender issues were literally "close to home,"
they made the war's impact in some sense culturally intelligible.[30] By
debating issues of gender identity, the French came to terms with a
postwar world that threatened to become unrecognizable to them.

Women's historians have overlooked this crucial function of gender in enabling postwar cultural reconstruction. In examining the impact of the war, they have tended to concentrate, in James McMillan's
words, on "the important question of whether or not the First War
represented a decisive stage in the process of female emancipation in
France." McMillan insists that the war brought about no permanent
change in the female role since, despite the more relaxed social behavior of postwar women, most still conceived their lives in terms of marriage and motherhood.[31] By contrast, Françoise Thébaud and Dominique Desanti have recently argued that the war signaled the
beginning of the modern, feminist era, in which the bourgeois French
woman "became aware that outside the home . . . lay the possibility
to take on new responsibilities, to be independent, and to widen her
horizons."[32] Despite their opposing views concerning the war's impact,
these historians all evaluate change in women's lives in similar terms:
as the degree of advancement in a particular era toward the "liberated"
woman of today. Change is understood in contemporary feminist
terms, that is, in terms of employment opportunities, wage scale, legal
status, and sexual freedom.

But by framing the argument in terms of the war's long-term effect
on women's status, these historians short-circuit exploration of how
contemporaries tried to understand change in women's lives: how they
used it to make other kinds of changes comprehensible, and how they
reconciled it with tradition. According to McMillan, French anxieties
concerning the war's effects—that French women were acting like
men and no longer wanted to bear children, that feminism had triumphed, that the war had emancipated young women—were "wrong"
from a purely structural viewpoint, that is, without statistical basis.[33]
Regardless of whether these anxieties were "right" or "wrong," however, they did preoccupy, worry, and even traumatize French men and
women. For this reason, they are cultural realities in themselves and
warrant our closest attention. The richest, most interesting questions
about the war's impact on women's lives revolve around how gender
both constructed and concealed change itself, as a "civilization without
sexes," as everywhere and yet nowhere.

The Essence of Every Culture

Why did Drieu la Rochelle link the fragility of a civilization with the blurring of a proper division between the sexes? There are two reasons why French men like Drieu la Rochelle made gender issues a discursive prism through which to envision the war's effects. First, gender identity played a fundamental ordering role in French society. Second, gender issues were central to how the war experience was understood by those who lived through it.

Like Drieu la Rochelle, Gaston Rageot, a well-known novelist, critic, and journalist, also saw civilization as tottering on the brink of disaster because of the war's supposed undermining of conventional gender relations. In a 1919 examination of women's wartime labor participation, Rageot asked, "Have women begun a new era of civilization by setting off to work? . . . If the essence of every culture is its notion of relations between the sexes, how will ours not be influenced by the day when women will no longer be seen as women?"[34] Because Rageot considered the "essence" of a civilization to be its notions of gender, he believed that the instability of gender relations could lead to profound cultural disruption: an end to an era of French civilization.[35] Rageot's argument here—that gender relations comprised the very foundation of a civilization—provides one important explanation for why the French debated gender issues as a response to rapid change.

Recent historiography has demonstrated that, at least in the modern period, gender relations served as a primary way of conceiving identity and power in French politics, culture, and society. Particularly in periods of profound upheaval, such as the Revolution of 1789, the restabilization of the terms and organization of gender was key to the process of legitimizing the new republican regime. Jacobin ideology precluded differentiation by birth or class, but sexual difference offered a way of ordering society that was more consistent with democratic ideals. Powerful symbolic categories linking power and masculinity helped to produce social hierarchies based on gender at a moment when their logic could have been refuted. Rousseau's republican ideal of virtue was based on homosocial bonds between men that relegated women to a private domestic realm.[36] During the crucial transitional period of the late eighteenth and early nineteenth centuries, the organization of gender—in particular, female domesticity—came to shape all modern French institutions, from the family to the state.[37]

Throughout this study, I use the term "traditional domestic ideal"

to refer specifically to the bourgeois ideal of female identity that flour-
ished in France throughout the nineteenth century: the self-sacrificing
"angel of the house" who slavishly devoted herself to the maintenance
of her home and the nurturance of her husband and children. As an
ideology or means of understanding sexual difference, domesticity
structured female identity in terms of a woman's role as mother and
wife. The social practice of domesticity supported sets of power relations as diverse as the sexual division of labor and the political system.[38]
As Michelle Perrot has noted, "domesticity had a fundamental regula-
tory function" in nineteenth-century French society; "it played the role
of the hidden God."[39]

Female domesticity became a crucial ideology and practice in a
bourgeois society where most professional and personal allegiances
found their source in the family.[40] As a result, throughout the nineteenth century, debates about female identity and women's role gained
broad significance. Debate concerning women played a crucial part in
the public discussion of other matters important to social, political, and
economic life—the problems of industrialization and urbanization,
and the construction of the welfare state, to name a few.[41] The postwar
debate on women simply continued a decades-long pattern in which
gender issues were at the forefront of French political, social, and literary discourse.[42]

In addition, the privileging of gender issues in the postwar confrontation with change has its historical roots in the war experience
itself. The blurring of conventional gender roles was one of the most
commented on of the war's effects. During the war, male combatants
communicated a feeling of exile, as they found themselves occupying
a barren, death-ridden no-man's-land on the very margins of civilization. At the same time, both soldiers and civilians expressed an acute
awareness that the war had changed women's lives in a dramatically
new way. As Henry Bordeaux, a prominent novelist and member of
the Académie française put it in 1922: "While the war may have nar-
rowed the horizon of men and limited their studies and culture . . . by
contrast, it helped to develop intelligence and initiative in women."[43]
When soldiers returned from the front, they saw their female kin,
friends, and lovers assuming traditionally male jobs and family responsibilities. On the streets, women served as tram conductors and train
porters; in the schools, they replaced the male teachers who had gone
to the front. The war generation of men found themselves buried alive
in trenches of death, at the same time that they witnessed the women
in their lives enjoying unprecedented economic opportunities.[44]

The intense anxiety of French men such as Pierre Drieu la Ro-chelle and Gaston Rageot can be traced to this collapse of conventional gender roles.[45] In addition, these men blurred this gender upheaval with a cultural one—confusing gender disruption with the demise of French civilization itself. This conflation of gender anxiety and a more generalized sense of cultural despair would persist in the way the war's impact was understood after the armistice, so that debates about the sexes also became attempts to address the meaning of the war. Even after 1918, the breakdown of gender roles continued to serve as a par-ticularly potent symbol of the war's sweeping cataclysm.

The Secret to the Complete Upheaval of Things

Three particular images of female identity—the "modern woman," the "mother," and the "single woman"—dominated the postwar debate on women. These three images can be defined generally as ways of imag-ining the female self. Although these images were idealized constructs, French men and women often presented them as the naturalized truth of what a woman is or should be. A dialectical logic linked these three images of female identity. The debate on women developed between the antithetical poles of the mother, a traditional icon of domesticity, and the modern woman. These images made changes associated with the war comprehensible to the French by offering them provocative, familiar symbols of the choice between old and new worlds. With her fast, loose ways, the modern woman—examined in Part One of this study—evoked the war's upheaval of conventional gender roles. Her power to shock was the trauma of rapid change. One respondent to a survey on the modern woman in 1925 described her in this way:

> The innocent young thing (l'oie blanche) of yesterday has given way to the garçonne of today. In this way as well, the war, like a devastating wind, has had an influence. Add to this sports, movies, dancing, cars, the unhealthy need to be always on the move—this entire Americaniza-tion of the old Europe, and you will have the secret to the complete upheaval of people and things.[46]

The modern woman provided a way of talking about the war's more general emotional trauma, as well as changes such as "Americaniza-tion" and a rapidly developing consumer culture.[47] In the debate on women, she became a "privileged symbol" of postwar cultural and sexual anxieties—a dominant representation of change in the postwar cultural landscape.

By contrast, the image of the domestic wife and mother—examined in Part Two—became a privileged symbol of both cultural continuity and traditional French ideals, such as family, self-sacrifice and discipline. George Duhamel, the prominent novelist who served at Verdun as a medical officer, recommended this retreat into the inner life as an antidote for cynicism and despair:

> Those who have the wisdom and the courage to retreat steadfastly into themselves have found their interior life ennobled, augmented, enriched. This interior life is the loyal wife who maintains a radiant home, is prepared to console, and who spins at her wheel behind the door, awaiting our return.[48]

Duhamel counterposed Valéry's Hamlet with a nostalgic Penelope. He used an idealized image of female identity to envision a restored interior life. The loyal, domestic wife promised a safe return or homecoming from the war's madness. A metaphor for moral constancy and inner peace, she assured the passage back beyond the postwar *crise de l'esprit*.[49] The image of the loving wife and mother provided a badly needed fiction of stability in a time of great turbulence and change.

If the modern woman served as a symbol of rapid change and cultural crisis, the mother created an illusion of continuity between the present and the past. She smoothed over the ruptures of the war experience. In this way, change, like the war itself, was everywhere and yet nowhere. Again, like Penelope, knitting and then unraveling the work that she had done, the postwar debate on women repressed as well as transcribed gender/cultural anxieties. This two-way movement of the debate resulted from a dual reaction to change on the part of French men and women. On the one hand, they expressed a belief that they stood "on the ruins of an overturned world," as Senator Chenu had put it. Traditional domesticity, they argued, had become an impractical and outdated ideal.[50] On the other hand, they signaled their profound anxiety concerning the passing of cherished ideals and social practices. In the decade after the war, legislators, novelists, social reformers, journalists, and feminists of all political stripes invoked the importance of a domestic and maternal role for women. They demonstrated a strong urge to return to a prewar era of security—a world without violent change.

Old and new worlds needed to be reconciled somehow. The third image, of the "single woman," helped French men and women to negotiate this conflict between tradition and change. The single woman was the name given to the estimated 1.5 to 3 million women who were believed "destined" to remain single because of the war's mortality and the resulting uneven sex ratio.[51] As a woman who was not expected either to get married or to bear children, the single woman symbolized female identity apart from traditional domesticity—and hence the changing socioeconomic conditions of postwar life. Poised at the frontier of changing female identities, the single woman symbolized the war's impact on the social organization of gender. If the single woman could not be a mother, would she be a modern woman? How could she live up to traditional domestic ideals and yet still be independent and support herself? How could women work outside the home and, in Rageot's words, still "be seen as women"? The image of the single woman provided French men with the opportunity both to express and to resolve the tensions inherent in the antinomy between old and new worlds, change and tradition, the modern woman and the mother. Out of these tensions came a new notion of gender identity, a "synthesis" of old and new.

Perceived in these terms, the postwar debate on women can be described as a dialectical effort to reconcile outdated domestic ideals with a changing social organization. Spiraling divorce rates, a vociferous feminist movement, adultery, and crimes of passion testify to the instability of domestic ideology from the fin de siècle onward.[52] Already precarious, domestic ideology became particularly shaky and volatile after the war. The postwar period witnessed profound changes in the nature of domestic life. A number of young middle-class girls broke with family tradition to enter the labor force because of depleted fortunes and inflation. Their entry had begun several decades before, giving rise to the image of the turn-of-the-century "new woman" who lived and worked independently of her family.[53] Yet like much else, the war drastically accelerated this trend, transforming work outside the home from an oddity to a commonplace for bourgeois women.[54] One could argue that, among many other things, the war made middle-class women working-class in the sense that they were pulled into the labor force in large numbers for the first time. Throughout the nineteenth century, the cultural authority of domesticity had been threatened by what has been called its "uneven development" across class. Bourgeois social reformers and legislators perceived the working classes as in need of "moralization" and tried to impose bourgeois domestic values on them. Yet many working-class women engaged in wage-earning both within and outside the home—an action that, whether voluntary or not, undermined the naturalized status of the bourgeois domestic ideal.[55] When more and more bourgeois women began to do wage work in the postwar period, the logic of class could no longer explain away the old contradictions plaguing bourgeois domesticity.

Still other changes further weakened the cultural authority of domestic ideology. Working-class women also increasingly left the household context in the postwar period. They abandoned domestic service and textile piecework for jobs in the rapidly growing tertiary sector. At the same time, middle-class housewives adopted new technologies, such as vacuum cleaners, sewing machines, and central heating, that freed them from dependence on domestic service. Finally, the rise of a mass media—including best-selling books and Hollywood films— threatened the integrity of the domestic sphere. In the transition to a mass, consumer economy, middle-class women were drawn outside the home in ever greater numbers and increasingly saw their domestic role in terms of a morally suspect consumerism.[56] In all these ways, the war's impact as well as the accelerated growth of mass consumer society created new socioeconomic conditions within which a rethinking of the female self had to take place. Like makeshift rigging, conventional notions of female identity had to be taken down and reassembled again.

"Woman"—Does It Really Signify Something?

Although the debate on women generally followed a dialectical progression, it had no simple or straightforward chronology. The debate began during the last years of the war. In 1917 six articles discussing women's future role appeared in French journals, which is why I begin the history of the debate with this year.[57] Various elements of the debate peaked in intensity at different times. For example, debate about Victor Margueritte's novel *La Garçonne* reached its height during the two years following its publication in 1922. The scandal surrounding postwar fashion came to a climax at mid-decade, between 1924 and 1926. At the same time, debates concerning the mother and the single woman stretched out over the period 1917 to 1927, changing very little in content over the course of this decade. In these cases, I treat documents from different years as parts of a single block of evidence. The last debate I examine in this study—educational reform—also takes place over the course of the decade. But only at mid-decade did educational reformers such as Louise Mauvezin and Germaine Montreuil-Straus achieve recognition for their efforts to rethink women's education. Mauvezin's first Congress on Vocational Guidance met in September 1926; Montreuil-Straus received state funding for sexual education in 1925. These dates suggest that by the end of the decade 1917–27, attempts were being made to reconstruct female identity on the horizon of a new generation.

Debate concerning women did not end in 1927, nor was any reconstruction of female identity decisively achieved during that year. Such chronological precision belies the true nature of the debate, which was an ongoing process rather than a clearly defined episode or event. As we have already seen, the postwar debate simply carried on a tradition in which concepts of gender structured public discussion of matters central to social, political, and economic life. The war initiated certain cultural and social tensions that were enacted on the field of gender, but that enactment itself describes an ongoing process. Because debate concerning gender issues had this continuing function in modern France, one cannot claim that this particular debate had either a sharp beginning or a clear outcome.[58] Hence I do not narrate the postwar debate on women as a decisive progression from French cultural despair to reconstruction. Instead I focus on the process by which the debate moved forward—how precisely the French used gender images to confront the problems of change and to resolve cultural and social tensions brought about by the war. As we shall see, this process was reiterative, multilayered, and often unexpected in its outcome. The same three images of female identity—the modern woman, the mother, the single woman—appeared and reappeared in various discursive forms, from novels to parliamentary debates. Their history as images was irregular, contradictory, and unpredictable.[59]

Nor do I determine one climactic moment in the postwar period when gender identities were reconstructed. Because such identities were cultural constructs, they were by definition unstable, and particularly so in the postwar period. The editor Jacques Boulenger seemed to recognize this instability when, in 1924, he asked:

"Woman"—does it really signify something? We know Marie-Louise, Yvonne, Françoise, Jacqueline, etc., that is, specific women, each with her own personality. But this abstraction "woman"—who has seen or known it? I know we agree on certain traits to define "the eternal feminine." But let's admit it—they're vague. Added to that, our era is particularly averse to such adventurous generalizations.[60]

While the debate on women did not decisively reconstruct gender identity, it can show us how this process of reconstruction took place—how the prewar abstraction of "woman" rubbed uneasily against the postwar reality of a Marie-Louise, making the postwar era "particularly averse" to "adventurous generalizations" concerning female identity.

My study, then, rests on several assumptions concerning gender identity in the postwar period. First, notions of female identity, such as the "modern woman" or the "mother," were culturally constructed rather than natural or prediscursive. Second, this construction emerged from a set of cultural parameters highly specific to the postwar period, including the traumatic emotional legacy of the war, acute concern over France's birthrate, and an infatuation with modern consumer culture. One of my aims is to explore these cultural parameters—why certain images of female identity emerged as dominant in the postwar debate, and how they helped the French to reconcile change with tradition. I do not pretend to explore how the individual French woman incorporated such images into her identity. Rather, I see this book as a necessary prelude to studies of this kind because it maps out the limited and conflicting possibilities of imagining the female self in the postwar period. By determining precisely what notions of female identity were available to individual French women, we can understand what cultural resources they drew on in conceiving and living a social self.[61]

My third assumption, then, is that the postwar debate on women helped to shape both identity and behavior, and thus must be recognized as having its own integrity as an object of historical investigation. I do not read the texts in this debate in order to determine the nature of women's lives—whether they smoked and had sex to a larger degree than in previous decades, whether they stopped wanting to have babies and sought careers instead. These issues are intriguing and important but cannot be resolved in a study using a debate as its primary form of evidence. The debate on women provides only a cloudy and distorted mirror of actual lives after the war because the relationship between texts, their subjects and their authors is so complex and multidirectional. In my analysis, therefore, I have tried to avoid sliding easily from what, for example, a French male author says to how French men as a whole might feel.

The French figure in this study as the readers and the authors of the debate on women. As readers of the debate on women, the French found certain books scandalous, others absolutely impossible to put down, and still others both outrageous and irresistible. By the postwar period, literacy was nearly universal in France, and more than one-third of the population were active readers.[62] The controversy surrounding a novel like Raymond Radiguet's *Le Diable au corps* (1923) signaled its ability to strike an important nerve in postwar French readers—to articulate previously obscure but profoundly felt emotions of some kind. I have tried to find out as much as possible about the French as readers of the debate on women by looking at reviews of books and accounts of parliamentary debates, by determining the number of copies a novel sold and how it was used in other contexts. This task was easy in the case of well-known novels, harder for more obscure ones, and hopeless for short articles and surveys.[63] Despite these problems of documentation, historians recognize the postwar years as a watershed period in terms of French readership. A new interest in reading among the French of all classes encouraged the sudden rise of the "best-selling" novel and a marked increase in print-runs of popular literature.[64] The weekly and monthly press also enjoyed a new popularity after the war and became more important in shaping public opinion.[65] More than ever, the French picked up popular novels, illustrated weeklies, and women's magazines in order both to entertain themselves and to decide how to think about various subjects. This growing readership underlines the cultural significance of the postwar debate on women.

A select and more easily identifiable group of French were the authors as well as the readers of the postwar debate. As James Smith Allen has recently argued about the history of reading in modern France, "authors and their texts are easier to document than their anonymous readers."[66] As authors, the French returned again and again to certain images and narratives; they shared many of the same worries and an uneasy feeling about change. In other words, their preoccupations and anxieties formed a shared pattern that can be laid out and analyzed. This shared pattern itself reveals a whole greater than its parts, because it tells us something about how the French processed change at a critical point of their history. For instance, because returning soldiers had trouble communicating openly or directly what they had seen and felt, and because the French often wanted to ignore the fundamental questions concerning the war's meaning, more oblique or "disguised" forms of symbolic expression such as novels became a popular outlet for debate. Hence, I have concentrated on novelists more than other type of writers. In addition, during the postwar period, literature far surpassed any other genre (history, sociology, etc.) in terms of the number of titles produced and sold.[67]

The authors of the postwar debate were mostly middle-class men, who had control of the press, sat in parliament, and dominated the literary world. Even so, no simple analysis by gender is possible. Certainly, the postwar discourse on gender sustained a system of domination that male voices in the debate tried to reaffirm. At the same time, however, the debate on women cannot be reduced to an effort by middle-class men to put women back in the home or reassert a dominant and oppressive ideology. Women joined men in condemning the modern woman and praising women's conventional domestic and maternal role. They formed some of the most conservative voices in the debate. Likewise, male novelists such as Victor Margueritte counted among the most radical voices and openly advocated women's sexual freedom. In addition, both men and women alike were bewildered concerning changes associated with the war. Rather than demand change in women's lives, feminists seemed more preoccupied with the response to it. Men and women cannot be located in predictable places on the ideological or political spectrum, nor can any one voice, such as that of the feminists, be privileged as telling the "truth" of the female experience. While feminists spoke out for women's rights with great courage and sincerity, they shared their preoccupations, their conceptual understanding of the problems at hand, and even their rhetoric with other participants in the debate, including their opponents. Because feminists formed their ideas within this shared universe of meaning, their arguments cannot be considered the "authentic" voice of women's experience.

PART ONE
LA FEMME MODERNE

1

"THIS BEING WITHOUT BREASTS, WITHOUT HIPS"

"Massacre des hommes, vie chère, voilà ce qui est à l'origine du triomphe de la femme moderne."
H. Mignot

A FTER THE WAR, writers and social observers produced a new image of female identity: *la femme moderne,* they called this new creature, or sometimes *la garçonne.* In 1924, Jacques Boulenger, the editor of the literary weekly *L'Opinion,* described her in this way:

> The war has undeniably had an enormous influence on young girls and young women; and I assure you, once again, that the *femme moderne* is above all a creation of the war.
>
> Without a doubt, she is freer in her behavior than women before the war. . . . Nestled in the arms of her partner, she dances without a corset; she swims in a maillot. . . . Above all, she has a taste or desire for independence, or rather . . . she is absolutely determined to be independent.[1]

This image of the modern woman—scandalous in her dress and manner, giddy with freedom—dances through most historical accounts of women in the 1920s.[2] Contemporaries saw the modern woman as "above all a creation of the war" that had allowed her to work and live independently for the first time. As a popular image, she can be traced to the "new woman" of prewar avant-garde circles. The new woman had embodied a modernist ideal of womanhood, pioneered by cultural radicals, and representing economic and sexual freedom.[3] But she had also been considered strictly a bohemian, avant-garde phenomenon, confined to the eccentric fringes of society, where her style of life served as a critique of Victorian bourgeois culture.[4] By contrast, the *femme moderne* could be the bourgeois girl next door. Here is how a young Parisian law student described her in 1925:

> Can one define *la jeune fille moderne?* No, no more than the waist on the dresses she wears. Young girls of today are difficult to locate precisely. If you want to be true to French tradition, it would be barbaric, in my opinion, to call our pretty *parisiennes* young girls.
>
> These beings—without breasts, without hips, without "underwear," who smoke, work, argue, and fight exactly like boys, and who, during the night at the Bois de Boulogne, with their heads swimming under several cocktails, seek out savory and acrobatic pleasures on the plush seats of 5 horsepower Citröens—these aren't young girls!
>
> There aren't any more young girls! No more women either![5]

For this observer, even the clothes that *la femme moderne* wore reproduced her inability to be defined within the boundaries of traditional concepts of womanhood. Her lack of a distinctly female form symbolized the unrestrained social and cultural space she seemed to inhabit—a space that was, above all, the creation of the war.

A "being" without a waist, without hips, and without breasts, she symbolized a civilization without churches, without palaces, and without sexes. In Mathilde Alanic's 1921 novel *Nicole maman,* the hero, Colonel Rémy, returns home joyfully after the armistice, only to become an outsider in his own family.[6] Overwhelmed by the difficulties of readaption to civilian life, he watched in bewilderment as his young daughter danced the tango with her boyfriends. Above all else, it was this young *femme moderne* who "made him conscious of the time that had passed, and of the sorrow that had changed his most intimate self."[7] For Rémy, the young woman embodied the war's impact on himself and the world around him. André Beaunier, best known as the literary critic for *La Revue des deux mondes,* produced the same image of the modern woman in his 1922 novel *La Folle jeune fille.*[8] Here Michel, another displaced and alienated veteran, interpreted his sister Sabine and her friends—young *femme modernes* all—as symbols of the "madness" of the age:

> You are crazy and I am crazy. Papa is crazy. What a family! And the others are equally crazy too. It's a mark of the times; one should predict the end of the world. . . . But if you really want to see the symbol of the era, it's in the absurd behavior that young girls are showing.[9]

Why did Michel consider the modern woman a symbol of the era? Why in these novels does she epitomize the madness of the age and the impact of the war? To answer these questions, we must go back a few years in order to analyze some of the ways in which gender issues figured in the French interpretation of the war experience. Gender relations during the First World War comprise an enormous and complex subject for historical analysis, which I cannot pretend to do justice to here. But even a cursory glance at both the personal and fictional literature of the war reveals that gender issues lay at the heart of how both soldiers and civilians made sense of the war and its devastating effects. This literature, then, can help to explain the genesis of the postwar debate on women.

Poor Strangers That We Are!

Memoirs and fiction written during the war reveal a persistant imaginative habit among soldiers—a tendency to understand the world in terms of gross oppositions and dichotomies, what Paul Fussell has called the "versus habit." According to Fussell, "prolonged trench warfare, with its collective isolation, its 'defensiveness,' and its nervous obsession with what the other side is up to, establishes a model of modern political, social, artistic and psychological polarization."[10] Obviously, French soldiers began by drawing a clear distinction between themselves and the Germans, but as the war dragged on, they made a second division as well—between the battlefront they inhabited and the homefront they had left behind. To a great extent, soldiers also "gendered" this division—that is, they opposed a "male" battlefront with a "female" homefront. Of course, no absolute gender boundaries of this kind could be drawn—politicians, older men, and war profiteers also populated the homefront. But because men and women inhabited largely segregated spheres during the war, soldiers did map their world in terms of an opposition between the sexes. The novelist Pierre Drieu la Rochelle described the front as a "country without women, where only man bears witness to man, where we suffer too much."[11] One wartime observer noted that by the end of 1914, Paris had become a "city of women."[12] As the historian Stéphane Audoin-Rouzeau has put it, the woman represented "the reverse image of the war, and that which gave it meaning."[13]

According to personal accounts of the war, the dramatic changes that men underwent at the front, their inability to relate the horror of

their experiences, the general ignorance about the war at home because of censorship—all led front soldiers to believe that they could
no longer communicate with the homefront.[14] Trench humor treated
this problem with biting sarcasm. In his "handbook" on *L'Art et la
manière d'accommoder et de raccommoder civ'lots et poilus*, George
Fabri, himself a soldier, set out to avoid "a new war: the war of *Poilus*
and *Civ'lots.*"[15] The engraving on the cover of Fabri's book portrayed
the civilian as a large, almost overwhelming, masculine-looking woman
(fig. 1). First published in trench journals during the later war years,
Fabri's manual offered advice to *poilus* on leave who became infuriated
when told by civilians that they "looked great"—an expression of
doubt, as they understood it, concerning the suffering they had endured. Make yourself look as dirty as possible before going home,
Fabri advised, dent your helmet, grow your beard, and fabricate heroic
stories. Excuse yourself for not being wounded, and if wounded, for
not yet being dead. (Perhaps you could bring this last happy news on
your next leave.)[16] Fabri warned his fellow soldiers not to be disap-
pointed if they could not impress a civilian with their war tales, because
in fact, to do so, "you must refer to something more horrible: the ra-
tioning of pastry or the closing of stores at 6:00 P.M., for example."[17]
Among the several "types" of civilians that Fabri described was the
reproachful, ungrateful *"dimineuse,"* who greeted the soldier with
these words: "Yet another leave? . . . But aren't you always on leave?"[18]
Fabri mocked what he saw as ignorance concerning the war: "With
great tact, let us inform those civilians who might not yet have noticed
at all that there presently exists a phenomenon that is called: the
war."[19]

Fabri's sarcastic suggestion of the wall separating (male) soldiers
and (largely female) civilians conveys his sense of pride and anger as
well as his alienation. This image of civilians—as indifferent to and
even scornful of the heroism of the front soldiers—appeared again and
again in trench journals during the years 1915 to 1918. Fabri's anger
was certainly not universal; many soldiers described their leaves as joy-
ful, happy times.[20] Still, Alain's cynical quotation—"Eight days of leave
is like a man getting hung two times over"—enjoyed popularity among
front soldiers.[21] By the end of 1915, civilians and soldiers alike were
voicing the belief that men and women had become strangers to each
other, separated by a wall of ignorance and experience.[22] In a 1917
account of a leave, the scholar Roger Boutet de Monvel also presented
the homefront as ignorant, indifferent, and self-absorbed. Women, he
argued, "do not dare admit it, but military exploits interest them little.

They prefer the '*cine.*'" Women's only reaction to the war, according to Boutet de Monvel, was: "It's lasting too long!"[23] The same year, another soldier told the story of how one young woman at a movie theater back home had declared a newsreel boring because "there were not even any corpses."[24] The biographer Michel Corday remarked in his Paris diary that year: "The fact is, Paris is remote from the war. The restaurants are crammed. What a contrast with those tortured towns of Eastern France, that endless stream of wounded down from Eparges into Verdun."[25]

In viewing the material contrasts between trench and civilian life, returning soldiers saw the homefront as a world of extravagence and luxury, whose pleasures they were largely denied.[26] No-man's-land entailed a daily battle with mud, rats, lice, and rain, as well as the German enemy. It was a cemetery of dismembered, unburied bodies, where life expectancy was often as short as three months. Surrounded by corpses, the front soldier expected and even desired death at any moment. The contrast with the homefront, particularly in large urban areas, could not have been more stark. Louis Huot, the well-known psychologist and doctor at the front, claimed that his "stupefaction was profound" upon returning from Senegal in 1915, and witnessing Paris "as joyously animated as in peacetime, . . . as fierce in the pursuit of its interests and pleasures." Huot referred to the "divergence" between the mentality of the combatants at the front, who were subject "to a rigorous discipline," and of the civilians "who tend to liberate themselves more every day."[27] On 15 June 1915, the trench journal *Le Pépère* portrayed the homefront this way: "Look at the theaters! You can't even begin to count the number of shows that feature skimpily clad women singing with false bravado about the glory of the allies."[28]

Maurice Donnay, the dramatist and member of the Académie française, wrote in his journal in February 1916 that the ways in which the people on the homefront passed their time during the war "shocked" and "offended" returning soldiers. A month later, he noted that men on leave in Paris "find that Paris is not contemplative enough, that there is too much luxury, gaiety."[29] In his 1917 *Carnet d'un combattant,* the historian Paul Tuffrau referred to soldiers who, upon returning to the trenches after a leave, "compared with bitterness their miseries with [the civilian's] pleasures."[30] "What struck me the most in Paris and elsewhere," wrote the novelist Georges Duhamel, "was the kind of unstable, unbalanced state into which all values—both material and moral—have fallen. . . . It's as if a good half of our contemporaries are swept away, uprooted by a whirlwind."[31] In 1919, Jean Finot, a veteran and the editor-in-chief of *La Revue mondiale,* argued that the war had had a double moral effect: on the one hand, heroism at the front had revived traditional values, but, on the other, corruption on the homefront had quickened their decline.[32]

Soldiers equated this corruption with war profiteers, who made fortunes in the armaments and other war-related industries. More important, however, they associated lax morals and Parisian gaiety with women, who dressed extravagently and became symbols of new wealth. In 1916, the trench journal *La Marmite* argued that "women have made the mistake of appearing thoughtless and carefree, and the skirts of 1916 look a little too lighthearted."[33] "You would never believe that we are at war," exclaimed one soldier in 1917, "The longer it lasts, the more they play: brightly lit stores, fantastic cars, chic women with little hats."[34] "For us and for History, this is the year of the war; for them, the year of short skirts," wrote the dramatist Abel Hermant the same year.[35] These writers would not deny that many women grieved and scrimped and kept their families together throughout the war. According to Audoin-Rouzeau, the devoted wife and mother outnumbered all other images of women in trench literature.[36] But to many soldiers returning on leave, this type of domestic woman was less visible than those who packed the theaters, cafés, and restaurants of Paris.[37] The relative comforts that women enjoyed at home seemed to throw into relief the hardships, sacrifices, and humiliations of trench life. A popular trench song called *"Les Petites femmes de mobilisés"* focuses on the contrast between the rigors of the battlefront and the pleasures of the homefront:

> Les Poilus s'en vont, le cafard au front
> trottinant parmi les cervelles
> A l'arrière, l'on voit la gaieté, la joie
> Et la guerre, nul s'en aperçoit
> > Concerts, cinéma, casino
> > Touts pleins de badauds
> > Qui ont la vie belle
> Nos femmes s'offrent du plaisir
> Elles peuvent s'offrir ce qui leur fait plaisir
> Elles rigoles des communiqués
> Les petites femmes des mobilisés.[38]

By the later war years, the gender divide separating the homefront and battlefront had become the subject of widespread commentary. A 1917 book of cartoons titled *Pourvu qu'elles tiennent* featured a woman angered by an offensive because it meant that she would be able to go to the theater only twice a week.[39] Another sketch, titled "Let's Make Sacrifices," showed a woman knitting a sock and grumbling about the "beautiful sweater" she could have made (figs. 2 and 3).[40] Even after the war, these images persisted. In 1919, one journalist created a picture of the war as a period in which a "taste for refined pleasures became a part of women's lives," and during which "they could live 'a bachelor's life' and its freedom seduced them."[41] In his sketches of wartime Paris, *Mado, ou la guerre à Paris* (1919), the writer and critic Maurice Level contrasted the frivolity of women's lives with the grave risks taken by the *poilu*. The cover of Level's book juxtaposes a woman applying makeup with the map of the Western front (fig. 4).[42]

In fact, women's lack of knowledge concerning the war can be ascribed to government censorship rather than to any "demoralization" of the homefront. Censorship of books and the press was primarily responsible for the rupture between soldiers and civilians. Military defeats, the horrors of the trenches, the 1917 crisis of morale—these stories of the war had difficulty reaching the French at home because of a censorship office more powerful than its counterparts in either Great Britain or Germany.[43] But, far from being contested, these unfavorable images of women found a receptive audience in literary Paris. For example, Rachilde, the literary critic of *Mercure de France*, accepted uncritically Level's portrayal of women as irresponsible in *Mado, ou la guerre à Paris*. She suggested that a large group of Parisian women be brought together in a theater so that the book could be read to them.[44]

If soldiers misinterpreted women's ignorance of the war as insensitivity, they exaggerated female wartime independence as a need to dominate men. In addition to complaining about women's frivolous lives, many soldiers expressed fear concerning their newly liberated ways. Soldiers returning to Paris confronted the sight of female postal carriers, tram conductresses, women ticket collectors, and even women street-cleaners clad in big hats and clogs, wielding heavy hoses.[45] As historians have argued, the economic and military exigencies of the war blurred conventional gender roles.[46] With 3.7 million of the active work force mobilized throughout the war, 1.5 million were left to do the work that normally employed 5.2 million.[47] Many working-class women quit traditionally feminine jobs, such as domestic services and textiles, to receive higher wages in the munitions factories, state railways, and the iron and steel industry.[48] They shoveled coal, fought fires, made grenades, drove motorcycles, collected tram tickets, and cleaned the streets of Paris. Middle-class women were also increasingly active outside the home. The number of middle-class women entering liberal professions such as law and medicine jumped dramatically during the war.[49] Women teachers enrolled in male lycées in order to replace the *agregés* at the front. For the first time, middle-class women were allowed to go almost anywhere, and by 1917, the sight of them alone on the streets at night was common.[50] Many older bourgeois women took over the businesses and trades of their husbands and often traveled extensively. The entry of significant numbers of women into higher education and traditionally male professions had, in fact, begun decades before, but the war accelerated these trends enormously.

While male combatants witnessed women taking on their jobs and family responsibilities, running businesses and even municipal governments, they themselves felt stranded on the edge of civilization in no-man's-land, where they became ciphers in a massive and mindless war machine. "During the torment," recalled a veteran in 1920, "life went on without us."[51] As he left the battlefront in July 1915, the soldier Paul Cazin related the sense that "little by little we are being brought back to civilization."[52] To the extent that women filled male roles, they collapsed conventional notions of sexual difference and reversed the boundaries of social marginality. Propelled from the margins of society, women had become the new "insiders," while men became the new "outsiders."[53]

The considerable personal literature of the war—memoirs, diaries, and journals published both during and after the armistice—presented this set of gender reversals as having a devastating psychological effect on front soldiers.[54] After a trip to the trenches in 1917, in which he talked to soldiers about life at home, the novelist and journalist Gaston Rageot reported:

> Most of them feared marital disgrace. Some said: "She'll wear herself out, and I'll have to take care of her"; others felt a confused humiliation in no longer being able to earn the money themselves. Finally everyone was convinced that they would not find their wives in the same condition as they had left them: either they would be dishonored or at best, they would become authoritarian, imperious, and act like bosses and drum-majors.[55]

Many soldiers expressed anxiety about reasserting their authority in the home at war's end. The trench journal *L'Horizon* asked in December 1918:

The returning victor . . . will he suffer to find a deserted home where his authority—so dearly paid for—will no longer be recognized? Upon his return, will he be told that there are no longer any political distinctions between men and women, that they are two beings equal in rights, two social units. . . . Can he bear to take part in civil and political battles with a woman? To find in her a rival and competitor for the same jobs that he wants, and that she leads him in obtaining?[56]

When asked why they wanted to survive the war, soldiers declared a desire simply to return to a safe and happy home. But soldiers also portrayed the moment of homecoming as traumatic because of their perception that wives and girlfriends had changed in dramatic ways. In Pierre Chaine's popular account of the war, *Les Mémoires d'un rat* (1917), the working-class *poilu* Juvenet is shocked when he returns home on leave and greets his wife, whose face is tinged with yellow as a result of working with melinite in a munitions factory. Chaine tells the story through a "rat" Juvenet has brought back from the trenches— a narrative device that also signals Juvenet's degraded sense of self. When Juvenet's wife takes the initiative of the first kisses, he feels shamed and dishonored: "this disgrace, added to all the other tribulations of the war, made the cup of his misery overflow."[57] In the 1936 preface to his very popular *La Guerre, madame,* originally published in 1916, the dramatist Paul Géraldy claimed that when the soldiers returned home, "they found women to be numerous, provocative, impatient." One man Géraldy knew trembled violently at the sight of his daughter dancing according to the new fashion. No less than Colonel Rémy in Mathilde Alanic's 1921 novel *Nicole maman,* the sight of this young modern woman dancing made him feel like an "outsider" in the postwar world.

According to the personal literature of the war, then, the homefront had become an object of both fascination and hatred, invested with hope and denounced with bitterness. This vision of the homefront also formed a central theme of the war's most famous and widely read fiction, in particular, Henri Barbusse's *Le Feu* (1916). Reputedly the greatest novel of the war because it dared to speak its truths, *Le Feu* examined the lives of soldiers in one military squad. Historians consider it astonishing that Barbusse's *Le Feu* passed the censors.[58] The object of enormous controversy, the novel even received the Prix Goncourt in 1916. Extremely popular, it sold 230,000 copies that year alone.[59] Throughout *Le Feu,* the distinction between the front and homefront, "a difference far deeper than that of nations and with defensive trenches more impregnable," irrevocably separates men and women.[60] One *poilu* in the squad reminisces how, in a town they had visited not long before, a woman "talked some drivel about attacks, and said 'How beautiful they must be to see!'" To this another soldier responds: "Beautiful? Oh, hell! That's like an ox saying: 'How beautiful it must be to see all those droves of cattle driven forward to the slaughter-house!'"[61]

Throughout the novel, Barbusse also presents the war as reversing the boundaries of social marginality, so that women become the new "insiders," and men the new "outsiders." At another point in the novel, Poterloo, also a *poilu,* tells the narrator how he had managed to sneak behind enemy lines to see his wife in occupied territory. Disguised in a German uniform, he was allowed only to circle his relatives' house and view her from a half-opened door. His happiness at being able to know her condition turned to shock and dismay when he discovered her in the company of a German soldier: "She was smiling. She was contented. She had a look of being well off, by the side of the *boche* officer."[62] Poterloo also noticed the widow of one of his recently killed friends in the room: "She knew he'd been killed because she was in mourning. And she, she was having good fun, and laughing outright."[63] In shaping his narrative, Poterloo dwells on "the lamp and the fire that emanated a familiar warmth" and gave the scene a golden look as he stood looking into the room.[64] The image of the combatant—peering into a brightly lit, cheerful room from the darkness outside and aghast at his own wife's complacent happiness—perfectly encapsulates his newly marginalized status. Once again, the experience is traumatic: "She was smiling, my wife, my Clotilde, at this time in the war! And why? Must we be away for only a short time before we do not count anymore?"[65]

The same symbolism appears later in *Le Feu* when several members of the squad go on leave in Paris after a particularly difficult battle. From the beginning, their experience of the homefront is alienating and upsetting. In a restaurant, they encounter a woman who describes what she thinks the war must be like: "Dear little soldiers . . . who can't be held back, who shout 'Vive la France' or who laugh as they die!"[66] At dusk, they watch the Parisians hurry home "toward the dawn of their lighted rooms." They pass a half-opened ground-floor window and "see the breeze gently inflate the lace curtain and lend it the light and delicious form of lingerie." Held back by the crowd, the men remain immobile on the sidewalk, "poor strangers that we are!"[67] Strangers to a feminine world of security, sensuality, and light, the combatants are once again outsiders looking in.

Cartoons also expressed male anxieties concerning the war's disruption of conventional sex roles. One appearing in *La Baïonnette* of 26 November 1915, featured a female train conductor who wanted her husband to come home from the front so that *he* could watch the children.[68] Another by Henriot, the cartoonist for *L'Illustration,* depicted a man knitting and looking terribly upset while his wife went out to work. The caption read: "Considering that since the beginning of the war women have replaced men in nearly every position, only women's work remains to the men."[69] Still another by Henriot portrayed a young woman boasting that "on top of the allocation, I'm getting eight to nine francs a day for making bombs . . . unfortunately, the war will not last forever" (fig. 5).[70] Because of high-paying war industry jobs and government allocations, working-class women were often much better off financially with their husbands at the front. But the belief that these women prized this situation above their husbands' lives signals anxiety about the war's upheaval of gender roles.[71] The conservative journalist Lucien Descaves shared this same fear in *La Maison anxieuse* (1916). Working-class women were quite happy to have their husbands away, Descaves argued, because they could spend more money on themselves. "When they see how we've been able to get along without them," he quoted one as saying, "these gentlemen will be less proud." As his title suggests, Descaves believed that anxiety pervaded relations between the sexes: "What I think is most sad about this provisional, relative emancipation of woman . . . is that out of the national war has come a precarious domestic peace."[72]

The work of Henriot and Descaves serves as a warning that wartime accounts depicting women as sexually and economically liberated cannot be taken at face value. They do not provide evidence that the war liberated women in contrast to men, as historians have sometimes read them.[73] Rather, they show that many male soldiers and civilians perceived a dramatic change in gender roles to be occurring and responded to this change in anxious ways—by exaggerating women's happiness or distorting their motives and reactions. Accounts by French women support this interpretation. Rather than present a happy picture of liberated life, French women record fears that their new "insider" status will have a demoralizing effect on the men in their life. Marguerite Lesage, a bourgeoise from Lille, indicated concern in her diary on August 31, 1917, in response to her friend's comment that men "will be embittered" when they return home. "Their pride will be wounded," she worried, "inasmuch as we knew how to take their place and save their interests, and then again we will have lost our 'femininity.'"[74] Another bourgeois woman, Madame Cloquié, predicted in 1915 that given the number of mutilated and wounded who would return after the war, the husband would have to stay home to care for the children while the wife "went to sit in the Chamber [of Deputies]." But Cloquié also warned her women readers: "Never forget that above all else you are a woman."[75]

Both Lesage and Cloquié seemed to understand that despite extraordinary circumstances, only their willingness to be women "above all else" would reassure their husbands of their manhood. Rather than celebrate their "liberation," these women expressed concern that changes in gender roles were causing men to feel angry, anxious, and dishonored. Colette related the same concern more indirectly in her wartime sketch of the bourgeois Sargent X. Arriving home on leave, he says he barely recognized his wife, a women he describes as having been "so womanly and so weak." He explains that with her coat styled after the French military uniform and her hair stuffed underneath her military hat, she looked like a man, not a woman. In addition, like Juvenet's working-class wife, she moved boldly forward to embrace him in "the most scandalous manner." All this, he confesses, created in him "the most intolerant, unjust exasperation."[76]

The literature of female indifference to male suffering and disregard for conventional gender roles must be considered alongside another wartime literature that sang women's praises. As the historian Françoise Thébaud has argued, never have women in France been so honored by so many prominent political and literary figures as they were during the war. Eulogizers proclaimed that women had revealed their moral and intellectual aptitudes not only to themselves but also to the nation, that they had cultivated new qualities such as patience and a sense of social engagement, and that in their loyalty and devotion, they had acted as a source of strength that counterbalanced the horrors of war.[77] In *La Revue* of May 1917, the lawyer and president of the Bar Henri Robert glowed about women in this way: "they have preserved their charm and elegance but at the same time lifted up their hearts to the heights of the drama where the nation's destiny played itself out. . . . They have done more! They have shown their heroism and their scorn for death."[78]

This literature was clearly propagandistic—attempting to paint a favorable portrait of French women abroad. But to a great extent, it was also probably sincere. The figure of the self-sacrificing nurse or domestic mother, who tirelessly attended the wounded and awaited her beloved's return, embodied an ideal of moral courage that helped the French to sustain hope and faith in the war cause. According to trench literature, the soldiers emphasized female recognition of their sacrifices as central to their sense of self-respect and power. The war was a profoundly emasculating, dehumanizing experience for the *poilu* or front soldier.[79] In memoirs of the war, novels, and trench journals, women's loyalty frequently allows the front soldier to recover some sense of himself as a husband, a lover, a fiancé, or a son—in other words, as an individual and a man. Eulogies to women's efforts on the nation's behalf represented women as nurses or mothers whose devotion lifted the hearts of the nation.

While these complimentary images of women served as propaganda, no evidence exists that the more negative portrayal of female wartime behavior, such as we have seen in trench journals, memoirs, and novels like Barbusse's *Le Feu*, was censored during the war. Two contradictory images of women—one "good" and one "bad"—coexisted in wartime literature, a polarization that has a long history in French culture. Pierre-Joseph Proudhon's description of woman as either "courtesan or housewife" provides one better known example. As the cultural historian Maurice Crubellier has noted, "the bourgeois male representation of woman assumes a curious duality" in the nineteenth century: images of women were split between the virtuous mother and the decidedly unvirtuous prostitute.[80] In light of this history, the good woman/bad woman duality of the war literature can be seen as simply updating an old theme. In addition, the soldiers' tendency to conceptualize their world in terms of gross opposites during the war probably helped to reinforce this dual vision of womanhood.

Whatever the origin of these images, my aim in examining them is not to determine which one—virtuous mother or ignorant pleasure-lover—appears more frequently in wartime literature, or more correctly "reflects" the "reality" of women's behavior during the war.[81] Rather, I would like to explore what symbolic work these images performed both alone and together—why they appear in wartime literature, what they symbolize in that context, and how they construct the larger meaning of the war experience itself. Because gender issues lay at the heart of how French men and women came to understand the war experience, these images cannot be reduced to mere "idealizations" or "distortions" of real women. Rather they are important in themselves as arbiters of cultural conflict and must be analyzed in that light.

She Is the Real Culprit

Far from canceling each other out, the two competing images of female identity that appear in wartime literature derive their meaning from the contrast set up between them. They were often juxtaposed in the same text, for example, in Chaine's *Mémoires d'un rat*. When Chaine's Juvenet discusses the hardship of trench life, his wife interrupts him with this question: "Do you know how many women perished in the factory explosion at Saint-Denis?" Silenced, Juvenet rushes to agree with everyone present "that women have been admirable." But soon after "by a strange revolution, the panegyric to women gave way to a violent diatribe against 'those who profit from the war in order to have a good time.'"[82] Similarly, Maurice Donnay's *Lettre à une dame blanche* (1917) presents two contradictory images of women's wartime behavior. The book consists of a series of imaginary letters to an angelic, virtuous nurse who has given up her life in Paris to tend to the wounded. But despite his eulogies to women's "courage and good faith" throughout the book, Donnay also scorns the nurse's cousin, Clothide, the self-indulgent *"président de l'oeuvre des désoeuvrées,"* who spends the war complaining and drinking tea.[83] Of interest here as well is the review of Donnay's book in *La Revue des deux mondes* by André Beaunier, author of *La Folle jeune fille*. Although Clothilde was a minor character in Donnay's book, Beaunier devotes his entire review to berating her and condemning "the ridiculous and sad comedy that some *dames moins blanches* perform in Paris, and with them, a good number of men who, on this point, are women."[84] Beaunier's fixation on the "bad" woman here again suggests that the French reading public was receptive to this image, and that as a symbolic category of wartime behavior, the "bad" woman also included the "bad" man of the war, such as the war profiteer or the draft evader.

To understand what symbolic work these two images performed by the contrast set up between them, let us examine in closer detail an example of their juxtaposition in a single text. In an article written on the eve of the armistice in September 1918, the novelist Louis Narquet began by praising women's patriotism: "Wife, mother, sister, fiancée. . . . She quickly overcame her own private, womanly grief in order to be united in the national danger, and this sacrifice of her wounded heart grew to total self-renunciation for the benefit and safety of the country."[85] As a symbol, the self-sacrificing wife or mother represents both civic patriotism and female recognition of individual men. Narquet presents her here not as a "citizen" but as a "wife, mother, sister, fiancée." He defines her civic identity in terms of her loyalty to the men in her life who were fighting the war. Her "total self-renunciation for the benefit and safety of the country" also affirms the dignity and courage of the individual husband, son, brother, lover engaged in the struggle. In a war that transformed its participants into anonymous ciphers, the woman's civic role was to reaffirm the personal identity of the soldier through her own "total self-renunciation."[86] In addition, by adhering to conventional female behavior—total self-abnegation for the sake of others—she reaffirms his manhood. As the historian Edward Berenson has argued, French notions of masculinity at this time depended heavily on just such conventional behavior: "The more [men] could persuade French women to conform to a masculine idealization of the *vraie femme,* submissive, obedient, emotional, unthreatening . . . the more French men could feel the virility to which they aspired."[87]

Likewise, the ignorant, frivolous woman symbolized a painful indifference to both the individual man and the war effort. Narquet goes on to bitterly denounce middle-class women who led lives of pleasure: "As for amusements, they plunged into them with a kind of frenetic energy, not giving any thought to the sadness of the wounded and mutilated." According to Narquet, the bourgeoise "insulted her husband in his deprivations and suffering" by spending enormous amounts of money on clothes and luxury items. Women "insulted" their men by denying them loyalty and respect at a time when they most needed it because of the dehumanizing conditions of the front. Like the women who performed male roles during the war, this bourgeoise failed to conform to conventional female behavior. In this way, she "insulted" the soldier's sense of manhood. Because male and female roles were intricately linked in a larger vision of social organization, changes in one profoundly destabilized the other. In addition, traditional female values—self-denial, obedience, submissiveness—sustained *both* conventional notions of femininity *and* the war effort. Women's disregard of such values thus signaled a double betrayal—of the individual man as well as the war endeavor. If a woman's civic identity was defined in terms of her personal self-renunciation and loyalty to individual men, her self-indulgence and disloyalty became signs of treason or patriotic indifference.

In war and postwar literature, the images of the "good" and "bad" woman blurred individual relations between the sexes—loyalty to or abandonment of the fighting brother, husband, lover—with a general, moral response to the war. The loyal wife or mother symbolized patriotic duty and civilian morality; the indifferent, independent working woman represented a moral abandonment of the war and the principles for which it was fought. This conflation of gender and moral categories also had a long history in modern French culture. For example, belief in the virtue of the domestic wife/mother secured her status as the moral paragon of French society and formed the basis of the nineteenth-century ideology of separate spheres. The virtuous wife, who assured the moral well-being of the soldiers and thus helped to sustain the war effort—this image was merely a variant of an old nineteenth-century theme in the discourse of gender. But, as we shall see, those who believed that the soldiers' moral well-being depended on women's loyalty left themselves vulnerable to the fragile nature of this formulation.[88]

According to wartime literature, women's indifference to heroism at the front was traumatic for the male soldiers. This trauma, in turn, became confused in his mind with the moral and emotional suffering of the war generally. Paul Géraldy's *La Guerre, madame* (1916) illustrates how in war fiction, a soldier's contact with female indifference triggered moral anguish. Immensely popular, this fictionalized memoir of the war went through 61 editions by 1922.[89] At a key point in the story, the front soldier Maurice visits an ex-lover in Paris before returning to the front. Completely unaware of what is going on in the war, she complains endlessly of all her "deprivations"—her inability to dress fashionably, her boredom with Paris at night, the tastelessness of the food. The visit to Paris plunges Maurice into a dark depression, in which anguish concerning the war effort is inseparable from anguish concerning his worth and dignity as a man: "And perhaps we are simply ridiculous, dirty, wretched, bearded, deceived. . . . Ah! I feel fainthearted. It's cold. The Germans are stronger than us. I should have died at Virton."[90] In Géraldy's account, Maurice's alienation from his ex-lover, who betrays him through her own indifference, kindles his profound despair concerning the war in general.

In less well-known wartime literature as well, women are endowed with enormous powers, symbols of the war's devastation and its hope for resurrection. In Gaston Rageot's novel, *La Faiblesse des forts* (1918), for example, the theme of marital infidelity confuses sexual betrayal with moral abandonment. In general, Rageot did not enjoy great success as a novelist, but *La Faiblesse des forts* sold well, going through seven editions in its first year of publication. In addition, Rageot was a prominent leader of the natalist movement. His treatise on the subject, *La Natalité*—also published in 1918—had an enormous impact on postwar natalist propaganda, examined in Part II of this study. As an important voice in the postwar debate on women, Rageot's wartime fiction merits close examination.[91] *La Faiblesse des forts* concerns two brothers, François and Marie Cordellier, both highly renowned doctors, who harbor a perfect faith in science and in the rational order of the universe. The war disrupts their union as brothers and their work as scientists because initially they respond to it in opposite ways. At least at first, François feels himself come alive as he works to keep soldiers alive.[92] Marie, however, almost immediately undergoes a profound moral crisis. He considers the war a futile, wasteful effort that throws into doubt his belief in scientific progress. Forced to remain home in order to recover from a wound, he suffers from "permanent lassitude, languor, . . . a sense of being nothing more than an obsolete object."[93]

By contrasting the two brothers, Rageot outlines two alternative moral responses to the war: an active embrace of its principles, or moral despondancy—Valéry *crise de l'esprit*. Furthermore, he connects these moral choices to the relationship both brothers have with the same woman—François's wife, Lise-Reine. With his brother away at the front, Marie seduces Lise-Reine, whom he comes to love and desire "like life, like light, like resurrection. . . . On a ground littered with bodies, what else remains to the survivor except to eagerly seize the woman he loves and to intoxicate himself with her?"[94] Marie endows Lise-Reine with a certain redemptive power, as if she alone were capable of "resurrecting" him from the wound of his moral anguish. But her destructive powers are stronger still. Although Rageot initially portrays François as energized by war work, as the war drags on, the latter's actions imply that his faith in science has been strained and even destroyed by the war.[95] But François's angst about the war finds expression only indirectly, in the obscure feeling that something is terribly wrong with his marriage. He "feels a heavy weight on his conscience, a constant constraint . . . something imperceptible and oppressive" that "takes away his force and his lucidity."[96] When he discovers the affair between his brother and his wife, he suffers a complete crisis, losing faith in his life's work as well as his love. Lise-Reine's sexual infidelity becomes not only a betrayal of a personal trust, but also a destruction of moral idealism.[97] François blames Lise-Reine, not his brother, for the sexual transgression: "the chance to destroy, to wreak havoc with a heart and an intellect, to annihilate an undertaking and the honor of a great name—admit it, this is what seduced you."[98]

While the war clearly has a destructive effect on his work and his ideals, François can only partly admit it to himself; he becomes aware only of an obscure, oppressive force weighing down his spirit. In addition, he projects his sense of disillusion onto Lise-Reine, whose sexual transgression becomes a symbol for the war's devastation as a whole. Quietly assuming the burden of guilt, Lise-Reine leaves in shame and then redeems herself by dying as a nurse at the front—the "good" woman of the war. Before she dies, however, she writes both brothers: "It was this devastating war that tore you from your work and from your union. She is the real culprit. . . . The woman who passed between you was only her instrument, perhaps her symbol."[99] In Rageot's novel, a woman's sexual transgresssion represents at once a personal betrayal and the war's betrayal of the very virtues—*savoir* and *devoir*—for which it was supposedly fought. For François, Lise-Reine's marital infidelity provides a compelling, familiar way of talking about something terrifying and abstract—the war's destruction of his liberal, scientific faiths. Lise-Reine herself accepts her role as a symbol of the war, but asserts that the war, not she, is "the real culprit."[100]

Lise-Reine's betrayal marks civilization's betrayal of itself. But she also acts as a symbol of "light, life and resurrection" to Marie when he is first wounded, and her death as a nurse at the front enables moral and emotional healing between the brothers to begin.[101] Her two guises here—as redeemer and destroyer of faiths—repeat the good woman/bad woman imagery prominent in wartime literature. This same opposition would continue to appear in the postwar debate on women, although in slightly different form. On the one hand, the French woman as devoted *mère de famille* served as the privileged symbol of moral virtue and male virility, both of which she affirmed by upholding the traditional domestic ideal. On the other hand, the French woman as newly independent *femme moderne* became the privileged symbol of the war's most destructive effects, which she reproduced through her own sexual transgressions. Let us begin to explore the way these images of female identity worked symbolically by examining how the "problem" of female sexual infidelity emerged during the war and became the subject of several popular novels published between 1919 and 1926.

She Lived It Up While I Was at the Front

In wartime literature such as *La Faiblesse des forts,* female betrayal of the fighting soldier took the form of sexual infidelity. Observations that women were engaged in extramarital affairs were almost always made in the context of comparison with the hardships of the war front. In 1916, Anatole France claimed that as many as 80 percent of French women were unfaithful and declared that their satisfaction in being far away from their husbands was one of the main causes of the lengthening of the war.[102] In Géraldy's *La Guerre, madame,* one woman tells Maurice: "But what women do know, all the same, is that their sons and husbands are dying. And at the same time, Maurice, they open their door to the first comer. . . . Women have been *infâmes.*"[103] Louis Narquet noted in 1918 that "too many French women" had indulged in marital infidelity, "an odious moral crime considering that the husband is in continual threat of death."[104] The same year, the psychologist Louis Huot provided a detailed medical explanation for the so-called increase in women's sexual desire—what he called the "more developed excitability of the genital areas." He lamented that "the sacrifice of heroes at the front has been paid with such a humiliating misfortune."[105] In the frontspiece of his 1919 book on wartime women, Lieutenant Georges Grandjean wrote: "The men of the front demonstrated the bloody heroism of voluntary death; [the women] of the homefront ought to have shown the heroism of fidelity."[106]

This commentary raises an intriguing set of questions: Did women's sexual activity increase during the war years? If so, why? If women were being unfaithful, with whom did they have sex? Other soldiers or civilians? Why were women, not their male partners, blamed? Historians disagree about how widespread female sexual infidelity was during the war, and why it might have occurred.[107] Once again, my aim in exploring the literary representation of female infidelity is not to determine the reality of women's wartime sexual behavior, but to analyze the symbolic work it performed in both war and postwar literature— how it acted as a provocative, familiar way for French men to express their moral and emotional trauma concerning the war. Sexual infidelity signified the wartime reversal of gender roles because in this case, women were free and promiscuous, while men were "confined" to the army and trenches. Hence sexual infidelity expressed the "difference far deeper than that of nations" between the sexes' war experiences. In addition, it signaled women's scorn for traditional female values—purity, morality, discipline, and self-denial. As we have seen, in wartime literature such a rejection of conventional femininity frustrated soldiers' attempts to affirm their heroism and their manhood. In all these ways, female infidelity symbolized the isolation, alienation, and emasculation of the male combatant.

Female betrayal forms a strong theme of the other highly acclaimed and popular novel of the war besides *Le Feu*—Roland Dorgelès's *Les Croix de bois*. Published just after the armistice, *Les Croix de bois* was a critical and popular success, praised for its "realism," particularly among war veterans.[108] Dorgelès himself was a veteran and already known as the author of *La Machine à finir la guerre* with Régis Gignoax. In Dorgelès's novel, marital infidelity causes the worst kind of suffering among front soldiers, far more painful than physical deprivation or the confrontation with death. Like *Le Feu*, the novel centers on one squad of *poilus*. In one extremely moving and climactic scene, a soldier named Bréval has been wounded and begins to sob uncontrollably. His wife, he confesses, has been unfaithful; he wants Gilbert, his friend, to tell her that he forgave her before death. Then, continuing to sob, he abruptly changes his mind and in great anguish, blurts out: "Listen, tell her that it's her fault that I was killed . . . you have to tell her . . . and tell it to the world, that she is a bitch, that she lived it up while I was at the front." Breval's outburst profoundly affects the other members of the squad: Sulphart sobs in one corner, his head buried in the folds of his arms; Lieutenant Morache "was livid. He was trying to control himself, but his lips and chin were visibly trembling." Crying as well, Gilbert cradles Bréval until he dies.[109]

The scene is prophetic because Gilbert and Sulphart also soon suffer the wound of female betrayal. On a hellish, rainy night in the trenches, Gilbert gets a letter from his wife, Suzy, in which she tells him about the "charming boy" with whom she frequently goes out. "That doesn't bother you, does it, my dear?" she asks.[110] The scene emphasizes Gilbert's sense of abandonment, which, in turn, prefigures his own death. Wounded in battle, yet overlooked and forsaken by the stretcher-bearers, he bleeds to death in a desolate forest. Also wounded in the same battle, Sulphart recovers in a hospital. His joy at having at last escaped the war is tempered by anguish concerning the cool tone and infrequency of his wife's letters. On the same day that he celebrates his medical release from the army, he receives a letter from his concierge telling him that his wife has run off with a Belgian and taken everything with her. Sulphart returns to a house now empty except for a bed, a chair, and a calendar he and his wife were given as a wedding present. Rejected by their women, Gilbert and Sulphart remain anonymous ciphers, the non-men of no-man's-land.[111]

In *Les Croix de Bois,* female sexual betrayal becomes a means of focusing the diffuse sense of anger and humiliation concerning the war that pervades the novel as a whole. Unable to get his own job back, Sulphart travels to Paris to find work. In the last chapter of the novel, ironically called "The Return of the Hero," he wanders an unfriendly Paris without money or a place to stay. His wife's betrayal becomes a symbol of a much larger desertion: of France itself in its attitude toward veterans. No less than Barbusse's Poterloo, Sulphart is a "poor stranger" in an indifferent world. A woman's treachery evokes the combatant's more general sense that he has been betrayed—by his elders, by his army officers, by his government, and by the French nation as a whole. Abandoned by army medics, Gilbert is left to die; abandoned by the homefront, Sulphart walks Paris alone and helpless. Sexually emancipated, the woman at home led a life that mocked the entrapment and isolation of her man in the trenches.

Female sexual betrayal comprises a central theme of another postwar best-seller published a few years later, in 1923—Raymond Radiguet's *Le Diable au corps.* The story concerns a young woman, Marthe, who has an affair with a sixteen-year-old boy, François, while her fiancé, Jacques, is at the front. Marthe gives birth to François's son when Jacques returns after the war and marries her. But Jacques, unaware of Marthe's betrayal, raises the child as his own after her death in childbirth. The novel contrasts the sexual freedom of Marthe and François with the grim constraints placed on Jacques. Radiguet portrays Marthe as insensitive and cruel to *"le pauvre Jacques,"* as he calls him.[112] Indifferent to the increasingly anxious, questioning tone of Jacques's letters, she throws them into the fire as she sits with François. When Jacques's leave is delayed, she is overjoyed; when he does come home, she retreats to a childhood room in her mother's house and refuses to sleep with him. Marthe's mother then blames him for her daughter's suddenly strange behavior. In Jacques's first letter to Marthe after returning to the front, he threatens suicide. But Marthe still responds passively, and it is François who dictates "the only tender letters that [Jacques] ever received from her" in order to prevent the tragedy.[113] Jacques then falls ill, but again unconcerned, his wife refuses to visit him unless accompanied by François, a demand that shocks even the latter. Indeed throughout the novel, François, despite his youth and infatuation, shows more sensitivity to Jacques's plight than does Marthe.

When *Le Diable au corps* first appeared, it caused enormous controversy.[114] "*Le Diable au corps* has exploded in the literary sky like the last cannon burst after the armistice," observed one critic, connecting the controversy to the war's unfinished business. To some extent, the media hype surrounding the novel's publication caused the public uproar. The publisher Bernard Grasset ran a huge public relations campaign, including use of the cinema and large photographs of the author, an upstart at the age of seventeen. Grasset played on Radiguet's youth and claimed to have discovered a new literary prodigy. But mostly the controversy centered on the novel's so-called immoral and cruel representation of marital infidelity.[115] Radiguet sent a copy of his novel to Roland Dorgelès. The author of *Les Croix de bois,* in turn, accused Radiguet of suffering from an "absolute lack of heart" in his casual treatment of Marthe's betrayal of Jacques: "I would not have had the cruelty to be so hard on the soldier . . . I loved them all too much."[116] When the novel won the literary Prix du nouveau monde in 1923, the veterans' Association des écrivains anciens combattants raised an outcry, claiming that the novel "profoundly wounds the feelings of veterans."[117] The scandal surrounding *Le Diable au corps* suggests that Radiguet's portrayal of Jacques's humiliation at the hands of Marthe struck a nerve in postwar culture. Five years after the armistice, veterans still claimed to feel the "wounds" of sexual infidelity.

In Colette's *La Fin de Chéri* (1926), still another popular postwar novel, a female writer expresses many of the same thoughts concerning the war's effect on gender relations. In *La Fin de Chéri,* sexual infidelity once more designates the veteran as the new "outsider" of postwar society. Colette intended the novel to be a sequel to *Chéri,* which she had written in 1919 after a short story completed several years earlier in 1912.[118] *Chéri* takes place just before the war and nostalgically evokes the extravagance and innocence of the vanished Belle Epoque.[119] The six-year romance between a young man, Chéri, and his aging courtesan, Léa, ends painfully when Chéri decides to marry a proper young heiress named Edmée. In *La Fin de Chéri,* which Colette began writing in 1924, she stresses the difference between the pre- and postwar worlds. The once vibrant and carefree Chéri returns from the war to wander Paris like a ghost, to live a life of self-indulgent debauchery, and to recall hideous scenes of the front.[120] At home he finds his wife, Edmée—a helpless, weeping child in *Chéri*—preoccupied with hospital work, inspired by a sense of her own importance, and most important, involved in a passionate liaison with a hospital colleague. (She thus combines both the "good" and "bad" images of female identity found in the war literature.) Edmée's affair and the changes in her life make Chéri feel lost and bewildered, in one critic's phrase, "even more of an outsider" in the postwar world.[121] In many ways, the two characters have reversed their prewar roles in *Chéri*. Edmée, not Chéri, is now engaged in an affair, and this new sexual assertiveness is central to her role as the new master of the house.[122] Chéri, not Edmée, now appears like a love-forsaken, lost child. His alienation and despondency send him back to the aging Léa, with whom his relationship is now long over. She has become a grotesque shadow of her former self, aged and fat. Colette compares her with Louis XVI and describes her as "straightforward, as jovial as an old gentleman." What Chéri notices, above all, is "that when she stopped smiling or laughing, she ceased to belong to any definite sex." Léa, the model of old-world femininity and sensuality in *Chéri*, has lost her proper sex altogether and is furthermore "virile and happy in that state."[123] Like Edmée, she creates an impression of power and self-containment that sharply contrasts with her feminine subservience in *Chéri*.[124] The meeting with Léa is fatal to Chéri; more desperate than ever, he commits suicide soon after. The reasons for Chéri's suicide are psychologically complex, but his inability to live in a "civilization without sexes" comprises a fundamental element of his postwar *crise de l'esprit*. In a 1926 review of *La Fin de Chéri*, the veteran and editor Jean Finot attributed Chéri's suicide to his inability to face the fact that "the past is dead; it cannot be brought back to life again."[125]

The Spiritual Sovereignty of Woman

Characters such as Colette's Edmée exemplify the modern woman image that emerged during the war years and became prominent in the debate on women. Because she could communicate moral as well as gender anguish, the modern woman came to symbolize the loss of everything familiar in postwar France. In short, then, the modern woman became a privileged symbol of change. But she cannot be understood apart from her "good" woman counterparts in wartime literature—the domestic wife or the self-sacrificing nurse who upheld morals through her loyalty and virtue. As we shall see in Part Two, the image of the

woman-as-redeemer reappears after the war, particularly in the literature of the natalist movement. Here let us examine the symbolic work
she performed in two novels—Jean Dufort's *Sur la route de lumière*
(1921) and Francis Forest's *Thé dansant* (1922). Neither of these authors enjoyed the popular or critical success of Barbusse, Dorgelès,
Radiguet, or Colette.[126] But their novels warrant our attention because
they neatly summarize several themes that dominated the postwar debate on women, for example, the marginal, war-ravaged veteran who
replaces the combatant as the new "outsider" of the postwar world.
Marc Sangnier, the founder of the Catholic Sillon movement and himself a veteran, expressed the veteran's dilemma in this way: "violently
torn away from our homes and our work for almost five years, we combatants, were exiled *[dépaysés]* in the most painful way, and seemed
like foreigners."[127] The veteran, like the angry combatant before him,
was the new "outsider" of the postwar world. In both Dufort's and
Forest's novels, it is woman who, as redeemer of faiths, has the power
to rescue these exiled and broken men.

In fact, however, in Dufort's *Sur la route de lumière*, woman first
acts as a destroyer of faiths. The soldier Olivier Mauret returns home
from the war without an eye and an arm, and struggles "to restore the
heaping ruins left by four years of systematic destruction." No less than
Valéry or Duhamel, he sees the war as "the monstrous fruit of an essentially industrial and scientific civilization" that presently lies in ruins,
"torn apart by doubt and suffering." Like Marie in *La Faiblesse des
forts*, Olivier has learned from the war's experience that "the supreme
good" is a woman's love.[128] But his fiancée Fernande, in whom he has
placed all hope of happiness, is repulsed by his mutilated body.
Throughout the course of the novel, she increasingly withdraws and
finally rejects him totally.[129] As she does so, his hope for a new life
disintegrates: "he was nothing more than a phantom, wandering amidst
other phantoms, in the sterile and cold agitation of the world."[130] Once
again, a woman's betrayal transforms the soldier into one of Valéry's
European ghosts—a Hamlet meditating on the life and death of
truths. When, after Fernande's departure, Olivier's friend Daniel asks
him if he still believes in "duty" and "personal dignity," he responds
"with bitter irony" that they are "merely pretty words. . . . I have given
all, sacrificed everything for these words. Now I know what they
hide."[131]

But in Dufort's novel, the redemptive woman ultimately triumphs.
Daniel offers Olivier hope by arguing that if the "solemn education of
the war" could engage the French "to come back to the most profound

sources of life," it would bring about "the rallying of wills to the service of civilization." When Olivier asks, "But whose voice . . . would be at once authoritative and persuasive enough to be heard by men?" Daniel "simply" responds, "That of a woman":

> Oh! without doubt, we will create marvellous air-machines capable of bringing us from one continent to another, we will dig eighteen-league tunnels under the seas, we will tear from nature more of its secrets . . . but if, first, we do not recognize the spiritual sovereignty of woman, we will not be guided in our labor by the great emotions that she alone can exalt and that alone are capable of making societies progress toward ever higher levels of civilization.[132]

Woman's "spiritual sovereignty" takes precedence over scientific technology (airplanes and undersea tunnels) as the guarantor of "civilization" and progress. If, as Paul Valéry and Georges Duhamel claimed, technology or *savoir* had betrayed civilization itself, woman alone, in her role as moral guardian, could save it. In terms of the novel's plot resolution, Dufort also presents "the route toward the light" as female salvation. Olivier and Daniel each marry extremely conventional, domestic women—"loyal wives," who like Duhamel's Penelope, assure their passage back from the postwar *crise de l'esprit.* "Without her, God knows how long I would have groped around under this still so pale, so indecisive light," claims Daniel at the novel's end.[133]

The same redemptive image of woman organizes the theme of moral crisis/resurrection in Francis Forest's *Thé dansant.* Its hero, the veteran André Chesnau, is once again a disaffected outsider unable to re-enter postwar society. The novel begins in the changing room of the *Académie d'armes,* where, in a strange postwar version of a Greek chorus, several older men scold the veteran for his inability to live his life once again.[134] One of the chorus of elders, the Marquis de Serquigny, urges Chesnau to go to a "tea dance" because:

> they reflect a certain state of things. During the war, women acquired a taste for independence. In addition, the education of children no longer plays a central role in their life. . . . Their little brains are given over to luxuries and pleasures.[135]

Serquigny repeats a truism of the war literature—that women have lost their way and succumbed to a life of luxury and pleasure. He identifies the *thé dansant* as the spatial metaphor of the postwar "state of things" and defines this new cultural regime in terms of women, who have rejected their traditional domestic role and become independent.

In the image of the "tea dance," women and the postwar cultural "state of things" merge into a single symbol of change.

Taking his elders' advice, Chesnau begins to frequent the *thé dansant* and becomes involved with a modern woman, Hélène Sézanne. She is a cagey, elusive character, mercurial in her movements, a play of surfaces. She lives to dance and dances to live; her life has no other purpose. But through Hélène, Chesnau himself begins to emerge from his ghostly withdrawal and to long for emotional commitment. When Hélène declares that she sees nothing more in him than a dance partner, he suffers from the by-now-familiar "wound" of betrayal. "The passing months had brought him only vain hopes and profound deception. His heart had opened itself up only to be wounded."[136] But just as his manhood is most grievously injured, Chesnau meets and falls in love with another woman—Madeleine LaPlane. When he first glimpses her, she is sitting quietly in a friend's parlor doing embroidery. With her head bent over in concentration and her entire body radiating serenity and virtue, Madeleine evokes the image of Duhamel's Penelope—the loyal wife who awaits the soldier's return.

Symbol of traditional domesticity and "the spiritual sovereignty" of woman, Madeleine will offer new life and moral resurrection to Chesnau. When he first meets her, she gets right down to business in a conversation concerning contemporary art: "You can be proud," she argues, "to belong to a country that affirms its genius and vitality, even in the wake of an unprecedented ordeal."[137] Brought up short, Chesnau surprises even himself by making this impassioned statement:

> We owe the glory of France to the common people. The peasant with his robust good sense, and the worker, rebel against alcohol and vice, are and always will be the living forces of the country. From these powerful trunks, in which a rich sap flows, the branches that bear the fruit you admire are born.[138]

Madeleine's sense of solidity and the clarity of her values begin to sew up the borders of Chesnau's world as soon as she appears, bent over her embroidery in the parlor. With a flash of her needle, she inspires Chesnau to resuscitate his masculinity through the mere suggestibility of language. By evoking the "robust" peasant/worker, in whose loins the "rich sap" of the future flows, he reasserts his own masculine power as well as the moral virtue of France.

After meeting Madeleine, Chesnau returns to the *thé dansant* and begins to think of Hélène, with whom he is still in love. Then, "suddenly, for some inexplicable reason, the image [of Hélène] disappeared and was replaced with that of Madeleine Laplane, thoughtfully embroidering."[139] Chesnau's mental substitution here identifies Hélène and Madeleine as competing female images, mirror opposites that construct each other. While Hélène lives to dance le shimmy and le foxtrot, Madeleine's philosophy of life, "one must make oneself useful," leads her to run a nursery for the children of working mothers.[140] If Hélène wants only a dancing partner, Madeleine embodies the desire for domesticity, marriage, and children. At the novel's end, Chesnau leaves Hélène for Madeleine, and the chorus of elders is again brought in to proclaim: "Happiness demands a stable foundation. . . . To have a goal, a lofty purpose, and to keep one's eyes fixed upon it: this is what I propose to you." The contrast between the chorus' advice to Chesnau at the beginning and the end of the novel marks the traveled path of moral restoration: from apathetic veteran to born-again Chesnau, from the fevered pursuit of pleasure to rock solid goals. The redemptive Madeleine, brandishing her needle and "the spiritual sovereignty" of woman, has upheld the values for which the war was fought, assured Chesnau's homecoming at last—and made the world safe for still another war.

In her roles as destroyer and redeemer, the French woman acted as the privileged symbol of postwar crisis and restoration. This dual view of woman had deep roots in French culture and emerged in wartime literature as a contrast between the self-sacrificing nurse and the sexually promiscuous wife. These two images represented not only different ways of imagining the female self, but also two competing moral responses to the war. The bad/good images of women in wartime literature blurred gender and moral anxieties in such a way that gender itself became a primary means of understanding the war's meaning and impact. Similarly, in the postwar debate on women, the symbolic presence of the modern woman and the domestic mother created an arena for acting out cultural struggle and tension. In particular, the modern woman—represented here by the mercurial Hélène—became the object of explosive controversy, largely because she symbolized both moral and gender trauma. The next two chapters explore the provocative, scandalous nature of la femme moderne by examining two controversies with which she came to be associated: first, the best-selling novel La Garçonne, by Victor Margueritte, and second, her visual presence, that is, the short hair, loose-fitting clothes, and low-cut dresses that comprise postwar fashion.

2

"SHE STOOD AT THE CENTER OF A SHATTERED WORLD"

IN 1925, A CATHOLIC COMMENTATOR on French fashion described the modern woman this way:

> We have to face the fact that women are not shying away from any means to make themselves look ridiculous.... Already we have the woman with the cigarette, the woman with the short skirt, the woman with the outrageously low-cut neckline and bare arms.... Now we have the woman without hair.... It is no longer only behind the bookstore window that one glimpses the *unfortunate* creation of an *unfortunately* famous author. It is also in our streets, our salons and even in our churches that we meet the rather uninteresting type, *"la garçonne."*[1]

The *"unfortunate"* creation referred to here is the protagonist of Victor Margueritte's infamous novel *La Garçonne*. Published in France in 1922, the novel depicts a modern woman who denounces her bourgeois family in order to lead an independent and promiscuous life in Paris. Banned by the Catholic Church, its sale restricted or forbidden throughout France, *La Garçonne* was nevertheless a best-seller and sold more than a million copies in France before 1929.[2]

The fear expressed here—that the novel, like a disease, was spreading from "fiction" to "reality"—typified a common prejudice concerning reading in the early twentieth century. The French widely believed that a book could be dangerous and have potentially catastrophic results. Books were endowed with considerable powers to trouble the senses and could even lead to a potential "loss of self,"

46

particularly in the case of female readers.[3] French men and women of all political persuasions shared the view that Margueritte's *La Garçonne* represented more than just innocent entertainment. For example, Renée Papaud, a radical feminist, had the same impression as the Catholic observer: "The suggestibility of a book is a fact. How many Werthers did Goethe produce, how many *garçonnes* are going to be born or have been born from the book of Margueritte!"[4] André Billy, the literary critic for the Radical daily *L'Oeuvre*, argued that Margueritte had succeeded in "giving form to a new feminine type." *La Garçonne*, in his opinion, acted as "an instigation and an excuse."[5] For these observers, *La Garçonne* played a definite and singular role in shaping postwar female identity.

The question of whether the *garçonne* was a "literary" or a "social" figure in the 1920s still concerns historians, who cite the scandalous banker Marthe Hanau and the journalist Louise Weiss as examples of "real" *garçonnes*.[6] But my own aim in examining Margueritte's novel is not to determine how much it influenced postwar social behavior. Instead, I want to explore the symbolic work performed by the novel— how the *garçonne* functions as a symbol of postwar cultural crisis and, through her own redemption, appeases both cultural and gender anxieties. Such a study must begin with the impact that *La Garçonne* had on French popular culture in the years after its publication in 1922. The fact that the novel became the focus of so much attention and controversy testifies to its ability to touch a nerve in postwar French culture—to address some issue beyond its superficial subject matter that resounded deeply in its readers. "An issue is captivating the reading public, fascinating even those who, ordinarily, don't even bother to read," reasoned José Germain, the literary critic of *Le Matin*, as a way of explaining the "fantastic" sales of the novel.[7] But what was this issue precisely? What was the source of the fascination and horror that *La Garçonne* offered to so many French men and women?

All Poetry, All Illusion Is Banished

La Garçonne was a publishing phenomenon (fig. 6). When it first appeared at the beginning of July 1922, it sold 20,000 copies in four days. Ten thousand copies were sold each week in August, 150,000 by the end of the summer, and 300,000 by the end of the year. In an age when the average printing for a novel by a popular author was 15,000 copies at best, these sales made news.[8] Furthermore, the phenomenal popularity of *La Garçonne* continued throughout the decade. As late as 1926 and 1928, it appeared in re-editions, and by end of the decade, it had sold over a million copies. The historian Anne-Marie Sohn estimates that, given that from three to five people read each copy of *La Garçonne* sold, 12 to 25 percent of the French population most likely read the novel in the 1920s.[9] Because the novel cost 7.5 francs (a figure beyond what an average worker could afford to pay for a novel), the audience was overwhelmingly middle class. Young women were also thought to form a large portion of Margueritte's readership.[10]

However, the success of *La Garçonne* cannot be ascribed to the interests of one age group. During the summer and fall of 1922, it was the book everyone was talking about.[11] The sales figures for *La Garçonne* become even more impressive when one considers that the book suffered restrictive marketing because of its condemnation by the Catholic Church. The archbishop of Paris denounced it as obscene, and conservative Catholic groups worked to have it seized from bookstores. When the first movie version appeared in 1923, there was such a violent struggle to censure it that the film was shown only once.[12] The translation of the novel into other languages (ultimately fourteen in all) caused further uproar, because French conservatives were horrified at the impression of French women it might produce abroad.[13]

The scandal also centered on the author Victor Margueritte, who was a member of the Légion d'honneur, honorary president of the Société des gens de lettres, and therefore a literary figure of some standing.[14] The son of a famous general who was mortally wounded in the Battle of Sédan in 1870, Margueritte spent most of his childhood in Algeria and came to Paris in 1872 after his father's death. In 1896, he left a military career to marry a woman whose dowry did not meet required military standards.[15] Soon after, he began his literary career with his brother Paul, and slowly gained a reputation as a social novelist with radical socialist leanings.[16] *La Prostituée,* a fictional portrayal of women's prisons, earned him entry into the Légion d'honneur. He had already provoked controversy in the postwar period for his book *Au Bord du Gouffre* (1919), which bitterly attacked French diplomatic and military incompetence both before and during the war. By December 1922, several natalist and veteran groups were demanding that Margueritte be denied his membership in the Légion d'honneur. His expulsion, which occurred a month later, again sparked a protracted discussion in the press, but that debate moved away from the book itself and focused more on issues of free press.[17] All this publicity fed sales of *La Garçonne,* and no doubt the controversy surrounding the novel contributed to its success.

Critical reviews of *La Garçonne,* published in daily newspapers and literary journals throughout the second half of 1922, provide clues concerning what about the novel readers found so scandalous and compelling. At the most superficial level, the debate centered on the sexual promiscuity of the novel's heroine and its explicit sexual passages. "This novel on young women is certainly not intended to be read by them," was the wry comment of Paul Souday, the well-known journalist for *Le Temps.*[18] Jean Guirard, the editor-in-chief of the Catholic daily *La Croix* called the novel "immoral" and reasoned that "if it has gone through numerous editions, this is because it awakens in man that which, more than anything else, reduces him to the level of beasts."[19] *Le Canard enchaîné* ran a satire meant to please even "the archbishop." Entitled *"La Glaçonne,"* it related the life story of a *jeune fille* who, *"naturellement froide,"* was born in *"Froidville"* and was greeted *"fraîchement"* by her father (a *glacier*) and her family.[20] Max and Alex Fischer, the novel's publishers at Flammarion, promoted this sexual aspect of the scandal in order to boost sales of the book. *"La Garçonne . . .* the most daring novel ever written," one advertisement boasted.[21]

To be sure, single, sexually active women had appeared in French literature before, for instance in Colette's novels, also extremely popular at this time. Most significant here was the fact that the *garçonne* of Margueritte's novel, Monique Lerbier, came from a "respectable" middle-class family. The satirist Georges de la Fouchardière argued that Monique's class origin was the "one mistake" that Margueritte made and the single cause of the novel's controversy.[22] Precisely the same argument was made by one elderly French woman, recently interviewed, who had read *La Garçonne* at the age of eighteen. Unlike the novels of Colette, she pointed out, the setting of the novel was not a bohemian world of music halls, artists, and intellectuals. Instead, it was *la grande bourgeoisie industrielle.*[23] The *garçonne's* middle-class background alarmed bourgeois feminists, who feared that their own cause would become associated with Monique's sexual misconduct. "The behavior of the *garçonne* is morally inadmissable," huffed Alice Berthet, the literary critic for the feminist *La Française,* in 1922. Berthet also worried about the impression that the *garçonne's* "liberated" life-style would make on young women. For her, Monique's independence seemed empty and bleak: "But this [Monique's] experience is unhappy . . . because a life from which all poetry, all illusion, all tenderness is banished, is an abyss of shadows and disgust."[24]

Berthet's comment that Monique lives in an "abyss of shadows and disgust" points up another aspect of La Garçonne that can help explain the intensity of its controversy: for, in fact, the phenomenal popularity of the novel cannot be understood solely in terms of its sexual explicitness—a common attribute of several other, much less successful novels of its time.[25] Complaints about sexual explicitness also do not explain why veterans felt strongly enough about the book to join their voices in the general outcry, nor why the book was so widely read, when prominent critics universally denounced it as lacking in any literary merit. As the literary critic Gustave Téry put it, "this so-called chef d'oeuvre is really just FILTH."[26] At best a second-rate novel, why did La Garçonne come to represent the raucous pleasures of "les années folles"? Why has it remained so central to the cultural mythology of the postwar era, even today?[27] The answers to these questions lie in the garçonne's role as symbol, her ability to embody a world of shadows in which, as Alice Berthet put it, "all poetry, all illusion, all tenderness" had been "banished."

She Bled Throughout Her Being

In the opening section of La Garçonne, Margueritte presents postwar bourgeois society as morally corrupt. The first scene revolves around a charity bazaar given by rich bourgeois patrons in the gilded ground-floor rooms of a ministry. The bazaar acts here as a parody of bourgeois charity, an ironic device intended to emphasize that charity—or social conscience of any kind—is the last thing on the minds of its organizers and patrons. Instead, it is a frenzied orgy "of every vanity and every corruption," in which what is for sale is not the small hand-crafted charitable items, but the marriageable daughters of rich men who sell them.[28] Given his own socialist political views, Margueritte's moral argument here—that capitalist greed had debased even family values—was not surprising. Still, many of the novel's critics chose to identify this postwar corruption with the war's destruction of bourgeois moral certainties. "In La Garçonne, Victor Margueritte has portrayed the society that the war has made," wrote Anatole France in his letter to the Légion d'honneur on Margueritte's behalf. "The immeasurable evils of a long war have produced abominable morals."[29]

In this first scene, Margueritte contrasts the opulent decadence enjoyed by the patrons of the charity bazaar with the difficult sacrifices endured by the war wounded it will benefit. The patrons include profiteers such as Léonida Mercoeur, who earned enormous wealth from the war at the same time that he avoided fighting in it, and rich, bloodsucking "aliens" such as Jean Plombino, a Jewish contractor, and John White, an American businessman, who also earned fortunes in the war. Monique, the young, single daughter of one of Paris's most prominent families, looks around her at the other patrons, and notes the unjust imbalance she sees between wealth and suffering. "The idea that one part of humanity bleeds while the other amuses itself and gets rich upset her greatly."[30] Glancing at the "luxury and stupidity that paraded" around the charity bazaar, she remembers the "atrocious vision" of the Hospice de Bois-Floury, where she went to visit the war wounded:

> all those remains of men, fragments of an intelligence, hope and love that once were, now nothing more than misshapen stumps, crushed faces, white eyes and twisted mouths. It was an unbearable memory. It pursued her with an unspeakable horror. The crime of war . . . that all the gold in the world, all the pity on the earth would never wipe from the bloody brow of humanity.[31]

The French reading public should have been familiar with this opposition between opulence and suffering because it appeared so often in wartime literature. However, here it is a woman, Monique, who suffers from her awareness of the war's agonizing contrasts. As if she possessed the moral awareness of the *poilu*, Monique angrily voices his old resentments concerning war profiteers of the homefront. In addition, she demonstrates an exceptional sensitivity toward "all those remains of men" the memory of whom pursue her "with an unspeakable horror."

In this way, Margueritte uses an unfamiliar voice (because female rather than male) to draw a familiar portrait of the society "that the war has made." From the start, he privileges Monique as the voice of moral conscience concerning both the war and bourgeois gender relations. She is deeply in love and engaged to the dangerous and dissolute Lucien Vigneret, who sees his marriage to Monique solely in terms of a share in her father's wealth. Monique's father, another war profiteer, supports Monique's engagement only because it assures him the necessary capital to support a new and lucrative investment. This "exploitation" of women on the marriage market Margueritte parallels to the buying and selling under way at the charity bazaar.[32] Despite the father's willingness to bargain his daughter away for his own profit, he is not beyond invoking the "family" as a means of persuasion: "Beyond our troubles and petty worries, there is only one thing that really counts: affection, tenderness . . . and the family!"[33] The moral bankruptcy of the Lerbier family, whose father sells his daughter to an unprincipled man and whose mother is interested only in appearing twenty years younger than she is, produces a picture of bourgeois society that is rotten to its traditional moral core.[34]

The second scene of the novel serves as a contrast and critique of the first. With her Aunt Sylvester, Monique visits the simple, austere office of Professor Vignabos, a celebrated historian at the Collège de France. The institution is described here as "an environment of sound ideology and free enquiry."[35] As Monique and her aunt enter Vignabos's office, three books about female identity sit on the table: Léon Blum's *Du Mariage,* Ellen Key's *Love and Marriage,* and Dr. Toulouse's *La Femme et la question sexuelle.*[36] All three were popular texts of turn-of-the-century cultural radicals, who criticized bourgeois marriage and demanded freer sexual expression for women. Blum, for example, argued that women had a polygamous instinct and should therefore be allowed to enjoy more sexual freedom before marriage.[37] The "new" or "bohemian" woman of the fin de siècle had supposedly embodied this cultural radical ideal of womanhood; she represented both economic independence and sexual freedom for women. Prewar critics considered these ideas signs of moral anarchy and national decadence, but they were taken up again after the war by writers such as Dr. Michel Bourgas and Marcel Barrière, who argued that since women's sexual needs were equal to men's, they were entitled to the same sexual freedoms.[38] During the course of her visit, Monique discusses the merits of these texts with Vignabos and his students Boisselet and Blanchet, all of whom are avid supporters of a woman's right to sexual and personal fulfillment both inside and outside marriage. By identifying these texts with a prestigious academic institution, Margueritte legitimates cultural radicalism for the bourgeois Monique, as well as for the bohemian new woman, for the insider as well as the outsider of bourgeois culture.

In the first two scenes, then, Margueritte contrasts two worlds—a morally decadent postwar culture, in which women are bought and sold on the marriage market, and a more radical, intellectual one, where women enjoy sexual freedom. Monique is aware of the corruption of the first, yet wary of the sexuality of the second. But when, by accident, she discovers that Lucien wants her only for her money, she is thrown into a frenzy of anger and makes love to the first man who picks her up on the street. When her parents object to her refusal to marry Lucien and casually dismiss his dishonesty, Monique is no longer able to ignore the moral bankruptcy of her own family. In the climactic final scene of the first part of the novel, she denounces bourgeois marriage as "nothing but a coupling of interests, a mutual contract of buying and selling."[39] With a fortune she conveniently inherits at precisely that moment—when her Aunt Sylvestre dies in a tragic accident—Monique goes off to live and work on her own in Paris. When we next see her, Monique is dancing in a jazz club, drinking cocktails, and engaging in an openly sexual affair with a woman.[40]

But precisely when she embraces radical gender ideals, they become problematic in two senses. First, Monique's so-called liberation is accompanied by a particularly agonizing personal upheaval. When she discovers Lucien's deception, "inner turmoil seized hold of her to such an extent that it obliterated everything else. She stood at the center of a shattered world."[41] She suffers from a "double wound," having first given herself sexually to Lucien before marrying him, and then having been cruelly deceived and betrayed by him. Thinking of this, "she bled throughout her being, . . . and wanted to be severed, immediately and forever, from what had only moments before been the reason for her existence. A part of herself amputated . . . spoiled illusion, . . . mortified flesh."[42] Far from finding happiness or fulfillment in her life as a *garçonne,* Monique lapses into a semisomnolent, depressed state, half-asleep and half-awake. "Despite some apparent healing, she remained an invalid, still anesthetized with chloroform on the operating table."[43] In this way, Monique's emotional wounds reproduce the physical wounds of the wartime combatant. No sooner do her sexual exploits begin than she begins to feel a sense of emotional emptiness, as if "an invisible worm was born in the magnificence of the fruit."[44]

As Monique rejects a more conventional feminine identity, it becomes problematic in a second sense. She finds herself forced to give up some traditional female prerogatives. Increasingly she takes on the appearance of a man—cutting her hair short and wearing tailored clothing. More important, she engages in a breathtaking series of sex role reversals. After engaging in an openly lesbian affair with a female music hall star, Monique dates only more "feminine" types of men, artists, entertainers, and dancers. She treats these men purely as objects, relishing them as instruments of sexual pleasure but forgetting them as soon as she tires of their tricks.[45] She reduces one lover first to a "glorious pleasure machine" and, later on, to a "breeder."[46] Furthermore, when Monique makes an attempt at (what is coded as) conventional feminine behavior, her efforts fail. As her feelings of apathy and malaise finally crystalize, she realizes that what she really wants is to bear a child. But after several affairs, her attempts to become pregnant are still unsuccessful. With a healthy sense of "*amour-propre masculin*,"[47] Monique first blames her failure on the men in her life. Ultimately, however, her doctor tells her that she is sterile, a fact that "made greater the desert of solitude within her."[48] Deeply depressed and isolated, she slides even further into a life of decadence and debauchery, retreating into her opium den every evening to sink into the recesses of narcotic oblivion.

Hence loneliness and despair weigh down Monique's supposedly joyous liberation. She begins to conceive of her life in this way: "She had won nothing with her freedom. Her work? What was the point if it only fed her loneliness? In pleasure, she had found only a pretense of love. If she could not have a child, what was left for her?"[49] Monique's sterility can be interpreted in several ways, first, as an attempt to reconcile her sexual freedom with the contemporary natalist movement. The natalists, intensified in numbers since the mass slaughter of the war, stressed the importance of woman's maternal role as the basis on which to rebuild France. Natalist doctors urged even single women to have children, declaring it inhumane and unhealthy to impose celibacy on them.[50] By making Monique sterile, Margueritte neutralized the meaning of her sexual rebellion in relation to natalist concerns. Since her reproductive apparatus was dysfunctional, she was no good to the republic anyway, and hence socially expendable.

One can also read Monique's sterility as the inevitable outcome of her decision to abandon conventional femininity. Having embraced a masculine life-style—identified with independence and sexual pleasure—Monique must cede the privileges of female reproductive power. In this way, erotic pleasure and maternal power remain separate, mutually exclusive ideals in *La Garçonne,* despite Monique's transgression of more superficial gender boundaries in appearance and behavior. Unable to become a mother, she remains woefully unhappy. Despite Margueritte's apparent embrace of cultural radical ideals, then, he reaffirms motherhood as the highest value of a woman's life, without which nothing else makes sense. The novel ultimately contradicts itself by denouncing as emotionally sterile female identity beyond a maternal role. In other words, Margueritte's radicalism is only skin deep.

In the last part of the novel, more prolonged relationships with two men, Boisselet and Blanchet, rescue Monique from her limbo of moral turpitude. The similarity in their names signals the parallel function of these two figures in the novel. Both are present in the earlier scene in Vignabos's office at the Collège de France, where they identify themselves as supportive of women's independence and sexual freedom. Because they, too, are attempting to redefine gender identity, they become eligible mates for Monique. Finally, both are veterans who fought bravely and survived the war only to experience difficulty in readapting to civilian life. Both, then, are the "new" men from no-man's-land. Together, as we will see, they represent alternative responses—one right and one wrong—to two cultural phenomena conflated after the war: the modern woman and the veteran's *crise de l'esprit.*

When we first meet Régis Boisselet in Vignabos's office, he voices a familiar bitterness and anger: "He still had on his heart the years of nightmare at the front, while behind the lines, in the hospitals and dancing halls, young girls like this [Monique] were playing the fool."[51] When Monique accidently runs into Boisselet again, his rancor seems not to have abated. He scolds her for her opium addiction and her self-pity, reminding her that others have suffered much greater sorrows than her own. To drive this point home, he tells her a story about a family with two sons; one was killed outright during the war and the other was permanently disabled. Aghast at the story, Monique is attracted to Boisselet's strong set of values. They begin a love affair, but it founders on Boisselet's inability to forget Monique's past of debauchery as a *femme moderne,* despite her pleas that "the past is the past. Neither you nor I can do anything about it."[52] Boisselet is troubled by his inability to reconcile himself to two kinds of pasts—that of his modern female lover and that of his own nightmarish war experience.

As Boisselet's jealousy becomes more violent, Monique begins to feel isolated and imprisoned by the relationship. At this point, she meets another lonely and depressed veteran, Boisselet's colleague Georges Blanchet. The two run across each other by accident at the Louvre, where each is viewing the ruins of ancient Babylonia. At the very moment she sees Blanchet, "in front of the winged bulls and giant friezes, Monique was thinking despondently of dead civilizations and the futility of her task."[53] A literal figuration of Paul Valéry's *crise de l'esprit,* the ruins act as a symbol for a dying bourgeois culture: "Myriads had been born, had suffered and had died. . . . And out of this whirlwind of evanescent dust, this is what remained: unfeeling stone, and a memory as deceitful as forgetfulness."[54] Seeing Blanchet plunges

Monique into a reverie about her own past, which she confuses with memory of the war and the psychic need for "forgetfulness." Blanchet congratulates her on attaining the equality they had discussed in Vignabos's office so long ago, but Monique bitterly replies: "Equality? . . . Yes, in annihilation! . . . Look at those! There's a lesson for you! . . . What ruination!"[55] By her own admission, then, Monique's embrace of a masculine life-style has led her into a no-man's-land of despair and annihilation, the ruins of a dead civilization.

But the ruins are also an ironic starting point for the future lovers' union, which will resurrect them and, by implication, bourgeois culture itself. By situating their first reunion there, Margueritte links the future of their relationship metaphorically to the fate of a dying bourgeois culture. When she and Blanchet begin to see each other, Boisselet, driven mad by jealousy, tries to kill Monique by putting a bullet through her heart. Because such a *crime passionnel* was a notoriously feminine crime in the early twentieth century, its commission by a man here represents yet another reversal in gender roles, one in which women certainly have the upper hand.[56] But precisely at this moment, when masculine self-possession collapses altogether, Blanchet resurrects male heroism, indeed masculinity itself, by placing his body between Monique and Boisselet's bullet and saving her life. Wounded, he loses consciousness and believes that he is back in the war hospital recovering from a trench wound. He awakens "another man" and sees before him "the re-emerging future in the white figure, the kind eyes, shining with life" of Monique, who, wearing a nurse's uniform, is nursing him back to health.[57]

Monique also experiences an awakening at this moment—to the shamefulness of her past and the loss of her childhood innocence. She wonders, "Was she worthy of such a love? Was she not bringing him a blackened soul, a profaned body?"[58] He reassures her by reinterpreting the debauchery of her past as a kind of moral suffering: "But I know! Yes, I know that you have suffered, like all hearts that thirst for the absolute."[59] Like Boisselet, Blanchet confuses his own moral suffering as a veteran with Monique's sexual exploits as a *femme moderne*. But unlike Boisselet, he is willing to forget her promiscuous past, *at the same moment* that he is finally able to put his own past, his own war experience behind him: "Think no more of the nightmares of the night! We are only beginning to live!"[60] Blanchet's second wound allows him to overcome his past and resurrect his own future and masculinity. Blanchet, not Boisselet, finds happiness *and* gets the *garçonne*.

Blanchet's second great awakening coincides with the resurrection of Monique's femininity. Nursing him back to health, Monique becomes the good girl of the war, the woman in white by the bedside of the wounded. When Blanchet reassures her about her past, she listens to him "as the Mary Magdalene listened to the Savior."[61] Interestingly, she feels no sexual desire for Blanchet at all. When he embraces her for the first time, "a sort of modesty [*pudeur*] that she had never felt before" overcame her.[62] The *garçonne* grows her hair long again, gives up her independent life and marries Blanchet. According to Berthet of *La Française,* she "becomes, quite simply, a woman again."[63] In the sequel to the novel, *Le Compagnon* (1923), Monique (not surprisingly) overcomes her sterility, has children, and dies, like a saint, attending the poor.[64] Her triumphant return to the traditional domestic ideal of womanhood here represents a compromise on Margueritte's part. On the one hand, Monique fulfills the radical ideal of Blum and others: she leads her *vie de garçon* before marriage, yet ultimately finds an accepting, forgiving husband. As Paul Souday of *Le Temps* put it, "normally she would have a much better chance of ending up in the gutter."[65] On the other hand, Monique's reaffirmation of conventional femininity can be read as a conservative impulse to redraw secure boundaries of sexual difference. This reconstruction of sexual difference takes on even more importance as we become aware of its redemptive power, that is, its ability to resurrect Blanchet's future out of the nightmare of the past. What else is at stake in this triumphant embrace of traditional femininity besides a happy ending for a bad girl?

Empty Suitcases

Let us attempt another interpretation of *La Garçonne,* one that reads the novel as a discussion of postwar cultural anxiety in general. In this reading, the *garçonne* Monique symbolizes the returning soldier who is freed at last from no-man's-land but who has rejected the bourgeois world that sent him to war. A look at other French novelists of the period supports this interpretation. Writers like Pierre Drieu la Rochelle, for example, portray returning veterans in much the same way as Margueritte does Monique. As we have seen, the war was a profoundly formative experience for Drieu la Rochelle. "Drieu is a writer who can't get out of the trench," argues critic Alice Kaplan.[66] The conclusion of the armistice brought him no great satisfaction. Deeply ambivalent about the world to which he had returned, Drieu plunged into Parisian social life and wrote novels about displaced veterans like himself, all of whom bear a striking resemblance to Monique.[67]

There are three clear parallels between Drieu la Rochelle's veterans and Margueritte's *garçonne*. First, Drieu's veterans return home thunderstruck and dazed by their experiences in the war. The soldier in the short story "La Prière d'Hargeville" (1918), for example, describes himself in this way: "War, like solitude you have obsessed me, you hold me in your grasp. . . . I am a poor child, fascinated and lost. Will I ever awaken from this mystical dream?"[68] Many of Drieu's young male characters, for example, Gonzague of *Plainte contre l'inconnu* (1924) or Gille of *L'Homme couvert des femmes* (1925), seem to be sleepwalking. Unengaged in life and uncommitted to any one person, they inhabit a dimly lit world of dreams and memories.[69] These veterans resemble, then, the "still anesthetized" Monique in her first days of freedom. Drifting in a kind of dream, Monique is also half-asleep and half-awake.

Second, like Monique, Drieu la Rochelle's veterans sink into a life of drugs and sexual promiscuity. Gille in *L'Homme couvert des femmes,* for instance, is described as "mad with pleasure."[70] Obsessed with death and sex, Gille and his friend Luc while away their hours in bars, salons, and opium dens. They engage in open sexual relations with prostitutes and single women. In "Nous fûmes surpris," a story that takes place not long after the armistice in the spring of 1919, soldiers go from café to café in Paris, drinking and talking rudely to women.[71] Guy, the main character, is "still attached to the principles that had sustained his parents," but "having no other guide than his disordered senses, he turns down dangerous roads, like a rebellious and lost blind man."[72] In "La Valise vide," Gonzague, another veteran, takes drugs as a way of "staying far away from Madame Lemberg, far away from women, far away from everything that was alive."[73] Drieu la Rochelle explains Gonzague's and his friends' behavior in this way: "Rather than being repressed altogether, their passions instead found unexpected outlets. Above all, it was necessary to disrupt unity and continuity."[74] Hence Drieu la Rochelle's veterans also resemble Monique in her life of debauchery. Monique's once honest passions, like those of the veterans, have been diverted into a blind rebellion against her parents' values.

Third, these veterans, like Monique, are sterile. Despite their many promiscuous relationships, they never have children and begin families. Gille, for example, cannot commit himself to either Finette or Jacqueline, the two women he loves. When he leaves Finette, she bitterly accuses: "the truth is, you are not capable of doing anything."[75] Gille's longing for a vaguely defined "ideal" woman, whom he never finds, reflects his quest for a new set of absolutes with which to reconstruct his life. The same emotional vagrancy characterizes Liessies, in "Le Pique-Nique" and Gonzague in "La Valise vide." These veterans pursue pleasure with an intensity that belies the spiritual emptiness it conceals: "all this freneticism was only depressing immobility, idle contemplation and sterile expectation."[76] Like Monique, their lives of pleasure bring them no sense of fulfillment or control.

If Monique's sterility marked her disavowal of female identity, that of the veterans was linked to the theme of emasculation. In *La Comédie de Charleroi* (1934), Drieu la Rochelle's narrator argues that the technological and bureaucratic aspects of modern warfare deprived men of the opportunity to be warriors and heroes. "In this war, one called but no one responded. I realized that after a century of running . . . I was no longer doing anything but crying and gesticulating. . . . I realized that and felt the man die in me."[77] Similarly, at the beginning of *La Suite des idées*, the narrator announces: "I am not a man."[78] Drieu la Rochelle uses the metaphor *"valise vide"* or "empty suitcase" to describe the veterans' spiritual emptiness, their impotence at beginning new lives. Unable to break out of his isolation and communicate with others (in particular women), Gonzague, the central character of "La Valise vide," attempts suicide. In Drieu la Rochelle's words, Gonzague "was everywhere and nowhere. He remained outside of everything."[79] The veteran, like the war itself, was everywhere and yet nowhere.

According to the literary critic Benjamin Crémieux, several other young postwar writers besides Drieu la Rochelle voiced this sense of *crise de l'esprit*. Crémieux analyzes four other postwar novels—*Détours*, by René Crevel; *Femme de paille*, by Léon-Pierre Quint; *Le Coeur gros*, by Bernard Barbey; and *A la dérive*, by Philippe Soupault—in order to create what he calls "a sort of composite portrait of the *jeune homme moderne*."[80] The heroes of all four novels, he argues, are identical in "their inability to grasp and then to hold onto whatever is there," most important, emotional attachments.[81] The hero of Barbey's *Le Coeur gros*, for example, oscillates between his friendship with Walt and his love for Walt's wife, Claude. Soupault's David "looked for a route without being able to make a choice."[82] Quint's hero boasts "no passion binds any part of me to anything."[83] These men are free for lack of being able to settle down, "abominably free" as the hero of *Détours* puts it.[84] Thus they resemble Monique in her emotional wanderings, her fondness for highly sexual and uncommitted relationships.

According to Crémieux, the women in these novels contrast sharply with their male counterparts in that they "know what they want and are capable of persevering in their designs or their whims with a tenacity that guarantees their success." In particular, they take on *"l'initiative de l'amour,"* beginning and ending relationships with men as these suit them.[85] Hence these novels demonstrate the same kind of sex role reversals that we have already encountered in Monique's willful sexual exploits, but with one important difference. In *La Garçonne,* Monique plays both the modern woman, capable of sexual initiative, and the veteran, incapable of emotional commitment. Monique as *garçonne,* as girl-boy represents both the modern woman and the "no-man," the man made frail or feminine by the war.

Understanding Monique as no-man as well as modern woman helps us to comprehend why, despite her relatively sheltered young life, she is haunted by the memory of the "remains of men, fragments of intelligence, hope and love" at the Hospice de Bois-Fleury and why she chafes at "the idea that one part of humanity bleeds while the other amuses itself." Her role as symbol of the veteran also clarifies why her rejection of bourgeois values, far from liberating her, places her "at the center of a shattered world," suffering from the "spoiled illusion" of her past. She reproduces the "double wound" of the combatant, having given herself voluntarily to Lucien, as the poilu gave himself to the war, only to be cruelly deceived, as the soldier was, by the illusion of honor. Suffering from these wounds, he, too, "bled throughout [his] being," having been "amputated" from all that had given life meaning before the war. Even after the armistice, "despite some apparent healing," he remained an invalid, like Monique, "still anesthetized . . . on the operating table." However, as the veteran Blanchet's wound is transformed into a mark of male heroism, he recovers consciousness and a sense of the future. Again, his reawakening coincides with that of Monique, who for one last time grieves the past, the loss of childhood innocence, the ruins of a dead civilization.

Margueritte's Monique can also be interpreted, then, as the symbol of a displaced and dreaming no-man. In Berthet's words, she lives a veteran's life, in which all poetry, all illusion has been "banished." She is not the only modern woman in postwar literature to act as a symbol in this way. Camille Englemann plays a similar role in Marcel Prévost's *Les Don Juanes,* another best-seller published in 1922 by a popular writer and member of the Académie française.[86] *Les Don Juanes* was often referred to in the same breath as *La Garçonne,* although Prévost's novel never enjoyed the spectacular success of Margueritte's. Otherwise the similarities between the two novels are striking.[87] *Les Don Juanes* also begins at the end of the war in an atmosphere of cultural and social dislocation. Prévost describes France in these terms: "ruins of houses, of factories and workshops, . . . ruins as well of what, in the home, could not be repaired with bricks and stones."[88] Like Margueritte's Monique and Drieu's veterans, Prévost's French seem to be sleepwalking: "Suffering from hallucinations, half-anesthesized, they wandered in the dark, not even asking where they went."[89] Promiscuous modern woman and bitter, uncommitted veterans also populate Prévost's novel. It concerns three *Don Juanes,* as they are referred to here, who in their relationships with men take what Crémieux referred to as *"l'initiative de l'amour."* Reviewers pointed out that since none of the three women has more than one relationship with a man, they are not true *"Don Juanes."* Still, the image of the sexually aggressive woman in the novel proved fascinating to critics. As Marc Varenne of *La Renaissance politique* put it, "They exist. No one would dare deny it. Why not, then, write their story?"[90]

Camille Englemann, the most vivid and interesting of the three *Don Juanes,* owns a large bank that she has taken over for her father (presumed dead) during the war. At the same time, Camille has somehow managed (and the improbability of this is significant) to volunteer in the army and be wounded twice. Hence, she reproduces the experiences of both sexes in the war. Like Monique, Camille is both modern woman and veteran. On the one hand, her male colleagues consider her "a man in terms of her intelligence and energy," and compare her with Elizabeth I or Catherine II in that she inspires "the same combination of esteem, admiration and naïve fear as those past destroyers of men [*consommatrices de mâles*]."[91] On the other hand, Camille's "ravaged face" and her skeletal, "wasted" body tell the story of where she has been, a story she tries to camouflage except in front of her own mirror. "Justly proud of her waist size before, she now was nothing more than a bony silhouette." One of Valéry's European ghosts, Camille is described as a "phantom" and a "frightening shadow of her former self."[92]

Prévost's portrait of the ravaged, sunken body of Camille contradicts her male colleagues' perception of her as a powerful, intimidating woman.[93] As a woman made man, she is able to intimidate others, but she inspires only revulsion and anxiety in herself. Prévost figures, in one body, postwar gender confusion in all its guises. Camille is at once the newly empowered "destroyer of men," who can inspire sexual fear in her colleagues, and the man destroyed by the war, anguished by his own emasculation. "I have sacrificed the woman that I was," she says to herself, "I have sacrificed the balance and joy of my life to an obscure impulse that I called my duty."[94] Rejected in love, she blames it on the hideous scars that the war has left and decides to commit suicide. "I can no longer endure the suffering from my wound and the operation I underwent," she writes in her suicide note, "I have acted like a courageous man; and because I am not a man, I am punished for my courage."[95] For Camille as well as Monique, then, the war's gift of freedom becomes a mixed blessing, "the sacrifice of the woman that she was." But unlike Monique, Camille fails to reconstruct a more conventional female identity, and this very failure leads to her suicide.

Camille's inability to return to a traditional model of femininity can also explain why *Les Don Juanes*, published the same year as *La Garçonne* and containing much of the same sexually explicit subject matter, never became as well-known or as widely read as Margueritte's novel. Even though *La Garçonne* was considered scandalous and outrageous, its ending had a pacifying effect. The novel worked simultaneously on two levels to soothe and to dispel postwar cultural anxiety. First, it normalized dramatic wartime changes in women's lives, and second, it reconstructed a rational future out of the nightmare of the war. In Margueritte's novel, Blanchet's war-devastated masculinity is able to recover thanks to the restoration of Monique's femininity. By ultimately embracing domestic femininity, Monique appeases the cultural/gender anxieties raised throughout the novel and covers over the ruptures of the war experience. Such a recovery does not take place in *Les Don Juanes:* here Camille, like Colette's Chéri, cannot reconcile herself to the past. Margueritte's figuration of postwar cultural crisis through the character of a promiscuous *femme moderne* accounts, in no small part, for the controversy surrounding *La Garçonne*. Likewise, by ultimately reconstructing a stabilized universe from the ruins of a civilization, the novel ensured its own popularity and its tenacity as a central cultural myth of the era.

3

"WOMEN ARE CUTTING THEIR HAIR AS A SIGN OF STERILITY"

FASHION WAS A HIGHLY-CHARGED ISSUE during the twenties. In 1925, an article in *L'Oeuvre* jocularly described how the fashion of short hair completely overturned life in a small French village. After the first woman in the village cut her hair, accompanied by "tears and grinding of teeth" on the part of her family, the fashion quickly became "epidemic: from house to house, it took its victims." A gardener swore he would lock up his daughter until her hair grew back; a husband believed that his wife had dishonored him. A scandalized *curé* decided to preach a sermon about it, but "unfortunately he had chosen the wrong day, since it was the feast of Jeanne d'Arc." As he began to condemn bobbed hair as indecent and un-Christian, "the most impudent young ladies of the parish pointed insolently at the statue of the liberator."[1] By claiming the bobbed-cut Joan of Arc as their mascot, these young women grounded their quest for "liberation" in the rich, tangled mainstream of French history. They appealed to the ambivalent, yet strongly traditional image of *Jeanne la pucelle,* at once patriotic, fervently Christian, and sexually ambiguous.

The fashion among young women for short, bobbed hair could inspire enormous tension within the family. Throughout the decade, newspapers recorded lurid tales, including one husband in the provinces who sequestered his wife for bobbing her hair, and another father who reportedly killed his daughter for the same reason.[2] A father in Dijon sought legal action against a hairdresser in 1925 for cutting the hair of his daughter without his permission.[3] "At present, the question of short hair is dividing families," argued Antoine, one of the hairdressers who pioneered the bobbed cut.[4] "The result," according to Paul Reboux, the editor-in-chief of *Paris-soir,* "was that during family meals, nothing is heard except the clicking of the forks on the porcelain."[5] One working-class woman, who was in her twenties during the era, remembered that her mother-in-law did not talk to her sister-in-law Simone for almost a year after the latter bobbed her hair.[6] René Rambaud, another prominent hairdresser in the twenties, recalled the story of a newly married woman who cut her hair, believing that she had the right to do so without consulting her parents. Her mother and father, in turn, accused her husband and his parents of the monstrous crime, leading to a rift so severe that the two families did not reconcile for twenty years.[7]

Why was bobbed hair such an emotional issue in the French family after the war? The outcry concerning the bob was only part of a heated debate on fashion that began during the later war years and peaked between 1924 and 1926.[8] The debate concerned fashions for women that emerged during the war—low-cut dresses, short skirts, pyjamas, the abandonment of the corset. The controversy surrounding fashion during these years can be explained, in part, by its novelty and unfamiliarity. Short hair exemplified the dramatic, provocative changes sweeping the world of French fashion. Notions of female fashion had undergone a profound transformation since the beginning of the century. According to the journalist René Bizet, for example, every aspect of female dress had not only changed, but become the mirror opposite of what it had been in 1900.[9] Both before and during the war, as the ideal of the voluptuous, curvaceous woman gave way to a sinuous, smooth, "modernist" one, the compressed structural lines and highly ornamental fashions of the previous century were radically simplified. Paul Poiret pioneered the new minimalist style within the elite world of *haute couture* during the first two decades of the twentieth century. Working-class and middle-class women began to adopt the more efficient approach to fashion during the war.[10] In the early twenties, the designer Coco Chanel created a sporty, casual style by further simplifying Poiret's fashions. Mass-produced and meticulously imitated throughout France, the Chanel look reached its peak of popularity by 1925 and held sway there until 1927 or 1928.[11]

The craze for short hair typified this chronology of change in the fashion world. At the turn of the century, excessive baroque hairstyles had dominated, and in the prewar years, only a few actresses, such as Caryathis and Eve Lavallière, cut their hair short.[12] Precisely who was responsible for popularizing the bob is a matter of dispute. Chanel, who cut her hair in 1916, is often credited with the revolution in hairstyles, as are two hairdressers, Antoine Cierplikowski and René Rambaud, who pioneered the style in professional circles during the early 1920s (fig. 7).[13] In any case, between 1918 and 1925, short bobbed hair "*à la Jeanne d'Arc*" or "*aux enfants d'Edouard*" grew in popularity and by mid-decade was sending shockwaves throughout France.[14] Particularly important to the popularity of the bob was the 1922 publication of Victor Margueritte's *La Garçonne*. According to René Rambaud, the novel inspired young women throughout France to cut their hair and otherwise follow the new style "*à l'allure garçonnière*."[15] After 1922, the new styles were associated with the young, sexy, independent modern woman.

The fashion styles that emerged in the 1920s dramatically differed from those of the turn of the century. However, since the new look emerged gradually, the fashion controversy cannot be explained solely in terms of its novelty. In looking back on the decade, memoirists invariably described the new styles as central to the spirit of the era, suggesting the broader cultural significance of fashion. "Short hair was not only a fashion, it was an epoch. It was a particular sign of a time," argued Rambaud in his memoir.[16] The "epoch" of short hair began immediately after the war, when the new bobbed cut first became an object of widespread controversy.[17] If we are to believe the radical feminist Henriette Sauret, the bob already preoccupied the French in 1919, when relatively few women were actually cutting their hair. During that year, Sauret made fun of male journalists who, faced with major stories such as the Paris Peace Conference, demobilization, and the Bolshevik "threat," still concerned themselves with women's hair. "This urgent question," Sauret cuttingly observed, occupies "a good third of their daily remarks." Short hair, she argued, "holds a certain interest for men that has gone undetected by us, because they deign to devote to it the precious emanations of their brains."[18] Although Sauret was obviously exaggerating, her remarks raise an interesting question. What "undetected interest" did short hair hold that it became the focus of so much emotion and anger? If fashion was a sort of "text," a complex visual language that postwar observers "read" in various ways, what about the new style gave so much offense? How did postwar observers—journalists, clergy, pamphleteers, designers, feminists—explain its dramatic and explosive power? Why was postwar fashion so central to the cultural mythology of the postwar period?

The controversy surrounding fashion can be explained by the fact that postwar observers "read" or interpreted it as a visual language for the war's social upheaval. As a result of changes in the world of fashion, a sizable debate concerning what women wore arose in the postwar period among journalists, novelists, sociologues, and social observers. A closer look at this debate can shed light on what precisely was so scandalous about the new style, or, in Sauret's words, what "undetected interest" it held to inspire so much attention. During the postwar period, fashion bore the symbolic weight of a whole set of social anxieties concerning the war's perceived effects on gender relations: the blurring or reversal of gender roles and the crisis of domesticity. Once again, it was the modern woman's role as symbol of the war's disruptive effects—her figuration of postwar gender/cultural anxieties—that lay at the heart of the controversy. In addition, postwar fashion figured in a larger struggle for social and political power. Feminists, designers (both male and female), and the women who put on the new fashions interpreted them as affording physical mobility and freedom. Because the new fashions were seen in this way—as a visual language of liberation—they also became invested with political meaning.

Nothing More Than a Rigid Straight Line

Before turning to the postwar debate on fashion, let us examine the social and economic context in which it occurred, as well as its place in the general history of French fashion. The centrality of fashion to a larger discourse concerning identity and power makes particular sense for France, where Paris had dominated the industry worldwide since the seventeenth century. In postwar France, more than anywhere else in Europe, fashion played a central role in the economy and as a form of cultural expression. The fashion industry itself had been ruled by the *haute couture* designers since the mid-nineteenth century.[19] Although only a minute fraction of French women could afford *haute couture,* it was widely imitated and disseminated throughout France and the world by the fashion press and the ready-to-wear industry. A proliferation of fashion journals and the rise of the department store also characterized the growth of the industry in the late nineteenth century. Trends initiated by French designers were enormously influential in deciding what the fashionable woman wore, but other factors, such as commercial promotion, methods of production, and consumer demand also affected changes in fashion.[20]

The fashion industry enjoyed a period of prosperity after the war.

Because of the diminution of European royal and aristocratic circles, Parisian designers found themselves catering to new customers, among them the nouveaux riches, writers and artists, and rich Americans.[21] Many new houses opened, including that of Coco Chanel, the first nationally and internationally known female couturier.[22] The influence of the *haute couture* designers became greater than ever after the war. Although mass production of fashionable styles had begun many decades earlier, postwar fashion was democratized in an unprecedented manner. As René Rambaud, the pioneer of the bobbed hairstyle, explained: "Until this time, fashion remained the privilege of a certain part of society; at this point, it penetrated all social classes, from *la plus grande aristocrate* to the humblest village dweller."[23] The ongoing transformation in the clothing industry toward mass marketing, as well as the development of the press and a full-scale advertising industry after the war, made fashion increasingly a product for mass consumption. The broad social dimensions of the postwar fashion controversy need to be understood against this background of a burgeoning consumer culture. When George Sand dressed as a man in the 1840s, she was likely to remain an isolated phenomenon; when Coco Chanel did the same in the 1920s, she was imitated throughout France and the world.

Within this social and economic context, a dramatically new style of women's dress arose during the first two decades of the twentieth century, a style most frequently associated with the designer Paul Poiret.[24] "It was the age of the corset," Poiret later reminisced, "I waged war upon it. It was in the name of liberty that I brought about my first Revolution, by deliberately laying siege to the corset."[25] Poiret here likened himself to a revolutionary storming the Bastille of Victorian fashion, thereby restoring to women their innate right to freedom of movement.[26] In addition, Poiret's art deco fashion plates, illustrated by Paul Iribe and then Georges LePape, revolutionized fashion illustration. Poiret was less concerned with transmitting information about the design involved than with conveying its "modern spirit" through a flat, highly decorative and abstract style. His illustrations were "cubist" inasmuch as the construction and detail of the dress remained vague and subordinate to the overall design. Poiret's idealized designs took on a life of their own, bringing fame to Poiret's styles apart from how they actually looked on women.

Despite Poiret's revolutionary achievements in the prewar world of *haute couture,* the new, more fluid style was above all—like the modern woman herself—a creation of the war. Although the new look emerged within the elite world of Paris *couture* long before 1914, working-class and middle-class women did not embrace it until after the war broke out.[27] In the somber spirit of the war years, the old ornamental frou-frous and decorative accessories were put away, and neutral colors adopted. Women doing factory work, for example, began to dress in simple sheath-like frocks and short, full skirts called *crinolines de querre,* or war crinolines.[28] Even after the war, large jewelry or ornaments of any kind that drew attention to itself remained out of fashion.[29] The taste for a more convenient, minimalist, pared-down look persisted, even as French women returned from the war hospitals and factories. By the end of the war, the visual appearance of the modern woman had begun to take shape.

In the early twenties, Coco Chanel, the youngest and most daring of the Parisian *couturières* after the war, further developed the new style.[30] Besides opening the world of *haute couture* to women, Chanel tried to create a look for the modern woman that was comfortable, practical, and compatible with an "active" life. "Chanel expresses the heart and soul of the modern woman," declared the title of a 1923 article in *Vogue.*[31] She used beige jersey to assure a loose, easy line as well as a sort of "poor" look for her designs.[32] Poiret jested about his postwar rival: "What did Chanel invent? *Pauvreté de luxe.*" In part because jersey was so difficult to sew, Chanel simplified and abbreviated her designs to an extent that Poiret had never dared, creating a sporty, casual look. She removed the waistline altogether, and radically shortened the skirt to well above the ankle (fig. 8). Chanel also adopted male fashions—short hair, ties, collars, long tailor-cut jackets, pyjamas—to create a boyish look.[33] Chanel's style of dress peaked in popularity at mid-decade and maintained its dominance in the fashion world until 1927 or 1928, when designers like Jean Patou and Elsa Schiaparelli began to reassert the waist and the bust.

The new style came to be known for its modernist spirit and its almost "Taylorist" efficiency of line.[34] In 1926, Maurice Prax, an editor of *Le Petit parisien,* argued that "[t]he weaker sex is completely destroying its charm, in order to be, from whatever angle one considers it, nothing more than a rigid straight line."[35] Whereas the encased, exaggerated female form of 1900 emphasized "womanliness"—a woman's breasts and hips—the new style relativized these as neither more nor less important than any other part of the female body. This body became a set of shifting, interchangeable planes and surfaces. According to a fashion writer for *Vogue* in 1923, the new style was also "the sign of an extreme modernism," because of its flat, cubist tendencies.[36] The well-known journalist and novelist Clément Vautel wagered in 1924 that a young modern woman "would no doubt consent, if fashion demanded it, to being nothing more than the intersection of two planes, like a geometric line."[37] In 1925, Colette described the new image as "short, flat, geometric and quadrangular."[38]

Although the new style followed a fashion cycle of growth and decline in the decade 1918 to 1928, its basic aesthetic and lines remained unaltered. Hence the period represents an internally consistent stage in fashion design, and the fashion commentary and debate from these years can be grouped together as a coherent body of evidence.[39] At the same time that Chanel's styles were popularized after the war, they became inscribed in a debate concerning the war and its perceived effect on gender relations. Because it was relatively consistent in content over the decade following 1918, this debate on fashion can be best explored thematically rather than chronologically, by analyzing the way in which the new fashion was interpreted first, by its critics, and, second, by its defenders.

Disguising Themselves as Men

The most vociferous critics of the new fashions included traditional conservatives, such as Catholics and natalists, as well as a smattering of journalists, writers, and fashion commentators whose social and political positions remain difficult to fix. Their invective concerning fashion began in the immediate postwar period and seemed to peak during the years 1925 to 1927. Most of these critics were men, but because many of fashion's most ardent supporters were also male, namely fashion designers and hairdressers, no simple historical analysis by gender is possible. The critics of fashion found two aspects of the new styles particularly offensive: first, their ability to blur the boundaries of sexual difference, causing women not only to look but also to act like men, and, second, their apparent lack of modesty.[40]

As early as 1918, Clément Vautel used a cartoon to express the first of these two critiques of fashion—its tendency to turn women into men (fig. 9). Vautel was a prominent novelist and journalist, well known for his natalist and antifeminist views.[41] His cartoon features a *midinette* being arrested "for the crime of wearing attire said to be feminine, including a skirt." The female police officers wear male uniforms and harsh, authoritarian expressions. In Vautel's fantasy of the future (the article is titled "Feminism in 1958"), women have seized political control from men. The cartoon relates the fear that women could no longer be "women" even if this were their wish, and that they were becoming indistinguishable from men, in their appearance as well as in their possession of traditionally male powers. The cartoon neatly illustrates the political stakes in the debate on fashion.

Above all, Vautel meant his cartoon to be funny. The lament that fashion erased gender boundaries often became the subject of innocent humor and sarcastic commentary. A 1921 column in the women's magazine *Fémina* told the story of a woman who was driving dressed in a riding outfit that made her indistinguishable from a man. When she caused an accident with another car by her own recklessness, the other driver, a man, emerged from his ruined vehicle. Enraged enough to mistake her sex, he slugged her in the jaw.[42] In 1922, Roger Boutet de Monvel, a fashion commentator for both *Vogue* and the highbrow *Gazette du bon ton,* used the example of Chanel's pyjamas to proclaim that women were "disguising themselves as men." "What gracious attention in our regard," he added sarcastically, "what kinder flattery than this, to so imitate us in all things?"[43] An article in the radical-socialist *Le Quotidien* (1924) worried that women who bobbed their hair might eventually suffer from baldness, that once strictly male source of anguish. Because medical wisdom at the time held that the shortness of one's hair caused baldness in some way, *Le Quotidien* wondered "if it wouldn't be necessary to pay dearly in a few years for this fantasy of young womanhood?"[44]

Elsewhere, however, the tendency of women to "disguise" themselves as men was not met with humor but with serious observation and invective.[45] "Smoking, wearing short hair, dressed in pyjamas or sportswear," complained the writer Francis de Miomandre, "women increasingly resemble their companions."[46] In 1925, an anonymous Catholic author declared: "Modern women shouldn't try to masculinize themselves, and thus to lose their sex.—A woman becoming a boy: No!"[47] Some critiques were grounded in fashionable scientific discourse, such as that on sexual perversion inspired by the translation of Havelock Ellis's work into French. "The species feels itself endangered by a growing inversion [*uranisme*]," the literary critic Pierre Lièvre argued in 1927, "No more hips, no more breasts, no more hair."[48] Evolutionary theory linked fashion trends to an ominous biological future. Fashion commentators predicted "the advent of the third sex" or the creation of a single one.[49] "I myself don't know if Lamarck had foreseen this transformation of the species," wrote the poet Jean Dars in a 1925 survey on the *jeune fille*. "It is not written in his *History of Invertebrate*

Animals that young girls were supposed to take on the appearance of boys so soon."[50]

In reading fashion as a visual erasure of sexual difference, postwar critics referred to the new female body and even "womanhood" itself as lacking clear definition or intelligibility. We have already heard the question of a Parisian law student in 1925: "Can one define *la jeune fille moderne*? No, no more than the waist on the dresses she wears. Young girls of today are difficult to locate precisely." This observer described the modern woman as a "being . . . without breasts, without hips."[51] The same year, the novelist Christiane Fournier called the young modern woman "a monster," explaining that "I only mean to say that she has been thrown by her time beyond the realm of natural law. We work [outside the home], and cause a great deal of trouble for ourselves . . . we aim for our ideal, which is to masculinize ourselves. Our hair is short, we are independent in both word and deed."[52] Both these observers emphasize the inability of the modern woman to be "located precisely" within the "natural laws" or traditions of French society. For both, the modern woman's rejection of the well-defined female form symbolized her lack of cultural intelligibility. Also in 1925, René Bizet noted how after the war, some designers had tried to bring back the old styles, "in vain, wanting to safeguard the charms of yesteryear and re-establish the frontiers, so to speak." According to him, the war, which had "overturned everything," made this impossible.[53] For Bizet, the loss of the old, well-defined female form became a visual sign of the war's disruptive effects—its wreaking havoc with the traditional "frontiers" or boundaries of sexual difference. The silhouette of *la femme moderne*—as a being without breasts, without a waist, without hips—visually expressed the erosion of traditional cultural categories.

In addition to the "masculine" nature of the new fashions, the critics found their apparent lack of modesty particularly offensive. In 1924, the illustrator George Barbier remarked dryly that in the park at Versailles, passers-by have the "good fortune of seeing for nothing what is so costly for a music-hall audience."[54] In a 1925 article entitled "Where will they stop?" one fashion commentator warned that "the divorce between fashion and modesty is very close to being pronounced."[55] "If your dress finishes too high," asked the civil engineer Gérard Lavergne, "doesn't it also start a little low? Aren't you afraid of getting a cold?"[56] The editor Maurice Prax warned in 1926 that "dresses are, in effect, getting so short that the time is coming when they can no longer be shortened—after all, nothingness does not get shorter."[57] Complaining of "flimsy dresses, too short, sometimes too open, clinging to the body," Cécile Jeglot, the Catholic spokeswoman for *Action populaire,* condemned modern women in this way: "With the recklessness and the intransigence of their twenty years, they . . . shave hair that is already cut short and shorten dresses that are already abbreviated both from the top and from the bottom."[58] In 1927, still another fashion observer dubbed the postwar years *"notre époque si déshabillée"* and condemned the "greedy couturier who unknowingly cuts away the last entrenchments of our virtue."[59]

Not surprisingly, Catholics and church officials led the crusade against the perceived lack of modesty in dress. At mid-decade, Catholics called modern women the *"déshabillées,"* or "the undressed ones," and expressed the fear that given current trends, "total nudity" would soon result."[60] In 1924, one Catholic spokesman quoted from the Bible Saint Paul's description of hair as a "natural veil, an expression or symbolic protection of feminine modesty."[61] By 1926, some priests and archbishops were refusing Holy Communion to young women who, in Father Vuillermet's words, came to church "more immodestly dressed than the pagans in their frenzied Saturnalia."[62] During that year, warnings were posted on church doors that women would not be served the sacraments unless they appeared in a specified style and length of dress.[63] One pamphlet published by the Catholic organization *Action populaire* went so far as to describe the new fashions as a free masonry plot to corrupt women and therefore the church.[64] Even the pope became involved, declaring postwar fashions "a veritable shame, from a human as well as a Christian point of view."[65]

Critics of the new styles also frequently inscribed their popularity within a socioeconomic context of *la crise du foyer,* women's so-called rejection of the traditional maternal, domestic role. Medical attention focused on the dire physiological effects of the new body image. In 1919, the natalist doctor François Fouveau de Courmelles claimed that the new styles had "reduced" women "to the state of eunuchs or sticks [*bâtons*], in which no supplementary being could find a place to live or be nourished." He dubbed postwar fashion "the fashion of non-nursing . . . the fashion of non-motherhood." For Courmelles, fashion itself besieged the set of norms, values, and social practices that had structured female identity in terms of a maternal, domestic role throughout the nineteenth century. Scanty dressed left the female body vulnerable to winds and drafts, so that women were bound to harm their reproductive organs. Postwar fashions, by transforming women into sexless eunuchs, non-mothers, and non-women, were the reason behind the falling birthrate.[66]

Such complaints continued throughout the decade. In 1920, the natalist Catholic pamphlet *La Mode est coupable* ("Fashion Is Guilty") described the new styles as physically dangerous and accused young women in this way: "Your children will suffer because of you, and the future generation, product of an age of pleasure, will not know how to preserve what our soldiers have defended."[67] Conservatives such as Roger Boutet de Monvel and Marius Boisson also condemned the new styles on these terms. According to Boutet de Monvel in 1922, the new styles caused a woman to ignore her family and home as well as encouraged a decline in *moeurs*.[68] "There is a repudiation of the womb, since she no longer wants to be a mother," wrote the novelist Boisson in 1925, as well as "a repudiation of breasts of any size . . . since if, by chance, she is a mother, she no longer wants to nourish her flesh."[69] Two other Catholic critics of fashion also argued in 1926 that modern women "do not want children because the short, new dresses no longer lend themselves to the disfigurements required by maternity"; consequently, "the most serious interests of the race are compromised."[70]

These critics voiced profound anxiety concerning de-sexed women and the erosion of traditional notions of femininity. Fashion preoccupied a disproportionate amount of attention throughout the twenties because critics interpreted it as a visual language that reproduced perceived changes in gender relations associated with the First World War: namely, the blurring of gender boundaries and *la crise du foyer*. The critics' interpretation of fashion as a symbol of alarming new postwar behaviors on the part of women—their so-called virilization and rejection of motherhood—explains the certain interest that fashion held in order to become the focus of so much emotion and anger. If we are to believe the critics of fashion, the new styles challenged traditional notions of gender difference as well as conventional modes of dress.

She is Completely Uncovered

Fashion's power to shock derived from its ability to figure not only shifts in gender roles, but also cultural upheaval in general. Some critics interpreted fashion as a visual expression of a larger cultural malaise—Valéry's *crise de l'esprit*. For example, in his classic postwar treatise of education, *Nouvelles lettres à Françoise* (1922), Marcel Prévost tried to comfort his niece, Françoise, who had two young daughters fast on their way to becoming *femmes modernes*. He acknowledged that

> it doesn't please you that skirts are so short that they show the knee, that the thickness of stockings has been so reduced that they are as transparent as tracing paper, and that evening dresses have been bared to the waist, both in the back and on the sides.[71]

Prévost admitted that the postwar woman was suffering from a "crisis of modesty" that had resulted from the war. But he tried to convince his niece that such a crisis was only skin deep, by distinguishing between *"vertu féminine,"* or female virtue, and *"pudeur,"* which for him meant modesty, ignorance, or innocence. Female virtue had remained intact, he reassured his niece. It was only *"pudeur"* that was a casualty of the war, in particular, of the war hospitals:

> For the first time, young French girls had to sacrifice the traditional modesty [*pudeur*] they had been taught in exchange for the tender pity that every woman feels for the young suffering man. In this place of physical misery, amid the suffering, the odor of blood and iodoform, a new communion of young women and men was established.[72]

Through the war experience, Prévost concluded, young women gained in moral strength, but, to a great extent, had lost their innocence. Hence, what he called the *"pudeur visible,"* or "visible modesty," that had characterized their prewar attire became, in this context, anachronistic, even though the "female virtue" of young girls remained untainted.[73]

In this way, Prévost linked the abbreviated nature of postwar fashions, which was so upsetting to many French men and women, with the "young suffering man" of 1914 and the "physical misery" of the war hospitals. He read postwar fashion as a visual language of the emotional exposure women experienced during the war—their innocence "sacrificed." Such a reading of fashion suggests that, for many critics, the appearance of the modern woman could have been troubling on a still deeper level, where it evoked not only Prévost's *crise de pudeur* but also Valéry's *crise de l'esprit.* When a critic of short hair argued, "It's a pity to think, believe me, that a woman would be voluntarily led to dispose of her own poetry," how did this phrase reverberate in a society so recently disposed of its own poetry—its own values, ideals, and notions of beauty?[74] When Drieu la Rochelle proclaimed that "this civilization no longer has clothes," was he referring to the *désha-billées*—the bobbed hair and short dresses of *la femme moderne*? Or was he thinking of a culture whose own innocence or illusions had been sacrificed?

Drieu la Rochelle provided a clue as to how he might answer this question in his portrait of the modern woman in "Le Pique-Nique" (1924). This short story, which concerns a disaffected war veteran named Liessies, contains the following description of Gwen, Liessies's girlfriend and a *femme moderne*: "She is extremely thin, mere skin and bones. . . . Women are cutting their hair as a sign of sterility. Sections of her hair are hidden under her handkerchief. She walks with empty hands; she wears no jewelry; she is completely uncovered."[75] The language Drieu la Rochelle uses to describe Gwen confuses her nakedness with other less tangible qualities—deprivation, barrenness, a lack of warmth and pleasure. As such, the language evokes a moral anguish that exceeds the boundaries of mere description. Like Monique's literal sterility in *La Garçonne*, Gwen's metaphoric sterility here represents the spiritual impotence felt by the veteran Liessies, with whom Gwen is involved. What Drieu la Rochelle finds of certain interest concerning the appearance of the modern woman is the way she evokes both a sense of exposure and a fundamental loss of innocence.

The same preoccupation with the starkness and sterility of the new fashions marks a later book titled *Reproches à une dame qui a coupé ses cheveux* (1927). The author Pierre Lièvre condemns his neighbor for bobbing her hair because in doing so, she has lost the ability to distinguish between those to whom her hair was always done up, and those to whom she let it down in the intimacy of her home. "One well knows that she can no longer transform herself in the bedroom: one knows her exactly as she is."[76] For Lièvre, then, short hair signified a new frankness and exposure in women's behavior, as well as the loss of a virginal intimacy, a domestic, private pleasure. Speaking of those husbands and lovers who had suffered from "the parricidal scissors" and "the cruel fashions that reign today," Lièvre concluded with this lament: "their intimacy has lost its crowning glory. They no longer awaken near a tousled lover, but instead, a friend with disheveled hair."[77] Short hair, as Lièvre presented it, was "cruel" in that it effaced a woman's femininity and "parricidal" in that it destroyed the world of the fathers—a familiar, parental world of domestic security.

The modern woman signified a colder, more impersonal world. In 1924, the novelist Magdeleine Chaumont critiqued her in this way:

Warped by life or only by fashion, we distance ourselves from what could be called somewhat disdainfully: tender feelings. . . . Observe in any public place the expression that all women wear upon their faces. Do we see one who is kind, dreamy, or satisfied? No, they all have features that are shut, hard, spiteful. . . . Put simply, women are becoming nasty, aggressive; one expects from them a cruel or disagreeable word. There is no longer either the heart of the mother or that of the daughter or lover. There is the dried-out heart of *la femme moderne,* the universal heart has become a desert.[78]

As in the case of Drieu la Rochelle and Lièvre, what charges this description of the modern woman is once again the replacement of a "dreamy," "tender" world of warmth and satisfaction with one that is colder, sterile, more exposed. Warped by life or only by fashion? The distinction was hard to draw, particularly as fashion itself took on the symbolic weight of anguish concerning the perceived loss of idealism and innocence. These components of a lamented prewar life—at once familiar and far away—were believed to be the hard casualties of the war as well as the new fashions. Even the physiognomy of the modern woman became a way of talking about the loss of the "dreamy" prewar era and the trauma of rapid change.

Fashion thus operated as a "text" that conveyed the same *crise de l'esprit* that Drieu la Rochelle, Paul Valéry, Romain Rolland, and other prominent writers made famous after the war. The beauty of the untouched and unseen, the mysteries of youth and intimacy—these were losses associated with both the war and the new fashions. But one could also argue in the opposite way—that the new fashions championed youthful innocence rather than signaled its demise. The ideal body type was no longer the fully mature woman, but a child whose body was not yet marked by her sex. "Nowadays," remarked the journalist René Bizet, "an adolescent makes a better mannequin than the Venus de Milo."[79] One cartoon of the era features a young modern woman sticking her tongue out at the Venus de Milo and challenging the statue to dress like her.[80] Because short hair had traditionally been a hairstyle for very young girls, it created an air of childish naïveté in a woman's silhouette, even though modern women appeared less innocent than ever in other ways. A 1925 cartoon named "Proprieties" plays on this paradox (fig. 10). A teacher tells a little girl that she is "too young to wear her hair so short." Dressed in men's pyjamas and smoking a cigarette, the mother/modern woman in the cartoon has a sexy, naughty air that distinguishes her from the sexless spinster. But at the same time, she is likened to the young girl through their similar hair-styles—a reassurance that, in fact, the modern woman knows much less than her appearance would lead one to believe. The new fashions also played with an image of female naïveté in an age of profound disillusion.[81]

Postwar observers "read" in fashion a visual language that reproduced some of the war's most commented-on effects: the blurring of gender boundaries and a loss of innocence among youth. Fashion operated as a "text" that conveyed the same cultural conflicts and tensions as Victor Margueritte's *La Garçonne*. But postwar fashion also operated in its own distinct, purely visual realm. As we shall see, the visual "beat" of fashion also communicated messages that could *not* be put into words, thus adding a depth and richness to the postwar debate on women that was all its own.

An Astonishing Ease Accompanied All of Her Movements

The critics' invective against the new styles suggests that they gained popularity in a socially conservative atmosphere. Given this social and cultural climate, how did those who liked the fashions—designers, merchandisers, young women, some journalists—defend and foster their development? The supporters of fashion, whose defense of the new styles seemed to peak at mid-decade, chose to praise it as a means of giving women a necessary freedom of movement and thus emancipating them from old social as well as physical constraints.[82] A young woman justified wearing such clothes by arguing that the modern woman "does not like to be restricted; this is why she is rejecting attire that could hinder her movements."[83] Defenders of the new look created a vivid image of a new kind of woman, who leads a mobile, athletic, and independent life. To do so, they adopted two discursive strategies. First, they associated the new styles with the aesthetic of modern consumer culture, defined in terms of mobility and speed. Second, they conflated physical and psychological qualities in their logic of human behavior: how one dressed encouraged behaviors analogous to the visual image produced. This confusion of the visual and the behavioral was key to the politics of fashion in the postwar era.

Supporters produced a notion of fashion as "emancipatory" by aligning the new look with the aesthetic of modern consumer culture. The rise of mass culture, the adoption of new forms of transportation and communication, and the growth of consumerism were socioeconomic developments well under way by 1914, but, again, intensely accelerated by the war.[84] Because fashion was by nature visual and dynamic, a constantly changing marketable mass of images, and because it represented the capitalist commodification of the body, it became integral to the new aesthetic of consumerism. As historian Bonnie Smith has argued, "fashion made women at once more desirable, more efficient, and in need of new goods."[85] The fashions of the modern woman were often linked with the new palladiums of pleasure in the postwar world—the tea dances and jazz clubs—as well as American consumer culture.[86]

The fashionably dressed modern woman was also linked to the new consumer plaything of the decade—the automobile. At mid-decade, advertisers, novelists, and social observers pictured women (much more than men, it seems) behind the wheel of the car, creating a visual image of female mobility and power (fig. 11).[87] In *L'Aventure sur la route* (1925), a popular novel about a modern woman who tours France in her new car, the heroine is described as a beautiful, sleek animal who moves effortlessly in the clothes she wears: "An astonishing ease accompanied all of her movements. It seemed as if her clothes imposed no servitude upon her; she moved with the glorious animal independence of gymnasts in their tights."[88] In 1927, the dramatist "Rip" described the modern woman in this way: "Athletic as well as capable of exercising most male trades, the modern woman, firmly installed behind thè wheel of the *torpédo* that takes her to her office, store or factory, has understood the superiority that severity of dress confers upon a man."[89] These advertisers and writers created the image of a woman who leads a busy, fast-paced, and independent life, and who is empowered by the "mannish" fashions she wears.

Like the automobile itself, these fashions created an ethos of mobility and speed in tune with the "freedoms" of modern life. According to an article in the fashion magazine *Fémina* (1924), modern women "dress in such a way so as not to be hindered in their gestures; they are adapting themselves to an era in which one must act quickly, walk with a hurried step, jump into a car, and proceed, in the least amount of time possible, from one occupation to another."[90] "Nothing stops her, nothing fills her with fear," wrote a female columnist for *Le Figaro* in 1925. "Intrepid, she drives her own car while waiting to pilot her airplane."[91] A year later, the designer Lucien Lelong shared the "secret" of the modern woman's fashions: "to be dressed in such a way so as to live for the speed—I would even say the electricity—of every passing moment. . . . *Tout est vitesse prodigieuse* and we appear in a dazzling film."[92] "Women want to walk, run, do sports," wrote the prominent aristocrat André de Fouquières in 1927. "Nothing can prevent them from doing so, nature is regaining its rights. . . . Suddenly, the noise of a motor! *C'est la realité présente!* life! movement! vertigo!"[93] By fusing the spirit of the new fashions with this modern consumer ethos of freedom, supporters of fashion were able to present it as liberated and liberating. As the journalist Paul Reboux put it in 1919: "What grace these soft curls and liberated necks have. . . . What an easy, comfortable charm! This look is so much preferable to those unstable edifices of hair that make women eternally apprehensive."[94]

Through fashion, the image of the modern woman became associated with the aesthetic of modern consumerism. Some historians have presented fashion as an agent of social control, which objectified and manipulated women as sex objects. According to this argument, as fashion became an intense preoccupation of women during this period, it facilitated their assimilation into mainstream patterns of behavior, erasing specifically female forms of cultural expression, and thereby defusing female political activism.[95] But, far from serving as a homogenizing force, modern consumer culture became the means by which women expressed a more liberated self. The visual alignment of *la femme moderne* with an ethos of mobility (embodied in the automobile) created a cultural landscape in which a vivid new kind of woman—powerful, active, and adventuresome—could be represented. The woman pictured behind the wheel of her *torpédo* was on the way to *her* office, store, or factory. In this sense, the impact of consumer culture on specifically female forms of cultural expression is both more paradoxical and complex than historians have believed.

In making their emancipatory argument, supporters of the new styles further relied on the unexamined assumption that what one wore affected how one behaved (and vice versa). Paul Reboux drew on such logic to defend the new bob. He began by reminding his readers of the political and symbolic importance of fashion in French history: "After the Empire, the struggle between advocates of the wig and those of emancipated hair offers a marvelous image of the Restoration." In the same way, Reboux argued, the short, bobbed cut signaled political and social changes in the postwar era. Speaking of the war, he claimed that: "in these four years, women were emancipated. . . . They have virile occupations. They are going to vote. It is quite natural that their hairstyle be adapted to this new condition."[96] Eight years later, in 1927, Reboux made the same defense of fashion, this time stating his argument more explicitly: "Free movement of the human body must accompany an age in which the individual is emancipated."[97] He continued to praise the bob as "the clearest symbol of female emancipation."[98]

Prominent designers also inscribed the new fashions within a socioeconomic context of change. In 1927, the designer Jacques Worth wrote: "The war changed women's lives, forcing them into an active life, and, in many cases, paid work . . . As the years pass by, women feel enamored by more freedom, hence the easier style of dresses." Another designer, Premet, agreed: "The woman of today has given up for good the restraints placed upon her."[99] In hindsight, the hairdresser René Rambaud explained the popularity of the new fashions in this way:

> The woman who took an active place in industrial, commercial, artistic, social life during what is called "The Great War" has in part conserved it. . . . Rapidly and not undeservedly, women are winning their right to freedom. And to equality perhaps . . . in a bold and impressive jump, this generation is surmounting the high barriers of tradition, prejudice and established morality concerning hair: she is having her hair cut.[100]

To Rambaud, bobbed hair was bound up inextricably with a broader fight for freedom, equality, and the attempt "to surmount the high barriers of tradition." One could argue that for designers and merchandisers, this emphasis on freedom and mobility was "cheap talk," merely an effort to sell women on the new styles, rather than a genuine promotion of freedom for women. Despite the possibility of such mercenary motives, the fact that these promoters felt called upon to make this kind of argument for the new styles becomes significant, inasmuch as it reveals their intuitive sense of what would attract women about the new styles—what image of themselves and of their lives they hoped to project through wearing them. Fashion acted as a presentation of self, in part, grounded in fantasy and wish fulfillment. What these designers felt they had to (and could) sell were images of fashion as change, liberation, and freedom from constraint.[101]

Although the origins of such images are impossible to determine, feminists were using them to describe fashion in the early 1920s, several years before they were adopted by the designers quoted above. The radical feminist Henriette Sauret described short hair in 1919 as "a gesture of independence; a personal venture." According to Sauret, the new fashions were not created by men to fulfill or further their ideal of female desirability; rather they were created by women themselves "to respond to our personal aesthetic or our need for convenience."[102] In 1921, Augusta Moll-Weiss, a well-known feminist and founder of the household rationalization movement, insisted that because women of all classes were now working, they demanded fashions "that one can put on easily, rapidly." Complicated fashions were no longer popular, she argued, because women "no longer tolerate impeding their freedom of movement for the benefit of laws whose omnipotence they no longer recognize."[103] In 1922, Jane Misme, editor of *La Française*, praised the new, more abbreviated swimsuits worn by young women for giving them ease and freedom of movement in the water: "anything that stands in the way of the harmonious and necessary development of the body can only be a false kind of grace and modesty."[104] By describing the old swimsuits as "false," Misme implied that the new ones more faithfully expressed a woman's "natural" self. Maria Vérone, a prominent postwar feminist leader and the editor of the bourgeois feminist monthly *Le Droit des femmes*, agreed with Misme. "The women who have preceded us," she maintained, "gave us the bad example of fake hair, false sentiments, marriage without love." By contrast, she argued, "we wear short hair, dresses that are not constricting, and we want to have a profession, in order to be independent."[105] Vérone believed that fashion played a fundamental role in shaping a woman's behavior. Fake hair encouraged duplicity in one's life as well as one's appearance, leading inevitably to "false sentiments" and loveless marriage. Likewise, the "nonconstricting" clothes of the modern woman created a visual analogue of liberation, encouraging an "independent" life-style.

The Illusion of Being Free

Historians have accepted uncritically the perception of postwar fashion as a sign of "the refusal of any constraint," the "emancipation of women," and "the affirmation of liberty."[106] They explain the trend among women toward short hair and a looser, more carefree style of clothing as a reflection of a new freedom of movement brought about by the war.[107] But feminists like Vérone presented fashion as a maker as well as a marker of change because it had the ability to encourage new behaviors analogous to the visual image produced. Can we say that fashion authorized feminist emancipation? Were the new fashions, in fact, physically liberating? Were they able to facilitate physical mobility and, therefore, a more independent life-style?

Freedom of movement is a relative concept, and certainly the new styles were liberating in comparison to the crimped, corseted fashions of the fin de siècle. Even a cursory glance at the narrow tubular skirts and the high heels of the period, however, casts doubt on the idea that such styles could afford women mobility, even if they were, by comparison to prewar fashions, easier to put on and more comfortable.[108] Although the designers, hairdressers, and *femme modernes* of the era interpreted fashion as honest, liberating, and carefree, in fact, achieving this idealized look required enormous time and effort. Writing on fashion in 1924, Jacqueline de Monbrison first proclaimed that "contemporary fashion is essentially comfortable, and that modern women will never accept a restrictive fashion." But some pages later, she admitted that the new styles of Jean Patou, for example, were "so narrow that 'madame' will not go very far, and would do well to have the car wait for her to return." She also confessed that dressing and undressing in the new styles presented an enormous difficulty: "By what miracle are we able to get into our dresses? . . . Mystery! and above all, yes, above all, by what other miracle are we able to get out of them?"[109] In *Reproches à une dame,* Pierre Lièvre disabused readers of the idea that comfort or freedom of movement had anything at all to do with fashion. Given modern conveniences, he argued, women had less need to move freely than ever before: "You are telling me that the woman who drives her little Citroën should not be restricted in her movements?"[110]

The new style was no more carefree than it was liberating. According to the historian Marylène Delbourg-Delphis, a new concept of beauty arose in the 1920s, particularly after mid-decade. This concept was based on faith in the body's malleability, its ability to be shaped and improved. As a result, she points out, women began to use more makeup and invest greater amounts of time and money in beauty products for their face, skin, and hair.[111] An article in *Vogue* (1923) commented on how much time women were spending in "*instituts de beauté*" and insisted that to achieve the look, the modern woman must "greet with a smile the incessant admonitions, the harsh instructions of the trainer, *masseuse,* professor: "Stand up straight, don't slump your back, eat little, don't drink, walk, get up, lean over . . . think of your health, of hygiene above all."[112] Several such *instituts de beauté* were established during the 1920s, especially in the later years of the decade.[113] Although women claimed that the new bob cut was "practical" and so easy to care for, in fact, as one commentator asked in 1924: "Can anyone argue that a few minutes every day devoted to the maintenance of long hair in the intimacy of the home, can compare with interminable periods spent waiting at the hairdresser's?"[114] In 1927 the political writer François de Bondy agreed that women spent their lives at their hairdressers, and remarked that "to pretend the contrary would be a little like saying that it was more practical for us men to shave every morning than to grow a beard."[115]

In addition, after 1920, the style of dress required excessive thinness, which could be achieved only by continuous, strict dieting.[116] A panoply of new products appeared on the market to help women shape their sometimes unwilling bodies into conformity with the new silhouette. These included such panaceas as Dr. Duchamp's *l'Iodhyrine,* "approved and recommended by the French and international medical body"; Dr. Jawas's "Mexican tea," "*L'Ovidine-Lutier,*" which promised a "marvelous result, without diet or danger"; Gigartina seaweed marine *dragées* to thin the chin, thighs, and waist; "Galton pills," also to rid women of double chins; and "Tanagra *dragées,*" containing thyroid to dehydrate women and produce "in no time an elegant and supple silhouette."[117] With a tone of great pity, a 1924 *Vogue* article described the regime of "*la malheureuse* who has resolved to maintain an ideal weight": "Hours passed in the gym, mornings devoted to the brutal hands of *masseuses,* thyroid pills taken despite the risk of permanently ruining one's health, masks or rubber girdles to slim down waists or faces."[118] Although traditional types of corsets were abolished, most women still wore constraining undergarments of some kind, such as the straight elastic girdle, the bust bodice, and the *ceinture réductrice.*[119] Poiret himself admitted in *L'Illustration* (1921) that the new look demanded some kind of girdle.[120] As *Vogue* exclaimed in 1923: "how seductive the straight line of our winter dresses is, how revealing the *sveltesse* of the female silhouette! But how ungracious when the waist is not shaped [*moulée*] by a corset-girdle, the indispensable complement of contemporary fashion."[121] Dr. Monteil's *ceinture-maillot*— cheerfully called "The Goddess"—was made entirely of rubber and cost a whopping 150 francs. There were also girdles for a woman's face, neck, and ankles, those for the latter advertised as "invisible even under the sheerest stockings" (figs. 12 and 13).

From this perspective, the new fashions look like an elaborate marketing ploy to feed the growth of a burgeoning beauty industry, including makeup and skin-care manufacturers, owners of *instituts de beauté,* hair salon owners, diet specialists, and the *haute couturiers.* In this sense, as feminist historians have claimed, postwar fashion represented a relatively new form of modern consumerism that exploited women in the pursuit of profit. Far from enjoying freedom, women who bought into this quest for beauty found themselves locked into a relentless and time-consuming set of physical and financial constraints. But if postwar fashion was not as "liberating" or "natural" as it appeared, why did feminists and the women who wore the styles present them as affording enormous mobility and freedom? According to the journalist René Bizet, who wrote a treatise on fashion in 1925, it was the *illusion* of freedom, if not freedom itself, that was the objective of the new look. In Bizet's words, "there was a tyranny of liberty in current fashion." Women went to desperate lengths in order to produce "the illusion of being free" through their clothes.[122] The fashion writer Jacqueline de Monbrison supported this notion in 1926 by referring to one Princess Irène, a woman who took no less than two hours with her maid to get ready for the evening. But, the desired result, according to Monbrison, completely disguised this effort: "The effect of extreme elegance that she produces would hardly lead someone to suspect that it took two hours to achieve, so much is it dependent on the triumphant appearance of simplicity."[123]

By conceiving of fashion as a language of movement and change, even when it was not, designers like Paul Poiret and Coco Chanel created a visual fantasy of liberation. Merchandisers sold the new styles by projecting an image of liberation from constraint because the women who wore them were attracted to this fantasy and wanted to express it as their own. In defining fashion in terms of personal emancipation, feminists such as Vérone and Misme also helped to define its cultural interpretation. The fantasy of liberation then became a cultural reality in itself that was not without political importance. The image of *la femme moderne* adopted by French women—as intrepid, powerful, active, and athletic—created a visual analogue of the freedom that many women of all classes had supposedly enjoyed during the war, when they had assumed traditionally male professions and responsibilities. By wearing these clothes, women could project a fantasy of an ideal, liberated self, one that moved freely in an unconstrained social space. In Moll-Weiss's words, such an ideal self could put on and take off new identities unrestricted by old prejudices, hierarchies, or "laws whose omnipotence they no longer recognize." Because the new look sharply contrasted with that of the turn of the century, it represented a visual declaration of sudden change in women's lives as well as in fashion.

The paradox of fashion in postwar France consisted in the strange and contradictory manner in which it was political. Despite the exploitative and regressive reality of the new styles, at the level of fantasy, they represented a visual image of personal freedom and emancipation. By mid-decade, the fantasy of fashion itself became invested with political meaning. To wear the new fashions was to embrace publicly the already established cultural meanings of fashion: as a visual erasure of sexual difference (the critics' view), and as a declaration of independence from prewar social constraints (the defenders' view). To buy and wear the new styles—at the workplace, on the streets of Paris, wherever social exchange took place—was to participate in a truly social fantasy of liberation. Fashion became a political language of signs used to herald the arrival of a new world; it formed a new, purely visual aesthetic of freedom.

French feminist historians have dismissed the young modern woman with whom the new fashions were associated as entirely apolitical. Perceived in terms of an "individualistic" or "life-style" approach to emancipation, the modern woman's quest for freedom has been seen as frivolous and self-centered.[124] Considering postwar fashion as a political gesture, then, raises two important questions. First, did women's participation in this visual fantasy of liberation produce any real political effects? Obviously, to look emancipated was not to be emancipated. Since the illusion of freedom could as much undermine as reinforce a liberated self-image, participation in this visual fantasy represented a political risk.[125] But despite these important qualifications, evidence does exist that the new fashions had a strong political effect—their ability to scandalize and infuriate postwar French men and women. If the new look did not in some way profoundly threaten traditional notions of female identity, why were fathers, mothers-in-law, and conservatives so up in arms about it? Why else did fashion divide families and destroy marriages if it did not touch some political nerve or challenge some prevailing signification of power?

Second, in considering fashion as a political gesture, we need to ask whether participation in this visual fantasy of liberation was a conscious political choice. Did women deliberately wear the new styles in order to project an image of personal freedom? Or were they just clotheshorses and fashionmongers? Exactly why women wore what they did was a complex issue, ranging from personal aesthetics to the desire to conform. The motivation of these women in adopting the new styles is especially difficult to ascertain because only rarely did they articulate their reasons on paper; fashion was something to wear, not to write about. These considerations of motive point up the possible weaknesses of fashion as a political or feminist strategy. The women who wore the new fashions were certainly rebellious, but if this act of rebellion was not a conscious political choice, was it likely to last or blossom into other forms? Were these women destined for an eventual relapse into conventionality?[126]

The answers to these questions lie beyond the scope of this study, but it is interesting to look at fashions during the 1930s with them in mind. After 1927 or 1928, rising stars of *haute couture,* such as Elsa Schiaparelli, began to reassert the waist and bust in dresses and to pioneer a gentler, more sculptured look. Typical of this new style were the *coiffures* that replaced the bob: framed by curls around the face, they had a softer, more "feminine" look. Fashion once again began to follow the contours of a woman's body and to delineate, even emphasize, sexual difference. The length of skirts, which gradually grew throughout the 1920s, stabilized at midcalf by 1930, and fashion generally grew more respectable and responsible. The notion of liberty and scandal in fashion disappeared.[127]

The period between 1918 and 1927 thus formed an exceptional time in twentieth-century French fashion, in which what women wore became invested with political meaning in a profound yet ephemeral way. The political significance of fashion did not inhere in the styles themselves; rather, fashion became political because of the way it was interpreted by contemporaries, how it was understood in the cultural imaginary. Wearing the new styles was in no way a form of organized feminism, as we are used to thinking of this term. Nor can they be said to have authorized "feminist" emancipation. Still, although sporting the new fashions did not get women the vote, it did help to maintain issues of female identity at the forefront of French life during a period of rapid social and cultural transformation. Speaking of the bob, René Rambaud asserted: "Never has any other [fashion] held such a place in the mind, in conversation, in events."[128] Through fashion, changes in female identity were debated, challenged, and embraced in multiple ways.

The "tyranny of liberty" in postwar fashion demonstrates the way in which the visual appearance of the modern woman figured in a political struggle for the redefinition of women's identity and power after the war. In *La Garçonne,* short hair "*à la Jeanne d'Arc*" is presented as a political strategy to assert female power. When the modern woman Monique Lerbier first reappears in Margueritte's *La Garçonne,* a friend has this to say about her hair: "Today for a woman, it is the symbol of independence, if not power. Once Delilah emasculated Samson by cutting his hair. Today, she believes she can make herself virile by cutting hers."[129] The myth of the biblical Samson crops up frequently in the debate on the bob. "Unlike Samson, who lost his strength in losing his mane," quipped the feminist Henriette Sauret, "we may gain total power in shorning our hair."[130] The myth gained particular relevance in the immediate postwar context because it formed the basis of the meaning of *poilu,* the French sobriquet for the trench soldier. Originally meaning "covered with hair" or "hairy," *poilu* eventually gained the connotative sense of *"homme robuste"* or simply *"homme"* precisely because of the myth of a virile Samson.[131] Another press name for the women's short bobbed cut was *"coiffure au poilu de 2ᵉ classe"* and the cloche hats of the 1920s have been closely compared with those of the *poilus* during the war.[132]

The investment of the female bob with a kind of virile power doubly inverted the *poilu*-Samson myth: first, because less, not more, hair granted power, and second, because women themselves became virilized Samsons—rather than shearing Delilahs! With the fashion of short, bobbed hair, *la femme moderne* became the new virile Samsonette or *poilue,* manipulating her visual appearance to reverse, once again, the hierarchies of gender. The inversions of power and gender in the *poilu*/Samson myth again reveal the link between the bob cut and social anxieties concerning the war's perceived reversal of gender boundaries. Fashion was not "politics" as we are used to conceiving it, but the debates over its meaning in postwar France were profoundly political. The fashions of the modern woman became central to the cultural mythology of the era, instilling at once envy, admiration, frustration, and horror, because they both provided a visual language for upheaval and change, and figured in the political struggle for the redefinition of female identity.

GEORGES FABRI

L'ART ET LA MANIÈRE

D'ACCOMMODER ET DE RACCOMMODER

CIV'LOTS ET POILUS

Préface de Léon FRAPIÉ

Dessin d'Adolphe WILLETTE

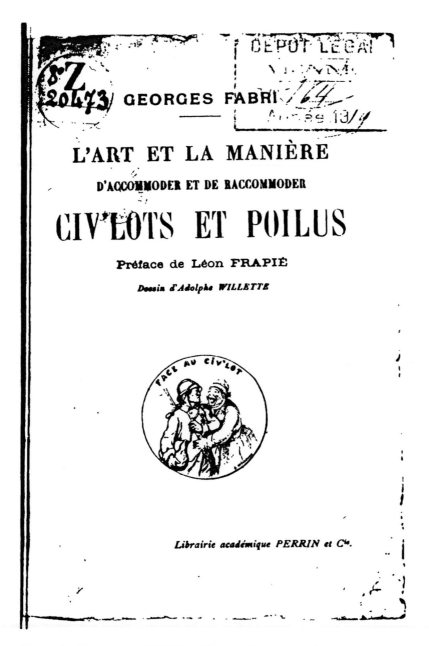

FACE AU CIV'LOT

Librairie académique PERRIN et Cⁱᵉ.

Figure 1. Cover page, G. Fabri, *L'Art et la manière d'accommoder et de raccommoder civ'lots et poilus* (Paris: Perrin et Cie, 1918), Engraving by Adolphe Willette

Figure 2. "During an Offensive."
S. Mazare-Aga, *Pourvu qu'elles tiennent*, 1917

Figure 3. "Let's Make Sacrifices."
S. Mazare-Aga, *Pourvu qu'elles tiennent*, 1917

MAURICE LEVEL

MADO

ou

la Guerre à Paris

ERNEST FLAMMARION, ÉDITEUR

Quatrième mille

Figure 4. Cover page, Maurice Level, *Mado, ou la guerre à Paris*, 1919

— Mais oui, en plus de l'allocation, je touche 8 à 9 francs par jour pour fabriquer des obus... malheureusement, la guerre ne durera pas toujours.

Figure 5. Henriot, *De L'arrière au front: Croquis de Henriot*, 1917

Figure 6. Cover Page, Victor
Margueritte, *La Garçonne*

Figure 7. "Coiffures Garçonnes," *Le Capillariste*, 1925. From
Catherine Lebas and Annie Jacques, *La Coiffure en France du
Moyen-Age à nos jours* (Delmas International, S.A., 1979)

Figure 8. Chanel's designs,
Vogue, November 1924

Figure 9. "The last *midinette* has been arrested by the guardians
of the peace for the crime of wearing attire said to be feminine,
including a skirt." Clément Vautel, "Le Féminisme en 1958," *Je
Sais Tout*, 15 May 1918. Dossier Anti-Féminisme, Bibliothèque
Marguerite Durand

LES CONVENANCES
— Non, elle est trop jeune pour porter les cheveux aussi courts...

Figure 10. "Proprieties," *Le Journal*, 1925. Dossier Coiffure,
Bibliothèque Marguerite Durand

Pourquoi ai-je choisi une CONDUITE INTÉRIEURE CITROEN?...
Mais, cher ami, regardez-la et dites s'il n'y a pas quelque chose de féminin dans son élégance..
Coquette et docile, nerveuse et souple, croyez-moi, c'est la voiture des femmes modernes.

Figure 11. "But, *cher ami,* look at it and say there isn't something feminine in its elegance. Coquettish and docile, responsive and agile, believe me, it's the car of *femmes modernes.*" Advertisement for Citroën, *Fémina,* January 1921

Figures 12 and 13. Advertisements from *Fémina* and *La Mode Practique*, 1924

Figure 13

Figure 14. Cover page, Paul Haury,
La Vie ou la mort de la France, 1924

Figure 15. "One of the profound causes of the present war has been our low birthrate." *La Femme et l'enfant*, 1918–20, p. 23

Figure 16. "What do I do to replace all those who have fallen if this continues?" *La Femme et l'enfant*, 1918–20, p. 4

Figure 17. "L'Infâme besogne." *La Femme et l'enfant*, 1918–20, p. 463

Figure 18. Clément Vautel, *Madame ne veut pas d'enfant*, 1924

Figure 19. "The Connecting Link." *La Femme et l'enfant*, 1918–20, p. 96

Figure 20. "Without Children, No Domestic Harmony." *La Femme et l'enfant*, 1918–20, p. 177

Figure 21. Cover, Emile Fenouillet, *L'Art de trouver un mari*, 1925

Pourquoi la Natalité diminue-t-elle ?

Parce que les pères de famille payent proportionnellement à leurs ressources des impôts directs et indirects bien plus élevés que les célibataires.

Figure 22. "Why is natality declining?" *La Femme et l'enfant*, 1918–20, p. 15

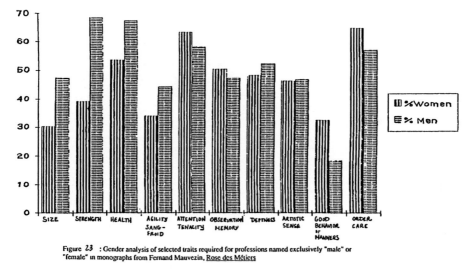

Figure 23 : Gender analysis of selected traits required for professions named exclusively "male" or "female" in monographs from Fernand Mauvezin, <u>Rose des Métiers</u>

Figure 23. Gender analysis of selected traits required for professions named exclusively "male" or "female" in monographs from Fernand Mauvezin, *Rose des métiers*

Figure 24. Logo of the Comité d'Education Féminine

Figure 25. Propaganda of the Comité d'Education Féminine. "Young girl, think of your future children—marry a healthy man."

PART TWO
LA MÈRE

THE MOTHER COMPRISED a second central image of female identity in the postwar debate on women. Unlike the image of *la femme moderne,* which was largely a product of the war, the image of the mother in French culture was old, multilayered, and complex in meaning. At the same time, the mother gained great cultural visibility in the postwar debate on women because she was linked to two historically specific themes—the veteran's anger toward women and the natalist's exaltation of maternity.

These themes and the relationship between them find precise expression in Pierre Drieu la Rochelle's *La Comédie de Charleroi* (1934). This largely autobiographical novel concerns the 1914 battle of Charleroi in Belgium, where Drieu la Rochelle himself fought during the war.[1] It explores the familiar postwar confrontation between the "authenticity" of the front and the "farce" of bourgeois civilian life. The narrator, a veteran of Charleroi, is charged with bringing a rich bourgeoise, Madame Pragen, to the Belgian battlefield where her son died in 1914. The trip takes place in 1919, just after the war. As they approach the scene of the battle, the veteran derides this woman's ignorance of the war and her preoccupation with social status. Then he makes this remark:

I looked at this woman glancing swifty and superficially over the battlefield with her lorgnette. And I shivered that shiver that I had known well throughout the entire war; no woman shares my suffering. But, then, do we know what they feel, when they carry and give birth to children?[2]

According to this veteran, maternity symbolized physical and moral suffering for women in the same way that soldiery did for men. Only through motherhood did women achieve status as an object of male sympathy.

Drieu la Rochelle was certainly not the first writer to draw a parallel between the soldier and the mother, nor was he the only one to do so in postwar France.[3] Postwar suffragists repeatedly argued that women's ability to bear children compensated for their exemption from military service and entitled them to citizen status.[4] Soldiery and motherhood represented differently gendered versions of the same *impôt du sang,* or blood tribute to the state. Natalist propagandists, who comprised part of an enormous postwar effort to raise the French birthrate, almost constantly played on the parallel between maternity and soldiery. Here motherhood meant a kind of reparation to be paid for male sacrifice during the war. The prominent natalist Gaston Rageot contended, for example, that if French women wanted "to disprove the sullen philosophers who consider excessive luxury, skimpy dresses and the tango to be a national danger," they would "make it a point of honor to conquer German women in peacetime, just as their husband and brothers conquered German men during the war. Now it is their turn!"[5] The belief that "maternity is the military service of women" was a truism of natalist discourse.[6]

The parallel between the mother and the soldier was hardly novel, but in postwar France it became freighted with a specific set of emotions associated with the Great War—anger, alienation, anxiety about change. In the larger history of the French natalist movement, postwar natalism distinguishes itself by its utter inseparability from the moral and sexual anguish of the war. In a speech delivered to the Senate in October 1919, Georges Clemenceau argued that:

> The treaty does not specify that France should commit herself to bearing many children, but that is the first thing that should have been written there. This is because if France renounces *la famille nombreuse,* you can put whatever fine clause in the treaty you want, you can take away all the armaments in Germany, you can do whatever you want, France will be lost because there won't be any more French people.[7]

According to Clemenceau, only a treaty affirming life could bring an end to the war's great holocaust. The inability or unwillingness to renew life would mean certain death for the French race. In this way, matters of life and death were inextricably bound in postwar France.

Already a topic of vehement debate in the decades before the war, the "crisis" of French natality became, in the words of one prominent French doctor, "the great preoccupation of thinkers, scientists and legislators" after the war.[8] Natalist values were so ubiquitous that counterdiscourses that might challenge their cultural authority were virtually nonexistent.[9] The enormous diversity of texts examined in the following two chapters—parliamentary debates, propaganda, sociological studies, novels, and short stories—suggests the pervasiveness of natalist rhetoric in postwar cultural life. Central to this rhetoric was the natalist figure of *la mère de famille nombreuse,* the natalist mother of a large family. Since the late 1860s, French fertility had been measured strictly in terms of the female population of childbearing age. Hence women bore a disproportionate responsibility in matters of reproduction; in short, they, not men, were blamed for the decline in fertility.[10]

The *mère de famille nombreuse* became an obsession in postwar France, in great part because of her powerful role in natalist discourse as the primary bearer of traditional bourgeois values. During the previous century, the figure of the mother had often embodied the possibility for orderly family and social life. As Joan Scott has shown, in the discourse of political economy, mothers "effected the transformation of others: under their tutelage children became moral, loving beings; men became responsible, disciplined husbands and fathers; even wages achieved their true value when "morale" prevailed in a household."[11] Similarly, in the postwar period, the mother played a morally constructive role: she became a symbol of rebirth, healing, redemption, and restoration from the war's moral trauma. By giving birth to healthy sons, the mother assured the military strength and demographic future of France. By acting in her role as a moral guardian, she embodied those values—honor, sacrifice, and devotion—for which the war had supposedly been fought. *La mère* was a redeemer in the same way that *la femme moderne* was a destroyer of faiths. In postwar discourse of all kinds, motherhood served as a panacea for an impressive host of postwar anxieties: demographic, military, economic, cultural, and sexual. It promised at once a strong birthrate and a strong nation, the foundation and renewal of moral virtue, and an end to gender confusion.

4

"A MATTER OF LIFE OR DEATH"

N 23 JULY 1920 A BILL WAS INTRODUCED before the French Chambre des députés. The bill would impose stiff penalties for any forms of propaganda—advertisements, articles, lectures, posters, the sale of objects—that encouraged abortion and the use of contraceptive devices.[1] The proposal met with little vocal opposition in the Chamber, except from two socialists, André Berthon (Paris) and Paul Morucci (Bouches-du-Rhône), who contested it on both practical and moral grounds.[2] Questioning the imprecise wording of the bill, Berthon asked if the text included "a condemnation of the prophylactics you see visible in every pharmacy window?" In light of the bill, he wondered, what might the Chamber do with the letters of Madame de Sevigné, which "as we all know, in fact give particularly precise advice on the way in which one should behave in the conjugal bed." These remarks, not surprisingly, caused an uncomfortable stir in the room. "Let us not forget that this debate is public," one member of the Chamber felt called upon to say.[3]

Nonplussed, Berthon went on to object to the bill on practical grounds, reminding his colleagues that "in order to have numerous children, one must first be able to feed them. Society must give assistance to single mothers, organize domestic assistance, and provide leaves of absence during pregnancy and after birth."[4] Berthon insisted that while he was not against the idea of legislative action to encourage natality, he objected to the hasty, and badly conceived way it was being dealt with here. These views were seconded by Deputy Morucci, who continued Berthon's verbal attack with a rather bad pun. "The good faith of our colleagues today is no doubt indisputable," he conceded, "but the ground on which they are standing seems to me to be hardly favorable to fertilization." He accused his colleagues of crude economic calculations and of seeking national health and happiness in "big numbers." Like Berthon, he demanded that "the state prepare the cradle before demanding the child." Finally, he defended women who aborted, arguing that they were not "criminal recidivists" intent on breaking the law, but the desperate poor, driven to take any risk in order to avoid the burden of another mouth to feed in an already destitute family.[5]

Despite the objections of Berthon and Morucci, which were met by a hostile, impatient audience in the Chamber, the bill passed the same day by an overwhelming majority of 521 to 55.[6] It was approved by the Senate without discussion six days later and became known as the *"loi scélérate"* against abortion and contraception, the most oppressive of its kind in Europe.[7] The apparent ease with which the bill passed the Chamber and the Senate is misleading, for it had already languished in parliament for almost a decade.[8] First proposed in the Chamber in 1891 by Radical Deputy Georges Trouillot, the bill was not even discussed in the Senate until 1914. Concern that certain of its provisions might threaten the principle of medical confidentiality prevented its passage at this time. It was not until immediately after the war, in January 1919, that these concerns were resolved and the proposal passed in the Senate. When the medical confidentiality issue once again began to delay progress in the Chamber, Edouard Ignace (Union Républicaine, Seine) extracted the texts of the bill already voted by the Senate and the Chamber commission, and pushed it through the Chamber in this form in July 1920.[9] After almost a decade of inactivity, the bill was introduced, discussed, and voted on in one day.[10]

Historians have interpreted the legislative victory of 1920 in two ways. First, they have seen natalist legislation as a logical gesture of the postwar conservative, nationalist Bloc national that came into power in the November legislative elections of 1919.[11] The Bloc national, a coalition of moderate and conservative groups, represented the first shift to the right in parliament since 1871. Yet while leadership from the more conservative wing of the Bloc national was no doubt important in bringing the bill to the Chamber floor in July 1920, it alone cannot account for its passage once there. As the Chamber vote shows, the natalist cause found widespread, almost unanimous support across the political spectrum; only socialists as a group spoke out against it.[12] Similar widespread support characterized the Senate vote as well. Clearly, then, its appeal was not specifically politically based, although the general atmosphere of political conservatism no doubt encouraged its success.[13]

A second explanation favored by historians has been to see the 1920 natalist victory as a response to an already serious demographic problem made worse by wartime casualties.[14] Between August 1914 and November 1918, an average of 930 Frenchmen were killed every day. If laid head to foot, those dead in the French army would have formed an unbroken line from Berlin to Paris three times over.[15] Proportionally, France's casualty rate was the highest in Europe: 16.5 percent (of those mobilized) compared to 14.7 percent for Germany.[16] In addition to the estimated 1.5 million casualties, there were 3 million wounded and 1.1 million who suffered permanent disability. Finally, the war also devastated the birthrate at least temporarily because, among other things, soldiers were not given leaves at its outset. The demographer Patrick Feisty estimates that the absence or death of men during the war period prevented 40 percent of the expected births from taking place.[17]

Postwar demographic realities were admittedly grim, and no doubt played an important part in spurring legislators to action. However, the demographic explanation becomes more problematic when we consider the composition of the law of 1920. As André Berthon pointed out, the law, for all its severity, did nothing to curb what were, in fact, the two most widely used methods of contraception: coitus interruptus and condoms. While the first of these was clearly beyond the legislators' control to legislate, prophylactics did remain widely available to men, supposedly to prevent venereal disease. Nor did the law provide in any way for the reduction of infant mortality, a major goal of social legislation in the past, such as the 1874 Roussel law regulating the wet-nursing industry.[18] In its punitive logic, the law of 1920 was exceptional; most postwar natalist legislation took the more positive form of trying to stimulate natality and lower infant mortality.[19] The original text of the 1920 law had actually included a measure to institute supervised obstetrical clinics; these would have given pregnant women pre- and postnatal care, thus reducing infant mortality. However, in preparing the bill in July for discussion in the Chamber, Deputy Edouard Ignace removed this clause, even though it had already been approved by the Senate.[20] Ignace eliminated the very provisions of the bill that sought to increase natality by more positive means.

If the aim of the law of 1920 was strictly demographic, as historians have assumed, why did it not target propaganda for prophylactics, "visible in every pharmacy window" according to Berthon? Rather, it sought specifically to bring women's sexual practices under legislative control by attacking abortion and female forms of contraception.[21] Why? Given the widespread use of coitus interruptus and male prophylactics as contraceptive practices in France, the deputies must have known all too well that it would have little effect on French population decline. "If you were bringing us the certitude of raising French natality both in quality and quantity, I would vote for your proposition with two hands," insisted Adolphe Pinard (Radical, Paris), a physician and widely acknowledged expert on natality. "But what you bring is only the shadow of a repression. In fact, what you bring is nothing."[22] Pinard was right—the law did nothing to raise the French birthrate.[23] Given Pinard's highly respected opinion, and his condemnation of the bill as merely repressive and ultimately ineffective, why did the deputies vote for it in such large numbers? Finally, the parliament of 1920, as one historian has described it, was "a body of men who had undoubtedly fathered fewer legitimate children than any other contemporary group of politicians."[24] At one point in the July discussion, Paul Morucci dubbed natalists "without progeny for the most part, or half-sterile."[25] Given their own Malthusian behavior, how could these deputies consider themselves defenders of a natalist policy? What import did natality have for them if not as a set of social practices that they themselves followed?

The answer to these questions lies in the specific historical meanings attached to concepts such as "contraception," "abortion," "depopulation," and "natality" in postwar France, as well as the particular metaphorical and rhetorical context in which they were articulated. Far from being transparent or transhistorical in meaning, the terms "depopulation" and "abortion," as used by legislators to debate social policy, were deeply imbedded in the trauma of the war and the tensions of postwar recovery. In many ways, the postwar natalist discourse used by members of parliament replicated that used by natalist groups from the turn of the century onward; they attributed depopulation to "egoism," or excessive individualism, and the degradation of paternal authority in French law.[26] At the same time, concepts such as "depopulation" and "abortion" changed subtly in meaning. In short, they became intimately associated with the war, caught up in an identity of holocausts that gave them unprecedented force and power.

The parliamentary debates that led up to the passage of the 1920 law were inscribed within a specific horizon of meaning, that is, they relied on a certain collective knowledge of the political system, a common conceptual understanding of the problems at hand (such as the "crisis" of depopulation), and a shared discourse and set of metaphors. This political culture, shared by all deputies and senators who participated in postwar parliamentary debates, made possible political exchange and decision-making. Parliamentary debate was based on belief in *persuasion* as the ultimate arbiter of political decision-making. Parliamentary persuasion, in turn, was grounded in the assumption that those involved in the debate inhabited the same universe of meaning. If not, they could not understand the terms of the argument being put forth, nor be aroused by the rhetorical and metaphorical devices used to convince them. In other words, they could not be persuaded of an argument if it was not, in some sense, culturally intelligible.[27]

Thinking about the debates in this way transforms them into objects of cultural history, a series of texts that can be analyzed by the historian for the specific cultural economy that they articulate. Such a historical analysis would define social policy (such as the law against propaganda for abortion and contraception) as a cultural construct, inasmuch as it is grounded in a certain conceptual ordering of social relationships. Giving attention to this specific cultural economy—what concepts such as "depopulation" or "abortion" meant to the legislator in all their historical complexity—illuminates a web of signification that, in turn, can explain the rationale for policy-making.

Demographers and historians of French depopulation have often argued that the drop in the birthrate was central to France's loss of political, military, and economic hegemony in Europe and that it resulted from some moral or economic decline in French society.[28] In part, this interpretation of French depopulation reflects contemporaneous natalist views. As we shall see, it was common among late nineteenth- and early twentieth-century natalists to make apocalyptic statements about France's future and to ascribe depopulation to moral decadence. More recently, the tendency has been to see French depopulation as not necessarily a bad thing, but rather a rational response on the part of the French to the demands of industrialization and urbanization.[29] In this light, the fact that many bourgeois Frenchmen saw depopulation as a profound crisis that threatened the very existence of France gains significance, not simply as "wrong" perception, but as a cultural reality in itself, a means of understanding what kinds of social practices inspired fear and anxiety. Let us, then, examine the cultural economy of the postwar parliamentary debates in order to understand

how Frenchmen interpreted the crisis of depopulation, and why it
stimulated both strong feelings and legislative action.

Something Changed in France

The sudden victory of the law of 1920 articulates two distinctive traits
of postwar natalism: first, the pervasive, almost universal support natalism enjoyed in bourgeois French society among both men and
women; and second, the new willingness of the French state to legislate on its behalf.

Far from being limited to the world of practical politics, natalist
values and ideals permeated all elements of postwar French culture,
from novels and short stories to the discourses of social reform, from
sociological studies of postwar French society to inquiries on demobilization, from editorials in the popular bourgeois press to medical literature in professional journals.[30] As the following chapters will show, natalist ideals assumed a myriad of specific forms, and were embraced
by various groups in different ways for disparate ideological purposes.
Only the most politically marginal figures, such as the socialist deputies
André Berthon and Paul Morucci, dared to denounce natalist policies
openly. In the same way, only extremely radical feminists, such as Nelly
Roussel and Madeleine Pelletier, dared to critique the natalist movement.[31] Roussel described the phenomenon in this way:

> For the last few months, we have been witnessing a crisis of "repopuli-
> dolatry" ["repopulâterie"], the like of which we have never seen before.
> Everyone, from superstar to bit player, is "breeding" at the same time.
> The president of the Chamber presides at the "Congresses of Natality."
> The old president of the Council makes his appeal for procreation from
> every lofty podium. At home, citizens receive sermons and exhortations.
> And the billboards intended for electoral posters are decorated with
> wild, bombastic fantasies concerning "Alliances" and "Leagues" already
> notorious for their obtrusive . . . and sterile agitation.[32]

Using the logic of inversion to undermine natalist rhetoric, Roussel
characterized the natalists as "sterile" in their efforts, and the crisis one
of "repopulidolatry" rather than depopulation. This "repopulidolatry"—the power of natalist ideology to achieve a degree of popular
consensus that was almost without opposition—characterized the
postwar decade in France. Because the 1920 law against propaganda

for abortion and contraception contributed to this consensus by silencing contrary voices, such as neo-Malthusianism, it deserves our closest attention.

The law of 1920 lay at the heart of postwar natalist efforts in a second way, inasmuch as it typified a larger pattern of aggressive state intervention in matters of natality and the family. For Roussel, a central element of the new "repopulidolatry" was the eagerness with which government representatives propagandized on the natalists' behalf. The postwar period represents a turning point in terms of the passage of natalist social legislation.[33] While depopulation was by no means perceived as a new problem in 1920, it received an unprecedented degree of attention from the state. Although before the war, the depopulation issue figured into the success of laws enacting maternity leave and benefits, in general, prewar attempts to enact natalist legislation had consistently failed.[34] Legislators in both the Senate and Chamber introduced but did not adopt measures to stimulate population growth. (Trouillot's 1891 introduction of what would become the 1920 law is only one example of this pattern.)[35] By contrast, after the war, natalist leaders sensed that the political climate had abruptly become more favorable to social legislation of the type that they had sponsored for decades before.

The so-called crisis of depopulation was a late nineteenth-century invention. A major drop in natality—what historians now call the "demographic transition"—took place all over Europe between 1850 and 1950, but France took the lead in this process. By 1911, France, which once held the predominant demographic position in Europe, had fallen behind Germany, Austria-Hungary, and the United Kingdom in population.[36] The drop in the French birthrate was considered unquestionably voluntary, an expression of what was then called "Malthusian behavior" on the part of the French.[37] Concern about depopulation began to be voiced as early as the 1850s, when deaths exceeded births in 1854 and 1855.[38] The French defeat of 1870–71 greatly intensified these early rumblings, as the discourses of nationalism and depopulation became linked in the minds of French politicians, demographers, and natalist propagandists. Although historians usually attribute France's humiliation in 1870–71 to ineffective and unimaginative military leadership, government officials explained it in terms of declining population.[39] Increasing awareness of demographic decline coincided with the realization of France's worst nightmare: the rise of a united, aggressive enemy to the east. Politicians and propagandists transformed this temporal coincidence into a causal determination, arguing that depopulation had, in fact, led simultaneously to the Prussian threat and French military vulnerability.

The depopulation issue achieved full political significance at the turn of the century, both in terms of the ferocity of the debate and its linkage to crucial issues of gender, feminism, and national regeneration. Debate concerning depopulation surfaced in antisuffragist literature, in tirades on the New Woman, in the discourse on decadence and degeneration, and even in popular novels such as Emile Zola's *Fécondité*.[40] Lobbying organizations emerged to advance natalist aims, including Auguste Isaac's La Plus grande famille and Paul Bureau's Lique pour le relèvement de la moralité publique, which had close ties to the Catholic Church.[41] By far, the most important of the new organizations was the Alliance nationale pour l'accroissement de la population française founded in 1896 by Jacques Bertillon. Bertillon, a renowned doctor and demographer, became the indisputable head of the natalist movement at the turn of the century, in part because his emphasis on the nationalist implications of depopulation popularized his cause with government officials.[42] Members of the Alliance were bourgeois businessmen, industrialists, and professionals (doctors and lawyers) who supported their organizations through dues, subscriptions, and donations. For the most part, their efforts consisted of publishing propaganda—brochures and periodicals as well as statistics on demography and studies on possible legislative actions. The Alliance also sponsored a variety of natalist legislation, involved itself in parliamentary commissions, and got local sections to put pressure on local representatives. Above all, the Alliance sought to forge official ties with the governmental powers who could realize its aims; it encouraged deputies, senators, and ministers to sit on its councils and administer its activities.[43]

After several decades of slow growth, the natalist movement came of age in 1919 with the First National Congress of Natality, held in Nancy.[44] The minutes of the first three national congresses—in Nancy, Rouen, and Bordeaux—demonstrate an increasingly complex organizational structure with a wide-ranging agenda of aims and projects.[45] Among the legislation proposed at Nancy were tax reductions, monetary allocations, and the construction of affordable housing for *familles nombreuses,* social assistance of all kinds for pregnant women and mothers, and reductions in military service and family suffrage for the *père de famille.*[46] Natalists also sought to reform testate law, which, following the nineteenth-century sociologist Frédéric Le Play, they claimed discouraged parents from having large families by mandating the equal partition of property inheritance. Natalist leaders lobbied for a system of financial bonuses for civil servants with large families and encouraged private patrons to adopt such bonus systems as well.[47] Finally, in 1919 they resolved to push through the proposal, already making its way through parliament, that would repress propaganda for abortion and contraceptives.

This elaborate legislative agenda reflected not only the coming of age of the natalist movement, but also the dramatic increase in support it began to enjoy from the French government. When the newly created minister of hygiene, social assistance, and prevention appeared at the Bordeaux Congress of Natality in 1921 in order to state the government's firm and unwavering support for the fight against depopulation, the longtime natalist leader Paul Bureau responded with surprise and delight. "Upon hearing this important government official's decisive words," he commented, "one could tell oneself that something had really changed in France."[48] Long dissatisfied with the government's indecision about the plunging birthrate, natalist leaders happily acknowledged new support among elected as well as appointed officials. In 1919, Georges Rossignol of the natalist monthly *Pour la vie* cheerfully proclaimed that the elections of that year "have not been as immoral as those of five years ago," in that many more defenders of the family had been elected.[49] Jacques Bertillon declared optimistically in early 1920: "Victory. The legislative elections are a triumph for *la famille nombreuse.*"[50]

If we take the record of natalist legislation passed in the 1920s as evidence of the French state's new commitment to the depopulation cause, these leaders had every reason to be optimistic. The legislature would soon prove that their unwavering verbal support for natalism was more than cheap talk. Besides the law against abortion and contraceptive propaganda, natalist legislative victories in the 1920s included a measure intended to increase the actual prosecution of women who sought abortions, passed in March 1923.[51] The decade also began the era of allocations and financial bonuses to large families; of social assistance to mothers to defray the cost of childbirth and postnatal care; and the establishment of state-run maternity institutions and educational programs *(puériculture).*[52] This legislation was sponsored by the Conseil supérieur de la natalité, created by government decree in 1920 from within the Ministry of Hygiene, Social Assistance, and Prevention. The role of the Conseil was to research and promote methods by which to combat depopulation and to act as official state protector of large families.[53] Also created by decree in May of the same year was the Médaille de la famille française, awards of bronze, silver, and gilded silver *(vermeil)* to mothers of large families (bronze for 5–7 children, silver for 8–10, *vermeil* for 10 or more). To the proud strains of "La Marseillaise," mothers were awarded these medals at public ceremonies staged by the local *hôtel de ville*.[54]

In the early twenties, the natalist leaders Paul Bureau and Jacques Bertillon sensed that "something had really changed in France" in terms of state support for their cause. The record of natalist legislation passed in these years—including the law against propaganda for abortion and contraception—proved them right. How can we explain this change? Why had the crisis of depopulation become more than ever, as Roussel charged, the object of sustained hysteria, sterile exhortation, and bombastic fantasy? To begin to answer these questions, we must examine the way in which the "crisis" of depopulation was presented in natalist discourse, what cultural meanings were attached to it, what it meant to the natalists and legislators who used it in postwar France.

We are Dying of Depopulation

In their consideration of the law of 1920, postwar legislators were clearly influenced by natalist propaganda, which they bought or received from the various natalist lobbying groups. The natalist propaganda that postwar legislators incorporated into their thinking of depopulation was remarkably consistent and homogeneous. Natalist treatises were exceptionally similar in structure, content, and tone. They began by stating the possible consequences of depopulation, moved on to discuss its causes, and then concluded by suggesting remedies to solve the problem. It is therefore possible to refer to "natalist discourse" as an internally consistent, even uniform body of literature.

One striking feature of natalist discourse was its apocalyptic tone. "The question of natality is the question of the very survival of our race," warned the prominent doctor Paul Carnot.[55] Depopulation was presented not only as a serious social problem, but as a "matter of life or death for the country" (fig. 14). As another propagandist put it: "Let us not forget that it's a question of France's very life!"[56] Such declarations not only argued for the utter gravity of the situation; they also produced an atmosphere of crisis in which to make the natalist argument for a rise in the birthrate. While the need to establish the urgency of one's cause is important to any social movement, the crisis of depopulation, with its proliferating death sentences and obituaries, must be understood as more than a means of self-legitimation. Propagandists such as Paul Haury warned: "fewer marriages every year and fewer children per marriage. Where are we going? Quite simply, to our death" and "we are dying of politics, we are dying of alcoholism; we are dying of depopulation."[57] How can we explain apocalyptic proclamations such as these?

In natalist discourse, the economic and political crisis of depopulation was based on a fundamental ideological linkage between population and national strength. According to the leading propagandist Gaston Rageot, "societies, like organic beings, live from a fixed capital of forces: social capital is measured by wealth in numbers of men. If this capital decreases, the vitality of a society ebbs away."[58] As La Plus grande famille leader Auguste Isaac succinctly put it, "Numbers are the first measure of the strength of peoples . . . the world belongs to large battalions."[59] In the dark apocalypse of a depopulated future, the lack of workers, farmers, and soldiers would inevitably result in the collapse of the French economy, in "industries without a workforce and without customers," and "business without prospects."[60] Wages and prices would rise because of the shortage of labor at the same time that national production in all sectors would diminish for lack of workers, engineers, businessmen, and scientists. Only massive foreign immigration could offset the shortage, a solution that natalists as a whole found unappealing.[61] Ultimately, France would be unable to maintain its colonies or compete on the international commercial market, and would therefore be vulnerable economically to exploitation by other countries.[62] Finally, the diminution of taxes would lead to a continuous fiscal crisis and the reduction of public services.

This image of an economically debilitated France was not new to natalist discourse. As an argument, however, it must have had a particularly strong impact on bourgeois French men and women in the years after the war, a time rocked by soaring national debt, franc devaluation, and inflation.[63] Propagandists conflated the inability to bear children with the inability to produce or be fertile in other ways. The landscape of the natalist nightmare was a rural wasteland of deserted homes and unfarmed fields. "For lack of workers, less and less can be cultivated year after year, the leprosy of unworked fields spreads," argued one propagandist at a 1920 natalist conference.[64] The physician Fernand Boverat warned that a day would come when the desertion of the countryside would leave the French unable to produce enough food even to feed themselves.[65] Particularly in the invaded regions devastated by the Germans, argued Bertillon, men were needed to reconstruct the farms and make the earth fertile again: "Intense, relentless and prolonged work alone can restore this immense land. But such work requires strong arms, and there are none."[66] In a classic treatise on depopulation that was recognized by the Académie française, Fernand Auburtin declared that "through lack of a sufficient natality, France does not reap from the soil all that she could, her factories do not produce all that they could, her foreign commerce is restricted, she imports when she should have exported, spends where she should have earned."[67]

In conflating depopulation with the inability to produce economically, natalist propagandists also exploited gender images. A France that cannot perform "intense, relentless, and prolonged" work, lacks "strong arms," and can no longer provide even for itself has lost its manliness or virility, and become economically impotent.[68] This France had become effeminate because it was dependent on others for its livelihood, and consumed rather than produced.[69] In Auburtin's words, "she spends where she should have earned." In addition, the argument that France lacks "strong arms" and can no longer provide for itself might have had a powerful effect on the thousands of veteran *mutilés*, those who knew them, and even those who simply saw them on the streets.[70] According to Gaston Rageot, France's population was "principally made up of old men," because "all that remained of the healthy and robust have either died or become invalids." Another propagandist defined depopulation as an expression of the "faltering will of a timid, mistrustful, resigned people, lacking a sense of daring, of new horizons" in their unwillingness to have children.[71] In this way, natalist propagandists exploited not only postwar economic worries, but also the gender anxieties and feelings of emasculation that pervaded those postwar novels explored in the first part of this study. This image of France as feminine, emasculated, and sterile recalls Drieu la Rochelle's veteran characters as well as that of the *garçonne* Monique.

The natalist argument concerning economic crisis also subtly undermined the logic operative in Malthusian family planning. The "leprosy" of unworked fields served as a metonym for France itself, mortally weakened by its own impotence, sterility, and loss of virility. These images of economic barrenness relied on an idealization of productivity and fecundity that, at the level of metaphor, condemned the Malthusian logic of family limitation, contraception, and abortion. Malthusian demographic theory, which was still espoused by some

French liberal economists at the time, held that prosperity grows as the population gets smaller, because each individual gets a larger "piece of the pie."[72] This, of course, was also the logic of the French bourgeois who limited his family size in order to maintain and enjoy his social status.[73] The natalist critique of Malthusian theory, although directed at the level of the nation as a whole, indirectly undermined the identical logic of French family planning.

Natalist propagandists most frequently applied the theory that "the world belongs to large battalions" in their assessment of French military strength. On the one hand, propagandists identified depopulation with post-1870 French military inferiority and the onset of the First World War. Conversely, they linked a strong population and a healthy birthrate, such as those of Germany, with national security and peace. At a congress of the Ligues de familles nombreuses in 1918, Bertillon declared, "the more numerous the French, the less one will dare to attack them." "Four and a half years of war, 1,500,000 dead, 300 [billion] in debt, this has been the cost of the lack of foresight among the French, who failed to understand what was only in their interest, and in that of their country," argued Boverat.[74] "We need not look further for the essential cause of the war of 1914," declared the demographer Paul Haury in a prize-winning essay, "because we had fewer and fewer children, the Germans saw in us a 'dying nation.' They believed that the moment had come to finish us off." In this way, postwar propagandists attempted to channel the combat-weary, often intensely pacifist sentiments of the French population into support for the natalist cause.[75]

This image of a Germany eager to finish off France rubs uneasily with the historiographical view of the war as caused, at least in part, by larger and more complex structural problems. The image also reveals a tendency in natalist discourse to script itself as melodrama. Natalists presented Germany as an angry, greedy aggressor who, unlike France, had survived the war's devastation without a scar of suffering and with its virility intact. This Germany is capable of revenge and conquest because of "the feeling of strength that results from an abundant population and a healthy natality." Its natality expressed "the deeply felt will of a vigorous and healthy, active and fertile people, well on their way to prosperity and growth."[76] Such a statement ignores the fact that depopulation was also perceived as a problem in Germany and produced an important natalist movement there as well.[77] The melodrama of a defenseless, damsel France at the mercy of a populated, powerful Germany again relied on gender imagery to gain force and meaning in the postwar context. A confident, virile German nation, held forth as an example "of the dynamism a race can achieve when it agrees to pass on life generously," countered an emasculated France, feeble "only by her own fault, by her very own fault."[78] As Victor Giraud, the literary editor of *La Revue des deux mondes,* put it: "Let us consider coldly, and in a manly way [*virilement*] the prospect of finding ourselves alone once again in a few years, and facing an overpopulated, and militarily, financially restored Germany, quivering all over with the desire for vengeance."[79] The image of a German baby-bully brandishing a rattle at the timid, effeminate French infant represents the fusion in natalist discourse of three key postwar fears—depopulation, German revenge, and gender anxiety. (See fig. 15 and note the decorative "feminine" touches, such as the bow and lace, on the French cradle.)[80]

In order to exploit precisely these fears concerning the war and its aftermath, natalist propagandists relied on an antiquated notion of military power, as based primarily on population. They excluded from their discourse any counterargument concerning military strength, such as the important roles of modern weapons technology in determining the outcome of the First World War. This explains in part how the natalists could produce an image of France as both weaker and more timid than Germany (because less populated), when in fact the former had just triumphed over the latter in war. In addition, natalist high anxiety concerning France's territorial integrity expressed fears concerning French status as a world power. At an October 1918 congress, Bertillon warned his audience that incipient victory, although sweet and deserved, was not totally French: "What would have become of us without the assistance of our English and American friends? Their aid saved us, but ought not to console us in our unpopulated and therefore weakened state. To owe her safety to the bravery of others— surely France is worth more than this."[81] In military as well as economic matters, the newly effeminate France had become incapable of taking care of herself and wholly dependent on others. This France, which figures again as a woman, is also arguably a displaced image of a castrated man, reduced, in Bertillon's view, "to the state of those diminutive peoples who live only through the charity of others."[82]

Although fiercely nationalist, natalist propagandists were forced into the ironic position of having to belittle France's strength and degrade her finest hour—the victory of 1918—in order to make their argument for repopulation. Clinging to the belief that the world belongs to large battalions, Bertillon was making a dangerously unpatriotic argument: that the French did not win the war, or at least could not have won it without the Americans and the British. Similarly, Paul Bureau asserted that the French were becoming contented "with being a Belgium or an enlarged Holland."[83] In the eyes of the Americans and the English, argued another propagandist, "France has ceased to be considered a truly independent Great Power," so that her existence "was henceforth at the mercy, not only of her enemies, but also of her allies."[84] In this version of the natalist melodrama, the United States, brandishing its new-found economic power, countered the "has-been" France, washed up on depopulated shores. "In the eyes of Americans, we are the country of days gone by."[85] At the same time, however, despite its tone of resignation, the natalist argument that "the entire world is getting used to considering us a second-rate nation" was capable of evoking pathos and hence a reaction of militant nationalist defiance on the part of the reader.[86] Ironically, natalist apathy was also able to produce a defiant nationalism, as if the nation needed to be lost in order to be found.

Natalist discourse, then, forged a chain of signification, breathtaking in scope, that linked depopulation to a long litany of postwar anxieties, including industrial and agricultural ruin, fiscal and monetary chaos, military vulnerability, German economic development and imperialist aggression, a loss of French international power and prestige, and gender confusion. These were all issues separate in themselves, also constructed as problems and crises in postwar France, and heavily debated in the parliament, in the street, and in the press. Natalist discourse effectively displaced these problems, took them up on its own terms, and subordinated them to its own cause. In this way, the crisis of depopulation became the master narrative of postwar economic, military, political, and gender anxiety.[87] By the early 1920s, "depopulation" as a natalist concept was forced to bear responsibility, at the level of discourse, for a host of other so-called crises. This, of course, would explain natalist discourse's apocalyptic tone, raised to a high emotional pitch by depopulation's charge of discursive meaning. The overdetermination of depopulation as a concept largely explains its becoming a site for anguish and anxiety in postwar France.

Natalist discourse frequently played on the metaphor of the body. Natalist propagandists presented France as a physically ailing social body that demanded immediate medico-legislative intervention. At the same time, they gendered this metaphorical body, most often as female. "France is dying. She is not dead, but she is dying," "France is seriously ill," and "France . . . is committing suicide" were common pronouncements of the literature.[88] "I do not know whether France will live or die, but what I do know is that her extremities are cold," warned Paul Bureau.[89] At times, the war was implicated: "Even her victory has left her bleeding and gasping for breath, weakened by all the sons she has lost."[90] Anemia, with its connotations of sterility, was commonly used by natalists to characterize the cause or effect of depopulation. France has been "rendered anemic by the deficit of her natality."[91] A propagandist for the natalist journal *La Femme et l'enfant* accused France of suffering from "an anemia of will" in her low birthrate.[92] According to Auburtin, the choice was between "an anemic, bloodless France, condemned by sterility to decadence and death, or a powerful, virile France, enriching [*fécondant*] the world with its genius."[93] Gaston Rageot compared depopulated France to declining elites who are "made anemic by rarefication, like a body that grows weak by wasting away."[94] France's wasting demographic body was also illustrated through maps, which compared a darkly colored "Healthy France" of 1801–1810 to a much lighter "Anemic France" of 1891–1900, to finally an almost white "Sick France" of the contemporary era.[95]

The metaphor of a bleeding, anemic France legitimized legislative action. "The sickness from which she suffers is so profound and serious," argued one speaker at a 1920 conference, that "surgical intervention . . . alone can save us." "Surgery is vital, it will be painful, but is this any reason to abandon it?"[96] As Fernand Auburtin claimed,

> as concerns this cardinal issue, in which the very existence of the race is at stake, it seems as if the country has lost its instinct for conservation, and that those organs naturally predisposed to the defense of the social body, that is, the legislative Chambers, the Académie de médecine, the Cour de cassation, have more or less abdicated their roles.[97]

Auburtin forged rhetorical links here between national self-preservation, human reproduction, and legislative action. Precisely because the French genital organs had "abdicated their roles," the French medico-legislative organs—among them the Senate and the Chamber—must rush to preserve the social body. By producing an image of France as a dying patient in need of legislative surgery, yet sluggish in its self-preservation, natalists legitimated their own intervention and that of the government representatives they elected and supported.

By framing the argument in terms of a female social body in mortal need of help, they authorized their right to control the female sexual body. In the case of the law of 1920 against propaganda for abortion and contraception, natalists sought an unprecedented degree of control over the woman's private right to choose between life and death. The right to control the female body in its reproductive role was balanced by the right of the social body to protect its own life.[98] To the extent that French legislators themselves internalized this metaphor of the social body and the role they were to play in maintaining it, the specter of a bleeding, dying France was to haunt their debates as well.

Fetuses Floating in the Seine

It was as protectors of life and death, of bodies, and the French race that legislators passed the law against propaganda for abortion and contraception in 1920. They discussed the so-called law relating to depopulation in three sessions of the Senate and two sessions of the Chamber between 21 November 1918 (only ten days after the Armistice), and 23 July 1920.

The Chamber that Ignace approached in July 1920 had recently undergone radical changes in terms of both composition and political allegiance. Fear of Bolshevism and electoral reform that favored the formation of coalitions had brought to power a new conservative bloc in the elections of November 1919. When compared to the united, nationalist center-right majority that emerged from the election, the left (including the radical-socialists and the socialists) came out badly divided and with their numbers severely diminished.[99] It is in this context, as embattled members of the left, that André Berthon and Paul Morucci challenged the bill against abortion and contraceptive propaganda. Their critique, which dominated almost the entire debate, was motivated in part by genuine conviction that the bill threatened basic French civil liberties and in part by a desire to challenge and even antagonize an intractable center-right majority. Put on the defensive in this way, the deputies in the Bloc national did not criticize or even discuss the bill among themselves; nor did they provide an articulate response to the left. Confident of their majority, they chose silence on the issues and responded with an increasingly hostile pattern of behavior toward Berthon and Morucci.

By contrast, in the Senate, which was less torn apart by political divisions of this kind, a thorough and often anguished reading of the bill took place. The emotional, agonized tone of the Senate debates cannot be overemphasized, even if we take into account that hyperbolic, highly colorful language is commonplace in French parliamentary debate. In many ways, the debates were theaters of anxiety, with the senators often using vivid and even gruesome images in order to make their points. They focused intensely on the "crisis" of depopulation and drew on both the logic and rhetoric of natalist propaganda. For example, they presented depopulation as a matter of life and death. "If France does not produce more children," threatened Dominique Delahaye (Right, Maine-et-Loire), "our country is destined to disappear gradually."[100] When Henry Chéron (Union Républicaine, Calvados) declared that Malthusian propaganda militated "against the very existence of the country . . . this is a question of life or death for France," he received enthusiastic signs of approbation from his colleagues.[101] Similarly, a comment made by Félix Martin (Union Républicaine, Saône-et-Loire) that "the race is threatened, France is in danger," evoked a torrent of *"très biens"* and applause from the other senators.[102]

The apocalyptic tone of the debates can be explained in part by the fact that here, as in natalist discourse, depopulation as a concept was forced to bear the emotional weight of displaced economic and military anxiety. "More than ever, we are going to need manpower," worried Senator Marie Debierre (Radical, Radical-Socialist, Nord), who, like natalist propagandists, preferred "to appeal to the French themselves" rather than to immigrant labor.[103] Like natalists again, these legislators founded their arguments on an antiquated notion of military strength as based on population. Paul Cazeneuve (Radical, Rhône) began his opening statement in November 1918 with a quotation from Adolphe Pinard, his colleague at the Académie de médecine, to the effect that "if our population had been equal to that of Germany, we would probably not have been victims of an invasion."[104] Making a similar point, Léon Jénouvrier (Gauche Républicaine, Ile-et-Vilaine) referred to depopulation when he warned "If we cannot put up a sufficient barrier against it . . . it will be in vain that our sons will have been killed."[105] The phrase "sufficient barrier" (somewhat ironic in this context) itself evokes the need for physical protection, a military barricade or Maginot Line. In the January debates, Chéron declared that if France did not raise its natality by efficacious means, "we are lost . . . and the victory that we have just won will have been fragile and precarious. In 15 or 20 years, our enemy will attempt a new invasion against which it will be impossible for us to defend ourselves. If France had had as many children as Germany in 1914, you can be sure that the war would not have taken place."[106] Like natalist propagandists again, these senators fused postwar fears concerning depopulation, military weakness, and German revenge, and appealed to the pacifist sentiments of the French public in support of the natalist cause.

Finally, like the natalists, the senators justified their own legislative intervention by using the image of France as a sick or dying body in need of urgent attention. The right to seize the female reproductive body was once again legitimated by the need to regenerate the social body. In the January debates, Eugène Reveillaud (Radical, Radical-Socialist, Charente-Inférieure) referred to a book *Les Malades sociales,* by the editor Paul Gaultier, and claimed that "the number of . . . social diseases is, alas, considerable." Their root cause, in his view, was the issue at hand, contraceptive propaganda: "France has suffered a great deal from this propaganda," he argued, terming its principles "theories of death."[107] Emile Goy (Radical, Radical-Socialist, Haute-Savoie) created this Spenglerian image of a dying French civilization:

> Civilizations are subject to the same processes as all things of this world: they have their moment of youth, of blossoming, and of maturity; then the germs of death that they contain within them, like any other living thing, develop little by little and lead to decrepitude and death.[108]

No less than Drieu la Rochelle, Goy, who lost a beloved son in the war, envisioned a dying, decrepit nation and the ruins of a civilization. Goy demanded "the addition of foreign, ethnic elements" to save France from this fate; these "younger, more robust" elements would "infuse" France with "new blood."[109] Goy's argument here for foreign immigration as a response to depopulation separated him from most natalists. But, as we have seen, his use of gender images to give his argument force and meaning was a common natalist device. If France could be compared to a dying old man or a desiccated old woman beyond her reproductive years, immigration would recharge him (or her) with new vigor, virility, and life.

The popularity of this natalist image of France as a dying body in need of medico-legislative attention was no mere coincidence: Goy and a sizable number of other senators were physicians (for example, Paul Cazeneuve, the *rapporteur-général* of the bill).[110] Because of this number as well as the complex implications of the law of 1920 on the French medical profession, medical issues characterized much of the debate in the Senate. In turn, the conflictual set of professional interests negotiated by the physician-legislators suggest larger political ambiguities in the history of Third Republic social policy and its relationship to the family.[111] On the one hand, as it was conceived in January

1919, the bill enabled physicians to gain institutional power as directors of state-supervised obstetrical institutions for unwed or poor mothers.[112] On the other hand, it threatened physicians' professional autonomy by undermining the principle of medical confidentiality. At stake here was Article 14, which obliged doctors to produce any information concerning abortionists, even if obtained within the context of professional confidentiality. The opposition to Article 14, led by Dr. Emile Goy and Léon Jénouvrier, argued that the principle of medical confidentiality "rests on a principle of utmost moral importance," which had been "instituted by virtue of a higher law."[113] Lawyers such as Henry Chéron were also stung by the proposed threat to professional secrecy. Chéron described the principle of confidentiality as "the safeguard of his profession." Only moments later, however, he also insisted that confidentiality was "enacted not in the interest of a profession, but in that of the public order and individual security."[114]

Inasmuch as these physician-legislators interpreted the issue of medical confidentiality as an issue of woman's privacy, they contradicted their own intentions in passing the law of 1920. The senator and physician Marie Debierre defended the principle of medical confidentiality on the grounds that he sought to protect "the secret of a family who has confided it . . . in utmost privacy.'"[115] Senator Goy also understood the issue in terms of a woman's physical and spiritual right to privacy. Compromising medical confidentiality, he argued, betrayed the woman "who has disclosed [dévoilé] all the secrets of her body and her soul." The example was given of a woman who, upon entering the courtroom, is shocked and dismayed to see the doctor "to whom this child has revealed [dévoilé] all her secrets, in whom she has confided as she does to her priest."[116] Ostensibly, the physicians were defending medical confidentiality as a central protection of a woman's privacy. Such a defense was odd or at least novel in a legal-cultural tradition that did not consider women as rights-bearing subjects. In fact, medical confidentiality was key to physicians' growing power as the new "priests" and confessors of the family, because it covered an undefined terrain and thus allowed them to intervene in matters outside medicine.[117] These physicians' sincerity in defending a woman's privacy was undermined by the fact that other articles in the bill that they would soon pass—those that outlawed all forms of propaganda about contraception and abortion—intruded on that same privacy. In the July debates, Deputy André Berthon critiqued the ban on propaganda as an invasion of privacy *in the very same terms* as these doctors defended the threat to medical confidentiality. He accused the legislators in support of the ban of seeking "to disclose [*dévoiler*] marital intimacies and to intrude upon conjugal privacy."[118] Defending women's right to privacy, these physician-legislators had simultaneously licensed intrusion on that privacy.

This contradiction, in turn, demonstrates a larger conflict between public and private authority in the history of Third Republic familial social policy. According to the historian Sylvia Schafer, from the 1870s onward legislators calling for increased state intervention in family life had relied on the metaphor of the French state as a *père universel*, or "meta-parent." For example, in the case of the 1889 law for the protection of morally abandoned children, legislators justified their intrusion in familial matters by figuring the state as a guardian who unselfishly intervenes to safeguard its children when they are themselves endangered by their own, morally corrupted birth parents. The social and political agenda of republican politics demanded that the private, familial ideal, as well as the paternal authority of the *chef de famille* (enshrined in the Napoleonic Code) be respected. Hence, when parents were believed to be morally deficient and unable to care for their children, the state felt called upon to justify its own intervention, by claiming the role of *père universel*. In this way, the fiction of private, familial authority was upheld at the same time that the state increased its control over this same terrain.[119]

By simultaneously upholding and undermining the right to privacy of their female patients, legislators such as Goy, Chéron, and Debierre followed in this double-dealing tradition. By upholding women's right to privacy, they also arrogated to themselves the right to police it though legislation such as the law of 1920. As members of parliament and as physicians, they considered it their duty to parent/doctor the child—in this case, not yet even born—whom the morally corrupt mother had endangered by her wish to abort. Paul Strauss (Gauche Démocratique, Seine) head of the commission for the law in the Senate, justified it in this way: "It is our duty and within our power to dry up at its source the major cause of abortions and crimes against childhood."[120] For Strauss—an activist in social legislation aimed at the family, including the 1889 law for the protection of morally abandoned children—there was little difference between the bill against abortion under discussion and other laws protecting childhood, such as that of 1889. Strauss and other senators justified this parental protection in their role as legislators and in their equation of the endangered child with the future of France itself. Chéron, for example, described propaganda for abortion and contraception as "propaganda against French natality, that is, against the nation."[121] Seen in this way, from within the larger history of republican social policy, the law of 1920 reveals the state's increasing role as the *père universel* of the French family and nation.

Yet the legislators' efforts to decide matters of life and death in the family were also fraught with ambivalence, not only because they threatened to undermine further *la puissance paternelle,* but also because of their radical implications in the war just passing.[122] Nowhere had such powers to decide matters of life and death been more tragically displayed than in the war, when the state had drafted hundreds of thousands of young men and led them to their death. These senators must have been acutely aware of such powers in these debates, some of which took place only weeks after the armistice. Consider, for example, these impassioned words of Léon Jénouvrier:

> If we cannot put up a sufficient barrier against [depopulation]. . . it will be in vain that our sons will have been killed; it will be in vain that France will have offered this most horrible holocaust that history has ever known to the defense of liberty and of civilization—1,400,000 killed, others say 1,800,000, a million severely disabled, all of which made three million victims out of eight million mobilized, more than a third, and what a third! The youngest and most courageous, a majority of whom should have been *chefs de familles,* fathers of families. How can we heal such a wound? How can we fill such a deficit? We must persuade the country that nations are depopulated less by men being killed than by men not being born.[123]

The specter of a wounded, bleeding France, exhausted by "the most horrible holocaust that history has ever known" haunted these debates. The legislators were all too aware that their power to decide life and death in the family had caused the death or mutilation of millions of potential *chefs de famille,* in all their youthful virility. If France had become an emasculated nation that had lost the best third of its "youngest and most courageous," was the state responsible? The rhetorical cadences of Jénouvrier's speech here bring into alignment those Frenchmen killed and those not able to be born, the "wound" that France has suffered from the loss of its virile core, and the "deficit" that numerically must be filled. The word "deficit" takes on more than a strictly demographic meaning here and becomes as well a repository of guilt, a reparation to be paid for the slaughter of innocents. Once again, when senators such as Jénouvrier aligned the holocaust of the war with Malthusian propaganda and depopulation, they echoed themes in natalist propaganda (figs. 16 and 17).

Inasmuch as the war was also a matter of life and death, something about abortion and malthusian propaganda became unbearable. In the cultural economy of postwar France, depopulation became linked to a whole other set of meanings that concerned the war, its traumas, and its sacrifices. In the eyes of the senators, haunted by the wounds of war and their own moral responsibility, abortion and Malthusian propaganda became searing affronts to the dead. When the senator and physician Cazeneuve was called on to defend the principle of medical confidentiality, he conflated the "terrible holocaust" of the war with the threat of abortion or Malthusian propaganda: "I am among those who believe that after the great ordeal that our country has suffered, after the attacks that certain criminals by profession inflict on the population," the doctor must tell what he knows.[124] In Cazeneuve's phraseology, "the great ordeal" of the war, and Malthusian, criminal "attacks" were again aligned and identified with each other. France was once again the victimized, female, social body of both: having "suffered" the war, she must now endure what abortionists "inflicted" on her. Cazeneuve's identification of abortion with the war's ordeal explains his graphic and highly emotional language in condemning the rise of abortions in recent years. Quoting a physician, he said:

> I advise all persons who are upset about the future of our country, from the point of view of its natality, to go look at the number of fetuses that are dredged up [ramènent] by sewer boats. Go see the thousands of victims who are carried away to the Seine, or who, on the way, become stuck in the iron bars of the sewers.[125]

It is tempting to connect Cazeneuve's tortured description, which formed a climactic moment in an already emotionally charged opening speech, with the "thousands of victims" to which Jénouvrier referred.[126] The power of a state to guarantee the life and health of the social body was joined in these legislators' minds to the other power of the state: to expose an entire population to danger and death. Victims of war or victims of abortion—both were marked by their innocence and struck down in mind-boggling numbers. Both were perceived as bearing on "the future of our country" and the "defense of civilization"; both represented "a matter of life and death." Both "inflicted" emotional and gender "wounds" that somehow must be healed. In the minds of senators like Cazeneuve, Malthusian propaganda was joined to the war at its most raw and deadly core: as a set of "theories of death," it, too, inflicted on France a most horrible holocaust: the slaughtering of innocent victims.

This flashing back and forth between the cradle and the tomb also characterized the conception of the bill in the Chamber.[127] The *exposé des motifs* (statement of purpose) of the original version of the bill, deposed on January 22, 1920, argued that "in a France that is wounded in her flesh, the situation calls for certain measures that will give her not only her former vitality, but also a power of expansion."[128] Once, again, the language of the *exposé* suggested a war-wounded and emasculated body-nation, whose virility and life force ("power of expansion") could be recovered only through natalist measures.[129] The second *exposé des motifs* presented by Edouard Ignace in July, also directly aligned the war with abortion and contraceptive propaganda:

> On the morrow of a war in which nearly 1,500,000 Frenchmen sacrificed their lives so that France had the right to live in independence and honor, it is intolerable that other Frenchmen have the right to make enormous amounts of money from the multiplication of abortions and from Malthusian propaganda.[130]

This identity of holocausts could have had a particularly mobilizing effect in the Chamber, which was dubbed the "Chambre bleu horizon" because so many of its deputies, freshly returned from the front, still wore the sky-blue army uniform. These deputy-veterans were particularly aware of the sacrifices made by their comrades so that France had "the right to live in independence and honor." They might have felt keenly the intolerability of those who made "enormous amounts of money" from death, a stock resentment of the *poilu* toward the war profiteer.

As concepts used by senators and deputies to debate the law of 1920, "depopulation" and "abortion," were historically embedded not only in the economic and military anxieties of a rocky postwar period, but also in the trauma and guilt of the holocaust just passing. How could one heal such a wound? To Cazeneuve the path of action was clear:

> Messieurs, after the great ordeal of this war, that has reduced by so much the number of our sons, that is, the most active element of our population, and in the presence of the appalling losses that we have suffered, we have the duty to do everything we can so that the country can be regenerated and repopulated.[131]

Given the cultural economy of postwar France—the specific horizon of meaning within which these parliamentary debates were inscribed—Cazeneuve could not have picked a more persuasive rhetoric. By framing the natalist argument within "the great ordeal" of the war, Cazeneuve and the other natalist legislators exploited a set of metaphors that enjoyed unequaled cultural force and that would resonate strongly with, and thus convince, their colleagues. If France lay wounded and dying, then the senator's role, as both legislator and (in the case of Cazeneuve, Goy, and others) as doctor, was to regenerate it by passing the law of 1920. The law itself had an ironic, double effect: it extended the state's right to control the family and the human body; but it also reversed, or at least seemed to reverse, the state's exercise of its right to kill. In this law, at least, the senators would be saving victims rather than creating them, at the same time that they reasserted their power to decide a matter of life and death. The law represented both a reassertion of the state's confidence in its own power and a way to appease what troubled that confidence, that is, the slaughter of 1.5 million men in the war.

In addition, the law provided a clear path of action to resolve what appeared to be a bewildering array of problems plaguing the state in the postwar era. The "crisis" of depopulation, as it was fashioned by natalist propagandists, appealed to legislators because it produced a coherent explanation, the identification of a single, fundamental cause, for a number of other "crises" that beleaguered them in the days following the armistice. In fact, the French state emerged from the war as much exhausted as it was victorious, and beset with unprecedented economic, social, and diplomatic problems.[132] Besides demobilizing one million soldiers, impatient to resume civilian life, the government found itself faced with the task of reconstructing 60 thousand kilometers of roads, 2,000 kilometers of canals and 6,000 kilometers of train-tracks.[133] The economic and diplomatic problems were enormous. Even the most basic foodstuffs—butter, sugar, and bread—could be bought only at exorbitant prices. The loss of the gold standard during the war and the enormous indebtedness of the state led to runaway, seemingly uncontrollable, inflation.[134] The legislators charged with solving the fiscal and monetary problems at hand were woefully unprepared for the task before them, as most were economically illiterate and had little or no experience dealing with a shaky currency.[135] The anxiety and sense of inadequacy felt by legislators in dealing with the economic situation was compounded by apprehension in the diplomatic realm. Fears of German revenge worsened considerably in

1919–20 as the French government began to feel isolated diplomatically and deserted by its allies. At the same time, the Soviet state rose like an ominous star on the horizon, striking fear and even panic in government circles.[136]

French legislators were thus plagued with immense, complex tasks, many of which they felt unable to solve or even to understand. As the historian Bernard Dubief has written, many of them coped by retreating into a web of illusions: believing that Germany would totally repay reparations, or that France would return to the gold standard and prewar economic parity.[137] Not least among these illusions, it could be argued, was the legislators' belief that France would be reborn economically and militarily through a simple increase in her natality. Although the problems facing legislators were confoundingly diverse, when they were linked together as various symptoms of one "social disease"—depopulation—they were rendered magically coherent, simple to understand. Natalist discourse itself generated anxiety, it is true, but only to resolve or "manage" it with its own simple, reassuring logic: "If only we would have children, these problems will be solved." The logical structure of natalist discourse was therefore cathartic: it mobilized anxiety only to resolve it, raising it to a fevered pitch (as we have seen in the Senate debates) only to produce a clear, uncomplicated path of action, as manifested in the law against abortion and contraceptive propaganda.

Despite the pervasiveness of natalist values, not everyone was convinced that raising the birthrate would magically cause *belle époque* stability to reappear. Never one to mince words, Nelly Roussel evaluated the effectiveness of natalist efforts in this way:

> Once again, all these gentlemen are wasting their time. No matter how stupid the people are—and they are, as the war and the legislative elections have so abundantly proved—you would nevertheless be hard-pressed to get them to admit that in the state of economic, financial and physiological "collapse" in which we find ourselves, threatened at every turn by famine and bankruptcy, and at a time when our shaken, exhausted race has hardly begun its convalescence after the terrible shock, that a multiplication of births would be a benefit for the country![138]

Like Berthon, Roussel tried to point out the feeble logic of the natalist argument. Yet even among feminists, most of whom were strongly natalist themselves, Roussel's view was largely condemned. Did this make feminists (and the French generally) as "stupid" as Roussel claims them to be? Perhaps the answer to this question lies in

Roussel's use of language, her evoking—no less than Senator Goy or propagandist Paul Bureau—the "shaken, exhausted" body of France, which "has hardly begun its convalescence" after the war. If the French were "stupid" about natalism, it was because of its magically healing effects, its power to soothe what Roussel called "the terrible shock" of war. And if French legislators were "wasting their time," as Roussel believed (and as the ultimate failure of the 1920 law indeed demonstrated), at least they had found a way to understand the baffling problems left by the war.

What maddened Roussel most about the natalists was that, in her words, "this gang of grotesque actors posing as moralists have found a way of composing their long harangues *without speaking of women and of mothers!* . . . These gentlemen may want children, but they don't seem to know how they're made!"[139] Again here, Roussel was both right and wrong: right in her assessment that natalists did not consider specifically female needs in their arguments, but wrong in her (admittedly ironic) belief that they had forgotten how children are made. The passage of the law of 1920 had everything to do with women and mothers, and it is to this aspect of the crisis of depopulation that we now turn.

5

"MADAME DOESN'T WANT A CHILD"

D URING THE JANUARY 1919 READING of the law against propaganda for contraception and abortion, Senator Léon Jénouvrier expressed the fear that French women no longer wanted
to have children. Quoting a recent article in the weekly *Le Radical*,
Jénouvrier lamented that while the aim of life had once been "to act,
to struggle, to be deserving," now "one wants 'to live one's own life,'
which often means refusing to give life to others."[1] The state, he resolved, should use all means at its disposal to teach "this country that
after the suffering and sacrifices of our soldiers at the front—indeed,
they did not try to 'live their own life,' but instead offered it up for
France's salvation—it is up to the people on the homefront to create
life."[2] According to Jénouvrier, "[a] country whose women do not know
how to produce children is a country struck at its very heart."[3]

Jénouvrier's language here suggests a dizzying web of connections
that is lost in translation. He declared that the French, and particularly
the French woman, was no longer interested in giving life *(donner la
vie)* because she wanted to "live her own life" *(vivre sa vie)*, that is,
lead a life of individual satisfaction and pleasure. Jénouvrier then compared this attitude with that of the soldier at the front who, rather than
"live his own life," chose instead to sacrifice it for his country *(donner
sa vie)*. For the purpose of rhetorical persuasion, Jénouvrier exploited
the similarities in language for motherhood, self-indulgence, and the
sacrifice of one's life for one's country; he connected the man who had
risked or given up his life, the woman who wants to "live her own life,"

120

and the mother who should, above all, give life. In other words, he linked three prominent postwar images: the veteran, *la femme moderne,* and *la mère.*

Jénouvrier was not the only postwar politician to express concern that women no longer wanted to give birth to children. In the same Senate debate, Jénouvrier's colleague, Emile Goy, attributed depopulation to the fact that "women dread the pains and suffering of maternity and fear that the child will mark their forehead with premature wrinkles."[4] In 1919, Georges Clemenceau remarked that the "merit" of a *mère de famille nombreuse* was "immense," but "not adequately appreciated. Too often, in fact, she is ridiculed!"[5] The same year, future prime minister Edouard Herriot argued in *Créer,* his evaluation of postwar France, that the war had brought about a "new life" for women, one whose "temptations" she had not been able to "resist": "even if one is not pessimistic, there is cause for worry. . . . What will become of motherhood . . . women's noble and eternal role?"[6] In the early twenties, Minister of Commerce Auguste Isaac explained the declining birthrate by accusing the French woman of being "more egoistic, more frivolous" and "less courageous than the German woman (who herself has five children)."[7]

For decades in fact, natalist propagandists, politicians, and doctors had voiced similar fears concerning the "egoistic" French woman. In his 1874 legislative effort to reform the French wet-nursing industry, Senator Théophile Roussel attributed population decline to the "weakening" of maternal love.[8] From its inception in the 1860s, natalist discourse equated population decline with women's unwillingness to have children. In natalist ideology, a woman's body had no integrity of its own apart from its maternal capacity, which itself was defined as a larger social function.[9] By contrast, the male reproductive role was ignored by natalist propagandists, in terms of both physiology and decision-making. The popular medical writer Dr. Gaston Cattier began his natalist pamphlet *Des Bébés, s'il vous plaît* (1923), by relating his friend's explanation for French depopulation: "The reason why there are so few children . . . is that women don't want them."[10] Gaston Rageot, a well-known novelist and natalist propagandist, argued that "the drop in natality is principally attributable to the French woman."[11] This aspect of natalist ideology, like much else, surfaced in the political rhetoric of the postwar years. In January 1919, Senator Henry Chéron attributed all family planning decisions to women when he argued that propaganda for abortion and contraception "consists in saying to French women: 'You will no longer have children.'"[12] The natalist elision between reproduction and the maternal body also explains why the law of 1920 targeted specifically female forms of contraception.[13]

When Jénouvrier expressed fear concerning the unwillingness of women to have children, he voiced an old natalist platitude, in no way unique to the postwar period. However, given the intensity of postwar trauma concerning gender identity—the fear of Drieu's sexless civilization—what particular resonances might such a fear have in postwar France? Did postwar French women reject motherhood? Was there, in fact, *une crise du devoir maternel,* or "crisis of maternal duty" as Gaston Rageot called it?[14] What relationship, if any, existed between Jénouvrier's concern that women no longer wanted to have children, and postwar gender trauma? And why, in the same breath, did Jénouvrier voice his fear concerning *la femme moderne* and his anger concerning the "suffering and sacrifices" of soldiers at the front? How were female egoism and male sacrifice linked in his mind?

Some evidence exists that motherhood was looked down on in the early twenties. In 1920, a natalist propagandist described women who had several children as "object[s] of scornful pity" and "pariah[s] in their own country."[15] Another commented in 1920 that "[i]n many circles, to have many children is an absurdity and is considered a folly and a blunder."[16] When in May 1920, the French state instituted medals to honor mothers of large families, the satirical newspaper *Le Canard enchaîné* responded by proposing an alternate skull-shaped medal that would honor "obstetrical laziness": "Quickly! a medal for bad *citoyennes,* and may every able-bodied man do his duty!"[17] A mother of fourteen who received the gold medal at the 1920 Rouen natalist conference told the editors of *Pour la vie* that "our neighbors have been telling us that we are imbeciles and are wrong to have children."[18] In a 1922 review of *La Garçonne,* the novelist Rachilde mocked Margueritte's heroine, Monique and her desire to bear a child: "Great God! Someone healthy in both body and soul, and eager for motherhood? You mean one actually exists in France?"[19] In 1923, the feminist Maria Vérone noted that the state's medal had been renamed *"la médaille de la mère Gigogne,"* which roughly translates as "the medal of the old woman who lived in the shoe."[20] In a survey on marriage appearing in *La Renaissance politique* during the spring of 1924, several respondants, including the well-known writer Colette Yver, claimed that "fewer and fewer women consent to be mothers."[21]

However, none of this evidence suggests that women, in particular, scorned motherhood in either rhetoric or action to any significant degree. Jokes about mothers and large families did proliferate in postwar France, but perhaps only as a nervous response to the intensity of natalist propaganda. If we are to consider feminist literature as one important voice of French women's views on sexuality, this literature neither contained a coherent, self-conscious attack on motherhood nor referred to such a position. Prominent liberal bourgeois feminists, such as Madeleine Vernet, Maria Vérone, and Jane Misme, all expressed strongly natalist views. Vérone herself thought motherhood "a rare enough sport," but she pleaded that it "ought not to be seen solely as a burden, but also a joy, and above all, never as a source of shame."[22] In 1917, Madeleine Vernet founded the monthly *La Mère éducatrice* in honor of the "indefatigable and loving . . . humble and devoted" working-class mother.[23] Feminists on the extreme left of the political spectrum, such as Louise Bodin and Nelly Roussel, strongly supported women's maternal role, even if they did not show sympathy for the goals of the natalist movement. The Communist Louise Bodin congratulated Vernet on the founding of *La Mère éducatrice* with this paen to motherhood: "At the very dawn of life, there is mother and child, and, in a society not lost to egoism, vice and crime, everything should contribute to the veneration of the mother and child."[24] Even Nelly Roussel, who became notorious in 1919 for inciting women to foment a *"grève des ventres,"* or "womb strike," upheld motherhood in principle. She urged women to strike or stop giving birth not because she scorned motherhood itself, but rather because of the impoverished and physically dangerous conditions in which women often gave birth.[25] In any case, Roussel certainly did not discourage women from having children so that they could lead lives of easy pleasure.

In addition, postwar demography does not completely support the notion of a *crise du devoir maternel.* The birthrate for the years 1920 to 1925 was 19.7 per 1,000 inhabitants, a figure historian Colin Dyer considers to represent "a healthy postwar revival" in demographic terms. The rate represented an increase over not only a wartime decline, but also the prewar figure of 18.2. After this initial postwar revival, the birthrate again began to gradually fall, dropping to 14.8 by the five-year period just before the Second World War.[26] The reasons for these demographic trends are complex and not reducible to women's assumed desire (or lack of it) to have children. Still, the birthrate during the early twenties (1920–25) distinguishes itself as the highest in the two-decade period surrounding it. If women were scorning motherhood, they were doing so less than they had in the prewar period or they would in the thirties.

Like the "crisis" of depopulation, the *crise du devoir maternel* cannot be understood solely in terms of demography or reproductive behavior. Whether or not the perception that women no longer wanted to bear children was "correct" from an empirical viewpoint, it gains significance as a cultural reality in itself, something that worried and preoccupied postwar French men and women. In other words, the *crise du devoir maternel* was as much a cultural as a demographic phenomenon in the postwar years. The old natalist argument that women were unwilling to give life in order "to live their own lives" gained intense resonance in relation to the heightened gender and cultural tensions of the period. The natalist condemnation of French women for their morally degenerate refusal to bear children channeled postwar fears concerning the erasure of sexual difference. Motherhood became a privileged site of moral regeneration and gender healing. Once again, moral and gender anxieties were conflated in the postwar debate on women.

The Sterility of Souls

Postwar natalists imbedded the fear that French women no longer wanted to give birth within a larger complex of ideas they referred to as the "moral problem of depopulation." From the mid-nineteenth century onward, scientists, demographers, and social critics of all political stripes blamed depopulation on national moral decay.[27] Jénouvrier voiced another old platitude of natalist literature when, in the Senate debate of January 23, he argued that the depopulation crisis was "moral in nature."[28] Once again, he was not the only postwar politician to do so. In 1918, for example, the future president of France, Paul Deschanel, described depopulation in this way: "it is a moral task that lies before us, it is the hygiene of souls that we must improve; it is the sterility of souls that we must attack." In 1920, Clemenceau declared that "the recovery of our natality depends above all on moral reform."[29]

Natalists defined the moral problem of depopulation in the highly abstract terms of such nineteenth-century sociologists and economists as Léonce de Lavergne, Fréderic Le Play, and Arsène Dumont.[30] According to these theorists, rising individualism lay at the root of depopulation. The desire for greater social status and a higher standard of living—what Dumont called *capillarité sociale*—led the French to limit the number of their offspring at the expense of demographic strength. In his seminal work *Dépopulation et civilisation* (1890), Dumont argued that a strongly democratic society, such as had character-

ized France since the Revolution, encouraged the individual to pro-
hibit himself from having children "out of egoism" and to ignore the
benefits to the country of a large family.[31] This immoral disregard of
the nation in order to advance self-interest comprised the moral problem of depopulation.

In the late war and postwar periods, prominent natalist propagandists such as Félix Auburtin, Gaston Rageot, and Paul Bureau emphasized this antimodern, antirepublican strain of demographic theory.
They defined the moral problem of depopulation in terms of modern
democratic individualism, or in Auburtin's words, "egoism in private as
well as public life: that is its definition. Everyone for himself: that is its
motto."[32] In *La Natalité* (1918), Rageot described modern democratic
society as nothing more than *"une juxtaposition d'égoïsmes"* and the
poor natality rate as symptomatic of a nation "inflicted with psychological decadence."[33] According to Bureau's journal *Pour la vie,* "a love
of well-being, an unwillingness to sacrifice any of one's comforts and
amusements, a growing need for luxury, vanity, a fear of complicating
one's life" was destroying the nation.[34] Love of children, argued Cattier
in *Des Bébés, s'il vous plaît,* "lies dormant, suffocated by egoism, the
taste for luxury, a thirst to live above and beyond one's means."[35] "Egoistic" was a postwar natalist catchword that propagandists applied to
anyone they considered self-serving or immoral.[36]

Natalists conceptualized their moral world in terms of two conflicting sets of values. The morally "sterile" decision not to have children implied personal vanity and ambition, as well as what Fernand
Auburtin referred to as "lack of initiative, fear of responsibility, scorn
for hard work, a desire for a peaceful and undemanding life-style."[37]
Advocates of *la famille nombreuse,* on the other hand," preach[ed] simplicity, a love of hard work and endeavor, a need to take risks, . . . confidence in life and in Providence."[38] Natalists particularly prized "a
rigorous conception of *Devoir*"—obligation or duty—that they counterposed to "egoism." "One word in particular rings clear and returns
at every turn like a refrain," argued Bureau, "this is the word '*devoir*'."
"We must restore the notion of duty to France and to French democ-
racy," insisted Georges Rossignol, a propagandist for *Pour la vie.* He
wanted the republican "Declaration des droits" to be supplemented by
a "Declaration des devoirs" in which familial discipline, sobriety, and
chastity would supercede equality and freedom as the highest values.[39]

In conceptualizing their bipolar moral world, natalists such as Rossignol drew generally on late nineteenth-century ideas of decay and
renewal. In order to define two other moral oppositions, natalists drew

more specifically on discourses of the war period. First, they contrasted wartime and postwar moral behaviors, drawing an opposition between the heroism shown by the soldier during the war and the moral dissipation shown by French society, particularly the French woman, after the war. Second, natalists polarized their image of the French woman into two separate types: the traditional, self-sacrificing *mère de famille nombreuse* and the selfish, pleasure-seeking *femme moderne* of the postwar era. In both these cases, natalists construed the logic of the opposition as the same conflict of moral values—duty vs. egoism, sacrifice vs. the pursuit of pleasure—that divided their moral world generally. Furthermore, the two moral oppositions were interrelated. Natalists expressed anxiety concerning the perceived contrast between the wartime spirit of sacrifice and the postwar atmosphere of moral decadence. For what set of values had the war been fought? How could the sacrifice be deemed worthy? Natalists resolved the anxiety generated by this first opposition by resolving the conflict in the second—that is, by transforming postwar *femmes modernes* into radiant mothers.

The first of the two contrasts—between wartime and postwar behaviors—was grounded in the natalist belief that the war had reaffirmed traditional ideals of heroism, discipline and sacrifice. In *La Natalité* (1918), which Rageot wrote during the war, he argued that "patriotism, religious sensibility, more attention to the realities of life and a new sense of moral values" were all "certain signs of this spiritual regeneration."[40] This optimism concerning spiritual rebirth persisted, although in a more troubled form, after the war. According to Paul Bureau in his classic natalist tract, *L'Indiscipline des moeurs* (1920), the war had revealed that despite fin-de-siècle malaise, France "had kept intact its tradition of warrior virtues."[41] "The sentiment of *devoir,* the spirit of devotion and sacrifice"—these were the passions that *La Femme et l'enfant* saw as reawakened by the war in 1920.[42] In sharp contrast to this spiritual regeneration of the war, however, stood the "excessive individualism" that characterized postwar society. France, propagandists claimed in 1919, could not "get control over its fever for instant, material pleasures. . . . A sort of frenzy is coming over all classes and bewitching all social circles: one no longer knows how to will *[vouloir],* but only how to desire *[désirer].*"[43] In 1920, Bureau argued that the country was traversing "an era in which the pursuit of happiness, of joy, or even simply of pleasure, enjoys an enormously important place in the life of individuals, and has become the sole guiding principle of behavior for a large multitude."[44] The same year, a journalist for *La Mère éducatrice* noted that the postwar frenzy of pleasures had left the war completely behind:

> The great stream of noise scattering death and tears is *forgotten*. The biting grief that tears at and consumes the mother's soul is *forgotten*. The gray crosses, distant testimonies of the sacrifice of our boys, *are forgotten*. A sort of mad pleasure holds the world in its grip.[45]

The anguished tone here permeates much postwar natalist discourse—a discourse twisted at its heart by the conflict between moral renewal and moral decay. According to natalists, the "fever" and the "frenzy . . . bewitching all social circles" undermined the so-called spiritual regeneration of the war. Caught in the uncontrollable grip of desire, bewitched by pleasure, France had forgotten the warrior virtues, the spirit of sacrifice, "the great stream of noise scattering death and tears."

In short, according to natalist propaganda, France had been both saved and thrown away; the task was to save it again in order to be worthy of the war's sacrifice. As Bureau put it in the introduction to *L'Indiscipline des moeurs:*

> The tenacious heroism of our chiefs and soldiers enabled us to impose defeat upon Germany on November 11, 1918. . . . A new and perhaps more difficult task demands our efforts . . . now we must organize the peace and merit its fruits with our painstaking labor. . . . As the incomparable warriors of yesterday, we must now create an organic, coherent society gifted with force, power and dynamism, in short, oriented toward life.[46]

The natalist vision of moral crisis—a frenzied, sterile pursuit of pleasure haunted by the specter of war—strikingly resembles the postwar *crise de l'esprit* expressed by Pierre Drieu la Rochelle and other veteran writers. These writers and the natalists shared the same anguished questions concerning the ultimate impact of the war. Had the wartime values of sacrifice and devotion been forgotten in the postwar frenzy of pleasures? Why then had the war been fought? How could its sacrifices be redeemed in the postwar world? To the extent that these questions remained unanswered, natalist propagandists bore down hard on the category of "woman"—privileging it as a symbol of both moral decay and regeneration.

The French woman played a strange double role in natalist discourse—as both modern woman and traditional mother. Her dual image comprises the second natalist opposition that drew on wartime discourses. As we saw in Chapter 1, two images of female identity—the ignorant, pleasure-seeking woman and the courageous, self-sacrificing nurse or mother—pervaded wartime literature. Natalists reproduced this dual image in their own propaganda. Most often (but not always), it had a distinct class element: the "bad" modern woman was bourgeois, while the "good" mother was working class.

Natalist propagandists defamed the bourgeois modern woman for her excessive individualism. In 1920, Paul Bureau referred to the "cold and selfish" *femme moderne,* who wanted only to "live her own life," who "prefer[red] jewels, clothes, or refined hands to noble familial tasks," and whose numbers (unlike those of babies) had grown "ceaselessly" since the war.[47] The same year, Emile Bocquillon, the chair of the Educational Committee at the Second National Natalist Congress, described the modern woman as morally "degenerate" because she wanted "a sweet, tranquil, calm life, without worry, suffering or difficulty," and filled with "all possible pleasures."[48] In this way, natalists identified the modern woman with the postwar "frenzy of pleasures" and the moral decay that this frenzy implied.

Although natalists had characterized the French woman as egoistic and pleasure-seeking since the previous century, the gendered geography of the war strongly reinforced their views. As we saw in Chapter 1, one important theme of wartime literature was the relative comfort of civilian to military life. Front soldiers saw the homefront as a world of pleasure and loose morality that threw their own life of sacrifice into stark relief. To the extent that the sexes inhabited a gendersegregated world during the war, the stark contrast between civilian and military life could also be perceived as a division between men's and women's wartime experiences. In 1918, the novelist Louis Narquet expressed a fairly common view when he argued that during the war the French woman had been "carried away by the frenzy of an unexpected freedom, by coquetry, vanity and pleasure. Even those who rigorously observed marital fidelity seemed unable to resist the contagion of this kind of vertigo."[49] The use of words such as "frenzy" and "vertigo" here echoed natalist descriptions of the postwar "frenzy of pleasures" during these same years (1918–20). The soldiers' comparison of their own wartime experience (hardship, suffering, sacrifice) with that of women (moral degeneracy, luxury, selfishness) mirrored the natalist moral conflict of values. Whether women actually demonstrated "egoistic" behavior during the war, this belief formed an important strand of wartime and postwar views on women. Clearly, natalists both were influenced by and contributed to their dissemination.

But natalists also referred to another kind of woman, contrasting the bourgeois *femme moderne* with another image, the working-class *mère de famille nombreuse*. Just as natalists identified the *femme moderne* with postwar moral sterility, they defined *la mère de famille nombreuse* as embodying those traditional values—honor, duty, sacrifice, devotion—for which the war had supposedly been fought. Paul Bureau, for example, seized on the occasion of Mother's Day (first celebrated in France in 1920) to praise the "special devotion" and "particular self-abnegation" of mothers who have "saved honor, the honor of their *foyer*, and that of their country, the honor of their husband, and that of their love."[50] Motherhood, then, became a privileged site of moral regeneration. Natalists invested maternity with the power to make the victory meaningful because it reinvigorated those traditional values for which the war had been fought. A speaker at the Second Natalist Congress in 1920 described the mother in this way:

> Choosing to remain at home, where she is upheld as an example of self-sacrifice, the mother is able to struggle effectively against moral wrong, more present today than ever before, and constituting a frenzy of pleasures. . . . By her life of continual self-denial, she becomes a living commentary on the renunciation of the moment, on the kind of self-abnegation that remains the sole and true source of familial and social virtue, the foundation of individual renewal, and the model of collective renewal.[51]

The mother was a living testimony to the principles for which the *poilu* had died: she made that death worthwhile. Only the mother in her traditional role of moral guardian—as the bedrock of familiar virtue—could overcome the excesses of postwar egoism. In 1919, a social Catholic propagandist urged women: "France's restoration rests with you much more than with men; it depends on you and the customs of life and devotion that you take up. I hope that . . . on the tombs of those who are no longer with us, you will lay down cradles."[52] Another argued in 1920:

> After the victory, grave moral, social and religious problems have presented themselves. The duty of the French woman is to participate in the work necessary to the regeneration of our country. At home, the woman must be a source of happiness, both by the material cares she gives her family and by the radiance of her strong virtue and cultivated intelligence.[53]

The sight of a loving, self-effacing mother soothed the souls of natalists not only because it promised an end to demographic vulnerability, but also because it represented a moral regeneration of familial and social virtue. The physician Jules Boudry ended his 1923 pamphlet *Le Problème de la natalité* with a long, lyrical "Call to the Women of France." Reminding his reader of how wartime nurses closed the eyes of dead soldiers, he continued:

> It is they who ask you to provide their replacements; respond to their call. The future of France is in your frail and yet so powerful hands! . . . And you will be greatly rewarded, when you feel the light touch of the breath of our dead souls, who will say to you: *"Petites mamans, Merci, vous avez bien mérité de la Patrie."*[54]

The French woman was central to France's *renaissance* in terms both of military strength and moral virtue. But it was also precisely the French woman who was under pressure in natalist discourse for her very *lack* of virtue. This splitting of the subject of "woman" aligned itself with the other oppositions—duty vs. egoism, self-sacrifice vs. pleasure, wartime vs. postwar—that comprised the natalist moral universe. As a subject of natalist discourse, the French woman was both the foundation and disrupter of virtue, the model of and obstacle to collective renewal. She was the focus of both hope and angry disappointment, but in all cases, the privileged symbol of the "moral problem" of depopulation.

In the cultural economy of postwar France, "motherhood," like "depopulation," became linked to a seemingly extraneous set of meanings concerning the war's traumas and sacrifices. Because of motherhood's role as a privileged symbol in this way, natalists read the so-called *crise du devoir maternel* not simply as a refusal to have children, but also as the rejection of a way of life, a set of ideals, and a sense of moral direction. They joined fears about motherhood and low natality to those concerning moral regeneration and the postwar *crise de l'esprit*. In a 1925 survey appearing in *Progrès civique*, a Parisian law student described modern women in this way: "These unhappy women do not want to be mothers because they do not dare to confess that they are sterile, sterile in their heart and in their feelings."[55] In *La Garçonne*, Monique Lerbier's physical sterility cannot be separated from the period of moral dissipation during which she experienced it. In the postwar period, "sterility" was a matter of heart and feeling, a "sterility of souls." Moral regeneration, demographic vitality, the war's spiritual legacy—all these could be assured if one could only transform modern women into loving mothers.

Still a closer examination of the debate on *la crise du devoir maternel* will reveal that motherhood guaranteed even more than this—that the mother could restore male virility as well as moral virtue. In order to understand this other prodigious power of the mother, we must take a close look at some examples of postwar popular literature. In the murkier, more oblique world of fiction, the crisis of maternal duty emerges as a crisis of sexual difference.

Pretty Women, Large Beefsteaks, and Brave Military Men

In 1924–25, the phrase "Madame doesn't want a child" became a cliché of the language. It was used as a sarcastic response to natalist propaganda. The phrase derived from the title of Clément Vautel's novel *Madame ne veut pas d'enfant* (1924), which concerned a *femme moderne* who refuses motherhood in order to lead an easy, pleasure-filled life.[56] Vautel was a prominent journalist and novelist, well-known for his natalist and antifeminist views.[57] His purpose in writing *Madame ne veut pas d'enfant* was propagandistic: to demonstrate the joys of a large family and the dangers to both personal and marital happiness implicit in the refusal of maternity. Vautel's novel was read in precisely this way. Gaston Picard, the literary editor of *La Renaissance politique*, called Vautel a "moralist" and described his novel as a "terrible denunciation" of a problem that will "weaken and exhaust France."[58]

Vautel delivers his natalist message both explicitly and implicitly. First, he engages anti- and pro-natalists in an explicit battle of words, giving the two sides a forum for their views through such plot devices as a neo-Malthusian journal, *Le Bonheur,* and a ceremony for bestowing *la médaille de la famille nombreuse.* More implicitly, Vautel expresses the natalist theme through character and plot. The unhappy fate of Elyane Parisot, the selfish, pleasure-loving *femme moderne* who refuses to bear children, once again drives home his natalist message. However, Vautel's plot resolution contains one interesting and important twist: it tells the reader more than Vautel himself perhaps intended about the relationship between natalism and male sexual anxiety.

Vautel's novel praises natalist, pro-family values. It boasts its own resident *famille nombreuse,* Monsieur and Madame Duverger and their six children. Although poor, this family presents a brave vision of domestic bliss. Messieur Duverger works fourteen hours a day to support his children, then mends their shoes at night for "pleasure." "Yes, his life was mediocre," comments the narrator, "he had neither the prospects nor the pleasures without which so many men are miserable, and yet, when among his children, he said to himself 'this is consolation enough for not having that'."[59] Duverger's wife, a glowing model of self-sacrifice, also considers raising six children "a pleasure" and cheerfully insists: "We're all doing fine . . . and if Father was only able to rest a bit, my God, that would be perfect!" As a family, the Duvergers taste "an intimate, profound, magnificent joy: that of working for their own, assuring their existence, being providers and protectors of the nest."[60] Vautel's description of the Duvergers' "intimate, profound, magnificent joy" demonstrates his acceptance of and contribution to natalist rhetoric.[61] But it is also interesting to note that "*verge*" means "rod" or "penis" in French. This detail suggests that Monsieur Duverger plays two roles in Vautel's novel—he is a symbol of virility as well as of paternity.

Vautel presents the neo-Malthusian perspective through the figure of Parisot, the owner of a magazine *Le Bonheur*. (During the course of the novel, *Le Bonheur* is transformed from a spiritualist to a Malthusian and finally to a family journal, whereupon it is retitled *Le Vrai bonheur*.) The journal runs advertisements, now forbidden by the 1920 law, concerning women "who surreptitiously offered to give 'medical treatment.'"[62] "Malthusia," its main author, writes such articles as "Tu n'engendras point" (probably a wordplay on another currently popular natalist novel, *Tu enfanteras*), and gives a public lecture on neo-Malthusianism: "In France, everything is coming together to help us: we no longer believe in either God or the devil, we love money more and more, silk stockings agree with wool ones that we must dread the children who would prevent us from having fun."[63] When none other than Monsieur Duverger valiantly defends the joys of a large family from his place in the audience, Malthusia shoots back: "What is motherhood if not the most heavy of servitudes?" In support of Malthusia's claims, a mob of women "clap their hands enthusiastically" and physically attack the poor Duverger. The women traduce Duverger's wife as "a victim" who "betrays her sex!"[64] This assault by a vicious gang of angry women again suggests that something more than natalism is at stake in Vautel's story, particularly if Duverger acts as a symbol of virility as well as paternity.

Like natalist propagandists, Vautel uses the logic of contrast to relate his pro-family message. He contrasts the happy, poor, and youthful Duvergers with the unhappy, rich, and elderly Provendiers, who have adopted a monkey, Albert, as their only "son." When Albert becomes incurably ill, the family doctor scolds his "parents" for having wasted their lives without children. Albert dies, "in the flower of his youth, and after a long and cruel illness," according to the formal death notice sent out by the Provendiers (and amply illustrated on a full page of the novel). He receives an elaborate funeral and is laid to rest by his bereaved, desolate parents in an expensive gravesite described by the narrator as "touching and ridiculous."[65] Vautel juxtaposes the funeral scene to another in which a beaming Madame Duverger receives *la médaille de la famille nombreuse* for her six children. "Bah! We have children because it's fun!" she remarks upon receiving it.[66]

Although by 1924 the French state had demonstrated sincerity in its efforts to support the natalist movement, Vautel ridicules what he sees as the government's hypocrisy in dealing with natalist matters. He presents the presiding government official as a *célibataire* who had "accepted this mission without enthusiasm, because he had hoped to spend his afternoon with his two little friends, both music hall dancers," but who nevertheless manages an effusive speech on motherhood.[67] He begins by heartily congratulating one of the women on the stage, who is then forced to tell him she is not a mother at all. During the ceremony, a group of "sterile ladies" (bourgeois in origin) look disdainfully upon (the working-class) Madame Duverger as she receives her medal, and cluck: "One or two, maybe. But six?! That no longer happens at all in certain circles." Vautel aims his attack at what he perceives to be a sterile, hostile, and morally decadent bourgeoisie. All but one of the six women receiving medals—"six of the last French women alive who . . . persist in their efforts to transmit life"—are working class in origin.[68] While throughout the nineteenth century the bourgeois class commonly perceived the working class as a threat to the moral and social orders, here the latter acts as the moralizing force of French society. This class reversal of moral properties was common in natalist literature.

The new tendency of the working class to serve as a moralizing force also describes the plot-line of Vautel's novel. The story centers on the marriage of Paul Le Barrois, a veteran who "had suffered so much during the war," to the spoiled bourgeoise Elyane Parisot, the daughter of *Le Bonheur*'s neo-Malthusian owner.[69] None other than Paul's working-class mistress, Louise, will ultimately save the marriage and the natalist day by serving as a strong "moral" influence on Elyane. In another strange twist of signification, Louise comes to speak for traditional female domesticity, and in this capacity, mentors Elyane. Similarly, Paul's uncle and mentor Prosper Boisselot represents a kind of confident male virility that the emasculated, insecure Paul himself sorely lacks. When Paul approaches him for advice about his upcoming marriage, he admits to doubts about the coquettish Elyane, but reassures Paul that "marriage will give her what she lacks. Motherhood does wonders for this type of little woman."[70] As we shall see, the end of the novel proves Prosper right.

Because of their crystalline sexual confidence, Prosper and Louise guide their youthful counterparts—Paul and Elyane—through the thickening fog of postwar gender confusion. Vautel's vision of such confusion emerges at a "spiritualist" lecture given by Professor Luminol and sponsored by the neo-Malthusian Parisot, Elyane's father. Luminol gives this ominous vision of the future:

> We are moving toward the suppression of the sexes. . . . The human being will soon be neither man nor woman . . . he will unite the attributes of both . . . and love, ceasing to be the clash of two conflictual, even hostile instincts, will be instead the harmonious and beautiful fusion of two identical bodies exchanging pure caresses![71]

"Like snails!" objects Prosper Boisselot, who speaks from the audience. But Luminol presses on, explaining how "the new Eve is flat, . . . in her occupations, her tastes, her ambitions, as in her physical structure, she is moving sharply away from the ancient Venusian model." Likewise, in "modern man," all "evident signs of . . . virility" are disappearing, as demonstrated by the "young men with delicate features" and "feminine ways," of which there are "several specimens in our midst." At this point, no longer able to control himself, Boisselot silences Luminol by loudly blurting out: "I am in favor of a clear demarcation between the masculine and the feminine sexes. . . . I am in favor of pretty women, large beefsteaks, brave military men, and *bon vivants*. . . . That is how I stand!"[72] With these words, Prosper proves not only that his own virility is "prospering," but also that he is willing to serve as a white knight against the darkening forces of postwar gender confusion—forces that will make his nephew Paul's life miserable.

Paul's mistress, Louise, also fashions herself as an heroic defender of "a clear demarcation between the masculine and feminine sex," the absence of which is clearly cause for considerable anxiety in Vautel's novel. When Paul tells Louise of his plans to marry, she rants and raves about Elyane in this way:

> she has that figure that is à la mode: nothing in front and not much behind! . . . A weakling, a shadow of a woman, a reduced model, a travel

accessory you can fold in two to put in your suitcase! But not me! *Tiens,* look at that! I've got it and I'm proud of it. *I'm* a woman, a woman with long hair, breasts and hips, a *real* woman, who doesn't cheat or play around with her sex![73]

Vautel portrays Elyane as the polar opposite of Louise—a *femme moderne* who summarizes her own notion of womanhood with this militant manifesto: "We go out alone, we go where we want, and we won't be bothered with a bunch of idiotic principles that have never been anything but *chiqué*."[74] Her general physiognomy and her clothing are indistinguishable from those of her husband on the novel's cover (fig. 18). In a review of *Madame ne veut pas d'enfant,* Gaston Picard described Elyane as "the young woman who follows fashion in all things: no child, etc."[75] While Elyane dances *le shimmy* at her wedding reception, Madame Parisot takes Paul aside and urges him never to get her daughter pregnant: "You know as well as I do that children complicate one's life . . . particularly the woman's life. One can no longer go out. And my daughter who adores her dinners in town, the theater, dance, traveling. . . . She has the right to have fun!" When Paul feebly protests that he has "the right and even the obligation *[devoir]* to give [his] wife one, two, three, four, ten children," Madame Parisot barks "You are a savage," and threatens him with a divorce until he relents.[76] Things go from bad to worse when the newlyweds find themselves alone on their wedding night. Elyane is cold and ungiving until she finds "mysterious objects" left for them by her mother at the bottom of the bed. Paul begins to suffer from a stomachache, headache, and (it is hinted at) impotence. He survives the night by dreaming nostalgically of Louise.

Inasmuch as the egoistic Elyane is not a *"real"* woman, she unmans Paul as well: he experiences all the physical symptoms of sexual anxiety. As his desperation increases, Paul goes crawling back to Louise in order to complain about his wife:

> My wife is implacable. On our wedding day, the mayor said: "The wife must follow her husband everywhere." Ah, but it's exactly the opposite that has happened. It is me who is obliged to follow her, and I assure you, it's exhausting. . . . And there's nothing to be done, no mercy nor amnesty to hope for! Do you understand, Louisette, she *wants to go out!*[77]

What Paul grieves most is the cozy domesticity of the home:

> Le Barrois dreamed of a quiet, cozy interior in which every evening, with his feet in his slippers, he could settle into the welcoming arms of

some big, comfortable chair, and peacefully smoke his cigarette, cigar or even pipe, all the while vacantly reading some article in his *Temps* on events in Nicaragua or the fall of the Norwegian minister.[78]

"My *Temps*!," he moans to Louise. In yet another startling reversal, Paul begins to assume just such a domestic existence with Louise, frequenting her home on a regular basis not to make love, as one would expect with a mistress, but to read the paper in his slippers. What can we say about the sorry state of the bourgeois *foyer* when a man must go to his mistress in order to read his *Temps*?

Like Victor Margueritte, Vautel portrays Elyane's modern womanhood as neither happy nor fulfilling. Despite her relentless, "implacable" pursuit of pleasure, she is also miserable. She becomes pregnant (an event that brings down the dark and terrifying wrath of Madame Parisot) and then gravely ill from an (illegal) abortion. Even after her recovery, Elyane grows "more and more nervous" and "irritable" as well as increasingly bored and depressed.[79] Suspicious of Paul's intrigue with Louise (if one could call it that), she hires a detective to bring her proof, and when he does, she buys a gun to shoot Louise in revenge. When Elyane reaches Louise's house, however, she can't go through with it, and so Louise makes her tea instead, while she lectures Elyane on the importance of making good pastries and controlling men without their knowledge: "You are making him lead an impossible life. Every evening, dinners in town, dancing. . . . No respite! . . . And to think that Paul got married in order to live a tranquil existence." She urges Elyane to have a child in order to win him back: "The arms of a woman are often less strong than the arms of a child for holding onto a man."[80]

The topsy-turvy state of postwar sex and class relations are obvious here, and were not lost on Vautel's readers and critics.[81] The mistress— in her newfound role as *devotée* of domesticity—urges the bourgeois wife to redeem herself morally by having a child. Seemingly unaware of this blinding set of reversals, Elyane unhesitatingly takes Louise's advice, reconciles herself with Paul, promptly gets pregnant, and bears a son coyly named *Désiré*. The baby becomes a miracle worker, curing Elyane of her vanities, reuniting Paul and Elyane in domestic bliss, and even softening up Elyane's mother, who is "initiated suddenly into the art of being a grandmother, conquered without a struggle by this little child."[82] At the baptism, one Dr. Sauvegrain issues a stern sermon on the demographic importance of babies to France, again driving home the explicit natalist message.

However, in Vautel's novel, motherhood delivers much more than Dr. Sauvegrain and other natalist propagandists promise. The night after the child's baptism, Paul receives his slippers in the mail from Louise. Domesticity has happily reinstalled itself in the bourgeois parlor where it belongs. Besides adding to France's demographic strength, the child manages to bring back into alignment more traditional gender and class relations: he cures Paul's sexual anxiety and restores the all-important bourgeois *foyer.* Boisselet, then, is right: "motherhood does wonders for this type of little woman." A war-weary veteran hungry for domestic tranquility gets a homecoming at last. Only the child can make the world safe again for pretty women, large beefsteaks, and brave military men.

Vautel's natalist message slips back and forth between two levels in his novel, revealing yet another set of meanings attached to the concept of motherhood in the postwar debate on women. On a more explicit level, Vautel reproduces the natalist bipolar moral world. He equates large families with humble self-sacrifice, and neo-Malthusianism with selfish egoism, particularly on the part of women. But on a more subtle, implicit level, Vautel identifies the "Madame who doesn't want a child" with a blurring of sexual difference—Luminol's ominous "suppression of the sexes." Contrary to Professor Luminol's predictions, however, such a suppression leads in the novel to neither androgyny nor harmony between the sexes, but rather, male sexual anxiety. Furthermore, Vautel interprets Elyane's suppression of her sex in moral as well as gendered terms: as an egoistic pursuit of pleasure. Vautel conflates gender and moral issues in such a way that Elyane as *femme moderne* commits a moral as well as a gender transgression when she refuses to be a *real* woman. Conversely, he presents motherhood as restoring traditional bourgeois moral ideals—domesticity, self-sacrifice—as well as traditional gender relations.

Proud of How We Had Proven Ourselves to Be Men

In Vautel's *Madame ne veut pas d'enfant,* natalism is linked to more general anxiety about postwar gender confusion. Fears about the moral crisis concerning maternal duty are confused with those concerning women who "cheat or play around with [their] sex." Vautel's condemnation of Elyane as 'egotistical' in her liberation echoes the moral problem of depopulation. Hence Vautel's novel raises two important questions about natalist discourse: first, why was gender confusion interpreted as a moral issue? Second, to what extent were gender anxiety and moral crisis confounded in postwar natalism generally?

The conflation of gender and moral issues in postwar natalism can only be understood by exploring notions of male identity in this period. As Robert Nye has shown, wartime medical literature connected the male capacity for physical courage with sexual virility. In a 1917 book on courage, the physicians Louis Huot and Paul Voivenel argued that the *poilu* had a "vividly imaginative phrase for anatomically expressing the chief quality of a warrior." According to these doctors, such a phrase evidenced a strong connection in the *poilu's* mind between honor, courage on the battlefield, and sexual potency.[83] Because of these links, the veteran's wartime sacrifice—his moral and physical courage on the battlefield—became joined in his mind with his ability to display sexual prowess. The war's moral worth and his own masculine worth became tests of each other. And to prove his manliness, the soldier/veteran could do no better than to sire a child.

To understand how the links between masculinity, sexual potency, and honor operated in postwar natalism, we must examine the so-called *crise du mariage* that arose during the war years. In December 1916, the combatant Jean Norton Cru (later a prominent literary critic) wrote in a letter to his sisters and mother: "Have you thought about crises resulting from the war? Here's one: *la crise du mariage*. Never since marriage became an institution among men has it undergone such a crisis."[84] As we have seen, combatants expressed these kind of fears concerning marriage and gender relations throughout the war. Sexual infidelity and marital disruption formed major themes of such well-known war and postwar novels as Henri Barbusse's *Le Feu* (1916) and Raymond Radiguet's *Le Diable au corps* (1923). Fears concerning a *crise du mariage* did not dissolve at war's end and, if anything, became more widespread. "It is becoming more and more banal to take note of the disastrous effect of the war on conjugal relations," argued Louis Huot in 1918.[85] A major "enquête sur la crise du mariage" appeared in the pages of *La Renaissance politique* throughout the spring of 1924, almost six years after the armistice. "The terrible years that we have survived," began the survey's editor, Maurice Duval, "have ruined homes [and] broken up households."[86]

How did French men and women define this so-called *crise du mariage*? An extraordinary source for answering this question is Henry Bordeaux's *Le Mariage, hier et aujourd'hui* (1921), a compilation of letters that the author received in response to an earlier article on the subject of the *crise du mariage*. Bordeaux was a prolific and influential popular novelist, a member of the Académie française, and himself a veteran of the war.[87] According to Bordeaux, the enormous amount of mail that his article prompted was evidence "of a widespread uneasiness" concerning gender relations in postwar society.[88] The *crise du mariage* arose during the war when women, having to manage for their husbands, "took on the independent ways of men." In the process, "many of them, little by little, began to disassociate themselves from their dead *foyer.* They came home as little as possible."[89] At the end of the war, they refused to give up their lives of independence and become simple housewives once again. According to one correspondent whom Bordeaux quotes: "The man demanded his old position, but the woman refused to bow her head any longer, and instead played the part of rival."[90]

Bordeaux's analysis of the *crise du mariage* echoes both the natalist analysis of the moral problem of depopulation and Vautel's characterization of Elyane Parisot. He quotes a letter from a French woman:

> Five years of war taught women that they could live without the support of the men who made them into eternal slaves. And our desire to create a home and children for our future happiness is no longer enough to make us lose our fear of male egoism, which has been all-too-well proven. Until now we have been merely passive victims, but there is an end to everything. Now we just want to live our own lives [*vivre notre vie*] without worrying about the fate of future generations.[91]

In her indictment of motherhood as inimical to women's freedom, this woman sounds like a radical (and marginal) feminist such as Nelly Roussel. But Bordeaux does not hesitate to generalize that the letter "very clearly indicates the new character of woman" in the postwar period: "She no longer possesses any spirit of sacrifice. . . . 'To live one's own life!' You cannot imagine how much damage has been caused by this short formula . . . as if the life of a woman who makes the *foyer* both shine brightly and endure is not a life worthy of being lived."[92] He defines this woman's rejection of the traditional female role in terms of her egotistical desire to live her own life. In fact, however, for the female correspondent above, the phrase "to live one's own life" meant something quite different. She confesses to a "desire to create a home and children for [her] future happiness," but also argues that even this is "no longer enough" to make "male egoism" endurable. For her, "to live one's own life" meant rejecting the "eternal slavery" that financial support from men required. She feared that such a rejection might

necessitate her foregoing the maternal role as well, but the happiness
that motherhood represented no longer compensated for the gender
oppression it seemed to entail.

What this woman relates as a changing attitude toward gender relations Bordeaux morally condemns as evidence of her "egotism" and
lack of "any spirit of sacrifice." We have caught him in the act, so to
speak, of interpreting changing gender relations in moral terms very
similar to those used by natalists and Clément Vautel. No doubt Bordeaux, who openly defended the cause of *la famille nombreuse,* was
familiar with natalist propaganda and used its rhetoric in his own analysis of postwar gender relations.[93] In addition, Bordeaux's use of the
notion of "sacrifice" here betrays another set of discursive origins—
the personal and fictional literature of the war. In other letters that
Bordeaux interprets, the dual image of woman prevalent in war literature—as courageous wife or pleasure-loving infidel—reappears. Bordeaux quotes one letter from an infantry soldier (which, he claims, resembles scores of others), who had "suffered tortures the exact nature
of which no pen could describe precisely." Riddled by moral doubts
concerning the war's purpose, he was able to sustain himself only by
evoking the vision of his devoted wife:

> We committed a stupid error. During the war, no doubt out of human
> frailty, we tried to re-establish our shattered moral and physical equilib-
> rium by mentally evoking a mirage. Oh! this blessed home where we
> would once again find our loving wives, compassionate concerning the
> way we had suffered, and proud of how we had proved ourselves to be
> men! . . . This was the voyage: you know the port. This was the dream:
> you know the awakening. How could anyone therefore be surprised if
> we felt disappointed and ridiculed![94]

According to this veteran, a vision of domestic female love served to
re-establish the soldiers' "shattered" moral equilibrium. As compas-
sionate, loyal wives, women became the measure of both the soldiers'
ability to prove themselves "as men" and the war's moral worth. Virility
and moral courage were tests of each other. By the same logic, then, a
woman's rejection of traditional domesticity "ridiculed" both her husband's virility and the meaning of his war sacrifices. According to Bordeaux, the soldiers "are dumbfounded by forgetfulness of services rendered and suffering endured." He referred to "the hideous injustice
on the part of these women and young girls, who after so little time
are already daring to negate the pain and anguish of this four-and-a-

half-year nightmare."[95] Once again, as in natalist propaganda, France had been saved only to be thrown away.

Bordeaux's veterans demonstrate once again the way in which the *poilu* interpreted women's loyalty or rebellion as a moral response to the war. The great unspoken question hovering over the letters of these veterans, like that of natalist discourse, was: "for what purpose, then, was the war fought?" A woman's rejection of domesticity ridiculed both the veteran's manhood and his sacrifice in the war. For this reason, such a rejection evoked a torrent of moral judgments that were unrelated (at least in a strictly logical sense) to her quest for independence. In reacting to the veterans' "tone of indignation" concerning "feminine ingratitude" for the war, Bordeaux asked: "As a woman represents tenderness and pity above all else, how can she remain so callous?"[96] The soldier/veteran's conflation of traditional gender ideals with the moral worth of the war raised the symbolic stakes in women's so-called rejection of domesticity. Like Senator Emile Jénouvrier, Bordeaux linked the soldier who had given his life with the woman who wanted to "live her life."

Bordeaux, like the novelist Clément Vautel, believed that only the woman who gave new life could save France from chronic gender/moral confusion. In a collection of stories entitled *Ménages d'après guerre,* published in 1921 (the same year as *Le Mariage, hier et aujourd'hui*), Bordeaux once again presents the child as a kind of gender/moral miracle worker. One long story in the collection concerns a deteriorating relationship between a war nurse, Madame Lhuys, and her veteran husband. "When I came back from the war," confesses Monsieur Lhuys, "my only thought was to rediscover my home and my work, well, that was my dream!" However, he complains, "she had her own life, her own work, her own obligations, habits, relationships . . . she was no longer willing to yield to my life and to me, as is natural." "No longer interested . . . in her home," Madame Lhuys, for her part, decides to leave her husband even though she is pregnant; she is deathly afraid that the baby will make her give up her work and force her to become more domestic. "A child no longer counts for much," laments the piteous and angry Monsieur Lhuys, "why should it count for more than the husband?"[97] All is saved at the end of the story, however, when Madame Lhuys has an intense flashback of her nursing experience at the front, during which she hears the wounded calling out in anguish against death. Overwhelmed by their suffering, she realizes suddenly that her pregnancy symbolizes "the communication of a life to come" and that she, no less than a soldier, is "mobilized" to deliver it.[98] Although still in the womb, Madame Lhuy's child plays the novel's most powerful role, forcing the errant mother to confront the war's sacrifice and reunite with her veteran husband. By providing a marker of male virility, the child redeems domestic harmony, male honor, and the war's sacrifice all in one powerful stroke.

The important links that Bordeaux establishes between moral and gender despair, the veteran's alienation and the *crise du mariage* also pervaded postwar natalist discourse. For example, these themes surface frequently in surveys, cartoons, and fiction published in the prominent natalist journal *La Femme et l'enfant* during the years 1918 to 1920. In 1920, *La Femme et l'enfant* conducted a survey on "The Home of Tomorrow" in response to concern about the "disorganized" state of the French family. "Returning home after five years of suffering, the *poilu* reckoned that he had earned the right to more tenderness than in the past, to more authority and perhaps also to more respect," argued one respondant, the dramatist Francis de Croisset, himself a veteran. But "the woman that the *poilus* rediscovered was not the same as the one they had left behind." No longer self-effacing or submissive, "the '*servante au grand coeur*' had become an associate" so that the reunited couple, "clashed, rebelled and separated from each other. This is the drama of innumerable homes."[99] Again, the solution was to bear children. Croisset concluded that "there is only one remedy, one resort: children."[100]

The editors of *La Femme et l'enfant* drove the same point home through two cartoons, "The Connecting Link" and "Without Children, No Domestic Harmony" (figs. 19 and 20). In these cartoons, the child is presented as the "connecting link" or guarantor of domestic harmony for otherwise troubled sexual relationships. The physiognomy of the woman pictured in "Without Children" undergoes a profound transformation when she becomes a mother—from cantankerous and disagreeable to angelic and harmonious. Her husband's gestures and expression relate a moral condemnation of her childless state. The well-known popular novelist Colette Yver offered the same message about the redemptive quality of motherhood in "Ménage d'Odette," a serial story that appeared in *La Femme et l'enfant* during 1918. Refusing "to be emprisoned by the four walls of an apartment," Yver's heroine insists on working even after her marriage to a young veteran.[101] When she becomes pregnant, she is horrified and he is ecstatic; she worries about their being able to live a life of comfort, and he thinks only of the child to be born. Their marriage begins to disintegrate. But after the child arrives and becomes gravely ill in the hands of a wet-nurse,

Odette gives up everything to become a full-time housewife and mother, and domestic bliss ensues.[102]

These natalist fictions inscribed a crisis in gender relations that linked soldiery, paternity, and virility. The veteran returns home expecting more respect and tenderness than the rebellious modern woman is willing to give him. So defeated in "proving himself a man," the veteran longs for a child, who represents the external mark of his manhood. As the child transforms an unruly wife into a loving mother, it helps to re-establish a blessed home, more traditional gender relations, and hence the veteran's shattered moral equilibrium. The *madame* who did not want a child frustrated not only natalists, then, but also veterans needing to prove their honor and virility. This gendered link between soldiery and paternity lies at the heart of the postwar natalist impulse. Although natalists gave obsessive attention to the importance of motherhood, the need *to father* clearly inspired their efforts.

She Wanted Her Vampire's Meal

I began the analysis of this second aspect of the postwar debate on women by noting the intimate relationship between differently gendered versions of the same *impôt de sang*—soldiery and motherhood. "To give one's life" and "to give life" constituted two themes in the postwar debate that were not only profoundly connected, but also freighted with such intense emotions as anger and anxiety. To both summarize these themes and show their power to evoke strong emotions in the postwar debate on women, I will conclude by analyzing one more novel published in the mid-twenties: Henry Fèvre's *L'Intellectuelle mariée* (1925).[103] Fèvre's novel typifies a genre of story that appeared in the years 1923–25 in the wake of Victor Margueritte's *La Garçonne*. Popular writers such as Fèvre hoped to exploit the phenomenal success of this novel by writing stories about young rebellious *garçonnes*.[104] Although less explicitly connected to the themes of war and natalism than the other fictions we have been studying, *L'Intellectuelle mariée* can be interpreted as an allegory of the war and the postwar moral problem of depopulation. Therefore, it provides a precise summary and conclusion to this second set of ideas concerning the mother and the soldier in the postwar debate on women.

On one level, *L'Intellectuelle mariée* contains the stock modern woman character of the twenties, an impetuous heroine who scorns

motherhood for a life of freedom. A young, headstrong philosopher
named Andrée arrives in Paris to give a lecture and becomes involved
with an older veteran of the war, Ricoeur. When he proposes, she
agrees reluctantly, afraid of losing her independence. Ironically, her
views as a philosopher concern the moral perfectibility of man through
purification of the soul. By contrast, Ricoeur (the veteran) is more cynical. When he refuses to be converted to her idealism, Andrée laments:
"No more ideals, voracious appetites, and vanities. Devotion, sacrifice?
Out of fashion." [105] Although Andrée initially appears to be just another
femme moderne, in fact she blurs the dual image of female identity
found in postwar natalist discourse. She guards her independence fe-
rociously, but defends progress, devotion, and sacrifice—natalist ideals
normally associated with *la mère de famille nombreuse*. In the same
way, she "selfishly" pursues her own philosophical work, defying all
Ricoeur's efforts to make her settle down, but she also condemns postwar egoism. *L'Intellectuelle mariée* also contains familiar elements of
postwar natalist discourse. Her husband launches a vicious and pathetic program to distract her from her philosophy, including attempts
to make her pregnant or enervate her with voluptuous nights of passion. ("Ouf," he congratulates himself one morning after, "if Andrée
can get going today I'd be surprised, after a night like that.")[106] When
Andrée greets his entreaties concerning a child with the confession
that "Perhaps I have other obligations, and children could distract me,"
Ricoeur responds: "From your mission? . . . What could be more important than populating France, which is in such desperate need?"[107]
He takes Andrée to the house of his friend, Madame Brunold, described as "a model mother" of five children and "*un chef d'oeuvre*
of maternity." Of all Ricoeur's friends, Andrée decides, only Madame
Brunold has been spared "a more or less empty existance." [108] Once
again Andrée's position is ambiguous; she hesitates to make a personal
commitment but embraces the moral importance of motherhood as an
escape from a meaningless, egoistic life.

Andrée's inability to decide between the roles of modern woman
and natalist mother provokes a familiar sexual anxiety in her husband
and leads to disaster in the novel. In a decisive moment, Andrée is
forced to defend her philosophical views concerning moral perfectibility against the redoubtable Sabine, a leader of the virulently feminist,
man-hating "Club des Amazones." The issue of motherhood is central
to the debate, although (significantly) its connection to Andrée's larger
philosophical views is attenuated at best. The Amazones obstinately

condemn maternity, and Andrée lectures in its defense, despite her own personal reservations. However, although Andrée steps forward to defend motherhood against the feminists, her impetuous need to pursue her selfish intellectual interests—the *femme moderne* in her— endangers her husband's life. Tension builds in the lecture hall, and Ricoeur, who is present, ultimately must defend Andrée's honor in a duel with a man who is rumored to have been her lover. After Ricoeur is gravely wounded, Andrée is convulsed by guilt and begins to regret her own idealism. Her ideas, she realizes, are nothing more than a "chimera," among many others—"chimera of glory, chimera of conquest . . . rash fool of war; social and political chimeras that create barricades. . . . And whole peoples are massacred."[109]

The reference to the "rash fool of war" here opens up another level on which to understand Fèvre's story—as an allegory of the war experience and its relationship to postwar gender anxiety. As he did in the war, Ricoeur fights in the duel for a set of traditional moral ideals— progress, spiritual perfectability—in which he himself has lost faith. To him, they have become senseless illusions by which "whole peoples are massacred." His profound doubt about these ideals is inseparable from his bitterness concerning the woman (Andrée) who represents them. When the duel leaves Ricoeur critically wounded, he finds himself thinking: "Yes, this was her fault, for her, because of her and her confounded ideas, that he was going to die a farcical martyr, a ridiculous victim."[110] Ricoeur duels for both a moral illusion and Andrée's reputation—once again, confusing moral and sexual honor. The ritual re-enactment of the war and the wound that results redeems both Ricoeur's manhood and Andrée's womanhood (much as the veteran Blanchet's wound does in Victor Margueritte's *La Garçonne*). Andrée "became the good little woman that she wanted to remain from that point on. She no longer had either ambition or vanity. She had dismissed her chimera." When Ricoeur finally awakens from a coma, he revealingly tells Andrée: "you have cared for me as you would your own child."[111]

Once again, however, Andrée wavers on the path to true womanhood, and Ricoeur pays the price. Although Andrée nurses her husband back to health like a good mother, the role is only temporary. She receives an offer to publish and decides to do so, demanding Ricoeur's support. At the same time, she becomes pregnant, and again expresses profound ambivalence about having a child. For this "relapse" into modern womanhood, Ricoeur is made to suffer enormously. In the surreal, highly symbolic last scene of the novel, Ricoeur's wound reopens while he and Andrée are making love. When she turns on the light, she witnesses this horrifying sight:

> Now Ricoeur, frothing and hiccoughing, was vomiting on the pillow, on the sheets, on the blankets, waves and waves of blood that refused to run dry, that were overflowing, soaking, drenching, inundating everything, engulfing the sheets and dripping onto the carpet. The bed became completely red; it looked like the scene of a massacre. And Ricoeur, drained of blood, arms thrown up, lay in this red pool, his face itself spattered in red, as if drowned in the blood that he still vomited, all his body's blood, gushing out as if from a bottle.[112]

In this scene, Ricoeur and Andrée's bed—a metonym of French gender relations—is transformed from a theater of passion to "the scene of a massacre," in which Ricoeur becomes the hapless victim, dead without a single drop of blood left in his veins.

Fèvre's macabre description again evokes another massacre—the war's great stream of blood and death. The "chimera" of idealism—and the woman who represents it—once again comprises both motive and blame for the massacre. According to the narrator,"[t]he first outpouring [of blood] was not sufficient, it had not satisfied or quenched the thirst of the chimera. She wanted her vampire's meal. She had it—copious, crimson, frothing, imperial."[113] As an idealist, a philosopher of chimeras, Andrée caused her husband's original wound. So had many soldiers, spurred on by the ideal of France and love of a woman, paid the voracious *impôt de sang*. But Andrée's guilt extends beyond this: her persistent desire to choose independence over her husband's desire for domesticity frustrates his recovery or homecoming. Despite Ricoeur's attempt to "prove himself a man" (by making love to Andrée), the modern woman reopens rather than heals the old wound; like a vampire she devours his strength a second time. As she watches her husband die, Andrée catches a glimpse of her own reflection in the mirror: "The blood had sullied her cheeks, her shoulders, her breast was red; her nightgown was stained; she had blood up to the hem, on her feet that had crossed the pool, on her hands that had leaned on the drenched linen, on her arms . . . as if she also had been bled white."[114] In this description, Fèvre implicates Andrée in her husband's bloody death and also names her penance—to be "bled white" herself, to pay her own *impôt de sang*.

Andrée pays such a reparation at novel's end when she decides to give up her work and freedom in order to bear Ricoeur's child. Grief-stricken and ravaged by guilt, she becomes a modern-day Lady Macbeth, haunted by the bloody image of herself: "She saw herself red, saturated with all this criminal blood: like the poet's blood, she could never wash it away." Momentarily, she considers returning to her work, but then remembers that she is pregnant: "she did not have the right, she was no longer free, Ricoeur rested there, in her child." [115] An identical logic, as we have seen, operated in the postwar natalist campaign against depopulation. Andrée's words here echo those of natalist George Blet in his 1921 pamphlet *L'Avortement: Est-ce un crime?* Here Blet argues that no Frenchman had "had the right to demand his own liberty" during the war, "even at the price of his own life." In the same way, then, "the mother cannot exempt herself from this kind of military obligation, that consists, for her, of bringing her pregnancy to term." [116] In deciding to leave behind her fateful modern woman ways and pay her own *impôt de sang* through motherhood, Andrée redeems her womanhood. More important, she redeems the manhood of Ricoeur, whose child gives proof at last of his own virility.

The themes that Fèvre explores in *L'Intellectuelle mariée*—the bloody and unrequited specter of the war's sacrifice, the anxious struggle to reassert virility in a rapidly changing postwar world, the redemptive promise of motherhood—lay at the very heart of how French natalists and writers understood the relationship between the war and postwar experiences. The *madame* who did not want a child, the modern woman who wanted to play with her sex, and the frustrated soldier who wanted to come home—these three images were linked again and again in postwar literature. The moral problem of depopulation was embedded in fears concerning the war's upheaval of traditional gender roles. Motherhood enjoyed miraculous restorative powers, capable of turning *femme modernes* back into *vraies femmes* once again. In postwar literature, maternity alone had the power to knit up the raveled sleeve of sexual difference.

PART THREE
LA FEMME SEULE

IN THE WAKE OF A DEVASTATING WAR, a strong natalist sentiment
pervaded France. Natalism expressed a need "to return to normalcy" and heal the wounds of war. In the postwar context, the
image of the mother served as a cultural representation of this longing
to heal and to forget. She symbolized a prewar era of relative security
and stability. At the same time, she seemed to extend these virtues into
the present, thus concealing changes brought about by the war. Like
postwar hedonism, the cultural image of female domesticity allowed
French men and women to elude some of the most agonizing questions raised by the war. Even as natalists presented domestic values as
endangered, they reaffirmed them as central to the moral, social, and
economic well-being of contemporary France. To proclaim paradise
lost was in fact a strategy to regain it. But could paradise be regained?
Could established bourgeois notions of female identity simply be reasserted?

While domestic values were too profoundly rooted in French culture to lose meaning as a configuration of identity, by 1917 many
French men and women believed that women's roles had irrevocably
changed and that their prewar identities could not simply be restored.
"One thing is sure," argued the lawyer and president of the Bar Henri
Robert in a 1917 lecture to the Ligue de l'enseignement, "for women,
the situation can never be tomorrow what it was yesterday. . . . The
reign of the woman-doll, ignorant of life and difficulties, happy to let
live and be pampered, is over."[1] In writing about the French woman

149

of tomorrow, both he and the novelist Louis Narquet used the French word "*fatale*," meaning "inexorable" or "fated," to refer to the evolution that women had undergone since the beginning of the war. Both seemed to ask their readers to face a reality that, if perhaps unpleasant, was nevertheless unavoidable.[2] The same year, the prominent writer Henri Spont noted women's "rapid, easy adaptation" to male professions and offered this final comment: "the social order is in such a profound state of upheaval that when one considers the future, a comprehensive revision seems imperative. . . . At present, everything has been called again into question."[3] Men and women of all political persuasions repeated these views in the postwar debate on women.[4] For the prominent Radical politician Edouard Herriot, for example, the war had made a greater impact on women's lives than half a century of feminist propaganda.[5]

If, as it seemed to many by 1917, conventional feminine ideals could not simply be reasserted, then they had to be reconstructed, recast, or remade. How was this to be done? We have seen how in postwar discourse, perceived changes in gender identity—Drieu la Rochelle's civilization without sexes—served as symbols of the war's impact on French bourgeois culture. But the debate on female identity must be analyzed in a literal as well as a symbolic sense. In other words, it must also be seen as a series of attempts to come to terms with what appeared to be a dramatically changing social organization of gender. While French men and women used the postwar debate to explore the war's general impact, they also focused more squarely on the changing role of women. The social transformation brought about by the war threw into relief the fragilities and contradictions of prewar female domesticity. Would the modern woman abandon motherhood altogether, as the natalists believed? Or would she define a new relationship between wage labor and domesticity, until now considered mutually exclusive fields of female activity? How were the contradictory images of *la femme moderne* and *la mère* to be negotiated?

Debating the fate of *la femme seule,* or "the single woman," a complex, ambiguous image of female identity, helped French men and women to answer these questions. The presence of a surplus single female population was by no means a new "problem." But French men and women perceived it as especially acute in postwar France, because of the lopsided sex ratio resulting from the war's holocaust. The "plight" of the single woman, discussed in postwar periodical, medical, fictional, and legal discourse, became much more than a demographic problem. Debate about *la femme seule,* who was seen as a direct product of the war, also represented a complex effort to reconstruct female identity in an era of "inexorable" change. A single woman unable by definition to fulfill the promise of traditional womanhood, *la femme seule* created a golden opportunity to debate female identity apart from a reproductive, domestic role. If *la femme seule* could not get married and bear children, what could she possibly do? How could she be a woman? In this sense, *la femme seule* represented the war's impact on conventional notions of female identity. Yet, as we shall see, the image of *la femme seule* was also used to reinforce a traditional domestic ideal.

In 1919, the well-known psychologist Dr. Edouard Toulouse voiced a common view when he glimpsed a "new world" taking shape on the ruins of the old. "A new world is born from the war," he declared. "Its advent will open for modern society an era as markedly different as the Christian era was from the ancient world."[6] On the emerging map of this new world, *la femme seule* moved back and forth unsteadily between two opposing poles of female identity—between *la femme moderne* and *la mère,* between independent wage worker and domestic mother. In sources as diverse as parliamentary records, novels and plays, career manuals, and educational treatises, debates about young single women constituted a series of attempts to reconcile changing socioeconomic circumstances with more traditional notions of female social roles. As we shall see, French men and women resolved the ideological conflict between independence and domesticity in a conservative way, by giving precedence to woman's maternal role over all other notions of female identity. Yet the very foregrounding of other more novel gender roles—the presence of the "new world" itself—had its own disruptive effect. The willingness to entertain, or simply the need to condemn, nontraditional gender roles created an indecisiveness concerning female identity that itself subverted the most conservative intentions. In the end, the antinomy between the old and new worlds itself undermined conservative efforts and assured that, in Henri Robert's words, "for women, the situation can never be tomorrow what it was yesterday."

6

"THERE IS SOMETHING ELSE IN LIFE BESIDES LOVE"

IN 1921, THE FEMINIST JOURNALIST Suzanne de Callias reported to her readers in *La Française* that a movement was afoot to import American husbands from California. Aware of the surplus of young, single women and "anxious to be of help to France," some wily Californians had come up with the idea of sending boys over to marry French girls. The California state government had done its part by offering to recruit men who could speak a little French, pass a medical exam, and furnish personal references. The state even promised to pay for the nuptial voyage. But their offer, alas, was greeted by the French Ministry of Foreign Affairs with a courteous, but firm "no, thank you."[1] Callias mused that this response was based on the ministry's ability to see "the vaudeville aspect of the affair," that is, "the landing of these contingents of fiancés, fanfares, banners: 'Nous voilà, Lafayette!' etc."[2]

While the importation of husbands may sound like a lunatic scheme, Callias urged her readers to consider it seriously.[3] Other well-known Frenchmen, such as the physician and professor Dr. Paul Carnot, did the same. In a 1920 article published in the bourgeois daily *Le Matin,* Carnot came out in support of the importation of husbands in order, as he put it, "to bring the sexes into equilibrium among peoples of the white race."[4] But Carnot favored the importation of husbands from Canada, not California, because Canadians already had French roots and spoke the language.[5] Nor was the California offer the only or most amusing plan to deal with postwar female celibacy. In 1924, a reader of the bourgeois daily *L'Oeuvre* wrote to the journal to propose that single women be sent to "little agricultural colonies" where they would live together and raise chickens.[6]

These schemes and proposals comprise only part of an enormous debate on the single woman, or *"femme seule,"* during the decade after the war. In the contemporary literature, numerical estimations of *la femme seule* varied widely, from 1.5 to 3.5 million women.[7] The demographer Michel Huber estimated that in 1921, marriageable women up to thirty years of age outnumbered their male counterparts by a ratio of six to four.[8] Whatever their number, single women in postwar French society became the object of endless commentary, which began in 1918 and persisted until 1926 or 1927, changing negligibly in content over these years. Novelists created scores of female characters who, unable to marry, led celibate, independent lives. Prominent bourgeois journals conducted surveys on the emotional and economic effects of female celibacy. Doctors worried about the health of the single women who would never become mothers—what were the medical consequences of celibacy? The debate focused on women from both bourgeois and popular backgrounds; it did not contain a distinct class element. Nor is any simple historical analysis by gender possible. The plight of the single woman drew a variety of opinions from both men and women. In short, *la femme seule* became the object of widespread and highly charged attention. The question to be answered, then, is Why? Why did female celibacy become the object of so much concern? Although the war certainly exacerbated the nation's uneven sex ratio, women had outnumbered men consistently in modern France. In addition, according to demographers, the numerical increase of single women after the war was not as great as expected because of a higher remarriage rate among male widowers and divorcés, and because many single women attached themselves to younger men and foreigners.[9] Why, then, the widespread concern?

Prince Charming Has Lost His Prestige

La femme seule drew unprecedented interest in the postwar period for several reasons, among them, natalist and feminist concerns. Most important, however, the single woman became a focus of debate because she symbolized shifts in the social organization of gender. French legislators, journalists, and feminists used the image of *la femme seule* to lament, affirm, or resist such perceived changes.

Postwar natalists, particularly in the medical community, focused on *la femme seule* as a possible solution to the flagging birthrate. In a 1920 inquiry on natality conducted by the professional journal *Paris médicale,* the medical community gave serious consideration to polygamy.[10] If French men were able to marry a number of women, reasoned Dr. Paul Carnot, the author of the inquiry, *la femme seule* could bear children and boost French natality. According to Carnot, "every French woman should bear children if she is able: this is her civic duty, just as the duty of men was to fight."[11] In this way, the medical community strove to reconcile the surplus of women with the state's supposed need for babies.

Polygamy also formed the subject of George Anquetil's 1923 treatise, *La Maîtresse légitime,* which that year went through two editions—the second with a preface by Victor Margueritte—and which continued to be reissued as late as 1951. Here Anquetil set out to abolish Article 340 of the code outlawing polygamy. He believed that the unmarried state of 3 million French women would have "disastrous consequences" for both the health of individuals and for more general questions "of natality and the race."[12] The idea of polygamy, Anquetil argued, was "in the air" and lay firmly within the boundaries of French tradition, given that Napoléon, Montesquieu, Voltaire, and Pope Gregory II were all enthusiastic adherents.[13] In fact, of course, polygamy lay completely outside French Catholic and cultural traditions. Support for polygamy to solve "the problem" of *la femme seule* demonstrates both the high degree of discomfort with female celibacy and the strength of natalist sentiment after the war. Despite the glaring weaknesses of Anquetil's argument, Jehan d'Ivray, the literary critic for *La Revue mondiale,* described polygamy as "a question that we must discuss and not simply smile about."[14]

La femme seule also commanded attention among feminists, who viewed her as a measure of women's new independence. In a 1919 editorial for *L'Oeuvre,* the feminist Jane Misme dismissed the innumerable "lamentations" she had heard concerning female celibacy since the end of the war. In fact, she remarked, French men were not automatically finding wives: "Ah! The time is past when you married the first well-groomed dog that came along just to be called Madame, wear diamonds, go out alone, and in particular, to guarantee your daily bread." Misme felt that a transformation in the image of *la femme seule* had been under way for a while, but that the war—"multiplying by the thousands the prospects of single life"—had dramatically accelerated it.[15] A few years later, in 1922, "M., *Dame célibataire,*" wrote in the feminist *La Française:*

But it needs to be said that the old maids of today do not at all resemble those of the past: the old type, created during the era when to work was to lower oneself, and when as a result, a woman had no other options than to marry and bring children into the world . . . this type is now disappearing.[16]

For feminists, *la femme seule* was the symbol of the notion, affirmed by the war, "that a woman ought to know and be able to behave, support, protect and entertain herself all like a man."[17] Much later in the decade in *Le Célibat, état supérieur* (1926), the well-known feminist Madeleine Pelletier announced that "Prince Charming has lost his prestige." While in the past, Pelletier argued, "the old maid remained so only by force of unhappy circumstance," today, "at the dawn of female emancipation, a number of young girls, understanding what the realities of marriage are for a woman, refuse to marry."[18] While Pelletier had a reputation in the prewar years as a maverick of extremely radical feminist views, in the postwar context she sounds unexceptional, not unlike Misme or "M., *Dame célibataire.*"

To generalize about changing mentalities in the postwar period is to assume greater homogeneity and consensus than was ever the case. Given the extent to which French men and women had defined female identity in terms of marriage and motherhood throughout the nineteenth century, they predictably viewed an exceptional number of single women as a "problem" to be solved. Portraits of pitiful, dazed *femme seules* persisted in postwar discourse and reinforced a conservative notion of female happiness as equated with male love and support. A poem about *la femme seule* written in 1918 contains stanzas that end: "we are the rose-tree imprisoned in the tower," "we will be the dry tree that is thrown into the fire," and "we will be the treasure that is thrown into the sea."[19] "What is going to become of these millions of women whom, whatever they do, life will pass by?" asked the novelist Clément Vautel.[20] According to Dr. Paul Carnot in 1920, they were "doomed to a sacrificed and sterile life."[21] Manuals published later in the decade, such as M. E. Fenouillet's *L'Art de trouver un mari* (1925), instructed women in the fine art of finding a husband so as to avoid what they called "la plus grande difficulté sentimentale d'après-guerre"[22] (see cover, fig. 21).

Despite such images, however, feminists and antifeminists alike perceived that a transformation in attitudes toward *la femme seule* was occurring.[23] To a 1920 *Eve* survey asking the question "Can a woman live without the support of a man?" the novelist Colette responded, "Women have abundantly, sufficiently proven that they can do without a man in constructing their lives and destinies."[24] When Jane Misme posed the question "Should French women marry foreigners?" to her *La Française* readers in 1921, their response, as she summarized it, was that it was far better not to marry at all than to marry simply to marry.[25] As one reader wrote: "most girls today no longer envisage marriage in that way. What pushes them toward marriage? Certainly not the need to assure their livelihood; they know how to earn a living, and they have learned to taste the pride of being independent."[26] Consequently, as another reader put it, they "do not look upon celibacy with horror; they do not consider it either a source of shame or a failure for the race."[27] A few years later, in 1923–24, the readers of *Eve* were no less optimistic in their letters to the bourgeois women's weekly.[28] One woman challenged her fellow readers to "take a good look around" so as to see "a large number of women living freely and independently," including many businesswomen and female professors from lycées: "Tell me honestly if you think they are ridiculous." Like Misme, this reader argued that women seldom "offer themselves to the first comer" and refuse to marry unless they find a man "worthy of them." Another writer to *Eve* distinguished herself from an "old maid" in this manner: "don't we, as *jeunes filles modernes*, enjoy numerous privileges, and wouldn't we require solemn promises of happiness in order to bind ourselves for life?"[29]

The new popularity of such terms as *célibataire* and *femme seule* also suggests that the war had accelerated a change in the image of the unmarried woman under way since the turn of the century. In his 1909 critique of the image of the "old maid" or *"vieille fille,"* the Abbé Louis Muzat claimed that there was no alternative to this term, despite his own distaste for it.[30] In 1922, "M" of *La Française* named herself *dame célibataire*, a term she claimed the novelist Marcelle Tinayre had recently coined and that she preferred because it "implies no value judgment; it simply defines the civil status of men and women: that is enough."[31] An *Eve* reader also referred to herself as a *célibataire*, explaining: "Women worthy of this name believe that there is something else in life besides love."[32] The term *"la femme seule"* was also fairly recent, most probably coined by the dramatist Eugène Brieux in 1912.[33] Like *dame célibataire* and unlike *vieille fille*, the term *femme seule* did not equate female adulthood with marriage.[34]

For feminists such as Pelletier and Misme, *la femme seule* provided proof of the independence they believed women had obtained in recent years. They created an image of *la femme seule* in terms that affirmed their own ideological goals. But antifeminists produced the same image of a feisty, independent *femme seule*, for example, in a survey on "The Crisis of Marriage" in *Renaissance Politique* during the spring of 1924. The literary critic Maurice Duval began the survey by quoting an article by the well-known natalist and antifeminist Gaston Rageot: "Many young girls today are convinced . . . that no boy is worthy of them and that marriage could be, for them, the worst form of servitude."[35] Colette Yver, another well-known antifeminist, argued that a young woman, "forced to consider that she might not marry, that it might be necessary for her to live without support and by her own means," had come to realize that "in fact, she can exist on her own. She no longer waits for a husband to provide her a living, as she once did."[36] In his antifeminist tract *Les Féministes françaises*, based on the 1923–24 *Eve* letters, Fernand Goland also conjured up an image of an independent *femme seule*. On the one hand, Goland incited his readers to pity the *vieilles filles* "who aspire to the happiness of a household" but who are condemned "to a pathetic and bitter solitude" by "the law of numbers, this terrible disproportion of the sexes."[37] On the other hand, Goland concluded that "the liberated woman, the 'superior' woman, the woman who assures her own livelihood, doesn't marry or only rarely so." These *femmes seules*, Goland accused, "voluntarily condemn themselves to a fruitless, selfish existence" in having "the puerile pride of all *parvenus*" and by considering their suitors from the "height of their ivory tower," from which they appear "quite small" or "inferior."[38] For Goland, the *femme seule* signified a new breed of women who "noisily demanded their place in the sun, set themselves up as direct rivals of man, and hoped to undermine him."[39]

Goland's contradictory vision of *la femme seule*—at once pitiful old maid and prideful modern woman—encapsulates the complex set of images assigned to young single women after the war. No less than Misme, Goland used the issue of female celibacy as a means to respond—in this case, anxiously rather than enthusiastically—to a more general set of changes he saw happening in women's lives: a new trend toward economic autonomy and the desire to devote time to career as well as marriage. Goland's reaction to such changes differed from that of Misme, but the terms of the argument were the same. For Goland, the freedom that the image of *la femme seule* sanctioned for all women's lives was menacing and disruptive. Other antifeminists, such as the novelist Colette Yver, described *la femme seule* as a threat to family life. Even if she could find someone to marry her, Yver argued, she would want to continue wage work, thus "obliterat-[ing]" the "model of *la femme au foyer*." Yver saw little difference between the working *femme seule* and the *femme moderne* who "lives like a bachelor" and is "dedicated to a purpose other than that of her children."[40] For Yver, *la femme seule* symbolized a threat to conventional gender roles and social practices. For feminists such as Misme, the same image signaled greater social and economic power for women. But both Yver and Misme identified *la femme seule* as a symbol of social change.

In sum, then, the single woman drew unprecedented attention after the war because she provided an opportunity to discuss perceived changes in all women's lives. Positioned on the horizon of changing gender identities, *la femme seule* served a double role in the postwar reconstruction of sexual difference. When she was perceived as a *vieille fille*, leading a death-in-life existence, she confirmed the emptiness of female life apart from male attention and sanctioned a traditionally conceived domesticity. But when she was presented as independent, even arrogant, she undermined the domestic ideal by subordinating marriage and motherhood to the quest for independence. *La vieille fille* and *la femme seule* represented shifting alternatives in the organization of social relations. Together they demonstrated the erratic movement back and forth in postwar discourse between optimism and anxiety concerning change, between proclaiming the new world and clinging to the old.

This chapter will examine two debates about the single woman that show her ability to symbolize change. The first debate concerns a relatively minor surtax imposed on single persons in 1920. The second debate spans the middle years of the decade, and centers on the issue of single motherhood—whether *la femme seule* should be encouraged to bear children for medical and demographic reasons. Both the surtax and the issue of single motherhood were taken up in popular literature and the bourgeois press, and became topics of widespread and intense debate. The surtax issue became a heated controversy in parliament and the press; similarly, medical support for single motherhood became the subject of several popular, well-known novels. Both debates rapidly gained in cultural complexity because the image of *la femme seule* provided an opportunity to negotiate social relations during an era of change.

This Young Girl Will Do What She Wants in Life

In 1920 the French government imposed a small surtax on the incomes of both male and female single persons over 30 years of age with no persons in their charge. The surtax was also placed on those couples who had been married for two years without any person in their charge. Exempted were disabled war veterans and parents of those men who had died during the war. The surtax was only one article in a much larger tax bill "having for its object the creation of new fiscal resources," a piece of legislation discussed in the Chamber of Deputies in mid-April and considered, in turn, by the Senate at the end of May.[41] The surtax aimed to create new sources of income for the government. A heavy burden of public debt and a wildly fluctuating franc had seriously drained and destabilized the government's resources since 1914.[42] When the new Chamber opened in January 1920, the government immediately began to explore ways to ameliorate what one spokesman later called "the very serious financial situation in which we find ourselves."[43] President Paul Deschanel made taxes a high priority in his inauguration speech early that year.[44]

Natalist considerations also influenced debate of the surtax in parliament. The surtax had long been part of the legislative program of natalist organizations such as Pour la vie and Bertillon's Alliance nationale (see fig. 22, *La Femme et l'enfant* propaganda).[45] Such organizations promoted the surtax as a way to distribute the tax burden more evenly by increasing the income tax of those who, without children, consumed fewer taxed goods. But critics of the surtax described it as a punitive measure. Léon Bérard (Radical, Basses-Pyrénées) called it "procreation by constraint or by legislative persuasion."[46] Although supporters of the surtax denied this charge,[47] the language natalist legislators used to describe the surtax betrayed moral disapproval of unmarried persons. For example, Senator Fernand Merlin (Radical, Loire) defended the tax as "rigorously and strictly fiscal in nature," yet also urged his colleagues to use it in order to teach single persons that "there is a notion superior to self-interest or selfishness, which is that of duty."[48] The surtax was only one way in which the natalists exerted their legislative muscle in the creation of new fiscal resources.[49]

Although the surtax was originally motivated by fiscal and natalist concerns, these were not the main focus of attention when it was debated in parliament and in the bourgeois press during 1920. Of greatest interest to both legislators and the press when debating the surtax was whether or not single women should pay the tax. Should a single woman be obligated to fulfill certain fiscal obligations? Or should she be exempted based on her own inability to change her celibate status? In discussing these issues of social responsibility, French legislators negotiated shifting notions of female identity. Were such women simply helpless children, whose adulthood was forever delayed by their celibate state? Or were they economically autonomous citizens?

When Article 7 of the tax bill—the section containing the surtax— came up for consideration in the Chamber on April 17, the issue of single women immediately dominated the discussion. In a speech described by journalists variously as "moving," "very witty," "touching" and "delightful," Léon Bérard defended the rights of widowers and particularly widows to be exempt from any surtax after the death of their spouse.[50] He described the widow as a "woman without profession, practically incapable of earning a living" and yet, he told the Chamber, "you are going to impose [on her] a courtesan's tax."[51] His remarks, greeted with the "lively applause" and cheers of his colleagues, ended in the exemption of widows and widowers. André Berthon (Socialist, Paris) then proposed a similar exemption for divorcées, arguing that "a woman is frequently betrayed and abandoned, left to her own resources, so that her life becomes singularly difficult."[52] But Berthon had little success in swaying the *rapporteur-général* Charles Dumont (Radical, Jura) and the other members of the Chamber. Dumont rejected Berthon's amendment, but fumbled when called upon to justify his decision. At first, he reverted to the vague, often repeated defense that "it should not be said of us that we are dealing here with punitive measures." He went on to complain that the law could not concern itself with "every particular case." Finally, he pointed to the relatively advanced age of the widow and noted that, by contrast, the divorcée had more options: "this young girl will do what she wants in life. But she should have no complaints about the law if it demands taxes of her for not having a child."[53]

The different fate of these two pleas for exemption is striking, particularly given the fact that Bérard and Berthon made almost identical arguments in their support. Both deputies reasoned on the basis of a woman's inability to support herself "left to her own resources" and "without a profession." Why, then, did Bérard succeed and Berthon fail? Berthon, as a socialist and a new member of the right-wing Chambre bleu horizon, was much less well-known and popular than the charming, witty, more politically moderate Bérard.[54] The impact of conservative French attitudes toward divorce presents another explanation. Berthon carefully specified that the exemption would apply only to those women who did not leave the marriage on their own accord and he presented the divorcée as "betrayed and abandoned . . . even though she has done her duty." But opponents such as Dumont still viewed her as a young, egocentric woman, able to "do what she wants in life."[55] Why was the younger woman seen as having control over her destiny while the older one was not?

These different perceptions of the widow and the divorcée reveal conflicting attitudes about female celibacy and economic autonomy. The deputies portrayed *la femme seule* as helpless, yet also capable (at least when young) of economic and emotional independence. These same issues preoccupied the Senate when the surtax came up for discussion there on May 26. The daily press described the session as "exceptionally animated" and even disorderly; one journalist noted that the question of the surtax seemed to have "violently upset" the senators.[56] Debate again centered on an amendment that exempted single women—referred to by Antonin Gourju as "the most interesting category of bachelors, those of the feminine sex." Gourju (Gauche Radicale, Rhône) introduced the amendment and presented *la femme seule* as a powerless victim of forced celibacy. While men often chose to stay single for honorable reasons, Gourju argued, "in the end, they are men, and it is because of their own volition, legitimate or not, that they remain unmarried." A young woman, however, "waits for someone to ask her, and if no one does, she remains unmarried with great reluctance, and perhaps with a broken heart. Moreover," Gourju asked his colleagues, "have you thought about all those [women] who will be plunged into forced celibacy forever by the war's uneven sex ratio?"[57] Speaking in support of Gourju's amendment, Fernand Merlin also brought up the case of the postwar *femme seule*. He estimated that 2.5 million women would be "doomed to celibacy, to a forced celibacy," as well as to "the search for a happiness that they would never find again." Under these conditions, "would you agree that a young girl . . . left to her own resources, isolated in the world, less capable than a man of making her way in life, should be stricken by your laws?"[58]

In debating the surtax in the bourgeois press, many journalists also presented *la femme seule* as a helpless object of pity. Although the surtax was only one of many amendments to a large and complex tax bill, it commanded considerable attention in the press during the spring and summer of 1920. What again was of particular interest to journalists was neither the fiscal issues nor the natalist undertones of the surtax, but its possible promotion of a new socioeconomic equality between the sexes. Prominent natalists such as Jacques Bertillon used the surtax to advance traditional notions of female domesticity. In words that echoed Gourju's, Bertillon argued that "most often, when a man doesn't marry, it's because he doesn't want to. By contrast, how many girls who ask for nothing more than the chance to lavish a husband with tenderness have not received it?"[59] Clément Vautel (author of *Madame ne veut pas d'enfant*) quipped in *Le Journal* that the surtax should be imposed only on the most recalcitrant women—those willing to sign the following declaration: "I could be proposed to by Prince Charming in person, and I would refuse his hand in marriage." In other words, according to Vautel, because most women had little power over whether they married, the exemption was unfair.[60]

But Vautel's and Gourju's vision of female powerlessness competed with another diametrically opposed one, put forth by feminists and other journalists of the bourgeois press. The Ligue française pour le droit des femmes, a bourgeois feminist organization, took this official position on the surtax issue:

> Women, say certain Ligue members, demand equality before the law, hence they ought not to shirk equality before taxes. The tax on single persons is not a penalty. Its purpose is to re-establish an equilibrium of social costs among all members of the collectivity. It matters little whether or not a woman has had the opportunity to marry. The sole fact that she lives alone, without a family, makes her *impôts indirects* less burdensome. As a result, she ought to supplement them.[61]

By clinging to the notion that the surtax was not in any way a penalty, feminists took the same position as the natalists, but for very different reasons. The natalists hid behind the argument that the surtax was "rigorously and strictly fiscal" in order to avoid accusations that they were legislating pro-family morality.[62] The feminists also played up a disinterested commitment to "an equilibrium of social costs." The woman subject produced here is an ungendered "member of the collectivity," a citizen whose sex in no way interferes with her fiscal responsibility. In other words, she was an ungendered equal before the law—an image that had distinct ideological advantages for feminists.[63] When, at the end of May, the surtax on single women was passed, members of another bourgeois feminist organization, the Union française pour le suffrage des femmes, wrote to the French minister of finances to argue that *la femme seule*'s inclusion in the surtax had created a precedent for equality before the law. Why not then give women the vote?

Feminists used the surtax to counter the image of women as pitiful children and to promote their civic identity. Other journalists in the mainstream bourgeois press produced still another image of *la femme seule*—one that recalls Charles Dumont's image of the young girl who "will do what she wants in life." An editorial on the surtax in the centrist *Le Temps* asked:

> Can't they [single women] also be accused of having refused more than one decent boy on the basis of the most futile pretexts? . . . The day is long gone when the young girl waited quietly in her corner for a suitor to notice her. . . . For those many who are now permitted to exercise a new profession, their independence will be assured and their selfishness will be strengthened, as they are given a sense of peace about the future. . . . In cultivating their spirit, education has permitted them to free themselves almost completely from male support.[64]

This journalist presents a young, haughty and economically autonomous *femme moderne,* who returns male attention and support with complete indifference.

To appreciate the novelty of this perception, we must read it against another press reaction to a similar surtax, imposed some twenty years before on single men in the grand duchy of Hesse, Germany.[65] In 1899 French journalists described the surtax as a "most brilliant legislative victory" with "a very real practical impact" for women, because it discouraged male celibacy and encouraged "obligatory marriage."[66] *Le Petit Journal* commented:

> When they are ready, our female contemporaries are nearly all pretty enough to find willing suitors. For such a system of "forced marriage" to work in France, we must await the century when our women will not be content being lawyers, doctors or professors. Once they are seated in Parliament, have become civil servants, academicians, or ministers, the worries of public life will make them so appallingly ugly that they will have to enact heinous laws to make us marry them.
>
> This will not be tomorrow.[67]

Although both *Le Temps* and *Le Petit journal* had a history of conservatism in relation to feminist issues, the contrast between the superbly confident, condescending tone of this 1899 editorial and that of its more anxious, even bitter 1920 counterpart could not be more striking.[68] The asymmetry of the new surtax—placed on single men but not women—went unchallenged in 1899 because, in contrast to the case in 1920, belief in marriage as the "saving grace" for women was not even questioned.

Although the surtax was only a minor part of a much larger tax bill, it touched on a subject that French men and women were eager to debate—changing relations of social organization. They gave the surtax their attention because it struck the nerve of something they wanted to talk about. French legislators and the press represented competing visions of *la femme seule*. They construed her as a pathetic child, an equal before the law or an insolent modern woman. In this way, the surtax created an opportunity to discuss changing notions of women's economic and emotional autonomy, as well as its impact on the social organization of gender.

Nature Has Created Them to Be Fertile

A second postwar debate concerning *la femme seule* centered on whether single women should be encouraged to bear children outside wedlock. This debate began during the war and peaked between 1923 and 1927 when several popular novels and plays on the single mother appeared. The origins of this second debate can be traced to the strongly natalist atmosphere of the twenties, as well as the degree to which female identity had been defined in terms of motherhood.

A convention of both pre- and postwar discourse on the single woman was that she should find appropriate social outlets, such as charitable good works, for her frustrated maternal instincts. In 1920, for example, the journalist Berthe Benage of *Le Journal des demoiselles* proposed "social" motherhood as an alternative to marriage for single women. She projected a maternal role onto professions such as social work, nursing, and teaching that many single women entered.[69] "Young girls of the postwar era, you will not all find someone to marry, and yet you will have to make a living. What will you do?" asked Benage. "Will you count yourself among the weary and discontented who, believing that they have missed their destiny, withdraw from active life and languish in an egoistic neurasthenia?"[70] Benage voiced a common fear, particularly among Catholics: that female celibacy would lead to the selfishness and materialism associated with the modern woman and the "moral problem" of depopulation.[71] To assure virtue, Catholics pressed "substitute" or "social" motherhood into service. The conservative Catholic vision of *la femme seule* emerges in *Les Inépousées* (1919), a novel by Geneviève Duhamelet, herself a popular Catholic writer. Duhamelet's story concerns two young women who reach the age of marriage just as the war breaks out. Facing the prospect of a life alone, Thérèse devotes her energies to taking care of a baby left behind by the maid; Marthe throws herself into hospital and charitable activities.[72]

In addition, in the years just after the war, many natalists began to take the notion of motherhood for *la femme seule* more literally. Despite their otherwise conservative moral vision, they began to support biological as well as social motherhood for single women. In 1919 the editors of the natalist journal *Pour la vie* reasoned that although the single mother, or *fille-mère*, "makes a mistake when she gives herself [to a man] outside marriage," she nevertheless "often has the right to leniency, ordinarily to pity, and to help when she is poor."[73] Natalist support of single motherhood, which gathered strength in the early years of the decade, often took the form of a simple softening of the moral and legal sanctions against women who had been seduced and abandoned. Bourgeois feminists also made some effort to criticize laws concerning paternity suits and illegitimate children in the military.[74] By mid-decade, several prominent doctors felt strongly enough about the social and biological value of single motherhood to argue for greater recognition of *la fille-mère*'s plight in more popular forms, such as a series entitled "Let Us Honor and Protect Every Mother" appearing in 1925 in the bourgeois daily *Le Matin*. Among these doctors was Adolphe Pinard—a prominent physician, a pioneer of social hygiene, a deputy representing the Seine, and arguably the "Dr. Spock" of his era. Pinard expressed his belief that any mother should be "honored and remunerated" no matter "the conditions in which she has conceived and given birth."[75] In the same series, Félix Jayle, the author of a highly acclaimed work on female anatomy titled *La Gynécologie: L'Anatomie morphologique de la femme,* also demanded that *la fille-mère* be given official recognition as a "Madame" in a ceremony at city hall.[76] Dr. Théodore Tuffier, a surgeon and member of the Académie de médécine, argued that if a mother deserved one medal, a single mother deserved two "for her courage in not prematurely ridding herself of her pregnancy, as so many others, alas, have done in her situation."[77]

Many doctors even campaigned for planned, systematic, and state-funded single motherhood. In 1920, the physician Paul Carnot asked the medical community in *Paris médicale*: "Can society itself replace the *chef de famille* by assigning a fairly large number of Volunteers of Motherhood to the mission of procreating, bearing, nurturing and raising a contingent of little Frenchmen?" Carnot targeted *les iné-pousées de guerre,* in particular, to form his army of volunteers and suggested that all costs be subsidized by the state, with bonuses paid according to "the good physical quality of the products."[78] In the 1925 *Le Matin* series, the obstetrician Louis-Jules Devraignes argued that *la fille-mère* should receive a small salary from the state for doing simple, physically untaxing work after her child was born.[79] Dr. Jayle also argued in *Le Matin* that *les inépousées de guerre* who wanted to have a child should have the right to do so, even if this required an illegal, temporary sexual union.[80]

The motivation for such radical schemes was undoubtedly natalist. In an early statement of the problem, *Mère sans être épouse* (1918), Martin de Torina declared that the population crisis was "a question of life or death" and that "only the French woman [could] save the country."[81] Estimating the number of single women at 3.5 million, Torina argued that if each one of these women had six children, there would be 1,050,000 more French children each year for twenty years, or 21 million in all.[82] Natalist concerns were avowed in the medical community as well. "To encourage motherhood by all means is, at present, a measure for the protection of the general public," argued Paul Carnot in 1920.[83] The articles appearing in the later *Le Matin* series were also strongly natalist. In addition, support for single motherhood reaffirmed a more conventional female identity. Doctors such as Tuffier couched their concern for the *fille-mère* in statements such as "all women are born to be mothers."[84] Tuffier's reference to "all women" here can be taken at face value: no strong class element marked the medical call for single motherhood.

The ideological campaign for single motherhood was conservative inasmuch as it sought to reassert conventional notions of female identity—the primacy of motherhood, maternal instinct—in what were perceived to be the exceptional social circumstances created by the war. But the notion of single motherhood entailed enormous moral risks for its conservative supporters. After all, *la fille-mère* had been a symbol of social and sexual disorder throughout the previous century.[85] As the historian Françoise Thébaud has argued, although a movement to support single motherhood gained some momentum during the postwar years, *la fille-mère* was still scorned and marginalized.[86] To endorse her required delicate negotiation of the behavior—particularly the sexual behavior—being prescribed for *la femme seule* outside marriage. There was only one way to get pregnant, and everyone knew what it was. A contradiction lay at the heart of the single mother as an image of female identity. On the one hand, she reaffirmed women's reproductive function and her conventional domestic role. On the other hand, she was sexually active outside marriage. As we shall see, the *excess* of sexual behavior implicit in the image of the single mother threatened to subvert conservative efforts to define female identity in chastely maternal terms.[87]

Many supporters of the single mother were well aware of the precariousness of their position. In 1919, one natalist called support of single motherhood walking on a tightrope. "To fall either to the right or to the left—the risks and the disadvantages are the same."[88] Although doctors like Tuffier and Carnot were willing to encourage motherhood "by all means" and "at any price," the question remained: How did these doctors contain the contradictions implicit in the image of *la mère seule* without falling "either to the right or to the left?" In other words, how did they seize an opportunity to raise the birthrate without openly advocating female sexual promiscuity? The natalists were largely unable to maintain control of the sexual meanings produced by their own project, and ironically it was they who helped to lay the grounds for the construction of a female sexual identity.

In order to negotiate the contradictions implicit in the project of single motherhood, the medical community grounded it in physiological terms, hence removing it from the more slippery and problematic moral terrain. During the war, a commission organized to study the "medical-physiological element" of the depopulation crisis and composed of several prominent members of the Académie de médecine, including Adolphe Pinard, Paul Strauss, Charles Richet, and Jacques Doléris, concluded that women who do not have at least one child suffer from the formation of "fibroma" or tumors composed of fibrous tissue.[89] According to Pinard, "a woman enjoys good health only if she is a mother and as much as possible before the age of twenty-five." In all his fifty-year career, Pinard claimed, "I have never seen fibroma in a mother of six children, and I've never seen an old maid in perfect health."[90] The theory of fibroma was based on the medical assumption that the uterus hypertrophied at birth in order to augment the number and size of its muscular fibers. These doctors believed that if the process of hypertrophy could not be carried out under "normal" conditions, that is, during gestation, it would manifest itself anyway, but abnormally, leading to a variety of pathologies in the uterus and adjoining organs, such as the formation of tumors. By contrast, the doctors emphasized the vigorous health of women who bore many children.[91]

By grounding their argument in physiology, these doctors transformed a morally uncertain project into a medical imperative. The members of the wartime commission concluded that failure to give birth was medically dangerous and that for humane reasons alone, "all mothers, whatever their civil status, will have to be protected, aided or assisted."[92] As Adolphe Pinard put it several years later in the *Le Matin* series: "The naked truth is this: childlessness *(sterilité)* is against nature: any legislation that encourages it is inhumane, hence contrary to morality."[93] Other prominent doctors in the series agreed. "It is a scientific and physiological truth that we must abide by, both in the laws of morality and in the civil code," argued Dr. Tuffier.[94] Dr. Jayle believed it would be "inhumane to impose childlessness" on single women "given that nature has created them to be fertile."[95] This belief in the dangers of *stérilité* seems to have been widespread in the medical community during the twenties.[96]

But even the argument for the medical necessity of maternity backfired inasmuch as it again produced a slippage between strictly reproductive and sexually promiscuous behavior. This slippage resulted from the correspondence in medical opinion between the hazards involved when women did not bear children, and those that arose when they abstained from sex. Although theories of continence were widely debated among French doctors throughout the pre- and postwar periods, it was a common belief of French medicine that abstinence, even for women, could lead to nervous illness and disorders of all kinds, including hysteria, nymphomania, and breast and uterine cancer.[97] Sexologists such as Richard von Krafft-Ebing and Henry Havelock Ellis, fairly well known in France at the time, reinforced these beliefs by arguing that celibacy could provoke diseases of the nervous system and the genital organs, and could rob one of energy and the capacity for work.[98] These beliefs were by no means confined to doctors. Even a relatively moderate bourgeois feminist like Maria Vérone admitted to them in an editorial on *la femme seule* for the *L'Oeuvre:* "Ask a doctor—he will answer you that a number of nervous illnesses, such as anemia and neurasthenia, often have no other cause."[99]

The theories of maternal and sexual deprivation shared a common medical assumption: that human organs that are not used or satisfied in "normal" ways assert themselves in any case, seeking pathological outlets.[100] According to the psychologist Charles Binet-Sanglé, this was certainly true in the case of sexual abstinence. Binet-Sanglé believed that "toxins" regularly excreted by the genital glands "accumulate in their cavity." If not "ejaculated" regularly through intercourse, they were reabsorbed into the circulatory system, where they produced a malaise "that grows little by little until it becomes unbearable," ending in onanism, sapphism, and hysteria.[101] In addition, the notion that the uterus hypertrophied at birth paralleled medical ideas concerning tumescence and detumescence, the vascular "accumulation" and "discharge" of sexual energy during intercourse.[102] Finally, the theories of maternal and sexual deprivation shared a similar logic as arguments for single motherhood: they presumed that social behavior should be determined on the basis of biological necessities, namely, the need of the woman for motherhood or sex. Given these similarities, was it possible to mistake a woman who suffered from not having a baby for one who suffered from not having sex? Could one distinguish "maternity-deprived" from "sex-deprived" symptoms? It was certainly difficult to do so in this speech made by René Biot, a prominent doctor and social Catholic for Lyons, at a *semaine sociale* in 1927:

> Nothing will be able to console [single women] in their grief concerning the cradles they could have filled. Instead, they will be confused by the multiple attractions that modern life offers to the senses, particularly in the city. One must say that in all likelihood, these women will have to struggle grievously against themselves.[103]

Biot's rhetoric here—his reference to the sensual attractions of modern urban life, the terminology of self-discipline and struggle—echoed Catholic exhortations against masturbation and sexual temptation. In this way, Biot seemed to assert the presence of a strong sexual as well a strong maternal instinct for women.[104]

Virgins' Consumption

This slippage between maternal and sexual needs emerges in fictions about *la mère seule*. Here I will examine three of them in detail: Léon Frapié's novel *La Virginité* (1923), Eugène Brieux's drama *Pierette et Galaor* (1923) and Marie Laparcerie's novel *La femme d'aujourd'hui* (1924). All three fictions revolve around unmarried heroines who want profoundly to bear a child—an attitude difficult to reconcile with the natalist fear, examined in the previous chapter, that women no longer desired children. But these popular fictions become much more than paeans to motherhood. Indeed, they inscribe a vision of gender relations that diverged sharply from that of the natalists. Rather than reinforce maternity as the primary destiny of female life, these fictions examine motherhood as part of women's growing economic and emotional autonomy in the wake of the war's upheaval. What they share with novels such as Clément Vautel's *Madame ne veut pas d'enfant* is their emphasis on the way such autonomy creates acute anxiety in men. Whether women scorned children or wanted them desperately in postwar fictions, their relationship to maternity seems to humiliate men.

Frapié's *La Virginité* was the first novel of a trilogy dealing with *la femme seule* and published in the years 1923–27. It had a print run of 18,000 copies in its first year of publication; this figure was above the average (10,000 to 15,000) for a popular novel by a well-known author. Profoundly ambiguous, *La Virginité* can be read simultaneously in two, almost diametrically opposed ways: first, as a conservative reaffirmation of motherhood and, second, as a much more radical statement of a woman's right to sexual fulfillment. Léon Frapié was a popular novelist best-known for his *La Maternelle,* which won the Prix Goncourt in 1905. He was viewed by his contemporaries as a social realist who modeled himself after Emile Zola and who was particularly interested in the "problem" of female celibacy, even before the war. A comparison of the women in Frapié's fiction before and after the war reveals a dramatic change in his representation of *la femme seule.* While Louise, the single, provincial teacher of *L'Institutrice de province* (1887), dies an early death of exhaustion and pain suffered from social hostility and alienation, Fanny and Honorine of *La Virginité* achieve at least some degree of professional and personal success. Whereas before the war Frapié was interested in *la femme seule* as a generic social type, after the war he became particularly concerned with the problem of female celibacy in relation to natalist values.[105]

On one level, Frapié's *La Virginité* is a tribute to motherhood as the single, overriding purpose of a woman's life.[106] Its publisher, Flammarion, advertised the novel as an examination of the "formidable problem" of "unmarried women without hope . . . condemned by misfortune to an external exile" even though their "essential purpose in life is motherhood."[107] The story revolves around two young women, Fanny and Honorine, who have been unable to find husbands because of the shortage of men. Both women are able to support themselves by working in a government office. But they have had more difficulty finding outlets for their emotional needs. Fanny writes novels as a way to ease her loneliness. With one of her manuscripts, she approaches a well-known novelist, Armand Prizeur, who himself has written on the *femme seule,* "deprived of legitimate love."[108]

The Prizeur household is used to reaffirm traditional maternal values in several ways. First, Armand and his wife, Suzanne, are experiencing marital difficulties because they have been unable to have a child, which "represented for them the pinnacle of human happiness."[109] They are being treated for their sterility by a midwife named Madame Le Guetteux, who is an outspoken advocate of motherhood for both married and single women. When Armand's maid becomes pregnant and is abandoned, both Madame Le Guetteux and Suzanne Prizeur encourage her to fulfill her "duty toward nature and society. Why is the woman creature on earth? What is her critical, most useful and beautiful function? Maternity."[110] Suzanne herself becomes pregnant soon afterward. Fanny and Honorine begin to frequent this fortunate house of fecundity, but to harmful effect, at least in Honorine's case. According to Madame Le Guetteux, the news of Suzanne's pregnancy is traumatic for Honorine and brings on a fatal condition known as *"la consomption des vierges,"* or "virgin's consumption." Its symptoms are a thinning, slumping figure, a loss of appetite, a general languor, and depression. Honorine's condition is curable, argues Madame Le Guetteux; one only has to "push her into the arms of a seducer who may give her a child," and she would blossom like a flower, much as Suzanne had done since she conceived.[111] When no such seducer arrives on the scene, Honorine becomes visibly weaker, manifesting a frantic, unhealthy love for Suzanne's child, crying out joyfully for his photograph, and worrying hysterically when he becomes ill. Her own condition becomes so grave (bad fibroma?) that she is sent by the family to a country home for fresh air. Armand seduces her in a garden there and, making her pregnant, "saves" her from certain death. Honorine begins to recover, so that when we eventually see her again in Frapié's next novel, *Les Filles à marier,* she "showed the freshness of a young mother, the tangible freshness of nature satisfied."[112]

In all these ways, Frapié's novel eulogizes motherhood. Why, then, is it entitled *"La Virginité"* and not *"La Maternité"*? The answer lies in a second reading of the novel, one that contradicts the first and that, appropriately, is grounded in a second novel-within-the novel, the novel that Fanny brings to Armand Prizeur as the story opens. Fanny's novel also concerns the problem of *la femme seule,* yet it praises virginity rather than motherhood. Its heroine, Gilberte, surrenders herself to charity work and a resolutely virginal state; in other words, she lives out the Catholic, conservative vision of female celibacy. In Frapié's larger story, Fanny's novel serves as a foil against which the perceived sexual needs of *la femme seule* are argued. When Madame le Guetteux first introduces the notion of *la consomption des vierges* in a discussion with Armand Prizeur and his friend Jérôme, she seems to refer to a sexual rather than a maternal need. According to her, consumption occurs when a "demand of nature" that "the freedom granted to boys tacitly recognizes" is denied to girls. Prizeur, in turn, remarks that while for many women virginity was not harmful, "for certain individuals . . . this decree of nature applies: *la fonction d'amour* during a normal time period, or death." [113] Woman's sexual need is ignored, Prizeur adds, "because in order to understand it, one would have to admit that the law of "love no matter how" is vitally necessary, and this concession would do away with the law of morality." [114] In a later scene suffused with sexual undertones and presented as a kind of verbal rape, Prizeur harshly criticizes Fanny for her fictional tribute to virginity. "After a certain age and a certain physical development, the virginal state is a state against nature, a state against happiness, against the very existence of an individual," he argues. [115] He calls Fanny's heroine, Gilberte, "a proud, cerebral woman" and "a monster who commits the worst possible abuse against feminine youth." [116]

Hence *La Virginité* can also be read as arguing that single women need more than babies, or at least that they satisfy another need while having them. Ambiguity permeates Frapié's condemnation of celibacy as an unnatural state: Is celibacy unnatural because it prohibits maternity or because it prohibits sexual activity? Madame le Guetteux describes Honorine as "defenseless against the snares of instinct . . . she must have love, with or without marriage." [117] Yet her "consumption" begins suddenly on the day Suzanne announces her pregnancy. When Armand momentarily hesitates to seduce Honorine, she is compared with a female animal who, "with an obvious need," attacks her prey. [118] But is that need sexual or reproductive?

This question remains unanswered in the novel, perhaps intentionally so. In discussing the problem of *la consomption des vierges* with his friend Jérôme, Armand Prizeur advocates secrecy as a strategy for change: "There are particularly useful moral dispensations that one need not annunciate. The public admits them on the condition that they seem to be ignored. An axiom, my dear Jérôme: sure progress is made in silence and even on the condition of silence." [119] Armand's statement could also be interpreted as a confession of the novel's narrative strategy. Frapié uses maternal instinct in the novel as a kind of veil to silence or make less threatening the existence of woman's sexual needs. The notion of female sexual instinct joins the natalist and sexological discourses running throughout the novel—a strained association indeed. When Honorine expresses moral qualms concerning the pregnancy, Madame Le Guetteux dismisses them with the argument

the "you cannot live on without being a woman" and that a "new morality" is taking shape: "the society in danger of death finally takes care to
harmonize itself with nature." [120] In an ironic mutation of natalist values, the midwife uses the depopulation problem to justify radical sexual behavior.

In this way, the image of *la femme seule* abetted the creation of a
sexual identity for women outside marriage and motherhood. In an era
when Sigmund Freud's ideas were just beginning to be known in
France, such an identity remained elliptical at best, as the thematic
fumblings of Frapié's novel attest. [121] Ironically, the grounds for the
construction of female sexual identity lay in the pervasiveness of natalist values. In needing to make single women mothers, postwar natalists (novelists as well as doctors) also made them sexual creatures.
And if we are to believe the feminist reviewers, it was as sexual creatures, not as mothers, that Fanny and Honorine caught the attention
of the public. In an editorial about *La Virginité* in the bourgeois daily
L'Oeuvre, the feminist Maria Vérone conceded that the novel could be
interpreted as immoral, then asked, "but how not to be moved with
pity by the physiological misery of those poor beings whom celibacy
kills slowly but surely?" [122] The bourgeois feminist Jane Misme recognized the strange mutation of natalist values in the novel; she described
Frapié's *fonction d'amour* as the old socialist doctrine of free love with
a new natalist twist. [123] Finally, the radical feminist Josette Cornec used
Frapié's novel (among others) to make a general defense of women's
sexual needs: "On the doctor's own testimony, virginity, if too prolonged, can retard intellectual and physical development." [124]

La Virginité creates an emotional as well as a sexual identity for
women outside marriage, inasmuch as it presents a vision of women's
emotional fulfillment independent of men. At the novel's end, Honorine and Fanny decide to raise the child together, finding great happiness in their love for each other and for Honorine's baby. But the trilogy generally moves away from the mutual support of female
friendship and toward the respectability and dependence on men implicit in marriage. In the second volume, *Les Filles à marier* (1925),
Armand Prizeur offers to provide for Honorine and her baby under his
own roof. He is devastated when Honorine instead decides to marry a
young middle-class man, Rénemy, who recognizes the child and wants
to raise it as his own. Rénemy is attracted to Honorine primarily for
"the maternal tenderness" that she lavishes on Zozotte, her child; in
his mind, such tenderness "undoubtedly offers the most definitive, the
most general revelation of the heart imaginable." [125] Prizeur's seduction

of Honorine is made legally respectable in *Les Filles à marier* in two ways: first, by the fact that she marries and, second, by a bill that Prizeur has introduced in parliament through a deputy friend. Prizeur's bill proposes that single mothers be able to claim the same legal privileges as widowed or divorced women so that their children would no longer be considered illegitimate.[126] Conversely, no marriage would be considered legal until the mother had a child. For some unexplained reason, when Honorine marries, she feels compelled to break completely with Fanny, who also ultimately marries in the third novel, *La Divinisée* (1927), after a period of trauma and isolation.

In the last two volumes of his trilogy, Frapié neutralizes the more radical implications of single motherhood by further emphasizing the maternalist strain introduced in *La Virginité*. *Les Filles à marier* opens on a defensive note, with Armand Prizeur's wife, Suzanne, trying to explain to friends why her husband seduced Fanny. According to Suzanne, maternal rather than sexual instinct was the primary motivating force. Her baby boy had grown seriously ill through some mysterious connection to Honorine's own suffering; Prizeur's seduction of Honorine saved her child's life as well. Honorine is also called upon to justify her act to a neighbor at the beginning of *Les Filles à marier*: she compares herself with a "sick child" cured by a "doctor" (Prizeur). Once again, as in the case of the natalist justification of single motherhood, Honorine grounds her argument in physiology in order to transform a morally uncertain project into a medical imperative. These justifications reflect defensiveness on Frapié's part concerning the more scandalous aspects of his previous novel. Such a defensive posture mirrors the disruptive potential of *la mère seule* as an image of female identity—her ability to figure changing notions of female sexuality.

Like Frapié's trilogy, Eugène Brieux's drama *Pierette et Galaor* (*L'Enfant*) uses the issue of single motherhood to explore shifting notions of female identity. A member of the Académie française and an internationally known playwright, Brieux, like Frapié, was interested in the problem of female celibacy even before the war.[127] Like Frapié, Brieux also considered himself a social realist. His plays took up contemporary issues and often became the focus of public scandal and debate. In 1901, for example, Brieux wrote a play called *Les Avaries* concerning syphilis that had a tremendous impact on public opinion about venereal disease. In 1912, an earlier play about *la femme seule* was equally polemical.[128] His decision to focus on single motherhood in *Pierette et Galaor*, first performed September 20, 1923 at the Vaudeville Theater in Paris, typifies his interest in topical, controversial subjects.[129] At the time of its opening, the play expected a run of 150 nights in a sizable theater (1,600 seats). As the drama critic for *Mercure de France* put it, "To get 1,600 spectators for 150 nights . . . what a sign of the nation's need to instruct itself on . . . the problem of the woman in postwar society!"[130] Because of Brieux's known ability both to discern and to shape popular opinion about topical subjects such as *la femme seule, Pierette et Galaor* merits close analysis.

Like Frapié's trilogy, Brieux's play represents an ironic, strained mutation of natalist values and points up the conflictual nature of the postwar debate on female identity. The play concerns a young bourgeois woman, Pierette, who, although "bursting with freshness and joie de vivre," is unable to find a husband because of the postwar shortage of men.[131] An engineer who manages a hydroelectric plant, she is financially and emotionally independent. Despite all this, however, her most fervent wish is to bear a child. She decides to seduce Henri, the nephew of her sister's husband, whom she has known for some time. Motherhood, in Pierette's case, represents not a surrender to a more conventional life, but the very grounds for happiness apart from men and marriage: an ironic rebuke of the traditional domestic role. The desire to bear a child leads Pierette, like Honorine, to construct a sexual as well as a maternal identity, so that the difference between these two is ultimately blurred.

The requisite sexual act, as recounted by Pierette herself, produces a concept of female sexual need beyond that of maternal instinct: "There was a savage, silent battle between us . . . a struggle of beasts. A female, a male, this is what we were, and this horror ended by a sort of rape to which I consented only when led by those primitive instincts that lie in all of us."[132] Pierette consciously decides to "save" herself by seducing a man and becoming pregnant. In this sense, she is a more sexually radical character than Frapié's Honorine, who willingly gives in to, but does not initiate, sex with Armand. But as in the Frapié trilogy, Pierette ultimately expiates her sexual activity by invoking the maternal instinct: "Finally, little by little, I succeeded in convincing myself that I was not without excuse, if I had need of one . . . the idea of devoting myself to my child gave me peace."[133] Still, at least one reviewer found this separation of maternal and sexual instincts unconvincing. Referring to Pierette's seduction of Henri, he argued that "it is the presence of pleasure in this affair that makes it so ticklish."[134] Another reviewer referred to the seduction sarcastically as "the completion of a ritual for which a degree in electrical engineering is perfectly unnecessary."[135]

Like Frapié's trilogy, again, *Pierette et Galaor* is characterized by the strange entanglement of a natalist sensibility with a fierce image of female independence. In contrast to the much older *mère Pincettes*, the pitiful "dry old maid" in the play, Pierette is able to obtain happiness separate from male love, financial support, and guidance. At the end of the play, Henri discovers that Pierette is pregnant and rushes back from Brazil to marry her. Yet she refuses even to see him and denies his rights as a father. Determined to raise the child on her own (something that her income as an engineer allows her to do), Pierette has already refused to marry another wealthy, older man, Brassol. "Indeed," she reasons, "some years ago, an old maid in my situation . . . would have been forced, so to speak, to consider your proposition as an unhoped-for opportunity. . . . But there was the war, Monsieur Brassol! There was the abolition of slavery . . . we've come to realize that we can walk all alone." [136] Although Pierette ultimately marries Henri, she does so for the sake of the child only: "What I've done, others will do," she explains, "they will be the volunteers for motherhood, volunteers who are necessary because the legitimate army refuses to do its duty." (Pierette's phrase here echoes Dr. Paul Carnot's call for "Volunteers for Motherhood" in 1920.)[137] Once again, natalist values serve as the legitimation for sexually unconventional behavior.

In Brieux's play, the single mother, like the modern woman, becomes a projection of postwar gender anxieties. The play's first lines, spoken by Brassol, frame Pierette's story within the larger context of the war's impact on sexual difference: "The women of France, having assisted their brothers and husbands during the war, now replace them in the work of the peace." [138] Pierette's profession—hydroelectric engineering—symbolizes the growing intrusion of women into traditionally masculine occupations. "One doesn't see that every day," comments Brassol. "But one will," responds Caroline LeGrand, Pierette's feminist friend.[139] The perception of women's new economic and emotional independence has a devastating impact on the male characters in the play. Brassol, whom Pierette refuses to marry, threatens to shut down the plant she manages, to take away her work and any motive she might have for not marrying him.[140] He eventually marries Caroline LeGrand instead, but remains timid and solicitous around her. Henri, the father of Pierette's child, is also a shrinking, impotent figure, no match at all for the powerful Pierette. One critic described Henri as "humiliated" around Pierette.[141] In love, yet too frightened to admit it, he remains unable to ask Pierette to marry him, forcing Brassol to plead his case. A depressed, alienated veteran who has exiled himself to Brazil,

Henri lurks in thresholds of doorways and on the very margins of the stage.[142] Pierette criticizes him as "without ambition," "skeptical," and the "enemy of effort."[143] When she refuses to marry Henri, his father defends him in a long speech on the veterans of the war:

> among the combattants, he is not the only one to have lost, with his blood, his energy and faith in life. . . . They were promised, at the end of their path of suffering, a France radiant with goodness and glory. . . . [Instead] they saw the scramble for money and pleasure. . . . They are reproached for shying away from marriage: [but] the attitude of women and young girls is not encouraging.[144]

Pierette et Galaor rehearses many familiar elements of discourse on the war—among them, male anxiety concerning the war's impact on gender roles, the veteran's bitterness upon his return, and the modern woman's indifference to the veteran's plight in her desire for independence.

Brieux also situates Brassol's and Henri's sexual anxiety in a larger landscape of changing gender relations. To give Pierette's story wider relevance, Brieux uses what could be considered almost a Greek chorus, one part male, one part female, whose attitudes serve as an indirect commentary on the play's action. The first chorus—three working, economically independent women—appears early on stage in traditional dauphinoise dress. The costumes, however, serve as a foil for these three women's attitudes, which are anything but traditional. They are happy to be working ("At least the money I've earned will be mine, and I'll no longer be forced to go wait for that scoundrel at the cabaret door"), and, if single, not at all in a hurry to get married: "There's no need!"[145] Their only regret is "that a husband is absolutely necessary to have a child!"[146] Ironically, in fictions such as Brieux's, the sexual behavior of men—not single mothers—is defined solely in terms of reproduction.[147] At the same time, the women are aware of the impact such attitudes have on their husbands: "The young men of today are humiliated if their wife earns more than them," says one, to which Caroline Legrand responds: "It compromises their authority . . . they can no longer claim to be protectors."[148]

The female chorus transforms Pierette's brassy economic and emotional independence into a more general phenomenon, evident in both single and married women. In the same way, the three-member male chorus, which appears later on in the play, generalizes Brassol's and Henri's fearful responses to such female autonomy, creating a virtual refrain of male anxiety. Escorted onstage by Brassol, the three men ask Pierette to fire their wives from their plant jobs because, according to them, it is "humiliating" to have a woman earn more than they did and because it is dispiriting to return home each night to an empty table.[149] For them, like Brassol, the hydroelectric plant, managed and run by women, is a symbol of their own rejection and uselessness as men. Again extremely timid and unable to speak for themselves, the three ask Brassol to argue their case for them, then slink offstage without a word when his anguished pleas fail to move Pierette.[150] Women are presented as capable of finding both professional and emotional fulfillment apart from men, who are therefore reduced to a merely reproductive role.[151] Inasmuch as these parallel choruses serve as two framing devices between which the play's action unfolds, the subject of Brieux's play ultimately becomes not *la femme seule* per se, but the growing economic independence of women and its effect on men. If we are to believe the critics, Brieux's audience understood the play in precisely these broader terms. The drama critic for the literary journal *La Revue des deux mondes* made this comment in relation to the play:

> It is true that the war has tangibly changed the social condition of women. Obliged to take care of herself and often to support her husband, the woman has become emancipated. She has entered new careers; a woman doctor, lawyer, engineer, painter, sculptor or composer is no longer a phenomenon. It is scarcely the exception to the rule.[152]

Brieux also deals with the theme of change more broadly through the mythic figure of Galaor, a symbol of tradition and constancy, who is counterposed to Pierette in the play's title. The myth of Galaor has been created by the Chalvet family, who own the hydroelectric plant, as a way of talking about the need for continuity from generation to generation. Although Galaor is sometimes presented as a neutral symbol of inherited wisdom, he is also described in more gendered terms, as the *"chef de famille* who never dies" and "the God of the home."[153] Pierette presents Galaor as her enemy: "I've spent my life struggling against him . . . a young girl who learns something else besides embroidery and piano! Galaor does not permit it! And my being an engineer! A young female engineer! Galaor smothers a scornful laugh!"[154] The conflict between Galaor and Pierette organizes tensions in the play between the competing discourses of natalism and feminism. Like many other postwar writers, Brieux attempted to negotiate the contradictory images of *la mère* and *la femme moderne.*[155] Like other postwar representations of women, Pierette moves back and forth between new and old, perhaps irreconcilable identities. Her marriage to Henri at the end of the play suggests a conservative reconciliation of these conflicts, one that appeases the gender anxieties raised earlier in the play. As the critic of *Mercure de France* argued, the ending was "a good old-fashioned trick devised to satisfy bourgeois morality."[156]

Marie Laparcerie's novel *La Femme d'aujourd'hui* (1924) provides a final example of how the image of *la mère seule* became the focus of debate concerning changing gender relations. Marie Laparcerie is best known as the creator in 1925 of the Tribune libre de femmes, an organization that served as a forum of debate for a variety of contemporary issues important to women. Hence her selection of single motherhood as a subject of importance shows once again how this issue pervaded public consciousness at mid-decade. Well-known within the feminist community, Laparcerie's novel provides a glimpse of how a prominent postwar woman viewed single motherhood.[157] As the story begins, the heroine Mathilde, the unmarried daughter of an impoverished middle-class family, is celebrating her twenty-eighth birthday by arguing with her mother over her future. Mathilde's mother wants her to remain at home with her older sister Armande, also unmarried. But Mathilde refuses, insisting that, unlike her sister, she wants to live a fulfilled, autonomous life: "Morality and men have compelled Armande to be chaste, something to which the woman of tomorrow will refuse to subject herself."[158] As in the Frapié trilogy, the meaning of "chastity" here is left ambiguous because of a slippage between maternal and sexual instincts. "Virginity is a state against nature," Mathilde argues, referring to "the free right to love and maternity."[159] Perhaps one could do without a husband, "but a child, maternity . . . what right does one have to deprive us of that?" Here Mathilde echoes the message of Brieux's female chorus: marriage is necessary for women for the sole reason that it secures them a child.

Throughout *La femme d'aujourd'hui,* marriage is presented as an anachronistic institution, withering away like Marx's state. Ignoring her mother's pleas, Mathilde leaves her bourgeois family and, with the help of a family friend, André, finds work as a secretary. Soon after, she begins dating a man whose marriage proposal she ultimately refuses because she believes she does not love him enough. At the same time, like Monique in *La Garçonne,* she decides to bear a child on her own and engages in a sexual relationship with Marc, a young Freudian intellectual, in order to become pregnant. Tales of other single mothers pervade the novel, including the story of one woman who, rather than marry, chooses "a handsome and robust man," becomes his mistress, has a son, and raises it without the father's help. Marc, too, is eventually made to feel, in his words, "like a stud."[160] After becoming pregnant, Mathilde all but dismisses him from her life, even though he offers to marry her. In a perfect conflation of natalist and feminist values, she defends her right to bear the child: "Here's the real crime: preventing women from blossoming, from completely realizing themselves, even forcing them to hide the proof of a courageous fertility."[161]

As a *mère seule,* Mathilde provokes a variety of gender anxieties: that women no longer need men emotionally or economically and that they plan to exploit them biologically, that women's real desire is to bear and raise children alone, and that marriage is a threatened institution. To some extent, the disruptive implications of her single motherhood are reined in and contained at the novel's end, when Mathilde, like Honorine and Pierette, marries after giving birth. Mathilde realizes not only that she loves her friend André, but that it was "because of him that she had achieved her dangerous dream of being an independent woman."[162] As in the case of Margueritte's *La Garçonne,* the domestic endings of these three fictions "cover over" disruptive changes in gender roles associated with the war. The image of *la mère seule* could both authorize discussion of the changing social organization of gender and then silence it through the heroine's ultimate embrace of conventional femininity.

But Mathilde, like Pierette, marries for the baby rather than for herself, a motive that, however praiseworthy from a maternal point of view, has the effect of humiliating the man involved. In the final moments of the novel, André is still anticipating the day when

> women, backed by legal reform as well as their own efforts, will no longer expect anything of the man except the gift of his heart or passion. Then they will hesitate before attaching themselves to a husband capable of destroying the happiness that could have been theirs alone, particularly when, like Mathilde, they have not waited for an official companion to satisfy their need for motherhood.[163]

Like *Pierette et Galaor* and the Frapié trilogy, *La Femme d'aujourd'hui* champions a brazen form of female autonomy and a vision of sexual relations sharply different from that of the natalists and their intentions for single motherhood.

La mère seule was a volatile mixture of two other competing images of female identity: *la femme moderne* and *la mère.* "Without a doubt," argued a review of Laparcerie's *La Femme d'aujourd'hui,* "Mathilde de Beauclinson is a modern woman, a woman neither frightened nor thwarted by anything."[164] The contradiction defining *la mère seule*—that she was idealized as a mother, yet was inevitably sexually promiscuous—resulted in a proliferation of subversive meanings around her. Because the number of illegitimate births fell rather than rose during the twenties, single motherhood does not seem to have come into vogue.[165] Neither did the idea of single motherhood receive widespread acceptance in postwar France, as the critics of the works by Brieux and Laparcerie demonstrate. "The 'volunteers for motherhood' do not always find 'volunteers for marriage' that can provide them with a happy dénoument," quipped the reviewer for *Mercure de France*. "And numerous cases of miserable single mothers," he continued, "testify to the fact that such matters are often less amusing than Monsieur Brieux pretends."[166] The significance of *la mère seule* in the postwar debate on women was ultimately cultural rather than demographic. Like *la femme seule,* the single mother provided an opportunity to discuss women's so-called new independence. In an era when gender identity was fluid and highly contested, a popular image like *la mère seule* had no fixed meaning. In the hands of novelists and dramatists, she was just as likely to mutate into a modern woman as to remain a natalist mother. Hence her presence in the postwar debate ultimately facilitated the creation of a sexual as well as a maternal identity for women outside marriage.

The call for single motherhood attempted to create an ideological continuity between past and present by imposing traditional values and sexual meanings on an unusual social situation created by the war. The enormous moral risks that such a campaign entailed for conservatives suggest the intensity of postwar natalist fears and the pressure to construct female identity in more traditional terms. If women had to be "modern," the logic went, at least they could be mothers. For certain members of the medical community, the notion of *la mère seule* served as a specific "solution" to the depopulation problem. As in the case of the surtax on single persons, the single mother became a complex cultural image that enjoyed considerable attention in postwar literature and in the press. Because she was necessary to many of those engaged in the debate, she was beyond the discursive control of any one group, such as natalists or Catholics. Her history as an image of female identity was therefore unpredictable, full of strange twists and mutations that both reproduced her contradictory nature and articulated her richness as a symbol of change.

7

"WE MUST FACILITATE THE TRANSITION TO THE NEW WORLD"

W HEN SIMONE DE BEAUVOIR WAS AN ADOLESCENT, her father took her aside and, in bitter tones, announced that she would have to work for a living because he could not assure her a dowry. Like many Frenchmen, Monsieur de Beauvoir had lost everything in the war. Although in Simone's words, he "thought it unseemly for a young lady to go in for higher education" and that "a woman's place was in the home," he could no longer assume that his daughter would marry. Despite their beliefs, de Beauvoir's parents gave her the financial and moral support necessary to enter the Sorbonne and pursue an advanced degree: only such an education would assure her livelihood as a single woman. For her part, de Beauvoir was ecstatic: "I infinitely preferred the prospect of working for a living to that of marriage; at least it offered some hope."[1]

Simone de Beauvoir's story illustrates how bourgeois parents had to abandon traditional expectations after the war and plan for their daughters' possible future as single women. The ruin of middle-class savings during the war, and the so-called surplus of single women because of high wartime mortality, forced parents to envision a future in which their daughters would live and work independently. Not surprisingly, then, calls to reform the educational system proliferated in the postwar period.[2] Both parents and educators feared that young girls were not being adequately trained for a profession by which they could earn a living either before marriage or throughout their lives. In 1924, for example, Minister of Public Education Leon Bérard made the fe-

183

male and male secondary school curriculums exactly alike so that for the first time, women achieved equal access to French higher education.[3] Bérard's reform resulted, in part, from an intense debate on women's education after the war—in professional journals and pamphlets, as well as surveys and articles in the bourgeois press.

This chapter examines two aspects of the educational debate: the call to give young girls vocational guidance so that they could choose an appropriate career and the demand to educate them in sexual matters so that they could venture safely outside the house unchaperoned. The first debate, concerning vocational guidance, began in the mid-twenties and gained momentum throughout the latter half of the decade. As a new field of expertise, vocational guidance developed rapidly after the war and signaled the rise in France of a growing twentieth-century preoccupation: the career. Beginning in 1922, the Ministry of Public Education instituted vocational guidance offices to work in cooperation with the schools and families of the student being counseled.[4] In an effort to meet the "special" needs of women in choosing a profession, Louise Mauvezin, the daughter of vocational guidance leader Fernand Mauvezin, pioneered women's vocational guidance during the mid-twenties. Mauvezin claimed that the growing necessity for women of all classes to work and the dizzying variety of professions opening up to them demanded a new expertise concerning women's labor and the professions. Her counselors promised to help young women choose a career by "scientifically" matching personal strengths with certain specified requirements of the profession.

The second debate, concerning women's sexual education, began in 1921, when Bérard circulated a questionnaire on the subject to all *maîtres* and professors in the primary and secondary system. The questionnaire asked whether sexual education should be taught in the state system, and if so, to whom and how.[5] It caused a heated debate in the press,[6] and in 1923, the Catholic Church felt called upon to officially condemn the institution of sex education in the schools.[7] Although sexual education for women remained a taboo subject before the war, in the postwar years, well-known doctors, sociologists, educators, and government officials debated it openly.[8] Because the Bérard questionnaire drew a negative response, the ministry chose not to institute sex education formally in the schools. Beginning in 1925, however, the Ministry of Hygiene, Social Assistance, and Prevention funded lectures on female physiology and reproduction given by Dr. Germaine Montreuil-Straus.[9] Like Mauvezin, Montreuil-Straus worked from within a larger organization, the Société française de prophylaxie sanitaire et morale (SFPSM).[10] In 1924, Montreuil-Straus created within the SFPSM the Comité d'éducation féminine (CEF), an organization devoted specifically to the sexual education of women.[11] After 1925, the state-funded CEF, composed of a small group of women doctors and Montreuil-Straus herself, gave public lectures to young girls of every class throughout France, published materials on female physiology and hygiene, and campaigned for the state institutionalization of sex education.[12]

The debates on vocational guidance and sexual education merit close attention because they show how the French dealt with the challenges posed by rapid change in the postwar era. The debates illuminate how the French confronted the shifting social organization of gender and attempted to reconstruct female identity on the horizon of a new generation. As Simone de Beauvoir's case demonstrates, the 1920s represented a period of transition in women's lives because of the war and changing socioeconomic circumstances. Bourgeois social observers of the twenties announced the passing of what they called *la vraie jeune fille*, who, like "a greenhouse flower," grew up sheltered within the home, her innocence and beauty protected, and who rarely ventured out, except under the watchful eye of her mother or governess.[13] According to Marcel Prévost, the main principle of prewar education had been that "the young girl should only rarely speak and move outside the mother's hearing and field of vision."[14] But in 1919, Edith Wharton, a long-time resident of Paris, observed that "the doing away of restrictions will be one of the few benefits of the war: the French young girl . . . will never again be the prisoner she has been in the past."[15] Simone de Beauvoir, for one, chafed against the restraints of her childhood during the twenties, then broke free—becoming a university student, a teacher, and a writer.

As the walls of the domestic greenhouse began to collapse, French parents and educators feared that young women were not prepared for the sexual freedoms awaiting them in the working world.[16] In a 1924 editorial, Paul Reboux, the editor-in-chief of *Paris-soir,* put it this way: "In an era of typists and car drivers, the innocence of a young girl is no longer imagined to be possible."[17] The same year, Marcel Prévost declared in *Nouvelles lettres à Françoise,* his classic postwar treatise on women's education, that "a type of young girl, the ignorant young girl, is gone. We might as well kiss her good-bye."[18] The new trend among young girls to venture beyond the greenhouse of domestic life motivated interest in women's sexual education. In the de Beauvoir household, for example, matters of sex remained shrouded in silence until Simone left Catholic school in order to prepare for the Sorbonne. With great embarrassment, her mother then volunteered to tell her the facts of life. The debate concerning women's sexual education reveals how the meaning of female sexuality was reconstructed after the war.

In the same way, the debate concerning vocational guidance offers an opportunity to explore how women's work was being redefined. The vision of *la femme seule* haunted postwar girls of all classes as they planned their educations and imagined their futures. By 1925, according to results of a survey on young girls' aspirations, the opinion prevailed that "the struggle will be hard" and that the young girl should be "sufficiently armed" to undertake it.[19] Even social conservatives such as Catholics and natalists affirmed grudgingly that the war's demographic and financial devastation was forcing many more women into the labor force. In his preface to a natalist career manual, Deputy Auguste Isaac (L'Entente Républicaine Démocratique, Rhône) evoked a biblical image: "This is the renewal of the sacred judgment: 'You will earn your bread by the sweat of your brow.'"[20] The postwar debate on women's education focused largely on *la femme seule* as a symbol of women's evolving economic and emotional needs. Proponents for both vocational guidance and sexual education used *la femme seule* as a way to justify educational reform. She represented a possible future for young women in which they would have to live and work on their own.

Both Louise Mauvezin and Germaine Montreuil-Straus represented new "experts" who emerged precisely when a set of social controls was giving way, as a result of the war and fears concerning female celibacy. Both reformers tried to recast women's education in terms of shifting economic and sexual relations for women. Both sought, through education, to discipline female behavior in new ways, that is, to "prepare" young women for a brave new world of work and love.[21] In their call for reform, both reconstructed the notion of female identity on which women's education was based. In particular, they redefined female domesticity in order to accommodate concerns about *la femme seule* and social change. But, like the natalists' promotion of single motherhood, the efforts of Mauvezin and Montreuil-Straus to recast female identity were rife with contradiction. The rationalizing methods of vocational guidance and sexual education were at odds with the tendency of both leaders to reassert asymmetrical notions of sexual difference, in particular, the primacy of a maternal, domestic role for women (and not for men). Their endeavors reveal the tentative, volatile compromises involved in the reconstruction of female identity after the war.

The debates on vocational and sexual education merit close attention for another reason: because they illustrate early attempts in the twenties to promulgate a new vision of social organization in the wake of the First World War. As the historians Jean-Jacques Becker and Serge Berstein have recently pointed out, the French began to realize by mid-decade that they could not bring back the world that the war had destroyed. Rather than languish in nostalgia for the past, technocrats on the right and the left began to conceive new ways to organize French society, the economy, and the state.[22] These men sought to respond to both the new demands of technology and the influence of American business trends such as Taylorism—the movement begun in American factories at the turn of the century that sought to "scientifically manage" the work process with the goal of promoting productive efficiency.[23] Their notion of a truly modernized economy was based on human engineering and the rational utilization of resources. According to Charles Maier, rationalizing tendencies were key to the process by which "security was apparently wrested from profound disorder and turbulence" in postwar France.[24] Technocrats and the republican state apparatus increasingly applied the standards of rationality, efficiency, and enhanced productivity not only to industry and the economy but also to other areas of French life—vocational choice, sexuality, health, and reproduction.[25] The debates on vocational guidance and sexual education demonstrate how this new rational, technocratic vision was applied to two areas of French life—work and sex—in the postwar years. Vocational guidance leaders aimed to "scientifically manage" career choice to achieve optimum efficiency and productivity; they shared many of the same methods and goals with such technocrats as Ernest Mercier. Similarly, Montreuil-Straus's campaign for sexual education, as part of the social hygiene movement, sought to rationalize sexual activity for productive and reproductive purposes.

The two debates reveal how the postwar French tried to reconcile the ongoing modernization of economic and social life with time-honored cultural traditions. As we shall see, gender roles—in particular, female domesticity—were key in this attempt to reconcile change with tradition. By reaffirming traditional domestic ideals, the French gave themselves a point of stability that, in turn, allowed them to come to terms with a world that threatened to become unrecognizable. The irony of postwar attempts to grapple with change lies precisely in the fact that the French reached back into an idealized past in order to bring a new future into being.

Any Job Is Equal to Another?

Louise Mauvezin developed vocational guidance during an era of women's work when the sexual division of labor was relatively fluid, at least compared with the prewar decades. During the first few years after the war, a spate of career manuals appeared, announcing a revolution in women's work, as indicated by both the number of single women working outside the home for the first time and the kinds of professions they were entering.[26] According to these manuals, the economic and social circumstances of the war had revealed the artificiality of the sexual division of labor by compelling large numbers of women to enter the labor force or unconventional occupations for the first time.[27] Hélène Bureau's 1921 *Guide pratique* began this way: "The question of female careers has become the focus of general attention in a way that is both singular and acute. If the number of women workers has grown, the number of the kinds of jobs they can fill has increased by the same proportion."[28] "The war has emancipated women, and the majority of professions that, up until now have been closed to them, are now opening" declared *Carrières féminines intellectuelles*, published in 1923.[29] These manuals gave long lists of schools recently opened to women in fields as diverse as commerce, electricity, public works, industrial design, electrical engineering, agronomy, transportation, and library science.[30] One editor, the feminist Suzanne Grinberg, expressed a common view when she declared that "the prejudice that commanded women to stay out of certain kinds of work—simply because they were women—is dead."[31]

Most historians agree that the postwar period was transitional in terms of women's work, but they consider the changes more qualitative than quantitative—having to do with the type of women working and the labor they performed rather than a numerical increase in the percentage of women in the work force.[32] When young bourgeois girls such as Simone de Beauvoir entered the working world, they moved into traditionally male professions—civil service, commerce (accounting, banking, retail sales), and the liberal professions.[33] Scores of well-known postwar novels and plays such as Marcel Prévost's *Les Don Juanes* (1922), Victor Margueritte's *Le Compagnon* (1923), and Eugène Brieux's *Pierette et Galaor* (1923) featured heroines who were lawyers, doctors, bankers, and engineers.[34] While the numbers of women entering untraditional fields were often extremely small, they enjoyed a disproportionate amount of visibility in French popular culture and in debates about women's work, so that the cultural impact of these new trends exceeded the actual numbers of women affected.[35]

The issue of visibility was also central to changes in working-class women's labor. Beginning in the first decades of the twentieth century, young working-class girls increasingly moved away from jobs in factories and live-in domestic service and to those in sales and clerical work in the growing tertiary sector.[36] By the postwar period there was much anguished talk in bourgeois circles about a crisis in domestic service, as deferential servants became increasingly difficult to find. In addition, as working-class girls moved out of the textile and clothing industries, engagement in domestic piecework, so long a tradition of women's labor, declined considerably.[37] Like their bourgeois counterparts, then, young working-class girls increasingly sought work away from home or apart from a household context. They entered a more visible, "public" sphere of activity in ever greater numbers, taking advantage of new professional opportunities and forms of leisure outside the home.[38]

It was during this transition in women's labor that Mauvezin developed women's vocational guidance. She and other vocational guidance leaders reacted to postwar changes in women's work in a contradictory way. On the one hand, they asserted that a woman should be able to choose any profession for which she was suited. They recommended career preparation for women of all classes and defined women's labor broadly—without attention to old boundaries based on the sexual division of labor. On the other hand, however, Mauvezin and other vocational theorists consistently reaffirmed the maternal role as woman's "true" destiny, to the exclusion of any other career. Influenced by the natalist movement, they aimed to preserve the sacredness of private, domestic life. Hence the twin concerns of work and motherhood formed two contradictory poles between which women's vocational guidance would develop.

At first glance, Mauvezin seemed to define women's labor as a necessary and dynamic field of activity. In developing career guidance for women during the mid-twenties, Mauvezin kept *la femme seule* uppermost in her mind. According to the bourgeois feminist paper *La Fronde*, the delegates of the First International Congress for Women's Vocational Education in 1926 were:

> unanimous in their recognition that the time is gone when a *demoiselle*
> of a good family had only to know how to embroider, sing, dance and
> play music; today a woman cannot brave life if she does not know a good
> occupation. She may not need to make use of it, but it the case arises,
> she ought to know how to earn her daily bread and all that comprises a
> woman's life.[39]

Mauvezin applied such an imperative even to the upper middle-class
girl whose financial future was secure, but for whom charitable works
alone "would not, in our day, satisfy an intelligent single woman's need
for activity."[40] Women's vocational guidance centers, instituted in the
twenties and thirties, were designed for young girls of all classes.[41]
Women's vocational counselors presented the young girl with a wide
open field of occupational choice in order to prepare her for her possibly celibate future.[42] Mauvezin's manual represented every conceiv-
able profession as accessible to women, as did the 1926 International
Congress of Women's Vocational Guidance. By making her program
broad-based in terms of both class and occupation, Louise Mauvezin
defined women's labor as free of sharp class or gender distinctions in
the meaning and type of work performed.

Mauvezin's notion of career choice for women answered a practical need: after all, unless there were many options for women, vocational guidance was not necessary. In addition, Mauvezin's concept of
women's career choice showed the influence of vocational guidance
theory, the parent field of expertise out of which her own ideology
grew. As it originally developed in France after 1922, vocational guidance was a government-sponsored program designed mostly for
working-class men who left school early to enter into industry or commerce.[43] Some years later, when Mauvezin set out to transform vocational theory into an ideology aimed at women (of both the middle and
working classes), she accepted vocational guidance's basic premise:
that access to professions should be determined scientifically and
based solely on personal aptitude.

The theoretical basis of vocational theory was that an occupation
need be a rational, scientific choice. The two founding fathers of vocational guidance, Julien Fontègne and Fernand Mauvezin, summarized
career choice in a mathematical formula: "Profession = Knowledge +
Aptitude × Force of Character."[44] Vocational guidance aimed to match
"scientifically" a man's skills, talents, and physical makeup with the occupation that best suited these. To this end, Fernand Mauvezin pioneered the development of "monographs" listing both the "moral qual-

ities" and the "indispensable aptitudes" needed for a specific occupation.[45] Major "characteristics and aptitudes" to be considered were size, strength, health, agility, attention and tenacity, observation and memory, artistic sense, bearing, and good manners.[46] The vocational guidance process began with a test to determine which of these characteristics the child or adolescent possessed; then the scientific matching began. Vocational guidance counselors claimed that they were replacing "pure chance" with "a scientific method" as the means of choosing a career.[47] Vocational leaders appropriated the metaphors and language of science, comparing vocational guidance to "a botanical classification" that "permits us to discover to which family belongs a particular plant, based on its characteristics."[48]

In this effort to systematize human choice for productive ends, vocational guidance leaders revealed their roots in Taylorism. Through such organizations as Redressement français, French technocrats like Ernest Mercier and Lucien Romier supported the application of Taylorist methods to French business and industry after the war. In response to advancing technology and the perceived need for modernization, such men sought to reform the values and practices of the business community, as well as the larger political and social structure. Their goals included the rational utilization of resources, a new faith in expertise and collaboration, and a centralized organizational structure directed by technicians like themselves in alliance with the state.[49] Similarly, vocational counselors applied Taylorist principles—efficiency, enhanced productivity, the elimination of waste—to issues of vocational choice. In 1919, *Le Temps* defined vocational guidance as "a methodical and rational utilization of the small number of men remaining to us in order to obtain from them the maximum output."[50] According to vocational leaders, the creation of a productive, efficient, and happy work force through the scientific organization of labor ensured the economic and moral regeneration of the nation.[51]

But the rationalizing methods of vocational guidance were at odds with Mauvezin's simultaneous need to reassert asymmetrical notions of sexual difference, in particular, the centrality of motherhood and domesticity to women's lives (but not men's). Mauvezin contradicted her own rationalized approach to career choice by declaring that "the destiny of the majority of women is to become wives and mothers," so that a woman's "duties as a mother of a family and her professional responsibilities are almost always incompatible."[52] At the 1926 congress, Fernand Philippart, the mayor of Bordeaux, reminded female delegates that motherhood, not wage-work, was woman's highest calling and that they really should not work outside the home.[53] It was on this principle that Mauvezin and other leaders limited the professions that a married mother could select. Vocational guidance, according to Mauvezin, "must take into account the principle that a woman's professional life is always a function of her familial role."[54] In a session on the medical profession at the first congress, for example, leaders stressed that family life would be impossible for a woman physician. "She will have to give up either the profession or the home, a dilemma that exists in many other professions, but perhaps not as acutely as it does so here."[55]

The same argument was put forth in sessions on other traditionally male professions, such as law and journalism; conversely, such traditionally female professions as social careers were praised, because they were said to prepare women for their maternal role.[56] For working-class families, guidance leaders supported *allocations familiales*, or family wage subsidies, given to the husband so that his wife could stay at home.[57] If a working-class wife was forced to work, Mauvezin encouraged her to do so within the household context, such as in piecework or domestic service, so that she could also watch over her children. In other words, she encouraged working-class girls to enter precisely those occupations from which they were increasingly moving away.[58]

Hence Mauvezin and her colleagues defined work both broadly and in a highly restrictive way. Why did they respond to postwar changes in women's work in so contradictory a manner? Implicit in how women's vocational guidance experts conceived work were contradictions rooted mostly in the origins of the discipline itself, from within the larger vocational movement. A scientific approach to vocational choice raised potential problems for Mauvezin because it ignored the large role class and gender played in determining a career. Was any job really "equal to another," as vocational guidance counselors claimed?[59] Assigning class and gender-neutral concepts such as "aptitude" and "force of character" as prerequisites for various careers concealed the large discrepancies in access, compensation, and status among these careers. If access to professions should be determined solely on the basis of personal aptitude and interest, it followed logically that no woman should be closed out of a career purely on the basis of sex.

The rationalizing logic of vocational guidance, necessary to establish the discipline's scientific credibility, contradicted the ideological basis of the traditional division of labor. Nineteenth- and early twentieth-century political economists and reformers had debated the meaning of women's work outside the home by framing an opposition between wage-earning and maternity, work and motherhood. This conflict, the focus of exhaustive discussion, was written into the sexual division of labor itself as a naturalized "fact" that upheld a whole series of hierarchies in wage and labor distribution.[60] Gender differences had come to organize divisions of labor, responsibility, and pay when several other kinds of differences—among them, labor markets, economic fluctuations, the·relation of supply and demand—could have served equally well. The central justification for such a division of labor was that male and female workers brought varying levels of commitment to the labor force. For men, this commitment was lifelong; for women, it must be interrupted by childbirth and child rearing.[61] In this way, the domestic ideal for women structured the division of labor.

By asserting that a career was a central human choice that should be rationally arrived at without attention to socioeconomic factors, vocational guidance experts challenged the assumption on which the sexual division of labor was based: that women have a less consistent commitment to wage labor because they bear children. If a woman's commitment to her career was as important as her reproductive, domestic role, could hierarchies in wage and labor distribution continue to be justified? At stake in vocational guidance was not only the social organization of labor but also the sexual meanings that supported that organization—in other words, issues of identity and power. As we have seen, during the postwar period both notions of female identity and the sexual division of labor were particularly volatile and fluid. In this context, the expertise that Louise Mauvezin tried to arrogate to herself became the power to reconstruct a notion of womanhood as well as a set of social relations in the process of transition. As the vocational leader Julien Fontègne put it, women's vocational guidance necessitated "a study of physical, physiological and psychical differences between the sexes, economic and social considerations concerning woman's role in modern life."[62]

In developing women's vocational theory, then, Mauvezin had to avoid undermining the traditional division of labor. She did so by focusing on the problem of *la femme seule* and.by affirming women's domestic, maternal role as primary. By concentrating her vocational efforts on *la femme seule,* who envisioned a future of celibacy rather than marriage and motherhood, Mauvezin was able both to promote career choices for women and to reaffirm reproduction as the primary focus of female identity. "The problem of making a living arises for a great number of women. Many of them will not marry," she argued in

1925, "It is prudent that a majority of young girls consider the possibility of celibacy and train for a position [*se créent une situation*]."[63] The single woman became a particular target of women's vocational guidance not only because her numbers were supposedly legion after the war but also because her professional identity was unproblematic relative to the dictates of domestic morality. By focusing on *la femme seule*, Mauvezin could reaffirm this morality, as well as the opposition between wage-work and motherhood that justified the traditional division of labor. Mauvezin presented the conflict between work and motherhood as a novel reality of the postwar age, thus ignoring its long history as a justification for the sexual division of labor.

In fact, the sexual division of labor was never truly "written out" of the vocational guidance theory that Mauvezin drew on in her own movement. While vocational leaders advanced sex-neutral categories such as "aptitude" in the determination of a vocation, they nevertheless reaffirmed the sexual division of labor in two ways. First, in his 1922 vocational manual, Fernand Mauvezin differentiated "occupations exclusively for women," "occupations accessible to women," and "occupations exclusively for men."[64] This gender categorization was based on a historically conceived notion of women's work as centering primarily in the needle trades (*lingère, couturière, modiste, brodeuse*) and domestic service (*femme de chambre*).[65] Second, Mauvezin's "monographs" of these occupations themselves advanced highly traditional notions of sexual difference. This bias is proven by a cross-gender comparison of the relative importance of the same set of aptitudes in professions designated "exclusive to men" or "exclusive to women"(fig. 23).[66] Not surprisingly, professions considered "exclusive to men" required strong physical qualities such as size, strength, and health. Also requisite for exclusively male occupations, however, were such "moral" qualities as mental agility and sang-froid—the ability to react to and control one's own environment and emotivity. These qualities preserved a conventional image of the male as rational, disciplined, and self-assured, fully in control of his faculties and environment. By contrast, professions either exclusive or accessible to women demanded less physical strength, but greater attentiveness, patience, good behavior and manners, orderliness, and care. Besides being stereotypically feminine attributes, these moral qualities sustained the popular image of woman as naturally fit for the unstimulating, repetitive, and highly fatiguing work associated with low-paying, low-prestige jobs.

The monographs effectively masked large discrepancies in skill, status, and pay between occupations, thereby reaffirming a traditional sexual division of labor under the guise of a seemingly neutral, scientific screening process. They did so precisely at a time when this division of labor was being critically challenged. Such a conservative effort may have been conscious on the part of vocational guidance leaders. In 1920, Jules Amar, whose research on women's work for the Académie des sciences formed a primary basis for vocational guidance theory, scorned "the permanent *remplaçantes,* pushed into degrading roles by the rhetoricians of the boulevard or the ignoramuses for equality." Unlike many others, Amar insisted that "the bourgeois style of life will not be modified." Although "its occupations will have been temporarily disrupted and transformed, they will become once again what they once were."[67] Similarly, in January 1922, the vocational leader Julien Fontègne demanded "a certain stabilization—one could even say a certain division of labor—that limits the activity of each occupation." In other words, Fontègne proposed "a rational organization of women's vocational guidance" that would establish "as clearly as possible" which professions would be exclusively feminine, which would be exclusively masculine, and which could be exercised by both sexes.[68]

Fontègne's desire to reestablish a clear sexual division of labor becomes particularly significant given the French state's institution of vocational guidance in 1922. Vocational guidance represented an important effort to limit a greatly expanded field of female occupational choice in a period when the sexual division of labor was relatively fluid.[69] But the ideology of women's vocational guidance developed by Mauvezin in 1925 yielded more than a reassertion of bourgeois domesticity or a prewar division of labor. The irony of attempts at educational reform such as vocational guidance lies in the way their very conservatism enabled a much more radical project. When Mauvezin defined career choice in terms of the primacy of woman's domestic role, she diverted attention away from the fact that she was also producing a radical and threatening image of female identity: the young *femme seule* who must choose, prepare for, and find fulfillment in an occupation. By giving priority to woman's domestic responsibilities, women's vocational guidance counselors reassured parents or others fearful that their daughters might "forget themselves" in their careers. In this way, they defused as well as diffused awareness that marriage was no longer the only career for middle-class women. In order to appear less threatening (and therefore in order to be pursued), female economic independence had to be represented in terms of a "last resort" to be undertaken when all other domestic, maternal avenues had been closed. The "fear" of female celibacy, in turn, provided young girls with a justification for pursuing a career. Although Simone de Beauvoir's father saw her career as a purely pragmatic "last resort," she used it to gain full economic and emotional autonomy.

Reasserting the primacy of motherhood in women's lives allowed vocational guidance leaders to rationalize the labor force without disrupting those notions of sexual difference that justified age-old hierarchies in wage and labor distribution. But the gender-neutral notion implicit in vocational theory—of occupational choice as a field bounded only by aptitude—was not wholly subverted by Mauvezin's attempts to accommodate woman's reproductive role. As stated in *La Fronde*, one of the major preoccupations of vocational guidance was "to discover in good time a young girl's abilities in order to put her on the path that will provide her with every satisfaction."[70] Put bluntly, the message of vocational guidance was that while a woman's gender became much more difficult to escape when she married (and her reproductive "aptitude" took first priority), a young single girl was free to follow her professional interests. Although woman's maternal role remained primary, the image of *la femme seule* persisted in reopening the horizon of female identity.

Science Anesthetizes What It Touches?

Like Louise Mauvezin, Dr. Germaine Montreuil-Straus had the image of *la femme seule* uppermost in her mind when she pioneered women's sexual education in the early twenties. In the preface to her classic treatise on the subject, *Avant la maternité,* her colleague and supporter Alfred Siredy wrote:

> In privileged families, where the young girl lives constantly under the surveillance of her mother and seems sheltered from every adventure, the value of sexual education is less obvious. But don't the sad examples that each of us witnessed during the war show that the dangers remain the same for all social classes? Even the most elevated morality, the most austere education centered on family traditions and religious enlightenment, has not been sufficient to protect young girls against sexual peril. And all these victims expressed the same complaint, the same regret: "If only I had known," they said![71]

At the end of the twenties, when Montreuil-Straus explained why she formed her Comité d'éducation féminine, she referred to the single young woman of the postwar period who could "no longer be kept under strict guard in an artificial atmosphere of ignorance," who was "called to go out alone and work outside the home" and hence "exposed to the dangers and seductions of the street." Like Siredy, Montreuil-Straus warned that the dangers of sexual ignorance applied "not only to young girls of working-class backgrounds, but to women of all social classes."[72]

In her call for reform, Montreuil-Straus, like Louise Mauvezin, used the image of *la femme seule* to raise awareness that the notions of female identity shaping women's education needed reconstruction. Montreuil-Straus's efforts to do this, like those of Mauvezin, were riddled with contradictions. On the one hand, she scandalized Catholic educators by taking a secular, scientific approach to sexual matters and by proclaiming the existence of a healthy, female sexual instinct. On the other hand, Montreuil-Straus reinforced as much as she dismissed Catholic morality, by defining sexual activity as acceptable only within a married, reproductive context.

The contradictions in Montreuil-Straus's theory of women's sexual education can be explained in two ways. First, they reflect her conflicting agenda in developing sexual education for women—her desire to establish professional credibility for her relatively new area of expertise while not offending delicate sensibilities on the matter of sex. Second, the contradictions in the way Montreuil-Straus conceptualized women's sexual education were rooted in the origins of the discipline itself—in social hygiene. Montreuil-Straus's vision of women's sexual education reflected her participation in the social hygiene movement, a group of doctors and legislators who sought to manage populations through rational means in order to eliminate disease, degeneration, and unhealthy children.[73] Like Mauvezin, Montreuil-Straus developed women's sexual education by applying a well-established ideology to the particular case of women. Dr. Alfred Fournier, a well-known expert on syphilis, had founded the Société française de prophylaxie sanitaire et morale several decades earlier in order to wage battle against venereal disease.[74] Sex education had already become an important part of the antivenereal struggle of that organization, composed of prominent bourgeois doctors, dentists, and pharmacists. But, much like vocational guidance, such education was almost exclusively aimed at young boys and men.[75] The SFPSM's notions of sexual education raised problems for Montreuil-Straus as she tried to apply them to the particular case of women. As was the case with vocational guidance, certain elements of the SFPSM's ideology threatened to undermine conventional notions of sexual difference—in this case, the sexual double standard rather than the sexual division of labor. Like the social hygienist, then, Montreuil-Straus took a rational, scientific approach to sexual matters. But at the same time, she reasserted conventional bourgeois morality, in effect upholding the sexual double standard.

Montreuil-Straus's task was to convince the French public and particularly the French government that an area of expertise that she alone possessed was of great utility to them. The bourgeois French family did not consider sex a topic of conversation for "respectable" girls and shrouded it in silence. Marcel Prévost expressed a common view when he argued that to speak about sex to a young girl was to strip her of innocence. Even the knowledge of sex, it was believed, destroyed a young girl's modesty. As a result of these prejudices, the French woman often came to marriage spectacularly ignorant of sex. One story concerned a turn-of-the-century bride who, on her wedding night, was baffled when her husband apologized for being unable to go beyond a first embrace. Her bewilderment continued the next day as he went off to see a doctor. "Could she already be pregnant?" she wondered.[76]

Montreuil-Straus's first attempts to lecture on female sexuality show she was fighting an uphill battle for legitimacy. Once after traveling by train to a small village in northern France in order to give a lecture, she arrived to find two young girls on the platform completely "terror-stricken" at the prospect of a talk on sexual matters. Their local hygiene organization had requested the lecture, but had somehow misinterpreted Montreuil-Straus's true purpose. Having misunderstood the precise contents of the lecture, the two girls were ready either to send Montreuil-Straus back to Paris or resign from the organization rather than "scandalize" their friends. Taking pity on the *"pauvres petites,"* Montreuil-Straus quickly devised a lecture that focused on infant mortality and in which female physiology was barely mentioned.[77] On another occasion, Montreuil-Straus arrived to discover that the title of her lecture, "Maternity and the Venereal Peril," had been omitted from the invitation cards. "You must understand," explained the organizers when she inquired into the matter, "our women have certain prejudices. We didn't want to offend them.[78]

"Offending" people was precisely what the CEF lecturers set out to avoid. They distributed a survey to seventeen écoles normales that they had visited, asking such questions as "Were your young girls offended?" and "Are you of the opinion that these talks have a demoralizing, or, on the contrary, a beneficial effect, in that they encourage a healthy and open discussion of questions formerly considered indecent and shameful?"[79] The two questions show how, in establishing their professional legitimacy as educators on sex, Montreuil-Straus and her colleagues fought the old prejudice that sexual knowledge would have "a demoralizing influence" on a young girl. In his preface to Montreuil-Straus's *Avant la maternité*, Alfred Siredy assured his young female readers that the author could instruct them in matters of sex "without offending their modesty, without awakening in them unhealthy thoughts."[80] Montreuil-Straus fought this prejudice by redefining the relationship between sexual innocence and knowledge: "at one time it was thought that ignorance was synonymous with purity. Experience teaches us, however, that ignorance, especially in sexual matters, can lead to all kinds of errors, sorrow and moral decay."[81] In this way, a young girl's purity became a function of knowledge rather than innocence.[82] The logo of the CEF featured a female St. George slaying (and thus saving) the blindfolded maiden of ignorance (see fig. 24). Hence the CEF's social mission drew on Enlightenment ideals of education. Montreuil-Straus conceived of sexual knowledge as an instrument of power that had been denied women and that they deserved to use for their own safety and happiness.[83]

While Montreuil-Straus had to proceed cautiously in order not to affront her audience, she also had to proclaim the existence of a healthy, female sexual instinct in order to justify her pedagogical project. Female sexual impulses, she argued, began in puberty, a phase she described as a "state of mental disequilibrium . . . engendered by the birth of a new instinct: the reproductive or sexual instinct. The blossoming of this instinct, more than any other, is capable of either ennobling or degrading life—hence, it ought to be recognized, surveyed and directed."[84] Montreuil-Straus's naming of a powerful and potentially ennobling female sexual instinct justified her own professional expertise as necessary to "direct" and "survey" it. Her notion of female sexuality suggests the influence of sexologists such as Freud and Ellis, whose work was just beginning to be translated into French.[85] Its direct genealogical roots, however, lie in social hygiene ideology.[86]

Montreuil-Straus expressed the social hygienist's utopian vision of society as highly rationalized, productive, and efficient. As was the case with vocational choice, the teaching of sex—once left to street whispers or the awkward confession of parents—had been an haphazard, unregulated, family affair. Social hygienists considered this method an inefficient social risk; sexual education required the intervention of the expert and the state. "The teaching of sexual hygiene to young girls," as Montreuil-Straus defined it in 1923, was "nothing but a scientific and rational preparation for marriage and maternity for the purpose of the preservation of the race."[87] She aimed for "a better social and legal organization of a function that is certainly of utmost importance to the State, because it assures the continuity of the race."[88]

In arguing for state-institutionalized sex education, social hygienists such as Montreuil-Straus consciously defined their position over and against that of the Catholic moralists. From the late nineteenth century onward, the social hygiene movement had fought a battle against the priest and his traditional power in the French family. Catholic moralists based sexual education on one central idea: "between the two elements that constitute a human being, between the flesh and the spirit, a struggle is inevitable, and in this struggle, the spirit must assure itself of victory."[89] Sexual education, Catholics believed, was safe only in the hands of parents and priests, and should be as vague as possible for fear that the young girl "will be offended, wounded in one of her noble qualities, modesty." While they acknowledged that "even for young girls, ignorance is more and more the exception," Catholics aimed to educate them strictly to encourage "purity" or self-control.[90]

Montréuil-Straus and her colleagues were anxious not to antagonize more socially conservative audiences, yet they conceived sexual education in opposition to these Catholic moralists.[91] The secular, scientific posture of social hygiene was congruent with the republican, anticlerical educational system where they sought access.[92] If the Catholics understood the aim of sexual education to be purity, Montreuil-Straus defined this goal as biological and social health. Although she agreed that sex education "must certainly lead to a higher morality," she also insisted that it "be above all based on the scientific study of normal phenomena, the anatomy and physiology of genital apparatus and the reproductive function, particularly in the woman."[93] If the Catholics required that the teaching of sex be a vague and moralistic enterprise, Montreuil-Straus demanded that it should be "honest," "open," "neutral," and "scientific." While Catholic moralists were convinced that such an education would "arm vice with scientific arguments," Montreuil-Straus and other social hygienists demonstrated a strong faith in the morally cleansing properties of science.[94] Defining their expertise in scientific, value-free terms would, they hoped, sterilize the potential seaminess of their subject matter.[95] "In every instance that it is treated scientifically, such an education will awaken neither romantic nor sensual images," assured Montreuil-Straus in 1922. She went on to quote a popular educator: "Science anesthesizes what it touches."[96]

But, as in the case of Mauvezin, the rationalizing tendencies in social hygiene also posed problems for Montreuil-Straus, as she attempted to apply the SFPSM's educational mission to the case of women. Once having created a female sexual instinct, Montreuil-Straus had to be careful not to lose control of it. In her own words, did it not demand to be not only recognized but also "surveyed" and "directed"? In particular, the positing of a healthy and ennobling female sexual instinct could validate women's sexual need or pleasure as an end in itself. Such a validation would challenge the sexual double standard that lay at the heart of the SFPSM's ideology of sex, their belief in the fundamental asexuality of the middle-class woman. In creating a philosophy of women's sexual education, Montreuil-Straus had to come to terms with the complex configuration of notions concerning sexual identity that had grounded the SFPSM's prewar antivenereal policies. In grappling with these notions, Montreuil-Straus avoided undermining the sexual double standard so fundamental to the SFPSM's ideology of sex, much as Mauvezin avoided threatening the sexual division of labor. Both women resolved the conflict in the same way: by privileging domestic, maternal ideals.

While the prewar SFPSM advocated premarital continence for both men and women, they subscribed to a sexual double standard: they created a notion of male sexual desire, but saw at least middle-class women as asexual. As Alain Corbin has argued, SFPSM antivenereal propaganda at the turn of the century represented a response to various forces—the extension of divorce and prostitution, the diffusion of neo-Malthusian ideas such as "free love," changing notions of continence—that decreased sexual inhibitions among young bourgeois men, and encouraged increased pre- and extramarital activity. In this way, male sexual desire comprised the "problem" to be solved; sexual, antivenereal education attempted to militate against increasing male sexual promiscuity.[97] Social hygiene propaganda continued in much the same vein after the war. For example, Dr. Paul Good, whose popular hygiene manual *Hygiène et morale* went through several editions during the twenties, urged young men not to turn to prostitutes in order to "satisfy their bad desires" while waiting to marry.[98] "No matter what moral armature an adolescent may be equipped with," warned the social hygienist Justin Sicard de Plauzoles in 1923, "he will always have to struggle against the currents of instinct and to endure the gusts of passion."[99] Even within their own ranks, social hygienists fought the fear that warning young men against such "appetites" would put the idea of debauchery into their heads.[100] In this way, they acknowledged their own power to construct as well as direct male sexual desire.

In defining female sexual identity, the prewar SFPSM had split along class lines. In the words of one SFPSM member in 1912, the bourgeoise was "above sexual preoccupations" and possessed "virginity of both body and soul."[101] When married middle-class women contracted syphilis, doctors such as Fournier assumed their sexual innocence and instead shifted the responsibility for contamination onto their husbands.[102] But while the members of the prewar SFPSM considered the middle-class woman asexual, they completely sexualized the working-class woman. On those rare occasions when they discussed the possibility of women's sexual education, they limited their attention to the young, single working-class *femme isolée,* who symbolized a world of social disorder and turbulent sexuality.[103] For example, the social hygienist Madame Leroy-Allais asserted in 1912 that a young working girl's protection posed a pressing need because, living as she did in filthy, lightless spaces, she was easily seduced and corrupted: "she is the object of so many diverse temptations that it is miraculous she can ever resist them."[104]

For two reasons, this dual image of female sexual identity—virtuous bourgeoise or sexualized *femme isolée*—was untenable in Montreuil-Straus's own postwar ideology of women's sexual education. First, as we have seen, Montreuil-Straus justified her project on the grounds that the chaste bourgeois ideal of adolescence was no longer feasible in postwar socioeconomic conditions. Her refusal to uphold the image of the virtuous young girl sheltered within the home in turn problematized that of the disorderly *femme isolée,* inasmuch as these two images had supported each other in a larger vision of social organization. In nineteenth-century social hygiene discourse, the public world became the realm of the disorderly Other: this image hinged on the ideological presence of an ordered, domestic, private world. As this notion of domestic order eroded, social hygienists could no longer sustain the existence of a marginal, chaotic, and immoral world beyond.[105]

Second, Montreuil-Straus wanted to include bourgeois girls in her program of education. She and her colleagues delivered lectures on sexual education to a wide variety of organizations and institutions, from women workers within the unions to teachers at the écoles normales.[106] Hence, she had to dissociate herself from any image of female identity that was coded as working-class. To link to sexual education such images of women as *la femme isolée* might alienate a middle-class audience. Just as Montreuil-Straus had given up the middle-class ideal of female sexual purity, so was she obliged to avoid the working-class image of the sexualized, disorderly woman.[107] She effaced traditionally sharp class distinctions, a signal, it could be argued, of the decline of bourgeois paternalist methods of reform. Because she tried to move beyond the Manichean conceptual universe of the prewar SFPSM, Montreuil-Straus took a more preventive approach to hygiene, one that stressed the engineering of the healthy body rather than the threat of the sick one.[108]

For these reasons, Montreuil-Straus rejected the SFPSM's dual image of female sexual identity. She also seemed ill at ease with the social hygienist's rationalized notion of sexuality—as a healthy and ennobling biological instinct—as much as she was committed to it in other ways. In *Avant la maternité,* she admitted that "although this volume has an exclusively scientific character," the reproductive function could not be studied in the same way as the digestive or circulatory systems: "because linked to the sexual instinct—and to the attraction that creatures of different sexes exercise on each other—is an entire world of feeling that constitutes love's foundation, and the fact of bringing a child into the world has a moral and social importance that goes far beyond that of a simple physiological fact."[109] Although Montreuil-Straus defined female sexuality as ennobling, she could not present it as an imperious and blind force (as the SFPSM did for boys), without undermining the sexual double standard. Speaking from the heart of the conservative medical community, excruciatingly conscious of the moral implications of her teaching, Montreuil-Straus had to validate her pedagogical project without upsetting conventional notions of female sexual innocence.

Like Mauvezin, Montreuil-Straus defused the explosive potential of the rational precepts grounding her discipline by reaffirming the primacy of the maternal role. In a perfect conflation of sexual and reproductive identities, Montreuil-Straus summarized "normal sexual life" in these words: "love, union, fatherhood, motherhood and family."[110] She conceived the object of her pedagogical project as the future mother: "in order to be prepared for her role as mother and wife, the young girl should know the composition of her body, the organs of maternity, their normal functioning . . . the precautions that she must take in order to stay healthy and bear healthy children." [111] In *Avant la maternité*, she described female genitals as "the group of organs destined to carry out the maternal function" and "the organs of motherhood, still called genital organs or female sexual organs." [112] She limited sexual expression to a married, reproductive context: "any union in which motherhood intervenes as a surprise, an accident, or even, let us say the word, a catastrophe, not only represents an error against social and moral laws, but also denotes a false understanding of happiness and the profound meaning of life." [113] Montreuil-Straus saw no contradiction between the traditional moral tone of these statements and her description of the volume as having a rational, medical, and scientific character. Despite all attempts to distance herself from the Catholic moralists, Montreuil-Straus reaffirmed a traditional Catholic morality of sex as strictly reproductive.

Montreuil-Straus had to change the rationale of prewar sex education in order not to project an image of single women as promiscuous. In the prewar era, sex education had been conceived as a form of prevention against venereal disease and as a project of dissuasion against sexual promiscuity among single young men, particularly in the military. Montreuil-Straus accepted current medical opinion that the male was the principal agent of contamination for the family in 95 percent of all venereal cases, so that justifying sex education for women on these grounds seemed foolish. In 1923, she dismissed the traditional strategy of the SFPSM on these terms: "it may be judged superfluous and even injurious to give adolescent girls lectures on chastity before marriage and on the harmlessness of abstinence, when for them, these have already been the rules of a natural morality for centuries." [114] By defining normative female sexuality as conjugal and reproductive, Montreuil-Straus could validate her project without producing a notion of female sexual desire. Like her predecessors in the SFPSM, Montreuil-Straus campaigned for the protection of the single woman from the dangers of ignorance in sexual matters. But by these dangers, she meant not sexual seduction or temptation, as had the prewar SFPSM, but unforeseen sterility, miscarriages, and other threats to future motherhood. [115] In this way, Montreuil-Straus justified sex education without disrupting the ideology of the sexual double standard. She did so precisely at a time when social and sexual constraints were breaking down, thanks to the increasing numbers of women of all classes working outside the household context. Under the liberal guise of "enlightening" women concerning sexual matters, the CEF sought to discipline sexual behavior of all kinds, "rescuing" sex from the fumbles and whispers of the streets and confining it to the clean rigidities of the conjugal bed.

Compared to notions of female sexuality being formulated by Freudian psychologists and sexologists in Great Britain and America Montreuil-Straus's reproductive sexual morality appears dramatically more conservative.[116] But her affirmation of a Catholic sexual morality diverted attention from the fact that she also produced a notion of female sexuality that was radical and new.[117] "It is natural, it is just," she argued, "that young girls want to know the joys of love and motherhood."[118] A young *normalienne* in one of the seventeen *écoles normales* that Montreuil-Straus surveyed responded, "It is a very natural thing to want to be able to taste one day all the happiness and the joys of the wife and mother."[119] By conceiving female sexuality in strictly reproductive terms, Montreuil-Straus seemed to be merely reinforcing traditional morality, but in fact she was also talking about sex in relatively subversive terms. The affirmation of female sexuality as reproductive and domestic enabled the production of a female sexual identity that was healthy and natural. Although Montreuil-Straus isolated the married woman as alone able to enjoy a sexual identity, one wonders whether such notions of female identity could remain so cleanly categorized. Their very contradictions imply a possibility of subverting boundaries, promising new identities for women, whether married or single.

By structuring her efforts in terms of the "neutral" transmission of a "transparent" body of knowledge, Montreuil-Straus also obscured the profound way in which she challenged patriarchal medical ethics. As Jill Harsin has shown, the prewar sexual ignorance of middle-class women, in particular, left them at great risk. They could contract syphilis and other venereal diseases from their husbands without even knowing it. The wife was then not likely to be treated properly because the husband guarded the secret of his infidelity at all costs, aided and abetted by the family doctor. Even Dr. Fournier of the SFPSM, a crusader for venereal education in other ways, adhered to a policy of confidentiality that left women at risk.[120] Montreuil-Straus explicitly attacked this willful neglect on the part of doctors and urged women to insist on venereal testing for their fiancés before marriage (see fig. 25).[121] That Montreuil-Straus was able to carry out this challenge to medical ethics from within Fournier's SFPSM itself testifies to how her conservative approach to sexual education enabled a radical project.[122]

Our Most Sanctified Customs Are Endangered

The education given young French girls such as Simone de Beauvoir after the war was based on contradictory principles. In short, it was marked with the ambivalence of a transitional era. Both vocational and sexual education reformers responded to the call for a redefinition in women's education during a period in which the old constraints of domestic morality seemed outdated. Using the image of *la femme seule* to signal change in women's lives, both movements attempted to reconstruct the notions of female identity that had shaped women's education. By exploiting bourgeois liberal notions of science and education, both sought to reimpose social controls that would discipline female behavior in conventional ways. While Mauvezin and Montreuil-Straus acknowledged the new socioeconomic circumstances of the postwar era, they also ultimately privileged a domestic, maternal role for women. But in both cases, *la mère de famille* served as a figure of stability that made acceptable other changes in female identity. Mauvezin promoted the image of a single woman who lives, works, and finds self-fulfillment outside a domestic context; Montreuil defined female sexuality as a healthy biological instinct. In this sense, both vocational guidance and sexual education represented attempts not to reassert conventional sexual meanings, but to negotiate a conflict between new and old worlds.

As educational reforms that arose as part of a changing social landscape, women's vocational guidance and sexual education bore a striking resemblance to each other. Both originated in larger male-dominated movements that had existed for some time in embryonic form, then achieved a new level of visibility immediately after the war. Both movements were pioneered by women who themselves modeled working careers outside the home, then helped to carry out a conservative project. Mauvezin's vocational guidance movement reaffirmed the traditional sexual division of labor in a period when it was relatively fluid. In the same way, Montreuil-Straus's social hygiene movement reinforced heterosexual, conjugal morality and the double standard during an era when the ideas of Freud and Havelock Ellis were beginning to be known in France. Women's vocational guidance and sexual education were highly sophisticated techniques of social management, part of a larger tendency in French society and the French economy to establish rationalized, corporatist bonds between public and private sectors and dissolve old divisions between family and state.[123] Such bonds were established through bureaucratically controlled, cooperative relations among state-funded "experts," families, and individual children.[124] These new experts sought to rationalize relations of work and sex in order to achieve maximum social efficiency. Vocational guidance counselors aimed for productive efficiency—the rational organization of a diminished labor force and a "chaotic" postwar economy. Social hygienists sought reproductive efficiency—a population capable of conceiving large numbers of healthy children, and thus remedying depopulation.

Our examination of educational reform efforts suggests that a profound transformation in social organization was taking place in the postwar years. Social hygiene, vocational education, and the scientific organization of labor represented various dimensions of the same vision of human engineering that was on the rise in postwar France. While this rationalizing trend had its roots in the late nineteenth century, it accelerated enormously during the twenties, as medical personnel and other experts, with the help of the state apparatus, managed the human body as a machine for optimum (re)productivity.[125] The dramatic rise in social hygiene efforts after the war illustrates this acceleration process.[126] Under the guidance of the first Ministry of Hygiene, Social Assistance, and Prevention created in 1920, a variety of new educational, social hygiene, and natalist programs were carried out, among them, *puériculture* and state-funded maternity care.[127] After the war, *puériculture,* or child-care education, achieved a new, intense level of popularity in the French medical body; in 1923 it became a mandatory subject for all schoolgirls. The leader of the *puériculture* movement, Adolphe Pinard, insisted that women needed detailed instruction and constant medical surveillance in order to raise their children correctly.[128]

The sudden postwar popularity of such movements as *puériculture* and sexual education demonstrate that postwar rationalizing trends extended far beyond the industrial, economic sphere. The growth of the natalist movement after the war can also be seen as part of this rationalizing trend. It enjoyed new ties with the republican state apparatus and promoted its methods in the name of social hygiene and a higher standard of reproduction.[129] The postwar proliferation of natalist programs signaled an intensification of an ongoing effort to rationalize sexual activity for productive and reproductive purposes. According to Françoise Thébaud, the Maternité Baudelocque, a state-financed institution for pre- and postnatal care built between 1919 and 1929, epitomized the transformation of maternity into a "rationalized operation in accordance with the knowledge and objectives of the mo-

ment."[130] Although here the focus was on hygiene rather than economic productivity, the impulse to manage populations through rational means in order to eliminate waste (in this case, unhealthy children)
strikingly resembles that of vocational guidance. After the war even
prostitution became "taylorized." According to Alain Corbin, rationalization, standardization, and sanitarism characterized the interwar
brothel.[131] Finally, in her "household management" or "domestic science" movement, Auguste Moll-Weiss tried to apply these same values
to housework and the individual home.[132] In all these ways, a new generation of "experts," often working in alliance with the republican state,
tried to rationalize sexual and family life.

This transformation in the vision of French social organization
after the war—toward human engineering for the purpose of social
rationalization and productivity—can answer an important question
raised by Mauvezin's and Montreuil-Straus's reform efforts: Why the
consistent reaffirmation of the primacy of domestic motherhood? At
the most superficial level, one could attribute it to the general postwar
atmosphere of natalism and the prevalence of fears about depopulation.[133] "If at present the country needs women workers, it needs mothers of families even more," began one vocational guidance manual.[134]
As the socially conservative journalist Henry Joly summarized the
"problem" of women's work in 1917: "we find ourselves in the presence, if not of an irreducible antinomy, at least of two equally imperious tasks. . . . We need children, many children in order to assure our
future, and we need manpower, a great deal of manpower, in order to
fulfill both our immediate and long-term needs."[135]

More important, however, reaffirming the primacy of the domestic, maternal role stabilized notions of female identity. This stability, in
turn, helped the French deal psychologically with the upheaval of the
war and the dramatic changes taking place around them. As we have
seen, these trends—the desire to "engineer" human capital in order
to enhance (re)production, and the breakdown of boundaries between
public and private sectors—affected social and familial as well as economic life in postwar France.[136] To evoke the figure of the loving, self-
sacrificing wife and mother was to evoke a figure of stability who assured that, despite the turbulence of the war experience and the
growth of rationalization and bureaucratization, a certain life and set
of customs would be preserved. Legislator and reformer became obsessed with the *mère de famille* not only because she promised to heal
the wounds of war and restore moral virtue/male virility, but also because she created a necessary illusion of continuity between the past

and present. If French men and women could convince themselves that a private family life was sacred, inviolable, and therefore unchangeable, then other changes might seem easier to accept. In a 1917 *Renaissance politique* article concerning "The Place of the French Woman after the War," the technocrat Henri Gabelle warned that overly rapid change would result in the French family becoming "a sort of hotel for passers-through": "As we can see, our old world is in the process of transformation. There is more than a slow evolution under way. We must facilitate the transition to the new world, while never losing sight of the great task that nature has bequeathed woman in society."[137] Here gender roles provide the stabilizing link between the new world and the old.

According to the historian Majorie Beale, interwar French men and women were deeply ambivalent about the potential impact of modern technology and scientific management techniques on French culture, fearing that these would destroy "conservative social and cultural values they nostalgically identified as traditional." While they cherished the opportunity to modernize French economic and social life, they worried that modernization would dismantle time-honored French cultural traditions.[138] Even such prominent interwar technocrats as Lucien Romier seemed nostalgically preoccupied with protecting nineteenth-century ideals. Romier's nostalgia is ironic because he himself sought through his work in Redressement français to bring labor productivity, technological efficiency, and modern corporate management to French industry.[139] In his well-known 1927 essay *Qui sera la maître, Europe ou Amérique?*, Romier expressed concern that the economic innovations he himself was helping to bring about in France were also effecting many potentially harmful changes. In particular, Romier voiced a familiar anxiety concerning *la crise du foyer*, a fear that the French family would dissolve into a kind of "barracks-life for men and women."[140] American technological and ideological "mastery" was inevitable, Romier conceded, but he wondered whether it would not "also result in the ruin of traditions, and in the birth, out of their ruins, of a new civilization that will have nothing in common with its predecessor?"[141]

Like Drieu la Rochelle and other postwar writers, Romier used the metaphor of a dead civilization to register the shock of sudden change. Like Drieu again, Romier considered the upheaval of gender roles a primary feature of this ruined civilization. The adoption of American technology and rationalization trends, Romier argued, had "worked such an upheaval in our morals that our most sanctified customs are endangered."[142] By "sanctified customs" here, Romier meant, among other things, nineteenth-century domesticity: "The economic upheavals have suddenly lifted [the French woman] out of her semi-secluded or sheltered ways and thrown her into the surging press of crowd life." Like postwar observers, Romier conceived of social change as ending women's enclosure within the domestic sphere. A modern woman either worked outside the household context or "ill at ease in her constricting home," she "goes out, looks for distractions."[143] The result, from the perspective of the French family, was this nightmare vision: "The private dwelling is no more. The family group is no more. The considerate relatives, the servants—all gone, save for temporary (or mechanical?) ones. . . . There is no frame in which things are fixed, no control, no lasting affections, no point of support, no moral example."[144] Even a technocrat such as Romier, well-known for his "forward" thinking about the economy and the future generally, feared the loss of fixity, stability, control, and moral example, all of which he equated with female domesticity.

By reaffirming domestic ideals, French men and women provided themselves with a "fixed frame" and "point of support" so as to grapple psychologically with the dramatic changes taking place around them. According to Beale, while the French ultimately did adopt modern technology and techniques of social management, they claimed to do so in order to preserve what they saw as traditional social relations and cultural traditions. In this way, "traditionalist and preservationist rhetoric generally served to cloak modernist designs."[145] Similarly, the reaffirmation of conventional notions of sexual difference itself enabled changes in women's lives and in French society generally to proceed forward. The domestic ideal played more than a conservative role in the postwar debate on women; it eased forward as much as it covered over social changes associated with the war.

Privileging woman's domestic role prevented the ruin of French civilization in more than a psychological sense. Such a reaffirmation, in turn, reasserted hierarchies of difference—such as the sexual division of labor and the sexual double standard—that had organized the distribution of labor, the rights of citizenship, legal status and property relations throughout the modern history of France. As we have seen in the case of vocational guidance and social hygiene, efforts to impose rational, uniform, normative standards in new areas of life threatened asymmetrical notions of sexual difference. *Not* to assert woman's difference or her maternal, domestic role as primary would lead to a profound transformation in the meanings of work, marriage, property, and politics in French society and culture. If a woman's primary role was no longer to bear and raise children, her unequal treatment in the labor market could not be justified, nor could her exclusion from accepted definitions of legal and civic identity, property rights, and suffrage. Woman's legal subservience under the Civil Code—her inability, in many cases, to manage her own property, or her debt of absolute obedience to her husband—depended on the notion of an economically dependent wife and mother in need of protection. In this sense, the domestic ideal, like the notion of a woman's sexual purity, supported the property system, through which the legitimate transmission of a man's property was guaranteed.[146] To ignore the essential way in which gender identities had organized economic, social, and political life in France would indeed, in Romier's terms, risk the ruin of sanctified customs and the eclipse of French civilization. The entire social and moral order would be threatened. By contrast, to invoke the primacy of woman's domestic role was both to counter and conceal the threat to asymmetrical notions of difference. In this sense, the "recasting" of bourgeois France ultimately relied on the reassurance of bourgeois domesticity.

Conclusion

"ARE WE WITNESSING THE BIRTH OF A NEW CIVILIZATION?"

Where is the world headed? Are we witnessing the birth of a new civilization? Have the institutions we have considered for centuries the fundamental basis of the social order suddenly and irrevocably become outdated? Or do they only need to evolve, to adapt themselves to the changes occurring in our morals, to the different notion we have of our rights and of the obligations that follow from social relations?[1]

These questions were posed by the literary critic Maurice Duval in 1924 at the beginning of a survey on "the crisis of marriage." They are marked by anguished uncertainty concerning the rapid social and cultural changes taking place during the postwar period—changes arising from both the war's impact and the accelerated growth of a rational, technocratic, mass consumer society. Debating gender identities allowed French men and women to understand painful social and cultural change as it took place and to negotiate it with cherished traditions. The debate on women, then, demonstrates how central gender was to postwar France's cultural self-representation, as well as to its organization of identity and power.

Gender enjoyed enormous symbolic power in postwar French culture. Various images of female identity—the modern woman, the mother, the single woman—provided compelling and meaningful symbols of change and tradition. As the symbol of the war's impact, the modern woman offered a focus for trauma concerning rapid change. Her power to shock lay in her ability to crystalize and communicate anguish of this kind. Even her fashions—the subject of unprecedented scandal during the twenties—visually evoked a civilization without sexes, without innocence, without idealism, without stable cultural and social boundaries. Gender ambiguity lay at the very heart of Victor Margueritte's bestseller *La Garçonne*, and explains the controversy surrounding its publication. Its heroine, Monique, represents not only the modern woman but the no man, displaced and disoriented by the war. By returning to conventional womanhood at novel's end, she saves both herself and him. The reconstruction of gender did more than normalize wartime changes in women's lives: it also appeased cultural and gender anxieties concerning the impact of the war itself.

In short, then, gender played a redemptive as well as an evocative role in the postwar confrontation with change. Fictions such as Margueritte's mobilized anxiety only to resolve it through the reconstruction of more conventional gender identities. Natalist legislation such as the law of 1920 against propaganda for contraception and abortion embodied the same cathartic logic. Postwar natalism generated anxiety concerning military and economic weakness only to manage it with a call to traditional motherhood as the panacea of all evils. Natalists sought to purge moral and gender anxieties as well as military and economic ones. Officially the movement interpreted the "crisis of maternal duty" as a moral problem, but in a more oblique way, it presented it as a symptom of postwar gender confusion. In novels such as Clément Vautel's *Madame ne veut pas d'enfant*, the resolution of this maternal crisis restored both male virility and moral virtue.

The conflation of moral and gender categories in the postwar debate on women explains why issues of female identity gained such profound symbolic importance in attempts to understand the impact of the war. In wartime literature images of "good" and "bad" women confused individual gender relations with a series of moral responses to the war. By adhering to traditional female behavior, a loyal wife who eagerly bore many children reaffirmed her husband's manhood, gave him an external mark of his virility, and upheld a set of values—self-denial, obedience, and discipline, among others—that sustained the war effort. Conversely, a woman's rejection of domesticity and motherhood frustrated a veteran's manhood and belittled the meaning of his war sacrifices. The conflation of moral and gender categories also characterized notions of male identity during the war. Both psychologists and the ordinary *poilu* connected sexual virility, for example, with the capacity for physical and moral courage.

The richly symbolic function of gender in wartime and postwar literature suggests several promising areas of historical investigation. More research on masculinity during the war can explain precisely how links between soldiery, virility, and paternity forged the meaning of the conflict for those Frenchmen who fought it. Attention to how moral and gender trauma became confused during wartime can also deepen our understanding of the history of the Second World War in France. For instance, why were the heads of French woman who had sexual liaisons with German soldiers publicly shaved? To what extent did these women's sexual transgressions become symbolic of France's moral humiliation concerning collaboration during the war? Finally, the postwar symbolic work of gender can illuminate contemporary American debate concerning a variety of issues. In what ways do disputes about the family and about morality also express fears about gender roles? What specific historical meanings have become attached to concepts such as "abortion," "family," and "motherhood" used by legislators to formulate and enact social policy? How does debating gender issues today, no less than during the 1920s, serve both to repress and to transcribe social and cultural anxieties?

In this study, change—"where the world was headed," to use Duval's phrase—has been defined as a cultural construction rather than a social, political, or economic reality. My purpose in emphasizing change as a cultural construct has been to destabilize the notion that "lived" or empirical reality can be studied apart from how people choose to imagine it. The meaning of change was the subject of great anxiety and contest in the postwar period—hence the intensity and volume of the postwar debate on women. As we have seen, most of the fears regarding change lacked a structural or statistical basis. It is debatable whether women's sexual activity actually increased significantly during the war, whether Margueritte's *La Garçonne* undermined morals, or whether fashions actually liberated women. Similarly, there is no statistical evidence that women rejected motherhood during the era or that France was headed for racial extinction. These fears could be considered "wrong" in that they did not correspond to a statistical reality. Nevertheless, inasmuch as French men and women conceptualized and understood change in these ways, such fears were extremely "real." The aim of this study has been to explore the meaning of these anxieties and their function as signals of postwar cultural crisis. Their impact extended beyond the ways in which change was imagined. Legislative concerns about depopulation, for example, inspired such policy as the law of 1920. The postwar cultural imaginary did not always begin by corresponding to an empirical reality, but it had enormous power in shaping that reality. For the historian, the "real" and the "imaginary" in postwar French society soon become impossible to separate.

The postwar debate on women was haunted by the figure of the childless young woman, sexually promiscuous, loose in her morals, free in her clothes, who wanted to "live her own life." Her presence does not constitute evidence that the war liberated women, as historians have sometimes concluded. Certainly the war's impact and the growth of mass consumer society created new socioeconomic conditions that transformed women's lives. But my attention to the issue of gender transformation has not centered on measuring the magnitude of change—to what extent the war altered women's lives in a permanent or significant way. Instead I have focused on the cultural production of change—the attempt to negotiate change with continuity, to reconcile old and new worlds. An anguished struggle between old and new lay at the very heart of the postwar decade. As the historians Serge Berstein and Jean-Jacques Becker have recently argued, the essence of the 1920s consists of a "dialectic between a visceral desire to return to the past in order to forget the war, and the practical impossibility of such a return due to the war's upheaval."[2] Nowhere was this dialectic more clearly operative than in attempts to reconstruct notions of female identity.

In this dialectic, the antinomy between old and new worlds itself created the possibility for change. For example, for certain members of the medical community, the call for single motherhood imposed conventional sexual meanings on a new social situation created by the war. But in the hands of novelists and dramatists, the image of the single mother created a sexual identity for women outside marriage; she represented a paradoxical and volatile mixture of old and new. Similarly, the vocational theorist Louise Mauvezin defined career choice in terms of the primacy of women's maternal, domestic role. But in doing so, she also produced a radical image of female identity: the young single woman who prepares for and finds fulfillment in her own career. Finally, when Dr. Germaine Montreuil-Straus defined female sexuality in strictly reproductive terms, she appeared to be merely reinforcing traditional Christian morality. But, in fact, she was simultaneously engaged in a much more revolutionary project: the affirmation of female sexuality as healthy and normal for both working-class and middle-class women. The more conservative elements of Mauvezin's and Montreuil-Straus's projects concealed their fundamental radicalism; the ideal of the traditional *mère de famille* served as a figure of stability that made acceptable more disturbing innovations in female identity. In reasserting the domestic ideal, the French, in effect, looked *backwards* to the future.

What this future might look like did not become clearly apparent until the thirties and forties. Historians now consider the postwar decade an important turning point in twentieth-century France.[3] By mid-decade, the French began to realize that they could not simply bring the old world back. As we have seen, young leaders such as Ernest Mercier and Lucien Romier began to imagine new ways to organize society and the state. They envisioned a technocratic government independent of political forces, and a mass consumption economy founded on low prices and expanding markets. The technocratic urge for rational efficiency, productivity, and human engineering achieved only moderate success during the twenties: it would be realized both more fully and more ironically during the next two decades. The links between Mercier and Romier and the right-wing political elite of the thirties and early forties are important to note in this regard. Mercier was a member of the Croix de Feu and a fomenter of the antiparliamentary riots of February 1934. Both men allied themselves with such leaders as Marshal Philippe Pétain, P.-E Flandin, and Pierre Laval. Romier was Pétain's closest adviser on social and economic affairs in Vichy France.[4] The contradiction that defined Romier's technocratic rhetoric in 1927—his belief, on the one hand, in the primacy of traditional domesticity and his encouragement, on the other, of a rationalized, modernized socioeconomic order—would culminate in Vichy social policy. In Vichy, too, one could argue, Pétain's program for "travail, famille, patrie" concealed its contrary drive for rational, impersonal, technocratic social organization.[5] Vichy social policy sought to legitimize itself by negotiating old and new worlds. In this way, it mimicked the postwar debate on women; it too promised a future both gloriously new and defiantly rooted in the past.

NOTES

Introduction

1. Gilbert Guilleminault, *Les Années folles* (Paris: Editions Denoël, 1958), p. 5. See also Pierre Faveton, *Les Années vingt* (Paris: Messidor-Temps actuels, 1982); A. Joffroy, *La Vie réinvitée: L'Explosion des années 20 à Paris* (Paris: Laffont, 1982); Dominique Desanti, *La Femme au temps des années folles* (Paris: Stock, 1985).

2. Maurice Sachs, *La Décade de l'illusion* (Paris: Gallimard, 1950), p. 17.

3. Barnett Singer, "Technology and Social Change: The Watershed of the 1920's," *Proceedings of the Fourth Annual Meeting of the Western Society for French History* 4 (1976): 321–29. On Josephine Baker, see Phyllis Rose, *Jazz Cleopatra: Josephine Baker in Her Time* (New York: Doubleday, 1989).

4. Elisabeth de Gramont, *Souvenirs du monde de 1890 à 1940* (Paris: Grasset, 1966), p. 319. Gramont also claimed (p. 320) that the hedonism of the postwar years owed to American influence, in particular, American soldiers who remained in Paris after the armistice. The following books provide a good introduction to the Great War in France: Jean-Jacques Becker, *France en guerre* (Brussels: Editions Complexe, 1988), or Becker's *Les Français dans la grande guerre* (Paris: Editions Robert Laffont, 1983); Marc Ferro, *The Great War, 1914–1918* (Boston: Routledge and Kegan Paul, 1973).

5. Robert Wohl, *The Generation of 1914* (Cambridge: Harvard University Press, 1979); C. G. Cruikshank, *Variations on a Catastrophe: Some French Responses to the Great War* (New York: Oxford University Press, 1982), p. 6. For England, see Samuel Hynes, *A War Imagined: The First World War and English Culture* (New York: Atheneum, 1991), chap. 1.

6. See Cruikshank, *Variations on a Catastrophe*, and Antoine Prost's brilliant and illuminating *Souvenirs individuels*, vol. 3 of *Les Anciens combattants*

et la société française, 1914–1939 (Paris: Foundation nationale des sciences politiques, 1977). These changes were Europe-wide. For Europe generally, see Modrus Eksteins, *The Rites of Spring: The Great War and the Birth of the Modern Age* (Boston: Houghton-Mifflin, 1989). For England, see Paul Fussell, *The Great War and Modern Memory* (New York: Oxford University Press, 1975); Eric Leeds, *No Man's Land: Combat and Identity in World War I* (Cambridge: Cambridge University Press, 1979); Hynes, *A War Imagined*. For Germany, see Eric Maria Remarque's classic novel, *All Quiet on the Western Front* (New York: Fawcett Crest, 1987; originally published in 1928); and Russell McCormmach's more recent *Memoirs of a Classical Physicist* (New York: Avon, 1982).

7. For this argument, see in particular Eksteins, *Rites of Spring*, p. 256; Jean-Jacques Becker and Serge Berstein, *Victoire et frustrations, 1914–1929*, vol. 12 of *Nouvelle histoire de la France contemporaine* (Paris: Seuil, 1990), p. 155. Becker and Berstein make the important point (p. 373), that the frivolity and hedonism associated with *"les années folles"* was confined to a relatively small Parisian elite. The large majority of peasants and workers, as well as the more austere provincial bourgeoisie, did not take part in the decade's debauchery.

8. Drieu la Rochelle (1893–1944) was born to a wealthy bourgeois family, yet the near ruin of his father's family fortune greatly attracted him to the nationalism of Maurras in the years before the war. When the war began in 1914, he was already enlisted, completing his military service. His political views were less clear directly after the war, when he befriended Louis Aragon, who would later become a Communist. He is best known for his later work, particularly *Gilles* (1939), which traces the career of his conversion to fascism in 1934. Much of the recent work on him in France centers on his fascism and collaborationism, as well as his death by suicide in 1944. See, for example, Marie Balvet, *Itinéraire d'un intellectuel vers le fascisme* (Paris: Presses Universitaires de France, 1984); Jean-Louis Saint Ygnan, *Drieu la Rochelle ou l'obsession de la decadence* (Paris: Nouvelles Editions Latines, 1984); Robert Soucy, *Fascist Intellectual: Drieu la Rochelle* (Berkeley: University of California Press, 1979); and Frank Field, *Three French Writers and the Great War: Barbusse, Drieu la Rochelle, Bernanos* (Cambridge: Cambridge University Press, 1975). The type of nihilism that Drieu voices here found its most famous expression in the Dadaist and Surrealist movements of the war and postwar periods. See Hans Richter, *Dada Art and Anti-art* (New York: Oxford University Press, 1965), and Maurice Nadeau, *Histoire du surréalisme* (Paris: Seuil, 1964), p. 33.

9. Pierre Drieu la Rochelle, *La Suite des idées* (Paris: Au Sens Pareil, 1927), p. 125. *La Suite des idées* went through four editions in 1927. Drieu la Rochelle voiced many of the same ideas in *Le Jeune européen* (Paris: Gallimard, 1927).

10. In *Rites of Spring* (p. 214) Eksteins talks about how the ruins left on

battlefields such as Ypres would soon be so flooded with tourists that "the ancient ruins of Pompeii and such places will be simply out of it." From this,
Eksteins concludes: "Ypres, despite its contemporaneity, had surpassed Pompeii, . . . as a monument of ruined civilization. Its scale of symbolism was in-
comparable."

11. For a general survey of this nineteenth-century malaise, see Eric Hansen, *Disaffection and Decadence: A Crisis in French Intellectual Thought,
1848–1898* (Washington, D.C.: University Press of America, 1982).

12. Other writers of this generation included André Breton, Louis Aragon,
Henry de Montherlant, and Philippe Soupault. See Wohl, *The Generation of
1914*, pp. 24–25.

13. See André Beaunier, "La Revue littéraire: Les Angoisses d'un combattant," *Revue des deux mondes*, 1 February 1923. A prominent literary critic,
Beaunier described Drieu's pessimism as a "testimony of incontestable value."
Here Beaunier was referring to Drieu la Rochelle's earlier work—*Mesure de
la France, Interrogation, Fond de cantine*—but the themes in these works are
identical to those expressed in *La Suite des idées*. According to Beaunier,
Drieu la Rochelle aimed his work at veterans between the ages of twenty and
forty. Beaunier ends his review with a plea for "the idea of continuity" between
present and past. Although the war seems to have "broken" continuity with
the past, he argues, it must serve as the "safeguard" of France's political, social,
and literary future. For another interpretation of Drieu la Rochelle's work as
an important testimony of his generation, see literary critic Nicolas Ségur's
review of *Plainte contre inconnu* in *Revue mondiale*, 15 January 1925.

14. Benjamin Crémieux, *Inquiétude et reconstruction: Essai sur la littérature d'après-guerre* (Paris: Editions R.–A. Corrêa, 1931), p. 18. Crémieux was
an infantryman throughout the war and was wounded three times. In 1924,
Marcel Arland, a critic for *La Nouvelle revue française*, described postwar literature as "the reflection of an upheaval that is leading an entire civilization
toward either its ruin or its resurrection." See "Sur un nouveau mal du siècle,"
Nouvelle revue française, February 1924: 158. As Charles Dedeyan put it in
Une Guerre dans le mal des hommes (Paris: Editions Buchet/Chastel, 1971),
"the war brought about the failure of civilizations, of civilization" (p. 312). In
Rites of Spring (p. 52) Modrus Eksteins argues that the revolt against the notion of "civilization" began before the war, and was articulated with the ballet
of Diaghilev, "The Rites of Spring," first performed in Paris in 1913. For an
intriguing analysis of many of the same issues in England, see Hynes, *A War
Remembered*, chap. 17, "A Botched Civilization." Combatants as well as writers mourned the death of civilization during the war. In 1916, the front soldier
Louis Mairet wrote in his diary: "Confronted by the spectacle of a scientific
struggle in which Progress is used to return to Barbarism, and by the spectacle
of a civilization turning against itself to destroy itself, reason cannot cope."
Quoted in Eksteins, *Rites of Spring*, pp. 215–16.

15. From an article by Romain Rolland dated 2 November 1916 and titled

"Aux peuples assassinés" in *A la civilisation* (n.p., 1917). See also Elie Fauré, *La Danse sur le feu et l'eau* (Paris: Crès, 1920), chap. 1: "De la civilisation."

16. Oswald Spengler, *The Decline of the West* (London: G. Allen, 1922). According to Barrie Cadwallader in *Crisis of the European Mind: A Study of André Malraux and Drieu la Rochelle* (Cardiff: University of Wales Press, 1981), pp. 32–33, Spengler's impact was strongest in France during the postwar decade. Spengler used the term "civilization" in a highly specific way, to characterize cultures in their decline, devoid of all creativity and approaching their death. European or "Faustian" culture, he believed, had become a "civilization"—or had begun to decline—at the beginning of the nineteeth century, when it came under the domination of the capitalist class. The holocaust of the war, according to Spengler, marked its ultimate demise. For a lucid explanation of Spengler's main theses in *The Decline of the West*, see John F. Fennelly, *Twilight of the Evening Lands: Oswald Spengler—A Half Century Later* (New York: Brookdale Press, 1972).

17. Georges Duhamel, *La Possession du monde* (Paris: Mercure de France, 1938: orig. 1919), p. 271. For another postwar attempt to define civilization by a prominent physician, see Charles Richet, "Qu'est-ce que la civilisation?" *Revue des deux mondes,* 15 March 1923.

18. See Georges Duhamel's *Civilisation, 1914–1917* (Paris: Mercure de France, 1918), particularly the title essay. The original essay appeared in *Mercure de France* on 16 September 1917 under the pseudonym of Denis Thévenin.

19. Paul Valéry, *Variété* (Paris: Editions de la *Nouvelle revue française,* 1924), 1:11–12. Valéry was a well-known poet throughout the twenties. For an interesting review of *Variété*, see Nicolas Ségur, "La Vie littéraire," *Revue mondiale* 15 October 1924 and 1 January 1926. See also Valéry's 1918 letter to Albert Mockel, a Belgian symbolist writer, quoted in Cruikshank, *Variations on a Catastrophe,* p. 167.

20. Ibid., p. 13. The translation is by Malcolm Cowley, *Variety* (New York: Harcourt, Brace and Co., 1927).

21. Ibid., p. 20; Cowley, *Variety.*

22. Anne-Marie Sohn documents this increase in "*La Garçonne* face à l'opinion publique: Type littéraire ou type social des années 20?" *Le Mouvement social* 80 (1972): 26. For the development of "les pages féminines" after the war, see also Claude Bellanger and Jacques Godechot, *1870–1940* of *Histoire générale de la presse française* (Paris: P. U. F., 1972), p. 481.

23. In May, 1919, the French National Assembly voted by an overwhelming majority to grant the vote to women; the Senate then defeated the suffrage bill in 1922. The legislative debates from these two parliamentary decisions are very long and fascinating. Although I read these debates during the course of my research, I decided that I could not do justice to their length and political complexity in a study preoccupied with so many other issues.

24. The history of the debate on male identity during the war and postwar periods needs to be written. For a beginning, see Annelise Maugue, *L'Identité masculine en crise au tournant du siècle* (Paris: Editions Rivage, 1987); and Marc Roudebush, "'Long Live Cowards and Fools!': World War I and the Construction of French Masculinity" (Paper delivered at the World War I: Culture and Society Conference, University of California at Berkeley, 15 April, 1990.)

25. See Eugen Weber, *France, Fin-de-siècle* (Cambridge: Harvard University Press, 1986), p. 2.

26. Charles Chenu in Suzanne Grinberg, "Le Rôle de la femme française après la guerre," *Renaissance politique*, 17 March, 1917. Charles Chenu was a well-known politician and lawyer who represented the Calmette family in the 1914 trial of Madame Caillaux. See Edward Berenson, *The Trial of Madame Caillaux* (Berkeley: University of California Press, 1992).

27. See Philippe Bernard and Henri Dubief, *The Decline of the Third Republic, 1914–1938* (Cambridge: Cambridge University Press, 1985), pp. 78–79. See also the helpful surveys by Paul M. Bouju and Henri DuBois, *La Troisième République, 1870–1940* (Paris: Presses Universitaires de France, 1975), and M. Agulhon and A. Nouschi, *La France de 1914 à 1940* (Paris: Nathan, 1971).

28. For an illuminating look at the French interwar economy, see Alfred Sauvy, *Histoire économique de la France entre les deux guerres*, 4 vols. (Paris: Fayard, 1965–70). For a thorough discussion of fiscal instability throughout the decade, see Bernard and Dubief, *Decline*.

29. For the desire for a return to normalcy, see Becker and Bernstein, *Victoire et frustrations*, p. 155; Marc Auffret, *La France de l'entre deux guerres* (Paris: Culture, Arts, Loisirs, 1972).

30. For the term "culturally intelligible," see Judith Butler, *Gender Trouble: Feminism and the Subversion of Identity* (New York: Routledge, Chapman, and Hall, 1990).

31. James McMillan, *Housewife or Harlot: The Position of Women in French Society* (New York: St. Martin's Press, 1980), pp. 99, 120–22. For a similar view regarding English women and World War I, see Gail Braybon, *Women Workers in the First World War: The British Experience* (Totowa: N. J.: Barnes and Noble, 1981).

32. Françoise Thébaud, *La Femme au temps de la guerre de 14* (Paris: Stock, 1986), p. 296; Desanti, *La Femme au temps des années folles*, p. 119.

33. See McMillan, *Housewife*, chap. 8 and particularly p. 163.

34. Gaston Rageot, *La Française dans la guerre* (Paris: Attinger Frères, 1919), p. 29. Rageot was the drama critic of *La Revue bleue* and an outspoken natalist, as we shall see in chap. 4. Rageot's belief that a proper division between the sexes was necessary to civilization reflected a widely held belief of late nineteenth century evolutionary science. See Jo B. Margadant, *Madame le Professeur: Women Educators in the Third Republic* (Princeton: Princeton

University Press, 1990), p. 29, and Cynthia Eagle Russett, *Sexual Science: The Victorian Construction of Womanhood* (Cambridge: Harvard University Press, 1989).

35. For other examples of postwar French men and women who believed that gender was a fundamental variable of French culture and civilization, see the antisuffragist Marthe Borély, "Enquête sur le féminisme de demain," *Je sais tout*, 15 January 1919: 37–40, and the feminist Jane Misme, "La Guerre et le rôle des femmes," *Revue de Paris*, 1 November 1916: 213.

36. For a theoretical explanation of the way in which gender constructs identity and power, see Joan W. Scott, "Gender: A Useful Category of Analysis," in *Gender and the Politics of History* (New York: Columbia University Press, 1988). For the new emphasis on gender differences in the eighteenth century, see Tom Laqueur, *Making Sex: Body and Gender from the Greeks to Freud* (Cambridge: Harvard University Press, 1990); Ludmilla Jordanova, *Sexual Visions: Images of Gender in Science and Medicine Between the Eighteenth and Twentieth Centuries* (Madison: University of Wisconsin Press, 1989); Londa Schiebinger, *The Mind Has No Sex? Women in the Origins of Modern Science* (Cambridge: Harvard University Press, 1989); and Denise Riley, *Am I That Name? Women as a Category in History* (Minneapolis: University of Minnesota Press, 1988). For recent historiography on the centrality of gender issues to the French Revolution of 1789, see the following works by Lynn Hunt: *The Family Romance of the French Revolution* (Berkeley: University of California Press, 1992); "The Many Bodies of Marie Antoinette," in *Eroticism and the Body Politic*, ed. Lynn Hunt (Baltimore: Johns Hopkins University Press, 1990); "Hercules and the Radical Image in the French Revolution," *Representations* 1:2 (Spring 1983); and "The Unstable Boundaries of the French Revolution," in *From the Fires of the Revolution to the Great War*, ed. Michelle Perrot, vol. 4 of *A History of Private Life*, ed. Georges Duby and Philippe Ariès (Cambridge; Harvard University Press, 1990). On the French Revolution, see also Sara Maza, "The Diamond Necklace Affair Revisited (1785–1786): The Case of the Missing Queen," in *Eroticism*, ed. Hunt; Joan Scott, "French Feminists and the Rights of "Man": Olympe de Gouge's Declarations," *History Workshop* 28 (Autumn 1989); Joan Landes, *Women in the Public Sphere in the Age of the French Revolution* (Ithaca: Cornell University Press, 1988). For Rousseau, see Barbara Corrado Pope, "The Influence of Rousseau's Ideology of Domesticity," in *Connecting Spheres: Women in the Western World, 1500 to the Present*, ed. Marilyn Boxer and Jean Quataert (New York: Oxford University Press, 1987).

37. See Landes, *Women in the Public Sphere;* Claire Moses, *French Feminism in the Nineteenth Century* (Albany: State University of New York Press, 1984), particularly chap. 2. See also the important critiques of Landes's work by Keith Baker, "Defining the Public Sphere in Eighteenth Century France: Variations on a Theme by Habermas," in *Habermas and the Public Sphere*, ed. Craig Calhoun (Cambridge: MIT Press, 1991); and Dena Goodman, "Public

Sphere and Private Life: Towards a Synthesis of Current Historiographical Approaches to the Old Regime," *History and Theory* 31: 1 (1992).

38. See Bonnie Smith, *Ladies of the Leisure Class: The Bourgeoises of Northern France in the Nineteenth Century* (Princeton: Princeton University Press, 1981); Smith, "The Domestic Sphere in the Victorian Age," *Changing Lives: Women in European History* (Lexington, Mass.: D. C. Heath, 1989); and Anne Martin-Fugier, *La Bourgeoise* (Paris: Bernard Grasset, 1983). For a useful discussion of the domestic ideal in Victorian Britain, see Mary Poovey, *Uneven Developments: The Ideological Work of Gender in Mid-Victorian Britain* (Chicago: University of Chicago Press, 1988).

39. Perrot, *Private Life*, p. 100.

40. The literature concerning bourgeois family and society in the nineteenth century is vast, but a sampling would include: Régine Pernoud, *Histoire de la bourgeoisie en France* (Paris: Seuil, 1962); Theodore Zeldin, *France, 1848–1945, Ambition and Love* (New York: Oxford University Press, 1979); "The Pretensions of the Bourgeoisie"; Marguerite Perrot, *La Mode de vie des familles bourgeoises 1873–1953* (Paris: Armand Colin, 1961); Adeline Daumard, *Les Bourgeois de Paris au XIXe siècle* (Paris: Flammarion, 1970), chap. 5; and Daumard, *Les Bourgeois et la bourgeoisie en France depuis 1815* (Paris: Aubier-Montagne, 1987). For a more contemporary source, see Edmond Goblot, *La Barrière et le niveau* (Paris: Presses Universitaires de France, 1967; orig. pub. 1925). For a completely different perspective, see Arno Mayer, *The Persistence of the Old Regime* (New York: Pantheon, 1981), chap. 2.

41. The literature on these topics is, again, vast, but for a sampling of how gender issues figured in these discussions, consult the following. On urbanization and industrialization, see Joan W. Scott, "L'Ouvrière! Mot impie, sordide . . .": Women Workers in the Discourse of French Political Economy, 1840–1860 in *Gender and the Politics;* Claire Moses, *French Feminism*, chap. 7; Alain Corbin, *Les Filles de noce: Misère sexuelle et prostitution aux 19e et 20e siècles* (Paris: Aubier, 1978); Jill Harsin, *Policing Prostitution in Nineteeth-Century Paris* (Princeton: Princeton University Press, 1985). For the construction of the welfare state, see Mary Lynn Stewart, *Women, Work and the French State: Labour Protection and Social Patriarchy, 1879–1919* (Kingston, Ont.: McGill-Queen's University Press, 1989); Joshua Cole, "The Power of Large Numbers: Population and Politics in Nineteenth Century France" (Ph. D. diss., University of California at Berkeley, 1991); Sylvia Schafer, "Children in 'Moral Danger' and the Politics of Parenthood in Third Republic France, 1870–1914" (Ph. D. diss., University of California at Berkeley, 1992).

42. As Berenson puts it in *The Trial of Madame Caillaux*, p. 11, "[d]uring the Belle Epoque private life and public preoccupation, sexuality and nationality, culture and politics, coalesced around the question of gender." See also Karen Offen, "Depopulation, Nationalism and Feminism in Fin-de-siècle France," *American Historical Review* 89 (June 1984).

43. Henry Bordeaux, "Les Jeunes filles nouvelles," *Journal des demoiselles,*

1 January 1922: 1. For more on Bordeaux's work, see chap. 5. Historian Gabriel Perreux echoes this sentiment in his *La Vie quotidienne des civils en France pendant la grande guerre* (Paris: Hachette, 1966), p. 67.

44. See Sandra Gilbert, "Soldier's Heart: Literary Men, Literary Women and the Great War," *Signs* 8 (Spring 1983). I am indebted to Gilbert's analysis here and throughout the first part of this study. But I believe that she paints an overly positive picture of the English homefront, as a close reading of Vera Brittain's *Testament of Youth* might show. For recent criticisms of Gilbert's thesis, see Claire M. Tylee, "Maleness Run Riot: The Great War and Women's Resistance to Militarism," *Women's Studies International Forum* 2: 3 (1988), and James Longenbach, "The Women and Men of 1914," in *Arms and the Woman: War, Gender and Literary Representation,* ed. Helen Cooper, Adrienne Minich, and Susan Squier (Chapel Hill: University of North Carolina Press, 1989). For two contemporaneous attempts to understand the psychological impact of warfare on the soldier, see Maurice Dide, *Les Emotions de la guerre* (Paris: Felix Alcan, 1918), and Louis Huot and Paul Voivenel, *La Psychologie du soldat* (Paris: La Renaissance du Livre, 1918).

45. According to art historian Beth Irwin Lewis, male anxiety concerning the role of women also pervaded German society after the war and is manifest in the work of such artists as George Grosz and Otto Dix. Lewis argues that a similar widespread debate about what she calls "the women question" takes place in Germany after the war. See her fascinating article *"Lustmord:* Inside the Windows of the Metropolis," in *Berlin: Culture and Metropolis,* ed. Charles W. Haxthausen and Heidrun Suhr (Minneapolis: University of Minnesota, 1990).

46. "Une Controverse: L'Emancipation de la jeune fille moderne est-elle un progrès réel?" *Progrès civique,* 13 June 1925: 840. *Progrès civique* was a fairly new review, which began in 1919 and was popular among radicals, socialists, and civil servants. The argument that *la garçonne* was a foreign, usually American, "import" was fairly common. See also C. Jeglot, "La Jeune fille et la malaise moderne," 26 June 1926 *Extrait des dossiers de l'Action populaire* (Evreux: Imprimerie de l'Eure, 1927), p. 3, 7.

47. On Americanization, see Paul A. Gagnon, "La Vie Future: Some French Responses to the Technological Society," *Journal of European Studies* 6 (1976). For a history of consumer culture in France, see Michael Miller, *Le Bon Marché: Bourgeois Culture and the Department Store, 1869–1920* (Princeton: Princeton University Press, 1981); Rosalind Williams, *Dream Worlds: Mass Consumption in Late Nineteenth Century France* (Berkeley: University of California Press, 1982); and Charles Rearick, *The Pleasures of the Belle Epoque: Entertainment and Festivity in Turn-of-the-Century France* (New Haven: Yale University Press, 1986). On the growth of mass culture in the 1920s in France, see Becker and Berstein, *Victoire et frustration,* pp. 381–82.

48. Duhamel, *Civilisation,* p. 18.

49. Alternate words used to describe "la crise de l'espirit," were "la fin de l'éternel," Julien Benda's phrase, and Marcel Arland's "le nouveau mal du siècle." See Barrie Cadwallader, *Crisis of the European Spirit*, p. 7.

50. See Suzanne Grinberg, "Le Rôle de la femme française après la guerre," *Renaissance politique*, 3 March 1917, the comments of Paul Painlevé in the March 17 installment (the same day he became foreign minister) and the remarks of the prominent doctor Adolphe Pinard in the April 14 installment.

51. Jean Rabaut estimates that there were 30 percent more women than men between the ages of twenty-five and thirty during the early twenties. See *Histoire des féminismes français* (Paris: Stock, 1978), p. 276.

52. For a discussion of some of the fragilities of domestic ideology in France in the *belle époque*, see Jennifer Waelti-Walters, *Feminist Novelists of the Belle Epoque* (Bloomington: Indiana University Press, 1990), pp. 8–9. For the debate on divorce and marriage at the turn of the century, see Berenson, *The Trial of Madame Caillaux*, chap. 3. For the French feminist movement in the late nineteenth century, see Claire Moses, *French Feminism;* Stephen Hause, with Anne Kenney, *Women's Suffrage and Social Politics in the French Third Republic* (Princeton: Princeton University Press, 1984); Laurence Klejman and Florence Rochefort, *L'Egalité en marche: Le féminisme sous la Troisième République* (Paris: des femmes, 1989). The prominent role that the prewar feminist movement played in challenging the social organization of gender is illustrated by the fact that the war, which appeared to have undermined this organization altogether, was often interpreted as a victory for feminism. See, for example, Henri-Robert in "La Femme et la guerre," *La Revue,* May 1917, p. 246, and Narquet, "La Femme dans la France," p. 273. For crimes of passion, see Joëlle Guillais, *La Chair de l'autre: Le Crime passionnel au XIXe siècle* (Paris: Olivier Orban, 1986); Ruth Harris, *Murders and Madness: Medicine, Law and Society in the Fin-de-Siècle* (Oxford: Clarendon Press, 1989). For adultery and other sexual transgressions, see Martin-Fugier, *La Bourgeoise,* chap. 4, "L'Avenir de la conjugalité."

53. For the debate on the "new woman," see Maugue, *L'Identité masculine;* Michelle Perrot, "The New Eve and the Old Adam: French Women's Condition at the Turn of the Century," in *Behind the Lines: Gender and the Two World Wars,* ed. Margaret Higonnet (New Haven: Yale University Press, 1987); Debora Silverman, "The 'New Woman,' Feminism and the Decorative Arts in Fin-de-siècle France," in *Eroticism,* ed. Hunt, pp. 144–63; Silverman, *Art Nouveau in Fin-de-Siècle France: Politics, Psychology and Style* (Berkeley: University of California Press, 1989).

54. McMillan, *Housewife or Harlot,* p. 20; Colin Dyer, *Population and Society in Twentieth Century France* (New York: Holmes and Meier, 1978); Françoise Thébaud, *Donner la vie: Histoire de la maternité en France entre les deux guerres* (Thèse du troisième cycle, Université de Paris VII, 1984), p. 289; and Hause and Kenney, *Women's Suffrage,* p. 198.

55. Poovey, *Uneven Developments*, p. 3. For bourgeois social reform in the nineteenth century, see Smith, *Ladies of the Leisure Class*.

56. See Louise A. Tilly and Joan W. Scott, *Women, Work, and Family* (New York: Holt, Rinehart, and Winston, 1978), chaps. 7 and 8; Sylvie Zerner, "De la couture aux presses: L'emploi féminine entre les deux guerres," *Le Mouvement social*, 140 (July-September 1987); Michelle Perrot, *Private Life*, pp. 669–72; Bonnie Smith, *Changing Lives*, chap. 10. For an argument that home appliances did not significantly reduce housework or free housewives from domestics, see Robert L. Frost, "Inventing the New Middle Class in Interwar France" (manuscript), p. 7.

57. The titles of these six articles include: Suzanne Grinberg, "Le Rôle de la femme française"; Henri-Robert, "La Femme et la guerre," *La Revue*, May 1917; J. Gabelle, "La Place de la femme française après la guerre," *Renaissance politique*, 17 February 1917; Henry Joly, "De l'extension du travail des femmes après la guerre," *Le Correspondant*, 10 January 1917; Frédéric Masson, "Les Femmes pendant et après la guerre," *Revue hebdomaire*, 3 March 1917; Louis Narquet, "La Femme dans la France de demain," *Mercure de France*, 16 July 1917.

58. For debates concerning gender issues in France, see Scott, *Gender and the Politics of History;* Hunt, *Family Romance.* For debates in England, see Judy Walkowitz, *City of Dangerous Delight: Narratives of Sexual Danger* (Chicago: University of Chicago Press, 1992); Leonore Davidoff and Catherine Hall, *Family Fortunes: Men and Women of the English Middle Class, 1780–1850* (Chicago: University of Chicago Press, 1987); Poovey, *Uneven Developments.* For Germany, see Biddy Martin, "Feminism, Criticism and Foucault," *New German Critique* 27 (Fall 1982).

59. For a similar view of historical change, see Michel Foucault, "Nietzsche, Genealogy, History," in *The Foucault Reader,* ed. Paul Rabinow (New York: Pantheon, 1984); Walkowitz, *City of Dangerous Delight;* Poovey, *Uneven Developments.*

60. Jacques Boulenger, "La Femme moderne: Devant le feu," *Illustration,* 6 December 1924.

61. For theoretical considerations concerning identity and the subject on which I rely here, see Theresa de Lauretis, "Feminist Studies/Critical Studies: Issues, Terms, and Contexts," and Biddy Martin and Chandra Talpade Mohanty, "Feminist Politics: What's Home Got to Do with It?" in *Feminist Studies, Critical Studies,* ed. Theresa de Lauretis (Bloomington: Indiana University Press, 1986); Joan Wallach Scott, "The Evidence of Experience," in *Critical Inquiry* 17 (Summer 1991); Felicity A. Nussbaum, *The Autobiographical Subject: Gender and Ideology in Eighteenth Century England* (Baltimore: Johns Hopkins University Press, 1989).

62. James Smith Allen, *In the Public Eye: A History of Reading in Modern France, 1800–1940* (Princeton: Princeton University Press, 1991), pp. 61 and 67 and Table A.7. Allen estimates the literacy rate for men in 1921 at 99.1

percent of the total population older than 14, the literacy rate for women at 98.4 percent of this same group, and the number of active readers at 36.6 percent.

63. The *dépot légal* system in France worked badly during the decade 1920 to 1930. It is therefore hard to give completely accurate information about editions of books and their conditions of production. See Henri-Jean Martin, Roger Chartier, and Jean-Pierre Vivet, eds., *Le Livre concurrencé, 1900–1950*, vol. 5 of *Histoire de l'édition française* (Paris: Promodis, 1986), p. 196.

64. Ibid., p. 86. See also Becker and Berstein, *Victoire et frustration*, p. 383, where they comment on "the extraordinary vogue of the popular novel during the twenties." Many of the novels examined in this study were among the first French best-sellers, notably Henri Barbusse's *Le Feu* (1916), Roland Dorgelès's *Les Croix de bois* (1919), Victor Margueritte's *La Garçonne* (1922), and Raymond Radiguet's *Le Diable au corps* (1923). See also Claude Jolly's "Les Pratiques de lecture," in *Le Livre concurrencé*, ed. Martin et al., pp. 565–71. Jolly argues that the postwar era was a turning point in terms of the breakdown of a two-tiered system of reading based on education and class. As reading became a mass activity, more and more people from all classes, except the extreme poor, began to read the same books.

65. Bellanger et al., *Histoire générale de la presse*, pp. 457–60. By contrast, titles of daily papers shrank in number, chiefly because of economic difficulties such as the increased expense of printing and paper. James Smith Allen also refers to the "much larger number of all periodicals" and the "bewildering variety of more freely available printed matter" by the outbreak of the Second World War. See *Public Eye*, p. 53. For the history of reading in modern France, see also Roger Chartier and Jean Hébard, "Les Imaginaires de la lecture," in *Le Livre concurrencé*, ed. Martin et al., pp. 529–41, and Roger Chartier, ed., *Pratiques de la lecture* (Marseilles: Rivages, 1985). On the cultural importance of the press in the years just before the war, see Berenson, *Madame Caillaux*, chap. 6.

66. Allen, *Public Eye*, p. 70.

67. See Martin et al., eds., *Le Livre concurrencé*, p. 84; Allen, *Public Eye*, pp. 50–51.

1. This Being without Breasts, without Hips

1. Jacques Boulenger, "La Femme moderne: Devant le feu," *Illustration*, 6 December 1924.

2. For France, see Dominique Desanti, *La Femme au temps des années folles* (Paris: Stock, 1985). For Europe generally, see Bonnie Smith, *Changing Lives: Women in European History Since 1700* (Lexington, Mass.: D. C. Heath, 1989), chap. 10. For the United States, see Rayna Rapp and Ellen Ross, "The Twenties: Feminism, Consumerism and Political Backlash in the United States," in *Women in Culture and Politics: A Century of Change*, ed. Judith

Friedlander (Bloomington: Indiana University Press, 1986), p. 55; Elaine Showalter, *These Modern Women: Autobiographical Essays from the 20s* (Old Westbury, N. Y.: Feminist Press, 1978).

3. See, for example, Léon Blum, *Du Mariage* (Paris: Albin Michel, 1908). In this book, Blum (later the architect of the Popular Front) argued that women possessed "a polygamous instinct" and should therefore be allowed, like men, to enjoy more sexual freedom before marriage. For his analysis of women's need for sexual pleasure and freedom, see particularly pp. 32–35. Blum's book was extremely popular and controversial, and went through 152 editions by 1937. According to Georges Anquetil and Jane Demagny in *L'Amant légitime ou la bourgeoise libertine* (Paris: Editions Georges Anquetil, 1923), Léon Blum was the first in France to argue for women's sexual freedom in this way.

4. For the historical literature on the New Woman, see my Introduction, note 53. For Bohemia, see Jerrold Siegel, *Bohemian Paris: Culture, Politics and the Boundaries of Bourgeois Life, 1830–1930* (New York: Viking Penguin, 1986).

5. M. Numa Sadoul, "Une Controverse: L'Emancipation de la jeune fille moderne est-elle un progrès réel?" *Progrès civique*, 13 June 1925, Dossier Féminisme, XXe Siècle, Bibliothèque Marguerite Durand (BMD).

6. Mathilde Alanic, *Nicole maman* (Paris: Flammarion, 1921). *Nicole maman* was only one of a larger series about this character, which continued into the forties with *Nicole mariée* (1947). Alanic's novel *Et l'amour dispose* (Paris: Flammarion, 1922) also concerned a young modern woman who wanted to live an independent life.

7. Alanic, *Nicole maman*, p. 44.

8. André Beaunier, *La Folle jeune fille* (Paris: Flammarion, 1922). *La Folle jeune fille* had a printing of 5,000 copies, a small number for that time. The average *tirage* for a new novel by a well-known author such as Henry Bordeaux was between 10,000 and 15,000. For more on Beaunier, see Fortunat Strowski, "La Vie littéraire: M. André Beaunier, et M. André Hallays," *Renaissance politique*, 24 September 1921.

9. Ibid., p. 85.

10. See Paul Fussell, *The Great War and Modern Memory* (New York: Oxford University Press, 1975), p. 76. See also Samuel Hynes, *A War Imagined: The First World War and English Culture* (New York: Atheneum, 1991), p. 116.

11. Drieu la Rochelle, *La Suite des idées* (Paris: Au Sens Pareil, 1927, 4th ed.), p. 28.

12. Quoted in John Williams, *The Other Battleground: The Homefronts, Britain, France and Germany* (London: Constable and Co., Ltd., 1972), p. 29.

13. Stéphane Audoin-Rouzeau, *14–18 Les Combattants des tranchées* (Paris: Armand Colin, 1986), p. 146.

14. See André Ducasse, Jacques Meyer, and Gabriel Perreux, *Vie et mort des Français, 1914–1918: Simple histoire de la grand guerre* (Paris: Hachette, 1969), p. 255. Ducasse, Meyer, and Perreux all fought in the war themselves. Audoin-Rouzeau argues, *14–18*, p. 143, that front soldiers from urban backgrounds felt the divide between warfront and homefront more keenly than those from rural backgrounds. On the separation between the homefront and the battlefront, see also the following oral history: Solange Bourrague and Renée Gourlaen, "Les Femmes dans la guerre: Recueil de témoignages, *Visions contemporaines* 4 (March 1990).

15. Georges Fabri, *L'Art et la manière d'accommoder et de raccommoder civ'lots et poilus* (Paris: Perrin et Cie, 1918), p. 1. He describes civilians and *poilus* as "two races, issuing from the same species but no longer understanding each other." *Revue de Front* and *Sans-tabac* are two trench journals in which Fabri's material first appeared. See the preface by popular novelist Léon Frapié, p. ix. For a critical review of *L'Art et la manière*, see *Mercure de France*, 16 March 1918. According to Audoin-Rouzeau, trench journals began to portray civilians in an unfavorable light beginning in early 1915; they continued to do so throughout the war period.

16. Ibid., pp. 2–3, 8, 44. In Pierre Chaine's equally sarcastic *Les Mémoires d'un rat* (Paris: L'Oeuvre, 1917), pp. 53–54, the returning soldier is also compelled to beg forgiveness for how good he looks.

17. Ibid., p. 39. Louis Mairet, another *poilu*, "was upset by those who, when told about some of the appalling conditions at the front and about the tenacity of the enemy, yawned and complained about the price of veal." Quoted by Modrus Eksteins, *Rites of Spring: The Great War and the Birth of the Modern Age* (Boston: Houghton-Mifflin, 1989), p. 227. Gabriel Perreux conjectures in both Ducasse et al., *Vie et mort*, p. 255, and in his *La Vie quotidienne des civils en France pendant la grande guerre* (Paris: Hachette, 1966), p. 258, that civilians were not interested in the "real" story of the front because they suffered from a *mauvaise conscience*—they were acutely aware of their safety in contrast to the danger their loved ones confronted.

18. Ibid., pp. 82–83. According to Perreux, *Vie quotidienne*, pp. 256–57, men were often reproached because they hadn't yet won the Croix de guerre.

19. Ibid., p. 5. He warned his fellows not to be bothered by "the prodigious quantity of civilians who crowd cafés," as these people were merely "cardiac and tuberculosis patients undergoing the *petit cure d'air*, while supporting economic recovery." See also Chaine, *Mémoires d'un rat*, p. 61.

20. Audoin-Rouzeau makes this argument in *14–18*, pp. 156, 159. To make his case, however, Audoin-Rouzeau quotes from a section of Fabri's *L'Art et la manière* that was published in the journal *Sans-tabac* in June 1918. In doing so, he distorts the meaning of the quotation, which concerns greeting loved ones upon arriving home. In particular, he ignores the heavily sarcastic tone of Fabri's remarks.

21. Quoted in Jacques Meyer, *La Vie quotidienne des soldats pendant la grand guerre* (Paris: Hachette, 1966), p. 356.

22. See Perreux, *La Vie quotidienne*, pp. 247–48; Ducasse et al., *Vie et mort*, pp. 254–55; Meyer, *La Vie quotidienne*, p. 350; Eksteins, *Rites of Spring*, p. 228. The split arguably began as soon as the war did. For example, in the fall of 1914, Georges Ohnet accused women of not yet knowing "that we are at war" and urged: "Allons! mesdames, disguise yourself as serious women, take on an appearance of gravity. . . . You are not bad, but you are thoughtless." See Georges Ohnet, *Journal d'un bourgeois de Paris pendant la guerre de 1914* (Paris: Société d'éditions littéraires et artistiques, 1914), pp. 324–25.

23. Roger Boutet de Monvel, *Carnet d'un permissionnaire* (Paris: Devambez, 1917).

24. Quoted in Audoin-Rouzeau, *14–18*, p. 129. The story appeared in *Le Crapouillot*, which means "trench mortar" in French.

25. Michel Corday, *The Paris Front: An Unpublished Diary, 1914–1918* (New York: E. P. Dutton, 1934), p. 78. See also novelist Henry Bordeaux's *Histoire d'une vie: Douleur et gloire de Verdun*, vol. 5 (Paris: Plon, 1959); and Perreux, *La Vie quotidienne*, p. 247.

26. Following the soldiers' lead, historians today continue to contrast the homefront and the battlefront in terms of an opposition between luxury and hardship. See, for example, Williams, *The Other Battleground*, p. 289; Meyer, *La Vie quotidienne*, p. 352; Ducasse et al., *Vie et mort*, p. 254; Perreux, *La Vie quotidienne*, p. 273. On pp. 338–39 in this last volume, Perreux explains the civilians' wartime penchant for luxuries and material pleasures as a result of several factors, among them, the influence of American culture. "From this moment," he claims, referring to the arrival of Americans on French soil, "a new civilization was born."

27. Louis Huot, "La Valeur morale des civils et la guerre," *Revue*, 1–15 August 1918: 258–60. See also his pamphlet *De Quelque manifestations de l'évolution psycho-passionnelle féminine pendant la guerre* (Paris: G. Roy, 1919), p. 5. He wrote several works on the psychology of the soldier with Paul Voivenel.

28. Quoted in Audoin-Rouzeau, *14–18*, p. 125.

29. Maurice Donnay, "Notes sur la guerre," *Revue hebdomaire*, 30 March 1918: 569, 574. These quotations are excerpted from the February and March 1916 entries of his war journal. See also Lieutenant Georges Grandjean, *De la dépravation . . . des femmes . . . des décadences* (Paris: La Maison d'art et d'édition, 1919), p. 63; F. L. Bernard, "La Psychologie du poilu," in *Grande revue*, April 1917; Maurice Demaison, *Croquis de Paris, 1914–1915* (Paris: Plon, 1917); L. Dumont-Wilden, "Journal de l'arrière," *Revue bleue*, 19–26 January 1918: 58; and Une Actrice de la comédie-française, *La Vie frivole pendant la guerre* (Paris: Flammarion, 1931), pp. 142–43.

30. Capitaine Tuffrau, *Carnet d'un combattant* (Paris: Librairie Payot,

1917), p. 151. Tuffrau fought in the war in the 246th infantry and, in 1930, coauthored a history of the Great War.

31. Georges Duhamel, *Entretiens dans le tumulte: Chronique contemporaine, 1914–1918* (Paris: Albert Guillot, 1949), pp. 153–54. Duhamel was the acclaimed author of *Civilisation* (1918) and *La Possession du monde* (1919). For more information on these texts, see the Introduction.

32. Jean Finot, "Pour la grandeur morale des français," *Revue mondiale*, 15 October 1919.

33. Quoted in Audoin-Rouzeau, p. 151.

34. Capitaine Tuffrau, *Carnet*, p. 150. At the opening of the Opéra in 1916, there was such a display of conspicuous wealth that the undersecretary of state for the fine arts was forced publicly to forbid ostentatious dress. A group of *poilus* who were "up to the ears in mud and proud to be there," congratulated him, crying "Bravo!" Quoted in Ducasse et al., *Vie et mort*, p. 261. In 1915, Michel Corday used the contrast between luxury and devastation to express the horrors of trench warfare, when he remarked in his diary: "At Caillot's, the costumiers, there are some jewelled gowns at 2,700 to 3,500 francs, intended for the gala at the Opéra on the 29th of December. And our men are standing in the trenches up to their waists in frozen mud." See Corday, *The Paris Front*, p. 126.

35. Abel Hermant, *Théophraste: Les Caractères français* (Paris: Editions de *La Vie parisienne*, 1917), p. 48.

36. Audoin-Rouzeau, *14–18*, p. 153.

37. In historian Philippe Bernard's words, "while grief and real suffering hid themselves, luxury and pleasure made a vulgar display." See Philippe Bernard and Henri Dubief, *The Decline of the French Third Republic, 1914–1938* (Cambridge: Cambridge University Press, 1985), p. 44.

38. Excerpted in Rémy Cazals, Claude Marquié, and René Pinès, *Années cruelles, 1914–1918* (Villongue d'Aude: Atelier du Gué, 1983), p. 48. I have chosen not to translate the song not only to preserve its original rhythm and rhyme, but also to preserve the double entendres. For example, "le cafard au front" can be translated in three ways. "Le cafard" was the special word that soldiers used to describe the endless waiting and boredom of trench life. In addition, "le cafard au front" can also be translated as "sorrow written on their brow" or "the cockroach at the front." For more on "le cafard," see Elizabeth Kahn, *The Neglected Majority: Les Camofleurs, Art History and World War I* (Lanham, Md.: University Press of America, 1984), p. 73. The word "rigole" is both a variant on the verb "rigoler," meaning to make fun of or to joke, and a noun meaning "trench."

39. The title here is a reference to a famous cartoon titled "Inquiétude" by Forain, which appeared in *Le Figaro* on 1 September 1915 and featured two *poilus* talking in the trenches. One says to the other: "Pourvu qu'ils tiennent!" and when the second asks: "Qui ça?" the first responds "Les civils." For other

references to the Forain cartoon in the war literature, see Jean Ajalbert, *Dans Paris, la grand ville* (Paris: Editions Georges Crès, 1916); André Beaunier, "Les Civils tiennent," *Revue hebdomaire*, 18 March 1916; Lucien Descaves, *La Maison anxieuse* (Paris: Georges Crès et Cie, 1916), pp. 53–54.

40. S. Mazare-Aga, *Pourvu qu'elles tiennent* (n.p., 1917).

41. Georges Lambert, "La Crise du foyer," *Opinion*, 9 August 1919.

42. Maurice Level, *Mado, ou la guerre à Paris* (Paris: Flammarion, 1919). In one sketch, Mado and her husband are looking through a magazine together that features stories about the war. Her husband is surprised and impressed by her apparent interest in the war until he realizes that she is really looking at pictures of women's fashion on the opposite page of the war story.

43. See Claude Bellanger and Jacques Godechot, eds., *1870–1940*, vol. 3 of *Histoire de la presse française* (Paris: Presses Universitaires de France, 1972), pp. 413–14, 425–26. The censorship office was managed through the Ministry of War. But however effective the office was in keeping "real" news about the war out of books and the press, the French became less and less credulous of what they read. The portrayal of the war in the newspapers angered the soldiers because they knew it perpetuated ignorance on the home-front. They dubbed the press *"bourrage de crâne,"* or "brainwashing." On this issue, see particularly Audoin-Rouzeau, *14–18*, "L'Arrière détesté." For censorship of published books, see Henri-Jean Martin, Roger Chartier, and Jean-Pierre Vivet, eds., *Le Livre concurrencé, 1900–1950*, vol. 4 of *Histoire de l'édition française* (Paris: Promodis, 1986), p. 189.

44. See Rachilde, *Mercure de France*, 16 December 1919.

45. Williams, *The Other Battleground*, p. 217.

46. See Françoise Thébaud, *La Femme au temps;* James McMillan, *Housewife or Harlot: The Position of Women in French Society* (New York: St. Martin's Press, 1981); Mathilde Dubesset, Françoise Thébaud, and Catherine Vincent, "Les Munitionettes de la Seine," in *1914–1918: L'Autre front*, ed. Patrick Fridenson (Paris: Les Editions Ouvrières, 1977). See also Perreux, *La Vie quotidienne*, chap. 4, "Les Remplaçantes."

47. Thébaud, *La Femme au temps*, p. 148.

48. By 1917, 684,000 women were working in munitions and arms plants in Paris. State railways employed 6,000 women before the war and 57,000 by 1917. See Williams, *The Other Battleground*, pp. 80–81; Stephen Hause with Anne Kenney, *Women's Suffrage and Social Politics in the French Third Republic* (Princeton: Princeton University Press, 1984), p. 198; Colin Dyer, *Population and Society in Twentieth Century France* (New York: Holmes and Meier, 1978), p. 35.

49. In 1919, there were ten times as many female law students and over three times as many women medical students as in 1914. Moreover, many women who were already doctors and lawyers gained clients as their male

counterparts left for the front. See Jean Rabaut, *Histoire des féminismes fran-çais* (Paris: Stock, 1978), p. 276, and Thébaud, *La Femme au temps*, p. 166.

50. Stephen Hause, "More Minerva Than Mars: The French Women's Rights Campaign and the First World War," in *Behind the Lines: Gender and the Two World Wars*, ed. Margaret Higonnet et al. (New Haven: Yale University Press, 1987), p. 102.

51. Paul Abram, *La Faiblesse de l'homme: Notes d'après-guerre* (Paris: Editions des Amitiés Françaises, 1920), pp. 9–10.

52. Paul Cazin, *L'Humaniste à la guerre* (Paris: Plon, 1915), p. 224.

53. Peter Gay has applied these terms to Weimar intellectuals. See Peter Gay, *Weimar Culture: The Insider as Outsider* (New York: Harper and Row, 1968), preface, p. xiv. Gay talks about postwar Weimar intellectuals and artists as "propelled by history into the inside for a short, dizzying, fragile moment." It is important to note that he does not include women in this group at all and that he is talking about the postwar period rather than the war itself. My analysis here is indebted to Sandra Gilbert, "Soldier's Heart: Literary Men, Literary Women and the Great War," *Signs* 8 (Spring 1983). Please see Introduction, note 44, for commentary and recent criticisms of Gilbert's work.

54. According to Marc Ferro, *The Great War, 1914–1918* (Boston: Routledge and Kegan Paul, 1973), p. 225: "There was also resentment against women who had also profiteered in their way from war because the men's departure made their emancipation possible." In *L'Identité masculine*, Annelise Maugue has argued convincingly that there was a crisis in male identity even before the war, because of the feminist movement and the growing number of women in higher education and the professions. She also examines the postwar period very briefly and conjectures that the crisis was resolved through the war because it exalted male virility and heroism. She bases her argument on an analysis of *La Garçonne*, but she concentrates only on the very end of the novel. In doing so, I would argue, she has overlooked the darker side of the war's effect on notions of masculinity. For an analysis of *La Garçonne*, see chap. 2. Michelle Perrot's argument in "The New Eve and the Old Adam: Changes in French Women's Condition at the Turn of the Century," Higonnet, ed., *Behind the Lines*, is based on Maugue's analysis.

55. Gaston Rageot, *La Natalité: Ses lois economiques et psychologiques* (Paris: Flammarion, 1918), p. 256. As Thébaud has argued, when French soldiers heard of women's entry into their previously exclusive domains, they expressed "fear in seeing themselves supplanted, in being the turkeys of a bizarre farce, in which some lost their lives, and others their virile prerogatives," See her *La Femme au temps*, p. 296.

56. Quoted in Audoin-Rouzeau, *14–18*, p. 141.

57. Pierre Chaine, *Les Mémoires d'un rat*, pp. 49–50. The book, which centers on the life of one *poilu* named Juvenet, is told from the perspective of a rat whom he has befriended in the trenches. Anatole France wrote the preface to the 1917 edition. It was then reissued by Payot in 1920, with new edi-

tions in 1923, 1930, and even 1934. Encouraged by the popularity of *Les Mémoires*, Chaine wrote a sequel titled *Commentaires de Ferdinand, ancien rat des tranchées* in 1918.

58. See Becker, *Les Français,* chaps. 2 and 11.

59. Henri Barbusse, *Le Feu (journal d'une escouade)* (Paris: Flammarion, 1916). In my translations here, I have sometimes used Fitzwater Wray's *Under Fire: The Story of a Squad* (New York: E. P. Dutton, 1917). In these cases, I have cited both the original text and the Wray translation. By 1927, Barbusse's book had sold 360,000 copies, a number that far exceeded the average *tirage* (10,000 to 15,000) of a novel at this time. Jean Vic, author of an early, massive bibliography on war literature, *La Littérature de la guerre: Manuel méthodique et critique des publications de langue française* (Paris: Les Presses Françaises, 1923), argues in vol. 3, p. 257, that "the book achieved an unequaled success" and that it was the focus of "passionate discussions." According to Albert Shinz in *French Literature of the Great War* (New York: D. Appleton, 1920), pp. 33–34, Barbusse's *Le Feu* was "by far the most-discussed book of the war." In *Témoins: Essai d'analyse et de critique des souvenirs des combattants edités en français de 1915 à 1918* (Paris: Les Etincelles, 1929), p. 557, Jean Norton Cru notes that "From 1917 on, it appeared to be an article of faith that Barbusse had written the greatest war novel, the one that proclaimed those truths that no one before had dared to speak." Contemporary reviews also emphasize the realism of the novel. See, for example, Rachilde's review in *Mercure de France,* 1 February 1917. On the issue of realism, see also Gerard Canini, *Combattre à Verdun* (Nancy: Presses Universitaires de Nancy, 1988), p. 192; Antoine Prost's *Les Anciens combattants et la société française, 1914–1939* (Paris: Foundation nationale des sciences politiques, 1977), 3:5; and Jean-Jacques Becker, *Les Français dans la grande guerre* (Paris: Editions Robert Laffont, 1983), chap. 11. Barbusse was a journalist before the war and had already published three books, including a collection of Symbolist poetry, when he authored *Le Feu.* He entered the war voluntarily in 1914 and fought for a year, despite the fact that he was forty-one and had a bad lung. He became a Communist in 1920 and served as literary director of *L'Humanité.*

60. Barbusse, *Under Fire,* p. 312; *Le Feu,* p. 327.

61. Barbusse, *Under Fire,* p. 339; *Le Feu,* pp. 357–58.

62. Barbusse, *Under Fire,* p. 163; *Le Feu,* p. 170.

63. Barbusse, *Under Fire,* p. 163; *Le Feu,* p. 171.

64. Barbusse, *Le Feu,* p. 170.

65. Barbusse, *Under Fire,* p. 163; *Le Feu,* p. 171.

66. Barbusse, *Under Fire,* p. 310; *Le Feu,* p. 325.

67. Barbusse, *Under Fire,* p. 312; *Le Feu,* p. 327.

68. Paul Ducatel, *Histoire de la IIIe République, Vue à travers l'imagerie populaire et la presse satirique* (Paris: J. Grassin, 1973), 4:92. See also the car-

toon of "Les Remplaçantes" from *Excelsior*, 6 November 1916, in the same volume, p. 113.

69. Henriot, *De l'arrière au front: Croquis de Henriot* (Paris: Fasquelle, 1917), p. 196. Henriot's real name was Henry Maigrot.

70. Ibid., p. 83.

71. Williams, *The Other Battleground*, p. 81. Many working-class wives of soldiers received 1 franc 25 centimes a day for themselves and 50 centimes for each child, thus enjoying a financial independence they had never known before, particularly if they were earning additional money doing war work. Historians argue that such an allocation did not in any way encourage women to want their husbands at the front. See the opinion of Gabriel Perreux in Ducasse et al., *Vie et mort*, p. 264, and Perreux's *La Vie quotidienne*, p. 65. See also Jean-Jacques Becker's interesting discussion of the allocations in *Les Français dans la grande guerre*, chap. 1. In *La Maison anxieuse*, p. 17, Lucien Descaves argued that the allocation varied in its meaning. For some women, it meant survival and for others, the movies two times a week. For the expression of a similar anxiety concerning rural women and their improved situation, see Audoin-Rouzeau, *14–18*, pp. 150–51.

72. Lucien Descaves, *La Maison anxieuse*, pp. 28, 30. Descaves was the drama critic for the conservative *L'Intransigeant*, and the literary director of *Le Journal*. For an intriguing analysis of his views considering gender relations before the war, see Berenson, *The Trial of Madame Caillaux* (Berkeley: University of California Press, 1992), pp. 120–21.

73. See Gilbert, "Soldier's Heart"; McMillan, *Housewife*. McMillan dismisses accounts of liberated women during the war as irreconcilable with factual evidence. In other words, because he reads such accounts at face value, he rejects their historical importance altogether on empirical grounds.

74. Marguerite Lesage, *Journal de guerre d'une française* (Paris: Editions de la Diffusion du Livre, 1938), p. 151. The wife of an *industriel* who was mobilized during the war, Lesage is from an occupied territory, so that her house and her husband's factory have been devastated. She writes on 31 August 1917.

75. Madame H. Cloquié, *La Femme après la guerre: Ses droits, son rôle, son devoir* (Paris: Chez Malone, 1915), pp. 7–14.

76. See Colette, "Modes," in *Les Heures longues* (Paris: Fayard et Cie, 1917), pp. 69–75. See also Colette's novel, *Mitsou, ou comment l'esprit vient aux filles* (Paris: Arthème Fayard, 1918).

77. Thébaud, *La Femme au temps de la guerre de 14* (Paris: Stock, 1986), pp. 36–39. See Léon Abensour, *Les Vaillantes* (Paris: Chapelot, 1917); Camille Bellaigue, "La Femme française et la guerre," *Revue hebdomaire,* 15 April 1916; Berthem-Bontoux, *Les Françaises et la grand guerre* (Paris: Bloud et Gay, 1917); Louis Barthou, *L'Effort de la femme française* (Paris: Bloud et Gay, 1917); Madame Camille Clermont, ed., *Souvenirs de parisiennes en temps*

de guerre (Paris: Berger-Levrault, 1918); Jules Combarieu, *Les Jeunes filles françaises et la guerre* (Paris: Armand Colin, 1916); Maurice Donnay, *La Parisienne et la guerre* (Paris: Georges Crès et Cie, 1916); Francis de Miomandre, *Méditation sur la femme de France* (Paris: Le Nouvel Essor, 1916); Jacques Vincent, *Parisiennes de guerre, 1915–1917* (Paris: Editions de la France, 1918). It is striking how many of these eulogies to women appeared in 1916 and 1917. However, Thébaud claims that the literature praising women was consistent throughout the war. For an American variant of the genre, see Louise Fitch's *Madame France* (New York: Woman's Press, 1919). For a fictional portrayal of the ideal mother/nurse during the war, see Charles Morice, *Par le sang de France* (Paris: Plon-Nourrit, 1921).

78. See Henri Robert, "La Femme et la guerre," *Revue,* May 1917: 244–46. Henri Robert (sometimes Henri-Robert) was the president of the Bar between 1913 and 1919.

79. For the literature on World War I as a dehumanizing experience, see my Introduction, note 6.

80. Maurice Crubellier, *Histoire culturelle de la France, XIXe–XXe siècle* (Paris: Armand Colin, 1974), pp. 111–12. For an illuminating view of the mother/prostitute dichotomy in the nineteenth century, see also Thérèse Moreau, *La Sang de l'histoire: Michelet, l'histoire et l'idée de la femme au XIXe siècle* (Paris: Flammarion, 1982). For the prostitute, in particular, see T. J. Clark, *The Painting of Modern Life: Paris in the Art of Manet and His Followers* (New York: Knopf, 1985).

81. Audoin-Rouzeau argues that in trench literature, at least, the image of the wife and mother is the most common and that of the frivolous, lighthearted woman, more exceptional. See *14–18,* pp. 152–53. This split between the "bad" and "good" woman parallels another division in the war literature that Gabriel Perreux points out in Ducasse et al., *Vie et mort,* p. 220. Here Perreux talks about how civilian war chronicles fall into two separate types. The first type is an exercise in civilian patriotism and optimism; it demands victory at any price "à la Barrès." The second type is more reserved and defiant, and tends "toward a reasoned pessimism" and a pacifism "à la Romain Rolland."

82. Chaine, *Mémoires d'un rat,* pp. 54–55.

83. Maurice Donnay, *Lettre à une dame blanche* (Paris: Société littéraire de France, 1917). I chose not to translate this phrase in the text because of the play on words between *"oeuvre,"* which translates roughly as "charitable organization," and *"désoeuvrées,"* which means "the idle ones." Examples of Donnay's eulogies to women's war effort can be found in the seventh and twelfth letters.

84. André Beaunier, "La Littérature de guerre," *Revue des deux mondes,* 3 October 1917. Beaunier's statement here contrasts with this one by Donnay on roughly the same subject: "many young women on the homefront will have shown more courage and good faith than have many men."

85. Louis Narquet, "La Française de demain d'après sa psychologie de guerre," *Revue bleue,* 21–28 September 1918.

86. See Audoin-Rouzeau, *14–18,* "L'Arrière qui fascine"; and Marc Roudebush, "'Long Live Cowards and Fools!': World War I and the Construction of French Masculinity" (Paper presented to the World War I: Culture and Society Conference, University of California at Berkeley, 15 April 1990).

87. See Edward Berenson's fascinating discussion of this issue in his *Trial of Madame Caillaux,* pp. 113–17.

88. See Ibid., p. 110, where Berenson makes the same point about Victorian men.

89. Paul Géraldy, *La Guerre, madame* (Paris: Editions Crès, 1916). Géraldy originally wrote the book anonymously, then made his authorship known in 1917, when the book had already enjoyed great success. On the popularity of *La Guerre, madame,* see Jean Vic, *La Littérature de la guerre,* and Perreux, *La Vie quotidienne,* p. 312. After its publication in 1916, *La Guerre, madame* went through 57 editions by 1919 and 61 by 1922. The book was reissued as late as 1936 in a new edition. For a review of the book when it first appeared, see Victor Snell, *Renaissance politique,* 5 August 1916.

90. Ibid., p. 36.

91. Gaston Rageot, *La Faiblesse des forts* (Paris: Librairie Plon, 1918). For an interesting review of the novel, see Nicolas Ségur, "Romans nouveaux," *Revue des revues,* 1–15 February 1919. Ségur compares the novel to a Greek tragedy in its sense of "inexorable fatality," but argues that it could not have taken place in any other era than that of the war—"that enormous cataclysm that, since 1914, has turned the world upside down." He describes Rageot as a "critic preoccupied with the great issues of the day."

92. Ibid., p. 147. François's "heart . . . had been seized with pity, but of the active kind."

93. Ibid., pp. 119–21. It is interesting that of the two brothers, he has the most "feminine" name.

94. Ibid., pp. 137–38.

95. Ibid., p. 155. For example, he becomes obsessed with the actual statistical percentage of the men that he can save. On a trip home from the front, he decides to transform the family's tuberculosis sanitarium into a refuge for war victims with nervous diseases. They are described in anguished terms as once beautiful and strong youths who are now mutilated, hysterical, or insane.

96. Ibid., p. 174.

97. Ibid. François interprets the affair as a symptom of "the demoralization of the homefront," which had betrayed the LeCordellier family's "sacred mission," the very thought of which now makes him laugh "loudly, like a lunatic, like one of his hysterics."

98. Ibid., p. 207. The dramatist Eugène Brieux outlines a similar dynamic between the front soldier and the woman of the homefront in his well-known,

controversial play *Pierette et Galaor (l'enfant)* (Paris: Librairie Stock, 1924), pp. 143–44. Here one of the main characters tries to explain why Henri, a veteran, is so disillusioned about the war and life in general: "I know: most French women have behaved admirably, but these admirable women are not the ones that [the returning soldiers] saw. They saw only the others. And the greatest crime these others committed was to sow the seeds of skepticism, doubt and desolation in the hearts of those who have just saved us." See chap. 6 for a more thorough examination of Brieux's play.

99. Ibid., p. 272.

100. She compares her seduction with "the madness of a man or of a people in destroying world peace." Ibid., p. 245.

101. Ibid., p. 274. Only Lise-Reine's ultimate death, like the end of the war itself, assures the restoration of harmony between the two brothers and the resumption of their work together, in the final scene, "as if . . . no trace of the storms of the heart had been left behind."

102. See Ducasse et al., *Vie et mort*, p. 264. This estimate is high compared to others made during the war by contemporaries. See, for example, Claude Laforêt, "La Mentalité française à l'épreuve de la guerre," *Mercure de France*, 16 February 1918: 585, and Hermant, *Théophraste*, p. 73, for a more moderate treatment of the subject.

103. Géraldy, *La Guerre, madame*, 1916 ed., p. 70.

104. L. Narquet, "La Française de demain," pp. 601–2. The novelist Henry Bordeaux also complained that women were not preserving their "dignity" and "fidelity" as the wives of servicemen. See Williams, *The Other Battleground*, p. 81.

105. Huot, *De Quelques manifestations*, p. 10. Huot blamed the "persistent nervous tension" and state of exhaustion that women suffered during the war, as well as their natural predisposition "to react to the slightest organic disturbance."

106. Grandjean, *De la dépravation*. The charge of female infidelity continued after the war. One French literary critic declared that for women, the war had served as a "bloody aphrodisiac." See H. d'Almeras, *La Femme amoureuse dans la vie et dans la littérature* (Paris: Albin Michel, 1925), p. 235.

107. Because the topic of female sexual infidelity forms such an important part of wartime literature, historians have tried to come to terms with the question of just how widespread it was. In *La Femme au temps*, p. 195, Thébaud argues that the war did increase illicit sexual activity for women. She refers to the high rate of prostitution during the war, as well as the effects of solitude and sexual abstinence. Yet she believes that the women who were not loyal were in the minority, basing her argument on the fact that there was no sharp rise in illegitimate birth statistics. More significant, in her mind, was the soaring divorce rate immediately after the war. Most of these cases were initiated by men, not women, and adultery increasingly counted among the reasons

given when such proceedings were initiated by both parties. However, in *La Vie quotidienne*, pp. 324, 329, Perreux accepts as truth the wartime perception of women as immoral and argues that the illegitimacy rate did increase. On p. 263 of *Vie et mort*, he justifies his view by reasoning that women, called to take on men's responsibilities, sought as well to assume their "traditional masculine prerogatives." In *La Vie quotidienne*, p. 210, Meyer also argues that female infidelity was widespread. See also Eksteins, *Rites of Spring*, p. 225. For England, see Sandra Gilbert, "Soldier's Heart." For the situation in Germany, see Stephen Kern, *Anatomy and Destiny: A Cultural History of the Human Body* (Indianapolis: Bobbs-Merrill, 1975), chap. 15: "Eros in Barbed Wire," and Beth Irwin Lewis, "*Lustmord:* Inside the Windows of the Metropolis," in *Berlin: Culture and Metropolis*, ed. Charles W. Haxthausen and Heidrun Suhr (Minneapolis: University of Minnesota Press, 1990).

108. Roland Dorgelès, *Les Croix de bois* (Paris: Albin Michel, 1919). In *Guerre et révolution dans le roman français de 1919 à 1939* (Paris: Klincksieck, 1974), Maurice Rieuneau argues (p. 20) that Barbusse and Roland Dorgelès wrote the two most important books of the war in terms of actual copies sold. According to Gabriel Perreux, *La Vie quotidienne*, p. 311, Dorgelès's novel enjoyed "great popularity among the veterans" and won the Prix Fémina in 1919. For the "realism" of the novel, see Rachilde's review in *Mercure de France*, 1 January 1920; Jean Finot's review of "La Reveil des morts," in *Revue mondiale*, 15 July 1923; André Beaunier's critical summary of Dorgelès's work in *Revue des deux mondes*, 1 September 1925.

109. Dorgelès, *Les Croix*, pp. 251–53.

110. Ibid., p. 276. According to some of his critics, Gilbert represented Dorgelès himself. See Rachilde's review in *Mercure de France*, and Gaston Picard, "Le Prochain Prix Goncourt: Des *Croix de bois* aux sept parmi les hommes," *Renaissance politique*, 22 November 1919. Dorgelès's later novel, *Le Réveil des morts* (Paris: Albin Michel, 1923), also deals with the theme of marital infidelity. Jacques, the main character, marries a war widow, Hélène, after the war is over, only to realize that he had been lovers with Hélène while her husband had been at the front. Dorgelès portrays Hélène as harsh and cruel; she tortures her husband during the war by not answering his worried and anxious letters. In one climactic scene, Jacques has a dream that all the dead awaken along the front and march on Paris, demanding justice from the war profiteers and women who have forgotten them. See Rieuneau, *Guerre et révolution*, pp. 48–50, and Finot, *Revue mondiale*, for a critical analysis of the novel.

111. See Gilbert, "Soldier's Heart."

112. Raymond Radiguet, *Le Diable au corps* (Paris: Gallimard, 1982; orig. pub. 1923), pp. 114, 116. For more on Radiguet, see Rieuneau, *Guerre et révolution*, chap. 5.

113. Ibid., p. 116.

114. Keith Goesch, *Raymond Radiguet* (Paris: La Palatine, 1955), pp. 34–

35. For an entertaining introduction to the scandal, see Christian Millau, "Raymond Radiguet: Le Diable au corps," in *La France de la Madelon, 1914–1918: Le Roman vrai de l'arrière,* ed. Gilbert Guilleminault (Paris: Denoël, 1965). See also the preface by André Berne Joffroy in Radiguet, *Le Diable,* and the discussion of the novel's controversy by Jean-Jacques Becker and Serge Berstein in *Victoire et frustrations, 1914–1929,* vol. 12 of *Nouvelle histoire de la France contemporaine* (Paris: Seuil, 1990), p. 174.

115. Keith Goesch quotes these words by reviewers in *Raymond Radiguet,* p. 43. For a positive assessment of the book, see Jean Cocteau's review in *Nouvelle revue française,* 1 April 1923: 703–5. For a negative review, see *Revue mondiale,* 1 May 1923. Radiguet, whose budding career was guided by Cocteau, died tragically at the age of twenty from typhoid fever.

116. Quoted in Goesch's *Raymond Radiguet,* p. 45.

117. Joffroy, "Preface" to *Diable,* p. x; Goesch, *Raymond Radiguet,* p. 44.

118. See Herbert Lottman, *Colette, A Life* (Boston: Little-Brown, 1991), chap. 19. The short story originally appeared in *Le Matin* in 1912. *Chéri* was first published in serial form in *La Vie parisienne* during 1921 and shortly afterward came out as a novel.

119. Colette later wrote in her memoir *L'Etoile vesper* (1946): "But life as it was prior to 14–18, gone forever and never to return.... People stopped reading or hearing or using droll nicknames like Félisque Faure or Nini Toutcourt, women seemed to have different names, their breasts and buttocks had been altered, demi-mondaines no longer lolled late in bed sipping frothy cups of hot chocolate and playing with their tiny dogs, they no longer poured half a liter of expensive perfume into their baths." Quoted in Michèle Sarde, *Colette: Free and Fettered* (New York: William Morrow, 1980), p. 300.

120. Colette, *La Fin de Chéri,* vol. 6 of *Oeuvres complètes* (Paris: Flammarion, 1949), pp. 163–64.

121. Elaine Marks, *Colette* (New Brunswick, N.J.: Rutgers University Press, 1960), p. 139. On pp. 140–41, Marks argues that Chéri's pathetic inability to live in postwar Paris "is only superficially connected with his war experiences or his domestic difficulties. It is very simply that he is incapable of living outside that world that Léa created for him." To argue that Chéri's behavior can be explained solely in terms of a postwar *crise de l'esprit* would undoubtedly be a reduction of the novel's psychological complexity. But the links here, I believe, are more than "superficial." See Sarde, *Colette,* p. 335, where he argues that Colette "managed to recall the atmosphere of the immediate postwar period" in *La Fin de Cheri;* and Margaret Davies, *Colette* (London: Oliver and Boyd, 1961), p. 53, where she praises Colette for having managed "to reflect and to anticipate in one of her main characters the whole spirit of the time."

122. As Joanna Richardson puts it in her biography, *Colette* (London: Methuen, 1983), p. 112, "Chéri returns to a world in which the rôle of the sexes seems to have been reversed. His womenfolk have a masculine sense of pur-

pose and they are the masters in the house. He himself no longer has a place." Richardson also notes the change in Chéri's mother as part of this phenomenon: she wears a uniform and is preoccupied with official duties, political intrigue, and financial speculation.

123. Colette, *La Fin*, pp. 212, 214, 219. For Léa as a symbol of prewar femininity and the "virilisation" of all the characters in *Chéri*, see Davies, *Colette*, pp. 59–62.

124. Sarde argues in *Colette*, p. 334, that trauma and anxiety concerning change—what he refers to as "the psychological crisis of the postwar period"—was primarily "a male crisis" rather than a female one. Women, argues Sarde, used the war to improve their status, take on new responsibilities, and acquire independence. Colette's writing during this period "expresses this kind of female post-war victory."

125. Jean Finot, *Revue mondiale*, 15 August 1926.

126. Jean Dufort, *Sur la route de lumière* (Paris: Librairie Plon, 1921); Francis Forest, *Thé dansant* (Paris: Aux Editions de Belles Lettres, 1922). Dufort's novel was published in 1921 and enjoyed a moderate success, going through six editions in a year. For a favorable review of the novel, see *Renaissance politique*, 5 February 1921. Dufort was born and raised in Lyon, where he was better known as a writer. He wrote several novels and won the Grand Prix de littérature de Lyon in 1930. The printing of Forest's novel was very small—only about three hundred copies.

127. Marc Sangnier, "Le Retour à la paix," *Revue Hebdomaire*, 30 August 1919: 582. For more on the Sillon movement, see Jean-Marie Mayeur and Madeleine Rebérioux, *The Third Republic from Its Origins to the Great War, 1871–1914* (Cambridge: Cambridge University Press, 1987), pp. 299–301.

128. Dufort, *Sur la route*, pp. 2–3, 17.

129. André Fage's novel *Les Demi-veuves* (Paris: Renaissance du Livre, 1919) shows how representations of wartime female infidelity reversed traditional sexual roles. In the preface to the novel, André Fage describes his inspiration as the plight of women whose lovers returned changed by the war: "deliverance restored to them nothing but a stranger, a face that forced itself to smile, a soul that disguised itself." But in the novel itself, the sexual roles of this postwar drama are reversed. Here the returning hero is a woman, Mounette, who arrives in Paris "a stranger" after four brutal years in German captivity. She finds her fiancé, Mareuil, having an affair with another woman. Here the woman, Mounette, is revolted by the casual disregard the city shows for the war's victims, and the man, Mareuil, is distant and indifferent. Mareuil's inner struggle to shake aside such indifference and commit himself to Mounette comprises the central conflict of the novel. Hence the story reverses Fage's own more conscious purpose in telling it—Mareuil, not Mounette, is the "soul that disguises itself" as he tries to overcome his doubts about Mounette. It is tempting to read such a reversal as an attempt to deal with female sexual infidelity by projecting its traumatic effects onto women themselves.

130. Dufort, *Sur la route*, p. 71.

131. Ibid., p. 127.

132. Ibid., pp. 17–19.

133. Ibid., p. 271.

134. Forest, *Thé dansant*, pp. 7–8.

135. Ibid., p. 21.

136. Ibid., pp. 205–6.

137. Ibid., p. 198.

138. Ibid., p. 19.

139. Ibid., p. 200.

140. Ibid., p. 209.

2. She Stood at the Center of a Shattered World

1. Anonymous, *Aux femmes chrétiennes: Le Scandale de la mode* (Besançon: Imprimerie de l'Est, 1925), p. 14.

2. Victor Margueritte, *La Garçonne* (Paris: Flammarion, 1922). Here I have used references from the 1949 Flammarion re-edition. All translations are mine unless otherwise indicated.

3. See Roger Chartier and Jean Hébard, "Les Imaginaires de la lecture," in *Le Livre concurrencé, 1900–1950*, vol. 5 of *Histoire de l'édition française*, ed. Henri-Jean Martin, Roger Chartier, and Jean-Pierre Vivet (Paris: Promodis, 1986), p. 530.

4. Renée Papaud, "Le Féminisme à travers le roman," *Bulletin des groupes féministes de l'Enseignement laïque*, February 1924: 13.

5. André Billy, "Les Livres qu'on lit," *Oeuvre*, 23 August 1922. Billy was also referring to Marcel Prévost's novel *Les Don Juanes*, which will be examined later on in the chapter.

6. See Anne Marie Sohn, "*La Garçonne* face à l'opinion publique: Type littéraire ou type social des années 20?" *Mouvement social* 80 (1972); and Françoise Thébaud, *La Femme au temps de la guerre de 14* (Paris: Stock, 1986), p. 299. On Marthe Hanau, see Dominique Desanti, *La Banquière des années folles: Marthe Hanau* (Paris: Fayard, 1968), and the obituary by Janet Flanner in *Paris Was Yesterday* (New York: Viking, 1972). For Louise Weiss, see her own *Ce que femme veut: Souvenirs de la Troisième République* (Paris: Gallimard, 1946).

7. José Germain, "Les livres qu'il faut avoir lus. Féminisme," *Le Matin*, 8 August 1922.

8. The figure of 15,000 represents a jump from the prewar average of 1,000 to 10,000. See Martin et al., *Histoire de l'édition*, p. 86. I have also surveyed the *tirages* for other Flammarion novels throughout the decade and come to the same conclusion. The average *tirage* for a new Flammarion novel by a

well-known author such as Henry Bordeaux was between 10,000 and 15,000. Even the *tirages* of Henri Barbusse's extremely popular and well-known *Le Feu* look skimpy in comparison with those of *La Garçonne*. By Flammarion's standards, *Le Feu* was definitely a "best-seller," but only 360,000 copies had been printed by 1927, eleven years after its publication. *La Garçonne* surpassed this number in its first year of publication.

9. Sohn, *"La Garçonne,"* p. 8. Gilbert Guilleminault, *Les Années folles* (Paris: Editions Denoël, 1958), pp. 123–24, 127–31. Among the many "spin-offs" of the novel were a hairstyle, a doll model, a perfume, and several films, the 1933 version of which starred Edith Piaf. See also Jean-Noël Jeanneney, *"La Garçonne"* et le *Gai Pied, Le Monde,* 14 August 1987.

10. For the argument that *La Garçonne's* readership was middle-class, see Sohn, *"La Garçonne,"* p. 8. Sohn argues that based on the fact that workers in transportation, for example, even in Paris, only made 15–16 francs a day, it is doubtful that they could have afforded such a book. For the argument that the readership was youthful and female, see Guilleminault, *Les Années folles,* p. 122.

11. See José Germain, "Les Livres." Anne-Marie Sohn counted 134 articles about the book in the French dailies and other periodicals from the time of its publication in July 1922 to the following January, when Victor Margueritte was expelled from the Légion d'honneur.

12. Guilleminault, *Les Années folles,* p. 135. Margueritte wrote the screenplay himself and the actress Frances Delhia played *la garçonne.* Margueritte also wrote a play version of the novel in 1927. See also Sohn, *"La Garçonne,"* p. 8.

13. Guilleminault, *Les Années folles,* p. 128. Many of the most controversial passages of *La Garçonne* were taken out of the English version.

14. For the Société des gens des lettres, see *Annuaire orange: Arts, lettres, sciences* (Paris: Aux Editions d'*Annuaire orange,* 1931), p. 352; and Martin et al., *Histoire de l'édition.*

15. Victor Margueritte, *Ainsi parla Victor Margueritte: Paroles recueillies par Maurice Roya* (Paris: Editions Nilsson, 1929), p. 17; Guilleminault, *Les Années folles,* pp. 125–26. Margueritte remarried in 1920 to a woman who was twenty years his junior.

16. Ibid., pp. 124–25. See also Sohn, *"La Garçonne,"* p. 10. Margueritte ran as a socialist of the extreme right in Ardennes in 1909.

17. Press reactions to Margueritte's expulsion from the Légion d'honneur varied according to political orientation. The right generally supported the move as a patriotic and moral act. See, for example, Jean Guirard, "Un Verdict salutaire," *La Croix,* 9 January 1923. In his review of the novel, Charles Maurras argued that although he considered Margueritte a "bad author" and the novel "without any literary value whatsoever," he was convinced that Margueritte's expulsion set a bad precedent in terms of freedom of press. See Charles

Maurras, "La Politique: La Liberté d'écrire," *Action française*, 9 January 1923. The Left, however, accused the generals of revenging themselves against Margueritte for his accusations of their incompetence during the war in *Au Bord du gouffre*. This was the accusation by young Communists such as Henri Barbusse, as well as the editors of the journal *Populaire*. Journalists across the political spectrum voiced the belief that Margueritte, who had a bad reputation for being egotistical, was simply making money from the scandal. See Marcel Martinet, "Les Lettres: *La Garçonne*," *Humanité*, 7 January 1923.

18. Paul Souday, *Le Temps*, 20 July 1922.

19. Jean Guirard's comments were made in response to Margueritte's expulsion from the Légion d'honneur. See "Un Verdict salutaire."

20. *Le Canard enchaîné*, 27 December 1922. See also the issue of December 13, where the editors gave Margueritte a prize for his "modesty."

21. Advertisement, *Oeuvre*, 3 August 1922. Margueritte's editors at Flammarion were Max and Alex Fischer, who themselves had rather shadowy reputations in the literary world. See Guilleminault, *Les Années folles*, p. 123.

22. George de la Fouchardière, "L'Affaire Margueritte," *Canard enchaîné*, 3 January 1923. In his celebrated memoir *La Décade des illusions* (Paris: Gallimard, 1950), Maurice Sachs mentions de la Fouchardière as one of the two best satirists of the postwar period. Clément Vautel, whose novel *Madame ne veut pas d'enfant*, will be examined in chap. 5, was the other. De la Fouchardière also wrote a satirical column for *L'Oeuvre*.

23. Desanti, *Années folles*, p. 25. Literary critic Fernande Gontier also argues that the novel's scandal can be explained by Monique's middle-class origins. According to Gontier, Monique breaks all bonds with the bourgeois world and enters "the world of Chéri." She calls *La Garçonne* "the incontestable best-seller of the twenties." See *La Femme et le couple dans le roman de l'entre-deux-guerres* (Paris: Klinksieck, 1976), pp. 79–82; Jean-Jacques Becker and Serge Berstein in *Victoire et frustrations, 1914–1929*, vol. 12 of *Nouvelle histoire de la France contemporaine* (Paris: Seuil, 1990), p. 364.

24. Alice Berthet, *La Française*, 2 September 1922. For a similar view of Monique, see Marc Varenne's review of *La Garçonne* in *Renaissance politique*, 29 July 1922. For another review by a well-known bourgeois feminist, see Maria Vérone, *Droit des femmes*, August–September 1922: 196.

25. See, for example, Fortuné Paillot, *Amant ou maîtresse? ou l'androgyne perplexe*, published by Flammarion the same year as *La Garçonne*.

26. Gustave Téry, *L'Ecole des garçonnes* (Paris: L'Oeuvre, 1923).

27. As recently as the 1970s, *La Garçonne* was republished in a paperback edition. See also Dominique Desanti, *La Femme au temps des années folles* (Paris: Stock, 1985), p. 25; Jeanneney, "*La Garçonne* et *Le Gai Pied*," which compares the censorship of *La Garçonne* to that of a homosexual magazine under the conservative Chirac government; Jody Shields, "Call Me Garçonne," *Vogue*, December, 1988.

28. Victor Margueritte, *La Garçonne*, p. 57.

29. Anatole France, "Lettre ouverte de Monsieur Anatole France à la Légion d'honneur," Preface to Margueritte, *La Garçonne*, p. x. In his own letter to the Légion d'honneur, same volume, p. xii, Victor Margueritte argued that he had been expelled precisely because he had criticized bourgeois corruption. See also Renée Papaud, "Le Féminisme à travers le roman," p. 13; and *Intransigeant*, 20 July 1922.

30. Margueritte, *La Garçonne*, pp. 35–36.

31. Ibid., p. 57.

32. Monique believes that prostitution reigns everywhere in Parisian upper bourgeois circles. See Ibid., pp. 96–97.

33. Ibid., p. 137.

34. Ibid., pp. 62–63.

35. Ibid., p. 81.

36. Léon Blum, *Du Mariage* (Paris: Albin Michel, 1908, 1937); Ellen Key, *Love and Marriage* (New York and London: G. P. Putnam's Sons, 1911); Dr. Toulouse, *La Question sexuelle de la femme* (Paris: E. Fasquelle, 1918). This title differs from the one that Margueritte wrote in his book: *La Femme et la question sexuelle*.

37. On Léon Blum, see chap. 1, note 3.

38. For commentary and critiques of Blum's book, see Emile Faguet, in *Le Féminisme* (Paris: Société française d'imprimerie et de librairie, 1910), pp. 219, 248; Marcel Barrière, *Essai sur le donjuanisme contemporaine* (Paris: Editions du Monde Nouveau, 1922); Dr. Michel Bourgas, *Le Droit à l'amour pour la femme* (Paris: Vigot Frères, 1919); Georges Anquetil, *La Maîtresse légitime: Essai sur le mariage polygamique de demain* (Paris: Les Editions Georges Anquetil, 1923); and Anquetil and Demagny, *L'amant légitime*.

39. Margueritte, *La Garçonne*, p. 126.

40. Monique's lesbian affair was considered one of the most scandalous aspects of the novel. In general, lesbianism appears frequently in postwar literature. See, for example, André Beaunier, *La Folle jeune fille* (Paris: Flammarion, 1922); Charles-Etienne, *Notre Dame de Lesbos* (Paris: Librairie des Lettres, 1920); J. J. Rosny, jeune, *Claire Tercel, avocate à la cour* (Paris: Grasset, 1924); and Fortuné Paillot, *Amant ou Maîtresse. La Garçonne* also became the name of a German lesbian magazine in the 1930s.

41. Margueritte, *La Garçonne*, p. 111.

42. Ibid., pp. 112–13.

43. Ibid., pp. 168–69.

44. Ibid., p. 195.

45. Ibid., p. 208.

46. Ibid., pp. 199, 211.

47. Ibid., p. 184.

48. Ibid., p. 210. The medical reason for Monique's sterility is interesting in terms of the theme of emasculation in *La Garçonne*. The doctor describes her condition as "*le col virginal*," which means that "even the most cunning sperms break their necks and cannot pass!"

49. Ibid., p. 213.

50. For a review of *La Garçonne* that focuses particularly on this aspect of the novel, see Rachilde, *Mercure de France*, 15 November 1922. For an extensive analysis of the issue of postwar single motherhood, see chap. 6 of this study.

51. Margueritte, *La Garçonne*, p. 85. Part of this translation is from the English version of *La Garçonne*, entitled *The Bachelor Girl* (New York: Alfred A. Knopf, 1923), translated by Hugh Barnaby.

52. Ibid., p. 295.

53. Ibid., p. 251.

54. Ibid., p. 254.

55. Ibid., p. 252. Translation, in part, from *The Bachelor Girl*.

56. See Joëlle Guillais, *La Chair de l'autre: Le Crime passionnel au XIXe siècle* (Paris: Olivier Orban, 1986); Ruth Harris, *Murders and Madness: Medicine, Law and Society in the Fin-de-Siècle* (Oxford: Clarendon Press, 1989). For another example of a *crime passionnel* committed by a man in postwar literature, see Charles-Etienne, *Notre Dame de Lesbos*.

57. Margueritte, *La Garçonne*, p. 363.

58. Ibid.

59. Ibid.

60. Ibid., p. 366.

61. Ibid.

62. Ibid., p. 367.

63. Alice Berthet, *La Française*.

64. *Le Compagnon* (Paris: Flammarion, 1923). The real heroine of this second volume, however, is Annik Raimbert, Monique's friend and a lawyer. The novel revolves around her live-in relationship with, and her child by a deputy for whom she works. She refuses to marry him and gives the child her own name. Margueritte also wrote a third volume, *Le Couple*, to complete a trilogy entitled *La Femme en chemin*. *Le Couple* concerns the children of the Blanchets and of Annik Raimbert, who also dies a martyr in this novel, trying to stop a train of soldiers on their way to war.

65. Paul Souday, *Le Temps*.

66. Alice Kaplan, *Reproductions of Banality: Fascism, Literature and French Intellectual Life* (Minneapolis: University of Minnesota Press, 1986), p. 94.

67. See Frank Field, *Three French Writers and the Great War: Barbusse, Drieu la Rochelle, Bernanos* (Cambridge: Cambridge University Press, 1975),

pp. 83–87. See also Marc Auffret, *La France de l'entre deux guerres* (Paris: Culture, Arts, Loisirs, 1972), pp. 128–29, and James McMillan, *From Dreyfus to DeGaulle: Politics and Society in France, 1898–1969* (London: E. Arnold, 1985), p. 83.

68. Pierre Drieu la Rochelle, *La Suite des idées* (Paris: Au Sens Pareil, 1927), p. 21.

69. Pierre Drieu la Rochelle's *Plainte contre l'inconnu* (Paris: Gallimard, 1924) went through five editions in 1924; his *L'Homme couvert de femmes* (Paris: Gallimard, 1925) went through two editions in 1925.

70. Drieu la Rochelle, *L'Homme couvert*, p. 22.

71. Drieu la Rochelle, *Plainte contre*.

72. Ibid., p. 27.

73. Ibid., p. 118.

74. Ibid., p. 88. Drieu la Rochelle's language here is strikingly Freudian, although Freud was just beginning to be known in France.

75.Drieu la Rochelle, *L'Homme couvert*, p. 220.

76. Drieu la Rochelle, *Plainte contre*, p. 84.

77. Drieu la Rochelle, *La Comédie de Charleroi* (Paris: Gallimard, 1982; orig. pub. 1934), p. 72.

78. Drieu la Rochelle, *La Suite, p. 13.*

79. Drieu la Rochelle, *Plainte contre*, p. 85.

80. Benjamin Crémieux, *Inquiétude et reconstruction: Essai sur la littérature d'après-querre* (Paris: Editions R.-A. Corrêa, 1931), p. 97. Crémieux was a veteran. See Introduction, note 14.

81. Ibid., p. 114.

82. Ibid., p. 118.

83. Ibid., p. 114.

84. Ibid., p. 117. Crémieux notes a difference in this literature from that of the nineteenth century in terms of the relationship between the hero and money. In nineteenth-century romantic fiction, he argues, the hero was poor but secure in his ideals. The struggle was to make it in the world. In postwar literature, however, the hero is well-off materially, but suffers from spiritual *inquiétude*. His battle to deal with this *inquiétude* forms the basis of conflict in the novel.

85. Ibid., p. 119.

86. Marcel Prévost, *Les Don Juanes* (Paris: Renaissance du Livre, 1922). The original press run for *Les Don Juanes* was generous—163,000 copies. In "*La Garçonne*," p. 22, Sohn mentions that 300,000 copies of the book were sold during the twenties. Flammarion brought out its own edition of the novel in 1925 and then reissued it regularly throughout the next decade. Prévost was also a literary critic, and the founder and editor of *La Revue de France*.

87. See, for example, Billy, "Les Livres qu'on lit"; Renée Papaud, "Le Féminisme"; Germain, "Les Livres qu'il faut."

88. Prévost, *Les Don Juanes*, p. 7.

89. Ibid., p. 5.

90. Marc Varenne, *Renaissance politique*, 1 July 1922. For another critical commentary concerning Prévost's use of the Don Juan metaphor, see Jean-José Frappa and H. Dupuy-Mazuel, *Revue des deux mondes*, February 1922.

91. Prévost, *Les Don Juanes*, p. 47.

92. Ibid., p. 86. For descriptions of her face and body, see also pp. 259–61.

93. Ibid., pp. 86, 261.

94. Ibid., p. 88.

95. Ibid., p. 325.

3. Women Are Cutting Their Hair as a Sign of Sterility

1. René Rambaud, *Les Fugitives: Précis anecdotique et historique des coiffures féminines à travers les ages* (Paris: René Rambaud, 1947), pp. 250–51. He quotes the article in *Oeuvre*, 29 May 1925.

2. Gilbert Guilleminault, *Les Années folles* (Paris: Editions Denoël, 1958), p. 121.

3. See Rambaud, *Fugitives*, p. 240, and Gaëtan Sanvosin, "La Jeune fille et les plaideurs," *Le Gaulois*, 6 November 1925, Dossier Coiffure, Bibliothèque Marguerite Durand (BMD). A good example of just how seriously fashion was taken during this era is the size and evidently careful research of Marguerite Durand's dossiers on fashion and hairstyles. Durand was a prominent feminist and a collector of a major archive on women, consultable today at the Bibliothèque Marguerite Durand in the 13th *arrondissement* of Paris. Her dossiers, which consist of articles carefully gleaned from the daily press and other periodicals, form a substantial part of the research of this chapter. Where possible, I have tried to verify the dates of articles and the accuracy of the quotations in the original publications. Besides using the dossiers on fashion at the BMD, my method has been to research systematically fashion, women's, and mainstream periodicals during the years 1918 to 1927, as well as to read all pamphlets and books published on the subject during these years.

4. A. Décaux, *Histoire des françaises* (Paris: Librairie Academique Perrin, 1972), 2:1007. See also Rambaud, *Fugitives*, pp. 205, 216, 231, and 240, where he refers to "this epic struggle" within families over short hair.

5. Paul Reboux, "Opinion: Cheveux coupés," *Oeuvre*, 11 January 1919.

6. Bonnie Smith, *Confessions of a Concierge: Madame Lucie's History of Twentieth Century France* (New Haven: Yale University Press, 1985), p. 57.

7. Rambaud, *Fugitives*, p. 240.

8. My chronology here is based on the number of articles I was able to find that concerned the wider social and behavioral implications of the new fash-

ions and that appeared in both fashion magazines and the wider bourgeois press from the late war years through the twenties. As far as I can tell, this type of article peaked in numbers during the years 1924 to 1926.

9. René Bizet, *La Mode* (Paris: F. Rieder et Cie, 1925). Bizet was literary director of *L'Intransigeant*. For favorable reviews of *La Mode*, see *Revue mondiale*, 15 December 1925, and *Renaissance politique*, 28 November 1925. See also *Vogue*, 1 March 1923 and 1 September 1924, and "L'Histoire de la mode féminine de 1900 à 1924: Huit des vingt-cinq poupées de Mmes. Lafitte-Désirat," *Illustration*, 21 June 1924, Dossier Mode, BMD.

10. Historian Valerie Steele argues that the Poiret, avant-garde style was popularized in the years just before the war, but she does not detail how except to say that it was promoted in avant-garde art. See her excellent *Paris Fashion: A Cultural History* (New York: Oxford University Press, 1988).

11. For two arguments that 1927 was a turning point, see *Mode des années folles, 1919–1929. Exposition. Paris, Musée du Costume de la ville de Paris, 1970–71* (Paris: Les Presses Artistiques, 1970) and François Boucher, *Histoire du costume en occident de l'antiquité à nos jours* (Paris: Flammarion, 1983). According to fashion historian Marylène Delbourg-Delphis, the new fashions evolved in the years 1920–23. The year 1923 was a turning point, after which the fashions took off in popularity. She notes slight variations on the style during the years 1924–30. See *Le Chic et le look: Histoire de la mode féminine et des moeurs, de 1850 à nos jours* (Paris: Hachette, 1981), pp. 102, 108–10.

12. It was the hairdresser Antoine who claimed to have cut off Eve Lavallière's hair. In his autobiography, *J'ai coiffé le monde entier! Présentation et propos recueillis par Jean Durtal* (Paris: Editions de la Table Ronde, 1963), pp. 104–7, Antoine tells the story of how he "discovered" the bob in trying to make this 40-year-old actress look young enough to play the part of an 18-year-old. Just as he was pondering what to do, he saw a young girl with very short hair bearing a letter for the actress. As legend has it, the actress Caryathis cut off her hair in 1913, as a response to a man whom she had failed to arouse. She tied a ribbon around her shorn locks and left them hanging from a nail in his home. See Edmonde Charles-Roux, *Chanel: Her Life, Her World, and the Woman behind the Legend She Herself Created* (London: Jonathan Cape, 1975), where the author credits Caryathis for inspiring Chanel to cut off her own hair (p. 164). Historians Catherine Lebas and Annie Jacques view Colette as one of the prewar pioneers of short hair, both because she cut her own and because she gave her fictional character Claudine short hair. See their *La Coiffure en France du Moyen Age à nos jours* (Paris: Delmas International, 1979), pp. 269–74, for a detailed history of the bob.

13. In her diary dated 30 May 1917, Misia Sert, the famous Russian musician, attributed the trend to Coco Chanel. See Edmonde Charles-Roux, *Chanel and Her World* (London: Hachette-Vendôme, 1981), p. 79. See also "La Coiffure," *Vogue*, 1 December 1924, where Chanel is credited with starting

the fashion of short hair. According to Lebas and Jacques in *Coiffure*, Antoine published the first short hairstyles in the professional press on 1 March 1919.

14. See Margarete Braun-Ronsdorf, *Des Merveilleuses aux garçonnes: Histoire de l'élégance en Europe de 1789 à 1929* (Paris: Editions des Deux Mondes, 1963), p. 207, for the names of the new bob. See also M. Bruyère, *Une Mode féminine: Les Cheveux coupés* (Avignon: Maison Aubanel Frères, 1924), p. 7. According to Paul Gerbod, the 1920s are now seen as the golden age of hairdressing because of the short hair and "la vogue de l'indéfrisable." See his "Les Coiffeurs en France, 1890–1950," *Mouvement social*, 114 (Jan.–Mar. 1981): 78.

15. Rambaud, *Fugitives*, p. 8. See also Lebas and Jacques, *La Coiffure*, p. 273. For the phrase "*à l'allure garçonnière*," see Magdaleine Chaumont, "Confidences," *Comoedia*, 18 March 1925, Dossier Mode, BMD.

16. Rambaud, *Fugitives*, p. 253. See also Smith, *Confessions of a Concierge*, p. 57.

17. The precise starting point of the bob controversy is difficult to ascertain. The earliest articles concerning the controversy that I was able to find date from 1919. Paul Reboux, "Opinion: Cheveux coupés" and "Longs ou courts?" *Oeuvre*, 23 February 1919; Pierre Chaine, "Autre opinion: Les Cheveux coupées," *Oeuvre*, 15 January 1919.

18. Henriette Sauret, "Préoccupations masculines," *Voix des femmes*, 30 January 1919. This article was, in part, a response to the series of articles in *L'Oeuvre* cited above. For another later commentary on how everyone was talking about fashion, see Eugène Marsan, "D'une Révolution du costume," *De la mode: Hier—Aujourd'hui—Demain (Les Cahiers de la république des lettres des sciences et des arts)*, no. 7 (15 July 1927): 49–50.

19. See Bruno de Roselle, *La Mode* (Paris: Imprimerie nationale, 1980), p. 50.

20. Valerie Steele, *Fashion and Eroticism: Ideals of Feminine Beauty from the Victorian Era to the Jazz Age* (New York: Oxford University Press, 1985), pp. 17–18.

21. Yvonne Deslandres and Florence Müller, *Histoire de la mode au vingtième siècle* (Paris: Somogy, 1986), pp. 115–16. Serge Berstein and Jean-Jacques Becker argue that whereas before the war, designers such as Poiret dressed the European aristocracy, after the war, they worked largely for the bourgeoisie. See their *Victoire et frustrations, 1914–1929*, vol. 12 of *Nouvelle histoire de la France contemporaine* (Paris: Seuil, 1990), p. 362.

22. For biographical information on Coco Chanel, see Charles-Roux, *Chanel* and *Chanel and Her World*.

23. Rambaud, *Fugitives*, p. 253. In the secondary literature, see Delbourg-Delphis, *Chic et look*, pp. 100–101.

24. Valerie Steele, *Paris Fashion*, p. 219; Braun-Ronsdorf, *Merveilleuses*, p. 201. However, in *Fashion and Eroticism*, p. 226, Steele also argues that Poiret's

personal influence on fashion has been exaggerated and that the new styles were pioneered between 1892 and 1908 in many of the big designer houses, such as that of Lanvin.

25. Quoted in Peter Woolen, "Fashion/Orientalism/The Body," *New Formations*, no. 1 (Spring 1987): 5–33; see also Steele, *Paris Fashion*, p. 10, and Elizabeth Wilson, *Adorned in Dreams: Fashion and Modernity* (London: Virago, 1985), p. 40. According to Wilson, Poiret claimed to have abolished the corset by 1908.

26. See Steele, *Paris Fashions*, pp. 219–23. Poiret's fame and fortune became a casualty of the war. He served in the army as a tailor, and when he returned to Paris in 1918, he was not able to recover his business, his popularity, or his marriage. See Yvonne Deslandres with Dorothée Lalanne, *Poiret: Paul Poiret, 1879–1944* (New York: Rizzoli, 1987), p. 57.

27. Much more research on class patterns of consumption needs to be done in order to arrive at a precise class analysis of fashion history in this period. In *Fashion and Eroticism*, p. 235, Steele downplays the importance of the war, arguing that the new styles might have emerged even without the influence of the war.

28. Ibid. See also Steele, *Paris Fashion*, pp. 237–9 and Gabriel Perreux, *La Vie quotidienne des civils en France pendant la grande guerre* (Paris: Hachette, 1966), p. 262.

29. Braun-Ronsdorf, *Merveilleuses*, p. 203.

30. See Jacqueline de Monbrison, n.t. (Paris: Société générale d'imprimerie et d'édition, 1926), p. 34. In *Histoire du costume*, p. 412, Boucher credits Chanel, Patou and Lelong with creating the models most typical of the new look.

31. *Vogue*, October 1923.

32. Jersey was a cheap fabric and at the time was considered to be unusable by most leaders in the textile industry. See Charles-Roux, *Chanel*, pp. 154–7. See also Wilson, *Adorned in Dreams*, p. 40, and Steele, *Paris Fashion*, p. 244. Charles-Roux links Chanel's "poor look" with her own childhood as a poor orphan.

33. Pyjamas had originally been used by fashionable Parisian women forced to appear in bomb-raid shelters in the dead of night; Chanel made them into a fashion rage.

34. At the turn of the century, Frederick Taylor began a movement to "scientifically manage" the work process in American factories. His goals were to promote productive efficiency and to eliminate on-the-job accidents. Taylorism became popular in some industrial circles in France after the war. For a more detailed discussion of Taylorism and other postwar rationalization trends, see chap. 7.

35. Maurice Prax, "Pour et contre," *Petit parisien*, 27 September 1926, Dossier Mode, BMD. For earlier commentaries on the simplicity of contemporary fashion, see Claire Lausnay, "Le Recueil des modes nouvelles," *Fémina*,

April 1921, and Nicolas Bonnechose, "Robes de bain," *Gazette du bon ton,* June 1922.

36. J. R. F., "Sur la simplicité," *Vogue,* 1 January 1923: 52.

37. Clément Vautel, "Etre mince ou ne pas être," *Art, goût, beauté,* 15 May 1924.

38. Quoted in Woolen, "Orientalism," p. 26.

39. In other words, I do not consider fashion commentary in the years between 1919 and 1926 so disparate as to warrant separate treatment or even chronological differentiation in my analysis.

40. This fear of masculinized or "desexed" women has a long history in the Third Republic and is not unique to the postwar period. See, for example, Gay L. Gullickson, "*La Pétroleuse:* Representing Revolution," *Feminist Studies* 17 (Summer 1991): 241–65.

41. The cartoon is from Clément Vautel's "Le Féminisme en 1958," *Je sais tout,* 15 May 1918. Dossier Anti-féminisme, BMD. For Vautel's natalism, see his article in *Le Journal,* 23 August 1923, which laments depopulation in the village of Montélimar, as well as his novel *Madame ne veut pas d'enfant* (Paris: Albin Michel, 1924). Vautel was also referred to as a formidable antisuffragist in the feminist monthly *Droit des femmes,* February 1919.

42. "De Petites choses," *Fémina,* May 1921.

43. Roger Boutet de Monvel, "Les Masculines," *Gazette du bon ton,* May 1922: 102–4. For another upper-class view of the "virilisation" of fashion, see Rosine, "A la Bayadère. A la garçonne," *Art, goût, beauté,* 15 April 1924.

44. "La Mode des cheveux courts rendra-t-elle les femmes chauves?" *Le Quotidien,* 3 September 1924, Dossier 391 Coiffure, BMD. The article has a serious tone, despite its comic effect.

45. Roger Boutet de Monvel, "Les Masculines."

46. Francis de Miomandre, *Notes et maximes: La Mode* (Paris: Hachette, 1927), pp. 40–41. He declares that same thing happened in 1700 and quotes from a book called *Le Théophraste moderne, ou nouveaux caractères sur les moeurs.* Controversies about fashion can be traced back to the early eleventh century; see, for example, Henri Platelle, "Le Problème du scandale: Les Nouvelles modes masculines au XIe et XIIe siècles," *Revue belge de philologie et d'histoire* 53 (1975): 1071–96.

47. Anonymous, *Aux Femmes chrétiennes: Le Scandale de la mode* (Besançon: Imprimerie de l'Est, 1925), p. 15. For still another example of the Catholic viewpoint, see Bruyère, *Mode féminine,* p. 17, where the author argues that in cutting her hair, a woman "will appear to have given up a privilege—she is less a woman."

48. Pierre Lièvre, *Reproches à une dame qui a coupé ses cheveux* (Paris: Le Divan, 1927), pp. 54–57. Lièvre chooses his word "uranisme" carefully here, which is why it is difficult to translate. He rejects "homosexual" because it "has a German connotation that should trouble the French reader." He also rejects

the word "nonconformist" because it carries inappropriate religious connotations and "sodomite" because it seems out of date. He argues, p. 58, that one master of these fashions, as well as the inventor of short hair, is an "obvious uranian." Havelock Ellis's *Etudes de psychologie sexuelle* (19 vols.) were translated and published continuously in France between 1908 and 1935.

49. See Gabriel Ferré, *Chroniques des temps d'après-guerre* (Paris: Editions Jules Tallandier, 1929), p. 17, and the poet Jean Dars, "Une Controverse: L'Emancipation de la jeune fille moderne est-elle un progrès réel?" *Progrès civique*, October 1925: 637, Dossier Féminisme, Vingtième siècle, BMD.

50. Jean Dars, "Enquête sur la condition et les aspirations des jeunes filles d'aujourd'hui," *Grande revue*, October 1925: 637–38. See also "La Mode masculine impose sa loi aux femmes," *Le Figaro*, April 1925, Dossier Mode, BMD.

51. Numa Sadoul, "Une Controverse," *Progrès civique*, June 1925, Dossier Féminisme, Vingtième siècle, BMD.

52. Madame Christian Fournier, "Enquête sur la condition," *Grande revue*, September 1925: 445.

53. Bizet, *La Mode*, pp. 8, 11.

54. George Barbier, "De la pudeur," *Gazette du bon ton*, no. 3 (1924–25): 117–20. See also Ferré, *Chroniques*, p. 154.

55. Hélène du Taillis, "Où s'arrêteront-elles?" n.p., 23 March 1925, Dossier Mode, BMD.

56. Gérard Lavergne, *Les Femmes d'après-guerre* (Nîmes: Chastenier, 1925), p. 13. For a similar comment, see Clément Vautel, *Fémina*, 1 February 1920. For the fear that women were going to catch cold or ill from the fashions, see also Albine Albaran, "La Mode et la santé," *Le Quotidien*, 11 November 1926, Dossier Mode, BMD.

57. Prax, "Pour et contre."

58. Cécile Jeglot, *La Jeune fille et la mode* (Paris: L'Action populaire, Editions "Spes," 1928), p. 16, and "Malaise moderne," p. 2. See also Jeglot, *La Jeune fille et le plaisir* (Paris: L'Action populaire, Editions "Spes," 1928); Taillis, "Où s'arrêteront-elles?" *Action populaire* was a conservative Catholic organization. Jéglot wrote a whole series of books on "La Jeune fille" for *Action populaire* in the late twenties; they each had press runs of 7,000 copies.

59. Princess Lucien Murat, "L'Influence de la mode sur la pudeur," *De la mode*, p. 26.

60. Anonymous, *Aux Femmes chrétiennes*, p. 9.

61. See Bruyère, *Mode féminine*, p. 10.

62. Fr. A Vuillermet, *La Croisade pour la modestie* (Paris: P. Lethielleux, 1926) p. 11. See Fr. Philippe de Jésus, *La Modestie et les modes féminines* (Lyons: Imprimerie P. Basacier, 1926), on how women were refused holy communion.

63. See "L'Eglise et la mode," n.p., 20 December 1926, Dossier Mode BMD. See also Rambaud, *Fugitives*, p. 241.

64. Anonymous, *Mode et modestie* (Paris: Action populaire, Editions "Spes," 1926). See also article by Georges de la Fouchardière in *Oeuvre*, 16 October 1926, which pokes fun at the church for interpreting fashion as a free-masonry plot. For other humorous treatments of the church's efforts in this regard, see the novelist and playright Abel Hermant, 'De la mode," in *De la mode. Hier—Aujourd'hui—Demain*, and Prax, "Pour et contre."

65. Quoted from *La Croix* of 17 February 1926 in P. Lemaître, *Deux questions angoissantes: La Mode et ses hardiesses, la danse et le spectacle* (Saint-Lo: R. Jacqueline Librairie-Editeur, 1926). Lemaître also provided examples of women being turned away from communion because they were "indecently" dressed (p. 67). The same treatment was given to improperly dressed women seeking audiences with the pope during these same years. See also "L'Eglise et la mode," for a reference to the pope's efforts concerning fashion.

66. Fouveau de Courmelles, "Modes féminines et dépopulation," *Revue mondiale*, 1 November 1919: 278–81.

67. Anonymous, *La Mode est coupable* (Tarbes: Optima, 1920), p. 3.

68. See Roger Boutet de Monvel, "De l'Influence des modes sur les moeurs," *Vogue*, 1 April 1922. See also "La Femme moderne: Vénus androgyne," *La Rumeur*, 1928, Dossier Mode, BMD.

69. Marius Boisson, "Pour nos ombrages," no periodical given. 15 July 1925, Dossier Mode, BMD.

70. Mlle. de Saint-Seine, *La Mode et la conscience chrétienne* (Paris: Secrétariat national français, 1926), p. 8; Fr. A. Vuillermet, *La Croisade pour la modestie*, p. 10.

71. Marcel Prévost, *Nouvelles lettres à Françoise* (Paris: Flammarion, 1922), p. 16. In his novel *Les Don Juanes*, Marcel Prévost referred to the women in *les dancings* as "half-naked." For more on Prévost's *Nouvelles lettres*, see chap. 7.

72. Ibid.

73. Ibid., p. 38. For another argument like Prévost's that women have not lost their virtue, see Hermant, "De la mode" and Murat, "L'Influence" in *De la mode*. See also Jacques Faneuse, "Simples propos," *L'Âme gauloise*, 1924?, Dossier Mode, BMD. Faneuse argues that it was not a loss of modesty, but a need to economize on fabric that made short dresses popular, since the modern woman liked to change her clothes so often. Lièvre in *Reproches*, pp. 20–21, interpreted the short dresses as a product of a ruined society and a faulty economic system. See also *La Mode pratique*, January 12, 1924, for another argument similar to Lièvre's.

74. "Paris: L'Enfer des cheveux," *Fémina*, January 1924.

75. Pierre Drieu la Rochelle, "Le Pique-Nique," *Plainte contre l'inconnu* (Paris: Gallimard, 1924).

76. Lièvre, *Reproches*, p. 16.

77. Ibid., pp. 9–10, 14,16.

78. Magdeleine Chaumont, "Les Elégances: Confidences," *Comoedia,* 17 June 1925, Dossier Mode, BMD.

79. Bizet, *La Mode,* p. 11. See also Vautel, "Etre mince"; Braun-Ronsdorf, *Des Merveilleuses,* p. 206.

80. Eugène Marsin, *Pour habiller Eliante, ou le nouveau secret des dames* (Liège: A la Lampe d'Aladdin, 1927), p. 34. See also "La Femme moderne"; Chaumont, "Confidences," 18 March 1925; Elsa Schiaparelli, *Shocking: Souvenirs de Elsa Schiaparelli* (Paris: Denoël, 1954).

81. For an intriguing discussion of the notion of "youth" in fashion, see Holly Brubach, "In Fashion: A Certain Age," *The New Yorker,* 5 November 1990, and a follow-up article, "Retroactivity," 31 December 1990.

82. Critics of fashion also sometimes spoke of fashion as emancipatory as well. See, for example, Jeglot, *La Jeune fille et la mode,* p. 11.

83. "Une Controverse," June 1925. See also Suzanne Callias, "La Liberté des cheveux courts," *La Française,* 7 May 1921; Bruyère, *Mode féminine,* pp. 25–26: Comte de Bondy, "La Mode et la vie," *De la mode,* p. 36; and J. R. F., "La Philosophie des coiffures de la parisienne," *Vogue,* September 1923.

84. See Barnett Singer, "Technology and Social Change: The Watershed of the 1920's" *Proceedings of the Fourth Annual Meeting of the Western Society for French History* 4 (1976): 321–29; Barnett Singer, *Modern France: Mind, Politics, Society* (Seattle: University of Washington Press, 1980); Paul A. Gagnon, "La Vie Future: Some French Responses to the Technological Society," *Journal of European Studies* 6 (1976): 172–89. See also Walter Benjamin's essay "Art in the Age of Mechanical Reproduction," trans. Harry Zohn, *Illuminations* (Glasgow: Fontana/Collins, 1973).

85. Bonnie Smith, *Changing Lives: Women in European History Since 1700* (Lexington, Mass.: D. C. Heath, 1989), p. 416.

86. See Deslandres and Müller, *Histoire de la mode,* p. 116.

87. In 1920, there was one automobile per 165 French inhabitants; in 1930, the figure was one per 28 inhabitants. See Singer, "Technology and Social Change." In order to determine when female images begin to predominate in car advertising, I looked at approximately ten French fashion and popular magazines between 1918 and 1927. For the link between the modern woman and the automobile, see also Delbourg-Delphis, *Chic et look,* p. 121.

88. Raymond Rienzi, *L'Aventure sur la route* (Paris: Flammarion, 1925), p. 14.

89. Rip, "La Mode de demain," in *De la mode,* pp. 89–90. See also Miomandre, *Notes et maximes,* p. 27, and "De Petites choses." For the "sportiness" of *la femme moderne,* see J. R. F., "Sur la simplicité" of *la femme moderne,* see J. R. F., "Sur la simplicité"; Monbrison, n.t., pp. 59, 64, and 67; André de Fouquières, "Les Tendances de la mode," *De la mode,* pp. 43–44; Marsan, "D'une Révolution du costume," *De la mode,* p. 80, and "La Femme sportive doit rester élégante," *Vogue,* July 1923.

90. "Paris, l'enfer des cheveux." See also Marc Varenne's review of René Bizet's *La Mode* in *Renaissance politique*, 28 November 1925.

91. Camille Duguet, "Critique de la mode," *Le Figaro*, 11 March 1925, Dossier Mode, BMD. See also the letter by Lucien Lelong to Duguet in response to this article: Lucien Lelong, "Lettre ouverte à Madame Camille Duguet," *Le Figaro*, 2 December 1924. Dossier Mode, BMD.

92. Lucien Lelong, "Un Plaidoyer pour les modes actuelles," n.p., 18 March 1926, Dossiers Mode and Coiffure, BMD. For a very similar statement, see Lelong, "Lettre." See also words of Cyber-Soeurs, in Marsan, "D'une Révolution du costume," p. 88.

93. Fouquières, "Les Tendances de la mode," *De la mode*, p. 45. See also Roubaix Prouvost, *La Mode en 1927* (Paris: Draeger, 1927), and Marsan, "D'une Révolution du costume," p. 70.

94. Paul Reboux, "Longs ou courts."

95. Many labor historians have stressed the negative homogenizing powers of mass culture. According to the "embourgeoisement thesis" of these historians, for example, mass consumption had the effect of assimilating workers into mainstream middle-class patterns of behavior and eclipsing a genuine working-class culture. For an excellent historiographical summary of this debate in American labor history, see Lizabeth Cohen, *Making a New Deal: Industrial Workers in Chicago, 1919–1939* (Cambridge: Cambridge University Press, 1990), p. 398, note 6. According to Arthur Marwick in *Beauty in History: Society, Politics and Personal Appearance* (London: Thames and Hudson, 1988), p. 29, the argument that fashion was an agent of social control was first voiced in Simone de Beauvoir's *The Second Sex.* (1949) It has been developed most fully in the historiography of American and English women. See Stuart Ewen, *Captains of Consciousness: Advertising and the Social Roots of the Consumer Culture* (New York: McGraw-Hill, 1976), chaps. 6 and 7; Rayna Rapp and Ellen Ross, "The Twenties: Feminism, Consumerism and Political Backlash in the United States," in *Women in Culture and Politics: A Century of Change*, ed. Judith Friedlander (Bloomington: Indiana University Press, 1986), p. 55. See also Elaine Showalter, *These Modern Women: Autobiographical Essays from the 20s* (Old Westbury, N.Y.: Feminist Press, 1978). For Europe generally, see Bonnie Smith, *Changing Lives*, p. 411. For an example of the way in which the notion of fashion as social control underwrites historiography of the period, see Maria-Barbara Watson-Franke, "I Am Somebody!'—Women's Changing Sense of Self in the German Democratic Republic," in *Connecting Spheres: Women in the Western World, 1500 to the Present*, ed. Marilyn Boxer and Jean Quataert (New York: Oxford University Press, 1987). For a refreshing revision of many of these questions, see Elizabeth Wilson's provocative "All the Rage," in *Fabrications: Costume and the Female Body*, ed. Jane Gaines and Charlotte Herzog (New York: Routledge, 1990).

96. Reboux, "Opinion: Cheveux coupés." See also the response to Reboux's first article, "Autre opinion," *Oeuvre*, 15 January 1919, by Pierre Chaine. Here

Chaine reminds Reboux that cutting women's hair has traditionally been a public humiliation for those women who have been "too friendly with the *boches*" and who are therefore considered guilty of treason.

97. Paul Reboux, "Grandeurs, variations et décadences de la mode," *De la mode*, p. 17. See also Marsan, "D'une Révolution," *De la mode*, p. 47. In his article, "Prosperity's Child: Some Thoughts on the Flapper," *American Quarterly* 21 (Spring 1969), Kenneth Yellis argued that the American flapper's abandonment of traditional female dress paralleled her rejection of a passive, sexual, social, and economic role from which such dress gained its meaning.

98. Reboux, "Grandeurs, variations," p. 16.

99. Quoted in Marsan, "D'une Révolution," *De la mode*, pp. 85–86.

100. Rambaud, *Fugitives*, pp. 237–39. See also Antoine, *J'ai coiffé*, p. 10.

101. For this idea of fashion as an expression of an ideal self, see Steele, *Fashion and Eroticism*, esp. pp. 45–48, and Sandra Gilbert, "Costumes of the Mind: Transvestism as Metaphor in Modern Literature," *Critical Inquiry* 7 (Winter 1980): 391–417.

102. Sauret, "Préoccupations masculines."

103. Auguste Moll-Weiss, "Les Femmes d'après-guerre et la mode," *L'Ecole et la vie*, 15 (1 January 1921): 235–36.

104. Jane Misme, "La Pudeur aux bains," *Oeuvre*, 3 August 1922, Fonds Bouglé, Articles de Journaux, Boîte no. 2, Bibliothèque Historique de la Ville de Paris.

105. Cited in Lebas and Jacques, *Coiffure en France*, p. 269. See also Camille Duguet, "Critique de la mode." Vérone was a lawyer and member of the Paris bar. She was the president of the suffrage organization Ligue française pour le droit des femmes between 1918 and 1938. She directed the journal *Droit des femmes* for the same period of time.

106. *Mode des années folles*. See also Decaux, *Histoire des françaises*, p. 1004; Annelise Maugue, *L'Identité masculine en crise au tournant du siècle* (Marseilles: Rivages, 1987), p. 86; Perreux, *La Vie quotidienne*, p. 345; Jacques Wilhelm, *Histoire de la mode* (Paris: Hachette, 1955); and Deslandres and Müller, *Histoire de la mode*.

107. See, among many other possibilities, Steven Hause, "More Minerva than Mars: The French Women's Rights Campaign and the First World War," in *Behind the Lines: Gender and the Two World Wars*, ed. Margaret Higonnet *et al.* (New Haven: Yale University Press, 1987), p. 102; Roselle, *La Mode*, pp. 157–58; *Mode des années folles*; Perreux, *La Vie quotidienne*, p. 345; Boucher, *Histoire du costume*, p. 411; Deslandres and Müller, *Histoire de la mode*, p. 115. Even those historians such as James McMillan who deny the reality of such a liberation argue that fashion was deceptive inasmuch as it "created a general aura of emancipation around women in the immediate post-war years." See James McMillan, *Housewife or Harlot: The Position of Women in French Society* (New York: St. Martin's Press, 1980), pp. 163–65. See also

Maïté Albistur and Daniel Armogathe, *Histoire du féminisme français* (Paris: Des Femmes, 1977), 2:586, for the argument that women's adoption of male dress and more "cavalier" manners did not necessarily mean that they sought or achieved emancipation.

108. Heels remained high, even though in January 1918 doctors Quenu and Ménard presented a lecture at the *Académie de médicine* on, in Gabriel Perreux's words, "the hazards of the high heel for the health of women." See his *La Vie quotidienne*, p. 267.

109. Monbrison, n.t., pp. 96, 100–101.

110. Lièvre, *Reproches*, p. 34.

111. Delbourg-Delphis, *Chic et look*, p. 118. Delbourg-Delphis makes no precise chronological analysis concerning this development of a new concept of the body. However, she seems to argue that it becomes particularly important after mid-decade. See also Steele, *Fashion and Eroticism*, pp. 241–42; Marwick, *Beauty*, pp. 298–99. For the American case, see Lois Banner, *American Beauty* (New York: Alfred Knopf, 1983).

112. "A la Conquête d'une nouvelle jeunesse," *Vogue*, 1 April 1923.

113. Delbourg-Delphis, *Chic et look*, p. 118.

114. Bruyère, *Mode féminine*, p. 26.

115. Comte de Bondy, "La Mode et la vie," in *De la mode*, p. 37.

116. See Delbourg-Delphis, *Chic et look*, p. 106.

117. See advertisements in *Fémina*, 1920, and *Mode pratique*, October 1922. See also Miomandre, *Notes et maximes*, in which he makes a reference (p. 26) to the "sometimes terrible means" by which women get thin.

118. "Traité de la silhouette féminine," *Vogue*, November 1924: 48. See also Vautel, "Etre mince ou ne pas être." In *Fashion and Eroticism*, p. 241, Steele describes how the era marked the *internalization* of the corset, as a new emphasis was put on strict dieting.

119. Steele, *Paris Fashion*, p. 235. Some fashion experts still argued for the traditional corset. See, for example, "Le Corset," *Mode pratique*, 27 September 1924. For a detailed history of undergarments during this period, see Elizabeth Ewing, *Dress and Undress: A History of Women's Underwear* (London: Batsford, Ltd., 1978); David Kunzle, *Fashion and Fetishism: A Social History of the Corset, Tight-Lacing and Other Forms of Body Sculpture in the West* (Totowa, N.J.: Rowan and Littlefield, 1982).

120. See "La Mode qui vient," *Illustration*, 11 June 1921. Poiret banished the traditional corset, but replaced it with a *"cache-corset* that would eventually become the *brassière*. He called postwar women "telephone poles." See Deslandres, *Poiret*, pp. 99, 149.

121. "La Ligne nouvelle," *Vogue*, December 1923. This article recommends several different kinds of corsets/girdles, each for one occasion (such as tennis or evening wear). See also Lucie Neumeyer, "Le Panégyrique du

corset," *Art, goût, beauté,* March 1925; Andrée Santeuil, "Dernières créations de la mode," in the trade journal *Les Elégances parisiennes,* no. 6 (1921).

122. Bizet, *Mode,* p. 17.

123. Monbrison, n.t., p. 41. See also p. 15, where she admits that women must diet, have massages, and wear corsets in order to achieve the line in fashion.

124. See Laurence Klejman and Florence Rochefort, *L'Egalité en marche: Le Féminisme sous la Troisième République* (Paris: Des Femmes, 1989), p. 343. As historian Bonnie Smith has defined it, the modern notion of womanhood "included efficiency at home and work, energy in sports and sexual life, companionship with her mate, and consumerism." The modern woman signified a preoccupation with sex, marriage, career, and shopping—not politics. See Smith, *Changing Lives,* p. 411. For definitions of French collective political engagement considered "feminist," see Claire Moses, *French Feminism in the Nineteenth Century* (Binghamton, N.Y.: State University of New York Press, 1984); Karen Offen, "Defining Feminism: A Comparative Historical Approach," *Signs* 14, no. 1 (Autumn 1988): 119–57. The British modern woman is also viewed as apolitical. As Deirdre Bedoe recently remarked, "the image of the flapper is partly an elaboration of the New Woman theme, but she is the New Woman stripped of her serious side and hell-bent on having a good time." See *Back Home to Duty: Women Between the Wars, 1918–1939* (London: Pandora, 1989), p. 10. For Great Britain, see also Olive Banks, *Faces of Feminism: A Study of Feminism as a Social Movement* (Oxford: Martin Robertson, 1981), p. 149; Sheila Jeffreys, *The Spinster and Her Enemies: Feminism and Sexuality, 1880–1930* (London: Pandora, 1985), pp. 148, 155. The argument that the modern woman was essentially apolitical has been particularly well developed in the American case. See William O'Neill, *Everyone Was Brave: The Rise and Fall of Feminism in America* (Chicago: Quadrangle Books, 1969), pp. 295–97; Mary Ryan, *Womanhood in America: From Colonial Times to the Present* (New York: New Viewpoints, 1975), chap. 6; J. Stanley Lemons, *The Woman Citizen: Social Feminism in the 1920s* (Urbana: University of Illinois Press, 1973); Sheila Rothman, *Woman's Proper Place: A History of Changing Ideals and Practices, 1870 to the Present* (New York: Basic Books, 1978); and Paula Fass, *The Damned and the Beautiful: American Youth in the 1920s* (New York: Oxford University Press, 1977). Historians of American women have begun to dispute these views. For example, in *Labor's Flaming Youth: Telephone Operators and Worker Militancy, 1878–1923* (Urbana: University of Illinois Press, 1990), p. 13, Stephen Norwood questions "the stereotype of the flapper as frivolous and apolitical" by demonstrating militant union organization among telephone operators, many of whom had strong links to the women's movement.

125. I am indebted to historian Estelle Freedman for this point.

126. As George Fredrickson and Karen Sawislak have suggested to me, the paradoxical life cycle of a fashion would seem to make such a relapse into

conventionality inevitable. A certain fashion becomes popular because it challenges convention in some way. For example, the short bob gained popularity largely because it represented a challenge to the old female convention of long tresses and elaborate coiffures. Yet the very popularization of this fashion, in turn, made it conventional—in the sense that "everyone" was having her hair cut.

127. See Delbourg-Delphis, *Chic et look,* pp. 110, 133–34, 148; Steele, *Paris Fashion,* p. 246; Caroline Evans and Minna Thornton, "Fashion, Representation, Femininity," *Feminist Review* 38 (Summer 1991): 49–57.

128. Rambaud, *Fugitives,* p. 253. See also Smith, *Confessions of a Concierge,* p. 57.

129. Victor Margueritte, *La Garçonne* (Paris: Flammarion, 1922), pp. 161–62.

130. Sauret, "Préoccupations masculines." *La Voix des Femmes* was a socialist feminist paper that became increasingly Communist after 1920.

131. See *Dictionnaire etymologique de la langue française,* ed. Oscar Bloch and W. von Wartburg (Paris: Presses Universitaries de France, 1950).

132. See Marcel Braunschwig, *La Femme et la beauté* (Paris: Armand Colin, 1929); Edmonde Charles-Roux, *Le Temps Chanel* (Paris: Grasset, 1979).

Part 2 La Mère: Introduction

1. Drieu la Rochelle, *La Comédie de Charleroi* (Paris: Gallimard, 1934). For the autobiographical nature of this novel, see Jean Bastier, *Pierre Drieu la Rochelle: Soldat de la grande guerre, 1914–1918* (Paris: Editions Albatros, 1984).

2. Ibid., p. 59.

3. See Nancy Huston, "The Matrix of War: Mothers and Heroes," in *The Female Body in Western Culture,* ed. Susan Suleiman (Cambridge: Harvard University Press, 1986).

4. See, for example, Jane Misme, "La Mère et le soldat," *Oeuvre,* 17 May 1923.

5. Gaston Rageot, "Les Impressions d'un occupant sur le femmes allemandes," *La Femme et l'enfant,* 15 April 1919. See also the insert in *Pour la vie,* December 1920, in which the language is almost exactly the same.

6. See "Maximes et pensées," *La Femme et l'enfant,* 1 September 1919. See also Dr. Toulouse, *La Question sociale* (Paris: Editions du *Progrès Civique,* 1921), pp. 217–18, 220, where he makes the same parallel. Motherhood itself was often described in militaristic language, for example, in Rossignol's "Le Jour de la française est arrivé," *Pour la vie,* January 1919, and Paul Bureau, "Le Jour des mères," *Pour la vie,* May 1919.

7. Speech delivered in October 1919 to the Senate, excerpted in Georges Bonnefous, *L'Après-querre,* vol. 3 of *Histoire de la Troisième République*

(Paris: Presses Universitaires de France, 1959), p. 58. See also the statement made by Clemenceau to Jacques Bertillon in "*La Femme et l'enfant* chez M. Georges Clemenceau, president du Conseil," *La Femme et l'enfant*, 15 December 1919.

8. Dr. J.-A. Doléris and Jean Bouscatel, *Néo-malthusianisme, maternité et féminisme, education sexuelle* (Paris: Maison et Cie, 1918), p. 2.

9. For the term "counterdiscourse," see Richard Terdiman, *Discourse/Counterdiscourse: The Theory and Practice of Symbolic Resistance in Nineteenth-Century France* (Ithaca: Cornell University Press, 1985).

10. See Joshua Cole, "The Power of Large Numbers": Population and Politics in Nineteenth Century France" (Ph.D. diss., University of California at Berkeley, 1991), p. 165.

11. Joan Scott, "L'Ouvrière! Mot impie, sordide . . .": Women Workers in the Discourse of French Political Economy, 1840–1860," in *Gender and the Politics of History* (New York: Columbia University Press, 1988), p. 157. See also Thérèse Moreau, *La Sang de l'histoire; Michelet, l'histoire et l'idée de la femme au XIXe siècle* (Paris: Flammarion, 1982).

4. A Matter of Life or Death

1. The penalties for propaganda concerning contraception were one to six months in prison and fines of 100FF to 5,000FF. The penalties for propaganda on abortion were six months to three years in prison and fines from 100FF to 3,000FF. See Robert Talmy, *Histoire du mouvement familial en France, 1896–1939* (Paris: Union nationale des caisses d'allocations familiales, 1962), 2:11, and Joseph Spengler, *France Faces Depopulation: Postlude Edition, 1936–1976* (Durham: Duke University Press, 1979). For a written text of the law, see *La Femme et l'enfant*, 1 September 1920. Statistics concerning the frequency of abortion are notoriously inaccurate and difficult to obtain. According to historian Jack Ellis, estimates about abortion ranged between 40,000 and 100,000 in the prewar years. See his *The Physician-Legislators of France: Medicine and Politics in the Early Third Republic, 1870–1914* (Cambridge: Cambridge University Press, 1990), p. 221. I have been unable to find statistics for the postwar years. For abortion in the prewar period, see Angus McLaren, "Abortion in France: Women and the Regulation of Family Size, 1800–1914," *French Historical Studies* 10 (Spring 1978), and McLaren's *Sexuality and the Social Order: The Debate over the Fertility of Women and Workers in France, 1770–1920* (New York: Holmes and Meier, 1983), chap. 9.

2. André Berthon was a deputy of Paris from 1919 to 1932. Although he had no official party affiliation, he was known as a socialist. He was elected for the first time in November 1919 and was therefore at the beginning of his career when the July 1920 debates took place. He became a Communist at the Congrès du Tours in 1920 and then ran as a Communist in 1924. Paul Morucci was a deputy of Bouches-du-Rhône from 1919 to 1924. A doctor, he was also

a socialist and a newcomer in July 1920. This and all other information concerning legislators in the parliament is taken from J. Jolly, *Dictionnaire des parliamentaires françaises, 1899–1940,* 8 vols. (Paris: Documentation française, 1960–1977).

3. *Journal officiel (JO), Débats parlementaires, Chambre,* 24 July 1920, pp. 3069, 3072. Berthon was most likely referring to Madame de Sevigné's letters to her daughter, Madame de Grignan.

4. Ibid., p. 3072.

5. Ibid.

6. "Vote de la loi réprimant la propagande malthusienne," *La Femme et l'enfant,* 1 September 1920.

7. Angus McLaren, *Sexuality and the Social Order,* p. 1; Françoise Thébaud, *Donner la vie: Histoire de la mère en France entre les deux guerres* (Thèse du troisième cycle, Université de Paris VII, 1982), p. 59. See also her *Quand nos grand-mères donnaient la vie: La Maternité en France dans l'entre-deux-guerres* (Lyon: Presses Universitaires de Lyon, 1986), pp. 19–20.

8. See Francis Ronsin, *La Grève des ventres: Propagande néo-malthusienne et baisse de la natalité française* (Poitiers: Aubier Montaigne, 1980), pp. 140–41; McLaren, *Sexuality and Social Order,* p. 169.

9. Edouard Ignace was a *deputy* representing the Seine from 1914 to 1924. He was an important member of the Commission de législation civile et criminelle, where the bill was first examined in the Chamber of Deputies.

10. See Talmy, *Histoire du mouvement familial,* 2:10–12; and Ronsin, *La Grève des ventres,* pp. 141–46, for a thorough history of the bill's progress.

11. Maurice Agulhon and A. Nouschi, *La France de 1914 à 1940* (Paris: Nathan, 1971), p. 22; Thébaud, *Donner la vie,* p. 60; and McLaren, *Sexuality and Social Order,* p. 169.

12. See arguments of André Berthon and Paul Morucci, *JO, Débats parlementaires, Chambre,* 24 July 1920, pp. 3069–74. See also Richard Tomlinson, Marie-Monique Huss and Philip Ogden, "France in Peril: The French Fear of Denatalité," *History Today* 35 (April 1985): 26. The antinatalist socialist position represented a change from before the war. For example, in 1887 Jules Guesde argued that depopulation would decimate the working class. After the founding of the Communist Party (PCF) in 1920, the socialist attitude became more ambivalent because abortion had just been legalized in the Soviet Union. In the 1930s, socialists (including Léon Blum, who was known earlier for his liberal views on marriage) once more became natalist. For the socialist view on natalism in the thirties, see Françoise Thébaud, "Maternité et famille entre les deux guerres: Idéologie et politique familiale," in Rita Thalman, *Femmes et fascismes* (Paris: Editions Tierce, 1987), p. 94.

13. In *Grève des ventres,* p. 146, Ronsin argues that the law's passage stemmed from the defection of certain groups usually allied to neo-

Malthusianism. Among them were the working class and those who argued on the basis of freedom of speech.

14. Ibid., pp. 144–45.

15. Colin Dyer, *Population and Society in Twentieth Century France* (New York: Holmes and Meier, 1978), pp. 39–40.

16. Ibid., p. 40. Theodore Zeldin quotes completely different figures: 17.6 percent for France and 15.1 percent for Germany. See his *France, 1848–1945* (New York: Oxford University Press, 1977), 2:1083. Between 1914 and 1918, France mobilized 7,935,000 men. Since there were only 8,570,000 men in the country aged 18–46, mobilization was nearly complete.

17. Patrick Festy, "Effects et répercussions de la première guerre mondiale sur la fécondité française," *Population* 39 (1984): 978–79. According to demographic historians Maurice Garden and Hervé Le Bras, the French population did grow by 6.2 percent between 1921 and 1936, but this was only because of the influx of foreign immigrants, up sharply from the prewar period. See their treatment of the impact of the Great War on the French population in "La Population française entre les deux guerres," in Jacques Dupâquier, ed., *De 1914 à nos jours,* vol. 4 of *Histoire de la population française* (Paris: Presses Universitaires de France, 1988), pp. 90–91.

18. For the Roussel Law, see George D. Sussman, *Selling Mothers' Milk: The Wet-Nursing Business in France 1715–1914* (Urbana: University of Illinois, 1982), and Josh Cole, "A Sudden and Terrible Revelation: Infant Mortality, Maternal Responsibility, and the Roussel Law of 1874," in "The Power of Large Numbers: Population and Politics in Nineteenth Century France" (Ph.D. diss., University of California at Berkeley, 1991). For the problem of infant mortality, see also Mary Lynn Stewart, *Women, Work and the French State: Labour Protection and Social Patriarchy, 1879–1919* (Kingston, Ont.: McGill-Queen's University Press, 1989), pp. 178–85.

19. Some of the more "positive" measures taken to encourage natality in the postwar period included improvements in state pre- and postnatal care and a variety of tax incentives to fathers of large families. See Spengler, *France Faces Depopulation,* p. 240, where he refers to "the exception" of the laws passed in 1920 and 1923 against neo-Malthusianism and abortion, and describes most other natalist legislation as assuming the form of "positive pecuniary aids to parents and of reductions in certain burdens incident on parents." See also Ellis, *Physician-Legislators,* pp. 221–22, where he discusses the more positive tenor of legislation passed to encourage natality in the prewar period.

20. When the bill was discussed in 1914, it included three measures designed to counter depopulation: two concerning propaganda for abortion and contraception and a third that provided for *maisons d'accouchement,* or supervised obstetrical clinics. For a more detailed explanation of the history of the *maisons d'accouchement,* which were instituted during this period (although not under the auspices of the law of 1920), see Yvonne Kniebiehler and C.

Fouquet, *La Femme et les médecins: Analyses historique* (Paris: Hachette, 1983), pp. 239–50.

21. See McLaren, *Sexuality and Social Order,* p. 182.

22. *JO, Débats parlementaires, Chambre,* 24 July 1920, p. 3070. Pinard's reputation as a doctor and scientist was extremely high. At one point in the Senate debates on the same bill, he was referred to as "a great doctor, professeur Pinard." He was a member of the Académie de médecine, and published many works on obstetrics and gynecology. He entered the Chamber of Deputies in 1919 and stayed until 1929 as a member of the Radical party. At the time of the debates, Pinard had been a prominent Parisan doctor for almost 40 years. In fact, however, in *Quality and Quantity: The Quest for Biological Regeneration in Twentieth-Century France* (Cambridge: Cambridge University Press, 1990), p. 37, William Schneider argues that the neo-Malthusians claimed Pinard as one of their own because of his critique of the law of 1920 and natalist policies in statements such as that quoted above. After Pinard made this statement, both Berthon and Morucci referred to it several times; they were obviously aware of Pinard's influence in these matters and wanted to use it to their full advantage.

23. See Ronsin, *Grève des ventres,* p. 193. Paul Paillat and Jacques Houdaille argue that despite the 1920 law, two out of every three births were prevented in the 1920s. See their "Legislation Directly or Indirectly Influencing Fertility in France," in *Law and Fertility in Europe,* ed. M. Kirk, A. Livi-Bacci, and E. Szabady (Dolhain, Belgium: Ordina Editions, 1975), p. 24. Spengler argues in *France Faces Depopulation,* p. 127, that the postwar parliamentary debates and the passage of legislation such as the Law of 1920 "evidenced little comprehension of natality-determining factors." In *Quality and Quantity,* p. 120, William Schneider attributes "limited success" to the law because although it did not solve the problem of the declining birthrate, it did eliminate, "at least temporarily, an organized birth control movement in France."

24. McLaren, *Sexuality and Social Order,* p. 1. See also Paul Bureau, *L'Indiscipline des moeurs* (Paris: Bloud and Gay, 1920), pp. 96–97, 227, for the contemporary view.

25. *JO, Débats parlementaires, Chambre,* 24 July 1920, p. 3074. According to William Schneider, natalist sentiments ran so high after the war that candidates for the Senate and Chamber put *"père de famille"* after their names and included the number of their children in the campaign literature. See *Quality and Quantity,* p. 119.

26. See Cole, "The Power of Large Numbers," chap. 4, and Spengler, *France Faces Depopulation,* for a full accounting of natalist arguments at the turn of the century. The division of property under the Napoleonic inheritance laws became a common explanation of the crisis of depopulation even in the 1920s. See, for example, Fernand Auburtin, *La Natalité: La Patrie en danger!* (Paris: G. Crès et Cie, 1921, 4th ed.).

27. For the term "culturally intelligible," see Judith Butler, *Gender Trouble*

(London: Routledge, 1989). For more on "persuasion," see Ellen Rooney, *Seductive Reasoning: Pluralism as the Problematic of Contemporary Literary Theory* (Ithaca: Cornell University Press, 1989), chap. 2.

28. See, for example, John Hunter, "The Problem of the French Birth Rate on the Eve of World War I," *French Historical Studies* 2 (1962): 492; Eugen Weber, *France, Fin-de-siècle* (Cambridge: Harvard University Press, 1986), p. 12. In *France 1848–1945*, 2:950, Zeldin makes the argument that historians look at the problem in this way, then tries to move beyond it in his own analysis.

29. According to McLaren, *Sexuality and Social Order*, p. 15, the most commonly accepted theory is that in a modernizing, industrial society, children are no longer seen by their parents as instruments of cheap labor, but rather expensive investments in terms of clothing, feeding, and education. Based on this change in the "utility value" of children, the theory goes, parents make a rational decision to limit the number of their progeny.

30. Philip Ogden and Marie-Monique Huss describe the interwar period as "the apogee of pronatalism." See their "Demography and Pronatalism in France in the Nineteenth and Twentieth Centuries," *Journal of Historical Geography* 8 (1982): 292.

31. Two prominent bourgeois feminists who were also strongly natalist were Madeleine Vernet and Maria Vérone. By Madeleine Vernet, see "Le Mensonge social et la maternité," *Mère educatrice,* December 1919; "La Science qui tue" and "A Toutes les femmes," *Mère educatrice,* n.d., Dossier Vernet, Bibliothèque Marguerite Durand (BMD). By Maria Vérone, see "45.000 francs pour les parlementaires, 180 francs pour les mères," *Oeuvre,* 10 August 1926; "La Répression de l'avortement," *Oeuvre,* 26 April 1923; and "Le Plus beau sport: La Maternité," *Oeuvre,* 29 November 1923, all in Articles de journaux, Boîte no. 6, Fonds Marie Louise Bouglé, Bibliothèque Historique de la ville de Paris (AMLB). For secondary sources, see Yvonne Delatour, *Les Effets de la guerre sur la situation de la française d'après la presse féminine* (Diplôme d'études supérieures d'histoires, Université de Paris, May 1965), pp. 67–68, where she argues for the strength of the image of the mother, even among the most radical feminists.

32. Nelly Roussel, "Posons nos conditions," originally written in December 1919 and posthumously reprinted in *Derniers combats* (Paris: L'Emancipatrice, 1932), p. 86.

33 See Thébaud, *Donner la vie,* p. 58, where she argues that, in sharp contrast to the prewar period, the interwar years are "rich" in pro-family legislation. According to Thébaud, France lagged behind other countries in terms of such legislation until the interwar years. See also her "Maternité et famille entre les deux guerres" and *Quand nos grand-mères,* pp. 19–23.

34. For how the depopulation issue figured into prewar legislative debates concerning maternity leave, see Stewart, *Women, Work,* chap. 8.

35. In *Quality and Quantity,* p. 41, Schneider uses the 1902 Parliamentary Commission on Depopulation to demonstrate the prewar legislative failure of

the natalist cause. The commission was requested by 133 senators acting in conjunction with Bertillon's Alliance nationale. It soon floundered because of a lack of funds and interest, so only a few reports were published. See also Spengler, *France Faces Depopulation,* pp. 8–9, 122, 126–27.

36. See Zeldin, *France 1848–1945,* 2:949; Dyer, *Population and Society,* p. 5. In 1800 France had 28 million inhabitants. The German states together had 22 million, and the United Kingdom 16 million. In 1871, France had 36.1 million inhabitants, the German Empire had 41.1 million, and the United Kingdom 31.8 million. In 1911, the figures were: France, 39.6 million, Germany, 64.9 million, and United Kingdom, 45.4 million. While Germany advanced at a rate of 57 percent in population between 1850 and 1900, France only grew 12 percent in these years. Its birthrate fell from 30 births per thousand in 1830 to 19 births per thousand in 1913, the lowest in Europe, compared with 29.1 births for Germany. Between 1900 and 1930, while the French population increased by only 3 percent, the German population grew by leaps and bounds at a rate of 36 percent. Angus McLaren provides the best review of the historical literature on the demographic transition in chap. 1 of his *Sexuality and Social Order.* He argues that "no one has as yet produced a completely satisfactory explanation" of this demographic phenomenon (pp. 14–15). See also Karen Offen, "Depopulation, Nationalism and Feminism in Fin-de-Siècle France," *American Historical Review* 89 (June 1984): 649–51; Hunter, "The Problem of the French Birth Rate"; and Ogden and Huss, "Demography and pronatalism," p. 284.

37. See Ronsin, *La Grève des ventres,* for a full treatment of the neo-Malthusian movement in the early twentieth century, and for the dissemination of Malthusian beliefs in the French population. See also Spengler, *France Faces,* p. 7.

38. Zeldin, *France 1848–1945,* 2:951–52. Among the most famous of the early natalists was Frédéric Le Play, who raged about the "problem" in 1855, blaming it on those clauses of the Napoleonic Code that divided property inheritance and therefore caused parents to have fewer children rather than split their property too many ways. According to Spengler, *France Faces,* pp. 111–13, the first critics of French population decline in the 1850s were C. M. Raudot and Léonce de Lavergne. For the latter figure, see also Cole, "The Power of Large Numbers," pp. 226–27.

39. For an explanation of the defeat of 1870–71 in terms of ineffective military leadership, see Gordon Wright, *France in Modern Times: From the Enlightenment to the Present* (New York: W. W. Norton and Company, 1987), p. 149. In *Quality and Quantity,* pp. 15–16, 39, Schneider also makes the point that in the early nineteenth century, when Malthusian views of population were in favor, a rise rather than a decline in population was the cause for alarm. As late as 1851, he relates, the Academie française offered a 3,000-franc prize for the best work on the subject: "Happy the country where public and private wisdom united to present the population from growing too rapidly." For an

excellent treatment of early nineteenth-century views on population in France and the transition from a Malthusian to a populationist perspective among economists in the period 1840–70, see Y. Charbit, *Du Malthusianisme au populationisme: Les Economistes français et la population 1840–1870* (Paris: Presses Universitaires de France, 1983).

40. For the term "full political significance," see Cole, "The Power of Large Numbers," pp. 249–50, where he offers an intriguing explanation for why natalist legislation failed to be passed even though the birthrate had become a political issue of great importance. See also Offen, "Depopulation, Nationalism and Feminism"; Spengler, *France Faces*, pp. 124–25. For the discourse on degeneration and decadence, see Susanna Barrows, *Distorting Mirrors: Visions of the Crowd in Late Nineteenth-Century France* (New Haven: Yale University Press, 1981); Robert Nye, *Crime, Madness and Politics in Modern France: The Medical Concept of National Decline* (Princeton: Princeton University Press, 1984); and Eugen Weber, *France: Fin-de-Siècle*.

41. Paul Bureau and his colleague in the Ligue, Georges Rossignol, were both important natalist propagandists throughout the 1920s. Besides contributing to *Pour la vie*, the Ligue's periodical, Bureau found time to write his long natalist treatise *L'Indiscipline des moeurs* (1920), which was considered so controversial that newspapers such as *Le Temps, Le Petit Parisien,* and *Le Petit journal* refused to advertise the book when it first appeared. See the reviews by Paul Chauvin in *La Femme et l'enfant*, 15 September 1920, and G. Rossignol, "L'Indiscipline française," *Pour la vie*, July 1920. Extremely orthodox in his Catholic views, Bureau was also a professor at the Faculté libre de droit de Paris, as well as the *Institut catholique de Paris.*

42. Ronsin, *Grève des ventres*, pp. 124–26, argues that Bertillon was incontestably the leader of the natalist movement throughout the beginning of the twentieth century. His treatise on depopulation, *La Dépopulation de la France* (1911), won the Prix Strassart awarded by the *Académie des sciences morales.* He was known as both a doctor and demographer and was the son of Louis-Adolphe Bertillon, also extremely renowned in the fields of medicine and demography. Bertillon served as the chef du service de statistique in Paris from 1883 to 1913 and published several works on demographic and natalist topics.

43. See Thébaud, *Donner la vie*, pp. 29–30, and *Quand nos grand-mères*, p. 19, for a full description of the Alliance's activities. On p. 88, she argues that the Alliance dominated the natalist movement from its creation in 1896 through the interwar period. For a natalist pamphlet that emphasizes legislative reform as a way to solve the "problem," see M. Galéot, *Avenir de la race, le problème du peuplement en France* (Paris: Nouvelle Librairie Française, 1918). See the *Bulletin d'Alliance nationale*, September 1921, for a listing of officers of the Alliance, many of whom were in the parliament or the ministry.

44. The first congress was held in Nancy because the Chamber of Commerce there was particularly active in natalist work. See Fernand Auburtin, *La Natalité*, p. 25. The Congress was held 25–28 September 1919. The officers

were: Auguste Isaac, president; J. Bertillon, vice-president; and Paul Bureau, *rapporteur-général*. For further information on the Congress of Nancy, see *Premier congrès national de la natalité, tenu à Nancy, Compte rendu* (Nancy: Imprimeries Réunies, n.d.); "Premier congrès nationale de la natalité," Nancy (25–28 septembre 1919), *La Femme et l'enfant*, 15 October 1919; "Le Congrès de Nancy"; "Programme provisoire du congrès national de la natalité et de la population, *Pour la vie*, July 1919, and "Rapport général de M. Paul Bureau, congrès de Nancy," *Pour la vie*, October 1919. William Schneider takes the fact that Isaac, president of the first natalist conference, also became minister of commerce in 1919, as a sign of the growing strength of the natalist movement. See *Quality and Quantity*, p. 121.

45. The second natalist congress was held at Rouen, 23–26 September 1920, and the third at Bordeaux, 22–26 September 1921. The second congress boasted the representation of 128 affiliated organizations, municipalities, and chambers of commerce. See "Liste des collectivités," *Deuxième congrès nationale de la natalité, Compte rendu* (Rouen: Imprimerie de la Vicomte, 1920). There were six commissions to do the work of the congress: enseignement, action religieuse, hygiène et puériculture, action législative, action professionnelle, and propagande. For the Third Congress, see *Troisième congrès de la natalité, tenu à Bordeaux, du 22 au 26 septembre 1921, Compte rendu* (Bordeaux: Imprimerie Cadoret, 1921). According to Spengler, *France Faces*, p. 128, the natalist movement included eight national associations and 62 regional associations by 1922.

46. Besides monetary allocations to large families, the congresses and the Conseil supérieur de la natalité proposed that the French government set up a "caisse nationale autonome de la natalité," an institution that would gather funds and redistribute them to supplement large families. Social assistance to pregnant women included pre- and postnatal care in state-run institutions, government *crèches*, or nurseries for working women, and monetary allocations to single mothers. "*Primes d'allaitment*" were financial incentives for women who chose to nurse their children and thus avoid the dangers of wet-nursing. Reductions in military service would be based on the number of sons that a father had. Family suffrage gave the father a vote for each of his children, as well as for his wife.

47. "L'institution obligatoire du sursalaire familial," otherwise known as the Loi de M. Mokanowski, was introduced in parliament on 24 February 1920. Its aim was to allow the working woman to return home from the factory by compensating her salary loss. By the time of the third congress at Bordeaux in 1921, the Committee on Professional Action was able to report on the existence of 75 "*caisses de compensation*" created by private employers to provide workers with a "*sursalaire.*"

48. Paul Bureau, "Le Congrès de Bordeaux," *Pour la vie*, October 1921. The Ministry of Hygiene, Social Assistance, and Prevention was created in 1920. The minister who appeared here was Leredu; he wrote one of the first

rapports on the law against abortion and Malthusian propaganda. See *JO, Chambre, Documents,* 1919 Annexe no. 6679, p. 2347. Certainly the feeling that "something had really changed" was not unanimous. For an alternative view, see Auburtin, *La Natalité,* pp. 27 and 333, and "Pour que les familles soient nombreuses," *Pour la vie,* April 1921.

49. Georges Rossignol, "Ce que la France attend de ses élus," *Pour la vie,* December 1919. He praised the election of Adolphe Pinard, Général de Castelnau, and Auguste Isaac. In another article, "Electeurs, vous avez le choix: ou nous écouter . . . ou périr," *Pour la vie,* October 1919, Rossignol was particularly optimistic about the new president of the Chamber, Paul Deschanel, whom he felt would be a banner-carrier for the natalist cause. See "Ce que nous attendons du Conseil superieur de la natalité," *Pour la vie,* March 1920, for Rossignol's critique of the government's prewar efforts. See also Rossignol's *Un Pays de célibataires et de fils uniques.* (Paris: Dentu, 1896).

50. "Message de J. Bertillon," *La Femme et l'enfant,* 1 January 1920. At the 1920 Congress of Natality, Deputy Auguste Isaac (Rhône, l'Entente Républicaine Démocratique) affirmed that electoral programs in the November 1919 election had included natalist propositions and that the candidates had assured voters that they cared about the *famille nombreuse.* See *Deuxième congrès,* p. 22.

51. The law "correctionalized" abortion, that is, put it under the legal jurisdiction of the Cour d'assises, where cases were heard by a judge, not a jury. Since juries in the past had pitied and acquitted women who had participated somehow in an abortion, it was believed that the change in jurisdiction would increase the prosecution rate. For a full explanation of the law, see Maria Vérone, "La Répression de l'avortement," *Oeuvre,* 26 April 1923, Boîte no. 6, Articles de journaux, AMLB.

52. For an extremely thorough explanation of family legislation in this period, see Robert Talmy, *Histoire du mouvement familial.* For a contemporaneous feminist view of the variety and extent of the new legislation, see "Au Parlement: Pour combattre la dépopulation," *Droit des femmes,* April 1921. For a fuller explanation of *puériculture,* the teaching of infant care and hygiene, see Kniebiehler and Fouquet, *La Femme et les médecins,* chap. 8, and the brief discussion in chap. 7 of this volume.

53. The creation of the conseil was the first administrative act of J.-L. Bréton, a leading natalist who had just become the minister of hygiene, social assistance, and prevention. (Leredu succeeded Bréton in 1921.) Bréton also created a comité nationale de propagande d'hygiène sociale et d'éducation prophylactique within his ministry. Natalist commissions in each department were established at the same time as the Conseil supérieur, to whom they reported on local matters. The conseil's first act was to sign a decree on February 3, 1920, that lowered the price of bread to families with at least three children. Besides proposing natalist legislation, the conseil examined all *propositions du loi* to make sure that they would have no harmful effects on natality. The edi-

tors of *Pour la vie* believed it was the presence of the conseil that accounted for the increase in legislation that year. Among the conseil's publications was *Le Livret de la famille nombreuse,* which summarized all the state-sponsored advantages of having several children. Among the original members of the conseil were Adolphe Pinard, Jacques Bertillon, Fernand Boverat, Paul Bureau, Georges Rossignol, industrialist A. Michelin, and numerous deputies and senators. Only one woman, Madame Witt-Schlumberger, was on the conseil. See "Contre la dépopulation: Un Conseil supérieur de la natalité," *Droit de femmes,* February 1920, and "Ce que nous attendons," *Pour la vie,* March 1920. For secondary literature, see Thébaud, "Maternité et famille," pp. 87–88, and Thébaud, *Donner la vie,* pp. 21–22.

54. Decree of 26 May 1920, as published in the *Bulletin d'Alliance nationale,* September 1921. The mother was judged not only on the basis of how many children she had, but also on how well she had fulfilled her maternal role. After 1926, the medals were bestowed as part of the annual Mother's Day initiated in that year and celebrated nationally every May. See also J. B., "La Médaille des mères," *Le Temps,* 3 June 1920; "Lois et decrêts: La Médaille de la famille française," *Droit des femmes,* June 1920; "Médaille de la famille française," *Bulletin d'Alliance nationale,* September 1921; Jacques Bertillon, "La Journée des mères," *La Femme et l'enfant,* 1 June 1919, and the pamphlet "La Journée des mères, Rapport au congrès de la natalité et des familles nombreuses," 10–13 October 1918.

55. Paul Carnot, "Enquête sur le problème de la natalité," *Paris médical* 36 (Partie médicale), 20 March 1920: 176. Carnot was a member of the *Académie de médecine* and a *professeur agrégé* at the Faculty of Medicine in Paris. See also G. Blondel, *Le Problème de la natalité et les espérances de l'Allemagne,* Conférence fait, Septembre 1920 à l'occasion de deuxième congrès national de la natalité (Paris, 1920), p. 7.

56. Georges Blet, *L'avortement. Est-ce un crime?* (Mâcon: Imprimerie J. Buguet-Comptour, 1921); Roger Cruse, *Le Problème de la natalité,* Conférence faite le 31 janvier 1920 (Bordeaux: A Michel, 1920), p. 29. M. S. Gillet uses similar words in "La Famille et le vote des femmes," *Action sociale de la femme,* April 1919. See also 'Il n'y a qu'une question importante," *La Femme et l'enfant,* 15 March 1920; Charles Benoist, "Ce Pays, qui n'a pas eu peur de la mort, a eu peur de la vie!" *La Femme et l'enfant,* 15 August 1920.

57. Paul Haury, *La Vie ou la mort de la France* (Paris: Imprimerie des Editions Médicales, 1924), p. 4; Georges Maurevert, quoted in "Il faut remoraliser la France," *Pour la vie,* April 1919, Haury was a professeur agrégé in demography at the University of Paris. *La Vie ou la mort de la France* won the 1923 Prix Michelin, sponsored by the Alliance nationale. Haury was a propagandist for the Alliance nationale well into the forties.

58. Gaston Rageot, *La Natalité, les lois économiques et psychologiques* (Paris: Flammarion, 1918), p. 115. This book was greeted favorably by the press. See for example the review in *Revue des revues,* 15 June 1919.

59. *Troisième congrès*, p. 1.

60. Haury, *La Vie ou la mort*, pp. 10–11.

61. See, for example, Paul Bureau, *L'Indiscipline des moeurs*, p. 195

62. See Ibid., p. 201: Jules Boudry, *Le Problème de la natalité, envisagé au point de vue morale, économique, et législatif* (Clermont-Ferrand: G. Mont-Louis, 1923), pp. 10–11. See "Au Travers la presse: Le Problème de la natalité," *Droit des femmes*, January 1921, the interview with A. Pinard for another expression of fears concerning a deficient labor force. In "La Diminution du nombre des mariages et sa répercussion sur la natalité française, Conférence faite à Rouen le 30 decembre 1921," Fernand Boverat makes many of these same points concerning economic crisis. See "La Diminution du nombre des marriages et sa répercussion sur la natalité française," *Bulletin d'Alliance nationale*, March 1922. For the argument concerning the French colonies, see Paul Bureau, "La Seule question," *Pour la vie*, June 1921, and his *L'Indiscipline des moeurs*, p. 195. See also Paul Haury, *La Vie ou la mort*, pp. 1–11.

63. The best brief history of the financial troubles of the postwar period is in Philippe Bernard and Henri Dubief, *The Decline of the Third Republic, 1914–1938* (Cambridge: Cambridge University Press, 1985), chaps. 9 and 11.

64. Roger Cruse, *Le Problème de la natalité*, pp. 7–8. See also Paul Haury, *La Vie ou la mort*, p. 10.

65. Boverat, "La Diminution," pp. 83–84. Boverat began writing propaganda for the *Alliance nationale* in the 1910s, and continued to do so into the mid-forties. For more on Boverat, see Cheryl Koos, "Gender, Motherhood and Nationalism: The Discourse of French Pro-natalism, 1930–1940" (paper delivered at the Society for French Historical Studies Meeting, Chico, California, 19 March, 1993).

66. Jacques Bertillon, "Le Salut de la France dépend de la femme," *La Femme et l'enfant*, 1 October 1919. See also "La Grande plaie de la France," *La Femme et l'enfant*, 15 June 1920, where Bertillon makes a similar argument.

67. Auburtin, *La Natalité*, p. 54. Auburtin was a member of the Conseil d'état. His book went through four editions by 1921. For other similar general statements concerning economic fears, see Gaston Rageot, *La Natalité*, p. 112, and "Courage et propagande," *Pour la vie*, June, 1922.

68. For helping to alert me to the gendered elements of natalist discourse, I am indebted to Sylvia Schafer and Ann-Lou Shapiro.

69. On the relationship between gender and consumerism, see Michael Miller, *The Bon Marché: Bourgeois Culture and the Department Store, 1869–1920* (Princeton: Princeton University Press, 1981); Rosalind Williams, *Dream Worlds: Mass Consumption in Late Nineteenth Century France* (Berkeley: University of California Press, 1982); Rachel Bowlby, *Just Looking: Consumer Culture in Dreiser, Gissing and Zola* (New York: Methuen, 1985); Ellen Furlough, *Consumer Cooperation in France* (Ithaca: Cornell University Press, 1991), and Leora Auslander, "The Creation of Value and the Production of

Good Taste: The Social Life of Furniture in Paris" (Ph.D. diss., Brown University, 1988).

70. Jean-Jacques Becker and Serge Berstein estimate that 1,100,000 of those wounded during the war received "*une pension d'invalidité.*" See their *Victoire et frustrations, 1914–1929*, vol. 12 of *Nouvelle histoire de la France contemporaine* (Paris: Seuil, 1990), p. 165. For a brief introduction to the discourse on the *mutilés*, see the prefaces of well-known dramatist Eugène Brieux in Paul Emard, *Dans la nuit laborieuse: Essai sur la rééducation des soldats aveugles* (Paris: Librairie J. Victorion, 1917), and prominent politician Edouard Herriot in Gustave Hirschfield, *Une Ecole de rééducation professionnelle des grands blessés de la guerre* (Paris: Berger-Levrault, 1917). See also Antoine Prost, *Les Anciens combattants et la société française, 1914–1939* (Paris: Presses de la fondation nationale des sciences politiques, 1977), 1:7–45.

71. Gaston Rageot, "Pourquoi la France repeuplera," in a special edition of *La Femme et l'enfant*, n.d.; Victor Giraud, *Le Suicide de France* (Paris: Editions de la *Revue des jeunes*, 1923), p. 19; Bureau, "La Seule question." See also Jacques Bertillon, "Sous quel auspices notre journal est venu au monde," *La Femme et l'enfant*, 1 November 1918.

72. See Bureau, *L'Indiscipline des moeurs*, pp. 209–11, where he criticizes John Stuart Mill for this view and mentions in passing that several French liberal economists still adhere to it.

73. See McLaren, *Sexuality and Social Order.* For a study on the logic of family planning in England, see J. A. and Olive Banks, *Feminism and Family Planning in Victorian England* (New York: Schocken, 1964).

74. Jacques Bertillon, "Séance de clôture des ligues de familles nombreuses et de repopulation, *La Femme et l'enfant*, 1 November 1918: 8; Fernand Boverat, "La Diminution," p. 79. See also Bertillon, "La Femme française," *La Femme et l'enfant*, 15 October 1918, and "Quatre ans de guerre," *Pour la vie*, December 1918; and "Prix Michelin de la natalité," *La Presse médicale*, 9 August 1922: "Depopulation is war, it is invasion, it is ruin."

75. Paul Haury, *La Vie ou la mort*, p. 13. For other arguments that numerical and military inferiority was a basic cause for the war, see Auburtin, *La Natalité*, pp. 13, 44–45; Giraud, *Le Suicide de France*, p. 21; Bureau, *L'Indiscipline des moeurs*, pp. 192–93. For the widespread pacifism in postwar France, see Modrus Eksteins, *Rites of Spring: The Great War and the Birth of the Modern Age* (Boston: Houghton-Mifflin, 1989); John Williams, *The Homefronts: Britain, France and Germany, 1914–1918* (London: Constable and Co., Ltd., 1972), p. 291; and Norman Ingram, *The Politics of Dissent: Pacifism in France, 1919–1939* (New York: Oxford University Press; 1991).

76. Blondel, *Le Problème de la natalité*, p. 5; Giraud, *Le Suicide de France*, p. 19. See also Boudry, *Le Problème de la natalité*, p. 9, and "Séance de clôture," p. 23.

77. On depopulation as an Europe-wide problem, see Bonnie Smith, *Changing Lives: Women in European History Since 1700* (Lexington, Mass.:

D. C. Health and Company, 1989), pp. 434–38, and Garden et Le Bras, "La Population française entre les deux guerres," p. 85.

78. The first phrase is from Paul Bureau, *L'Indiscipline des moeurs*, pp. 212–13, and the second, spoken by Georges Maurevert, is quoted in Rossignol, "Il faut remoraliser." See also "La Propagande néo-malthusienne est d'origine étrangère: Un Document accablant," *La Femme et l'enfant*, 15 September 1920.

79. Giraud, *Le Suicide de France*, p. 24. See also "Premier Congrès de la natalité," p. 557; Jacques Bertillon, "C'est par la femme que la France doit être sauvée," *La Femme et l'enfant*, 15 September 1919, and Bias, "Neo-malthusien," *La Femme et l'enfant*, 15 August 1919.

80. This tendency to express fears about Germany in terms of gender and sexuality had a history in modern France. Edward Berenson has found the same phenomenon in debate about the Franco-Prussian War at the end of the nineteenth century. See his *The Trail of Madame Caillaux* (Berkeley: University of California Press, 1992), p. 115–7.

81. "Séance de clôture," pp. 23–24. See also Bureau, *L'Indiscipline des moeurs*, p. 193.

82. Ibid.

83. Bureau, *L'Indiscipline des moeurs*, p. 241. See also his "La Seule question," for a similar argument.

84. Giraud, *Le Suicide de France*, p. 10. See also *JO, Débats parlementaires, Chambre*, 12 December 1923, Comments of Deputy Roulleaux-Dugage for a similar argument concerning France's relative strengths, and Haury, *La Vie ou la mort*, pp. 1, 6.

85. "Pour que les familles soient nombreuses." See also "Le Sabotage de la nation," *La Femme et l'enfant*, 1 July 1919, and "La Bourgeoisie en péril," *La Femme et l'enfant*, 15 December 1919 and 15 January 1920.

86. Giraud, *Le Suicide de France*, p. 21. See also Boverat, "La Diminution," p. 75.

87. See, for example, the anguished questions of Fernand Boverat in "Metallurgie et dépopulation," *Bulletin d'Alliance nationale*, September 1921: "Will France be able to pick itself up from the terrible ordeal that it has just undergone? Will it be able to restore its devastated riches, to bring its production level up again to prewar levels? Won't it give way under the weight of its enormous debt, the financial burden that weighs down on it and that seems to preclude any hope for prosperity for a long time?"

88. Giraud, *Le Suicide de France*, p. 5: "Il faut remoraliser la France," and Gaston Rageot, "Une grande nation va-t-elle s'éteindre?" *Oeuvre*, 11 September 1920; Cruse, *Le Problème de la natalité*, p. 5; Phédon, "Le Sabotage de la nation," *La Femme et l'enfant*, 1 July 1919; "La Grande plaie de France"; Rageot, *La Natalité*, pp. 1–2, 72; Madame Claude d'Habloville, "Le Suicide

national," *La Française,* 12 May 1923; and "Aux educateurs," *Pour la vie,* n.d., Dossier Natalité, BMD.

89. Bureau, *L'Indiscipline,* p. 194.

90. Giraud, *Le Suicide,* p. 57.

91. Bureau, *L'Indiscipline,* p. 195.

92. See Blondel, *Le Problème de la natalité,* p. 8.

93. Auburtin, *La Natalité,* pp. 38–39,

94. Rageot, *La Natalité,* pp. 111–12.

95. "Le Bel avenir de vos enfants."

96. Roger Cruse, *Le Problème de la natalité,* p. 29. See also Boudry, *Le Problème de la natalité,* p. 11, and Rageot, *La Natalité,* p. 19.

97. Auburtin, *La Natalité,* p. 333.

98. Foucault would argue that the natalists were trying to exercise power over what he called the "species-body," or "the body imbued with the mechanics of life and serving as the basis of the biological processes: propagation, births and mortality, the level of health, life expectancy and longevity." See his *Introduction* to *The History of Sexuality* (New York: Random House, 1980), p. 139, for a discussion of the state's "calculated management of life and death."

99. Gordon Wright considers a "fluke" the 1919 shift to the right in the Chamber. He attributes it to a change in the electoral system made that year that favored electoral coalitions. The right managed to form such coalitions under the label "Bloc National," but the left did not, as it was torn apart by inner divisions concerning Bolshevism. See *France in Modern Times,* pp. 334–35. For the same interpretation, see also Agulhon and Nouschi, *La France de 1914 à 1940,* pp. 19–23. Georges Bonnefous believes that the electoral changes were only one factor in the victory of the Bloc national. Also at stake, he argues, was the "discipline" and energy of the right organizationally, the desire for renewal that encouraged the entry of new deputies, and anti-Bolshevism. See his *Histoire de la Troisième République* (Paris: Presses Universitaires de France, 1968), 3:59–67. Socialists and radical socialists suffered the greatest losses in the election of 1919. Socialists went from 101 to 72 in numbers, radical-socialists from 288 to 138 deputies. The left would remain severely divided until 1924.

100. *JO, Débats parlementaires, Sénat,* 22 November 1918, p. 776. Delahaye was the senator of Maine-et-Loire from 1903 to 1932. He had a reputation as a royalist and as a volatile, temperamental senator.

101. Ibid., 29 January 1919, p. 49. Chéron was deputy from Calvados from 1906 to 1913, and then the senator from 1913 to 1936. He was a consistent advocate of *la famille nombreuse* during his long tenure in the parliament.

102. Ibid., p. 50. Martin was the senator of the Saône-et-Loire from 1887 to his death in 1924 at the age of 84.

103. Ibid., 25 January 1919, p. 30. Marie Debierre was the senator of the Nord from 1911 to 1932. He was a practicing physician and a member of the

Academie de médécine. Before his political career, he taught anatomy and physiology at the French universities in Lyon and Lille.

104. Ibid., 22 November 1918, p. 776. Many illegitimate and orphaned children, Cazeneuve went on to argue, "have made courageous soldiers" who have been decorated with the Croix de Guerre and have died "bravely doing their duty." Paul Cazeneuve was deputy from the Rhône from 1902 to 1909, and senator from 1909 to 1920. Hence he was at the very end of his career when appointed as *rapporteur-général* of the law in 1918–19. He had a brilliant reputation as a scientist and doctor as well as a legislator.

105. Ibid., 25 January 1919, p. 32. Léon Jénouvrier was the senator of Ile-et-Vilaine from 1907 to 1932. He was a lawyer and a fervent Catholic. In his *Dictionnaire des parliamentaires françaises,* J. Jolly names Jénouvrier's role in these debates as one of the landmark moments in his career. In 1921 he would become vice-president of the Senate.

106. Ibid., 29 January 1919, p. 49.

107. Ibid., pp. 51–52. Reveillaud was the senator from the Charente-Inférieure from 1912 to 1921. He was a lawyer and, according to Jolly, spoke out openly against neo-Malthusian propaganda and abortion as early as 1910. Paul Gaultier was a member of the Institut de France and the Légion d'honneur, and an editor of *La Revue bleue.*

108. Ibid., 25 January 1919, p. 30. Emile Goy was the senator from Haute-Savoie from 1910 to 1925. He was a doctor and a member of senatorial commissions on teaching, hygiene, and social assistance.

109. Ibid.

110. Cazeneuve claimed that there were approximately 100 doctors in the Chamber and the Senate in 1919. See *JO, Débats parlementaires, Sénat,* 29 January 1919, p. 40. Historian Jack Ellis's numbers are more conservative: 44 doctors and 5 pharmacists. However, Ellis argues that doctors were second only to lawyers in terms of their relative representation in the national politics of the Third Republic, a phenomenon that "had few counterparts in other societies." See his *Physician-Legislators,* pp. 3–5. Ellis argues that the postwar period was a political turning point for the physician-legislator, marked by "a conservative drift among the older republican groups on the left, especially as they became outflanked by socialists and Communists."

111. Ibid., pp. 12–14, 139, 240, and chap. 6. According to Ellis, "far from viewing political activism as an abdication of their role, many physicians welcomed it as a means of furthering efforts to enhance medical power and authority." Their activity in questions of public health and hygiene, such as depopulation, infant mortality and alcoholism, formed a long tradition.

112. The *maisons* would be administered by "competent medical direction," either a doctor or midwife, who would be chosen by the Ministry of the Interior. The medical director would then be obliged to cooperate with various administrative assistants, who in turn would be surveyed by the police. The

minister of the interior would appoint the directors based on nominations from France's most prestigious medical institutions, such as the Facultés de médecine and the Facultés mixtes de médecine et de pharmacie, which were at this time dominated by male physicians rather than midwives. Hence the *maisons d'accouchement* would most likely have privileged doctors over midwives, their competition in obstetrical and gynecological medicine.

113. *JO, Débats parlementaires, Sénat*, 25 January 1919, pp. 29, 31. The principle of medical confidentiality was also referred to (p. 29) as "a principle of natural law." The Commission justified the article by citing the gravity of the depopulation crisis.

114. Ibid., pp. 30, 35. See also the remarks of Debierre and Milliès-Lacroix, same day, p. 30.

115. Ibid., pp. 29–30.

116. Ibid., p. 32.

117. See Ellis, *Physician-Legislators*, p. 76, and McLaren, *Sexuality and Social Order*, pp. 44–45. Both McLaren and Ellis believe that the doctor had replaced the priest as the main confessor of the family by the end of the nineteenth century. According to Ellis, the doctor "no longer considered himself a mere healer or hygienic adviser; he was also a councillor and intermediary, a voice of reason and reassurance helping resolve the most private conflicts." See also *JO, Débats parlementaires, Sénat*, 29 January 1919, p. 42, remarks of Senator Empereur, who also compares the doctor to the priest.

118. *JO, Débats parlementaires, Chambre*, 24 July 1920, p. 3071. Medical interests were ultimately defended, as Article 14 of the final Senate version required doctors to denounce abortionists only if it did not compromise the medical confidentiality of an individual. On the other hand, however, when Article 14 continued to delay progress of the bill, bogging down discussion in the Chamber commission, it was eliminated from the streamlined proposal (along with the *maisons d'accouchement*) that Edouard Ignace presented to the Chamber on 23 July 1920.

119. See Sylvia Schafer, "Children in 'Moral Danger' and the Politics of Parenthood in Third Republic France, 1870–1914" (Ph.D. Diss., University of California at Berkeley, 1992), chap. 2.

120. *JO, Débats parlementaires, Sénat*, 25 January 1919, p. 28. Paul Strauss was the senator from the Seine from 1897 to 1936. He became minister of hygiene, social assistance and prevention in January 1922 and held the post until March 1924. For more information on Strauss, see Ellis, *Physician-Legislators*, pp. 174–75, and Robert Nye, *Crime, Madness and Politics*, p. 236.

121. Ibid., 29 January 1919, p. 49. Such an equation of the child with the future of France characterized natalist discourse from its conception. See Cole, "The Power of Large Numbers," p. 193.

122. For the ambivalence that marked the Third Republic's social policy

toward the French family, see Schafer, "Children in Moral Danger," pp. 99–116.

123. *JO, Débats parlementaires, Sénat,* 25 January 1919, p. 32.

124. Ibid., p. 37.

125. Ibid., 22 November 1918, p. 777.

126. See also Paul Bureau, "L'Avortement," *Pour la vie,* June 1919.

127. Given the sparsity of actual discussion of the law in the Chamber on 23 July 1920, I have tried to piece together related documents in order to determine whether it was conceived in the same way as in the Senate.

128. *JO, Documents parlementaires, Chambre,* Annexe no. 201, Séance 22 Janvier 1920, F713955, Malthusianisme, 1919–1920 Archives Nationales.

129. Here and elsewhere in my analysis of the sexualized nature of this language, I am indebted to the observations of Ann-Lou Shapiro in her comment on my paper, "How Can We Ever Heal Such a Wound?": Pronatalism, Cultural Crisis and the Abortion Law of 1920," (Paper delivered at the Society for French Historical Studies Meeting, Vancouver, British Columbia, 23 March 1991.)

130. *JO, Documents parlementaires, Chambre,* Annexe no. 1357, Séance du 23 juillet 1920, p. 2065, Exposé de motifs, presentée par M. Edouard Ignace.

131. *JO, Débats parlementaires, Sénat,* 22 November 1918, p. 780.

132. For a Europe-wide survey, see Charles Maier, *Recasting Bourgeois Europe: Stabilization in France, Germany and Italy in the Decade after World War I* (Princeton: Princeton University Press, 1975). See also Edouard Bonnefous, *Avant l'oubli: La Vie de 1900 à 1940* (Paris: Editions Fernand Nathan, 1985), pp. 186, 202; and Adeleine Daumard, *Les Bourgeois et la bourgeoisie en France depuis 1815* (Paris: Aubier-Montaigne, 1987), p. 278. The immediate postwar period was also a time of considerable worker unrest. Strikes in early 1919 led up to an attempt for a general strike beginning May 1. The Confédération Générale de Travail experienced enormous growth as those employed by the war industry lost their jobs. See Agulhon and Nouschi, *La France de 1914 à 1940,* p. 18.

133. For property destroyed, see Bonnefous, *Avant l'oubli,* p. 187; for reconstructive work, see Agulhon and Nouschi, *La France de 1914,* p. 18. The best treatment of demobilization is contained in Antoine Prost's *Les Ancien combattants,* 1: chap. 2.

134. See Bonnefous, *L'Histoire,* 3: 26, where he quotes the "Témoignage de Louis Marcellin," concerning the scarcity and expense of charcoal, butter, eggs, sugar, and meat. For other contemporary views on postwar inflation, see "Les Vainquers sous le joug," *Oeuvre,* 2 February 1919, and "La Bourgeoisie française dans la lutte pour la vie," *Renaissance politique,* 24, 31 July 1920. Among the secondary literature, see Daumard, *La Bourgeoisie.*

135. Between 1919 and 1920 the franc fell by 50 percent, and by 1924 it had fallen to less than 10 percent of its prewar value. For a full description of

the crises in the franc that plagued France throughout the decade, see Bernard and Dubief, *The Decline of the Third Republic*, particularly pp. 94–107. In *La France de 1914 à 1940*, p. 32, Agulhon and Nouschi point out that the instability of the franc was absolutely unprecedented in French history and had its roots in the war, which had drained all federal reserves. All these historians emphasize that this was a fiscal situation that legislators did not have the economic literacy to truly comprehend. See also Wright, *France in Modern Times*, pp. 364–65, for the economic illiteracy of the politicians.

136. See James McMillan, *From Dreyfus to DeGaulle* (London: E. Arnold, 1985), p. 95. Recent diplomatic historiography emphasizes the wartime and postwar periods as ones of decline in international power and prestige for France. For a summary and evaluation of this material, see Michael Carley, "Le Déclin d'une grande puissance: La Politique étrangère de la France en Europe," *Canadian Journal of History* 21 (1986).

137. Bernard and Dubief, *Decline*, p. 125. See also Maier, *Recasting Bourgeois Europe*, p. 144, and C. Fohlen, *La France de l'entre-deux-guerres* (Paris: Casterman, 1972). C. Fohlen calls the postwar period "Les Temps des Illusions."

138. Roussel, "Posons," p. 86.

139. Ibid., pp. 86–87.

5. Madame Doesn't Want a Child

1. *Journal officiel (JO)*, *Débats parlementaires, Sénat*, 25 January 1919, pp. 33–34.

2. Ibid., p. 34.

3. Ibid., p. 32. Jénouvrier claimed to be quoting "Monsieur Roosevelt, one of our great friends, dead yesterday unfortunately." Journalists expressed similar fears. See, for example, Henry Joly's remarks in "De l'extension du travail des femmes après la guerre," *Le Correspondant*, 10 January 1917: 27, and the corresponding chapter in Joly's book, *L'Avenir français* (Paris: Bloud et Gay, 1917).

4. *JO*, *Débats parlementaires, Sénat*, 24 January 1919, p. 30. See also the opinion of Dr. Jayle in "Honorons et protégeons toutes les mères: L'Opinion du Docteur Jayle," *Le Matin*, 22 August 1925.

5. Quoted in *"La Femme et l'enfant* chez M. Georges Clemenceau," *La Femme et l'enfant*, 15 December 1919.

6. Edward Heriot, *Créer* (Paris: Payot et Cie, 1919).

7. This is cited in Juliette Françoise Raspail, "Si la France se dépeuple, dit un homme, c'est la faute des femmes!" *La Française*, 24 March 1923. The statement was probably made sometime in 1922 or 1923.

8. See Cole, "The Power of Large Numbers: Population and Politics in Nineteenth Century France" (Ph.D. diss., University of California at Berkeley, 1991), pp. 165–6.

9. Ibid., pp. 202–3, 252–55. For motherhood as a social function, see also Mary Lynn Stewart, *Women, Work and the French State: Labour Protection and Social Patriarchy, 1879–1919* (Kingston, Ont.: McGill-Queen's University Press, 1989), pp. 177–78.

10. Docteur Cattier, *Des Bébés, s'il vous plaît* (Paris: Plon, 1923), p. 7. Dr. Gaston Cattier was a member of the Institut urétrologique de Paris and the author of several popular medical books in the twenties and thirties.

11. Gaston Rageot, *La Natalité, les lois économiques et psychologiques* (Paris: Flammarion, 1918), p. 211.

12. *JO, Débats parlementaires, Sénat,* 29 January 1919, p. 49.

13. See Cole, "The Power of Large Numbers," pp. 202–3. Cole also names several other natalist measures that were geared specifically at the female population, namely, the encouragement of breast-feeding, maternal financial assistance, and regulation of female employment, including mandatory maternity leave. For the last of these, see Stewart, *Women, Work,* chap. 8.

14. See Rageot, *La Natalité,* p. 209.

15. Michel Planter, "Ce que nous devons aux mères françaises," *Pour la vie,* May 1919.

16. "La Lutte contre la dépopulation," *La Femme et l'enfant,* 15 April 1920.

17. "La Bonne médaille," *Canard enchaîné,* 23 June 1920. The theme of *citoyenne* was also played on in a natalist poem by René Buzelin, "Il n'y a plus d'enfants!" *Canard enchaîné,* 4 February 1920. One stanza went like this: "Malgré le danger pressant/La femme est souvent rebelle/Comme si l'état, pour elle/Cessait d'être intéressant."

18. Paul Bureau, "Deuxième congrès de la natalité," *Pour la vie,* October 1920.

19. *Mercure de France,* 15 November 1922.

20. See Vérone, "Le Plus beau sport: La Maternité" *Oeuvre,* 29 November 1923, Articles de Journaux, Boîte no. 6, Sa-Ve, Archives Marie Louise Bouglé (AMLB). *La mère Gigogne* was a dramatic character created for the theater in 1602. She was represented as a large woman with a huge skirt, from which emerged a large number of children. Balzac used the *mère Gigogne* in his *Mémoires de deux jeunes mariées* as a derisive word for a woman who has or is surrounded by many children. See *Le Grand Robert de la langue française,* 2nd ed., vol. 4.

21. Maurice Duval, "Une Enquête sur la crise du mariage," *Renaissance politique,* 5 April–24 May 1924. See the remarks of Gaston Rageot and Maurice Duval in the 5 April installment, those of Yvonne Sarcey in the 19 April installment, and those of Colette Yver in the 25 April installment.

22. Vérone, "Le plus beau sport." See also Jane Misme, "Maternité, ménage et profession," *La Française,* 20 May 1922, and "La Maternité, est-elle une vocation?" *La Française,* 29 April 1922. For an interesting explanation of why so many feminists of the day were natalist, see Françoise Thébaud,

"Maternité et famille entre les deux guerres: Idéologie et politique famili-ale," in *Femmes et fascismes*, ed. Rita Thalman (Paris: Editions Tierce, 1987), pp. 95–96.

23. Excerpted in Louise Bodin, "La Mère éducatrice," *Voix des femmes*, 12 September 1918, Dossier Education Sexuelle, 1898–1938, Bibliothèque Mar-guerite Durand (BMD). For more information on Madeleine Vernet, see Dos-sier Madeleine Vernet, BMD.

24. Ibid. For more examples of the radical feminist view on maternity in the 1920s, see also "La Journée des mères," *Voix des femmes*, 22 May 1920, and *Au Pays des repopulateurs: Une Campagne pour l'adoption des enfants assistés* (Paris: Société mutuelle d'édition, 1922); *Bulletin des groupes fémi-nistes de l'Enseignement laïque* 10 (April 1924). One constant complaint among feminists that is voiced in this last article is the fact that only one woman sat on the Conseil supérieur de la natalité.

25. See "Posons nos conditions," in *Derniers combats* (Paris: L'Emancipa-trice, 1932), and "Pour la France?" n.d., Dossier Nelly Roussel, AMLB. Nelly Roussel was not the first Frenchwoman to propose such a strike. See Elinor Accampo, "Anarchism and Gender Relations: The Birth Control Movement, 1890–1920," Paper given at the Western Society for French History, Orcas Island, Washington, October 1992. For another radical feminist view, see Séverine, "La Grève des ventres," *Humanité*, 9 April 1922.

26. Colin Dyer, *Population and Society in Twentieth Century France* (New York: Holmes and Meier, 1978), pp. 50, 78. In 1926–30, it was 18.2 per 1,000 inhabitants; in 1931–35, it was 16.5; and in 1936–38, it was 14.8.

27. See Eric Hansen, *Disaffection and Decadence: A Crisis in French Intel-lectual Thought, 1848–1898* (Washington, D.C.: University Press of America, 1982), p. 4, where he cites both Ernest Renan and prominent scientist Mar-celin Berthelot as making this argument at midcentury.

28. *JO, Débats parlementaires, Sénat*, 24 January 1919, pp. 33–34.

29. "Appel à l'action: Discours de M. Paul Deschanel,' *Pour la vie*, October 1919, reprinted in Jacques Bertillon, "Séance de clôture des ligues de familles nombreuses et de repopulation, *La Femme et l'enfant*, 1 November 1918, p. 26; "*La Femme et l'enfant*, chez M. Georges Clemenceau." For other French legislators and officials who spoke in this way, see, for example, the remarks of Georges Leredu, then minister of hygiene, at the third national natalist con-gress in 1921, *Troisième congrès de la natalité, tenu à Bordeaux, du 22 au 26 septembre 1921, Compte rendu* (Bordeaux: Imprimerie Cadoret, 1921); Mar-quise de Moustiers, "Les Conceptions morales de la française," *Action sociale de la femme*, 23 April 1920. For similar statements from natalist propagandists, see "Premier congrès nationale de la natalité," Nancy (25–28 septembre, 1919), *La Femme et l'enfant*, 15 October 1919; Cornet, "Un Congrès de la natalité," *Paris médicale*, 26 July 1919; "Courage et propagande," *Pour la vie*, June 1922; Mme. Claude d'Habloville, "Le Suicide national," *La Française*, 12

May 1923; Paul Bureau, *L'Indiscipline des moeurs* (Paris: Bloud and Gay, 1920), p. 263.

30. For Léonce de Lavergne, see Cole, "Power of Numbers," pp. 226–28 and Angus McLaren, *Sexuality and the Social Order: The Debate over the Fertility of Women and Workers in France, 1770–1920* (New York: Holmes and Meier, 1983), pp. 9, 21. According to McLaren, Léonce de Lavergne gave a "typical" argument when, in 1857, he attributed the fall in fertility to "shameful calculations of egoism." See also Theodore Zeldin, *France, 1848–1945*, 2:962–64.

31. Arsène Dumont, *Dépopulation et civilisation* (Paris: Lecrosnier et Babé, 1890), pp. 113, 127–30. The socialist Dumont argued that the natality rate stood in an inverse ratio to *capillarité sociale* and that only a strengthened family structure and a socialist government could raise the natality rate once again by reducing the individual's *capillarité sociale*. For an excellent analysis of Dumont's theories and their influence on late nineteenth-century natalist discourse, see Cole, "Power of Numbers," pp. 353–55.

32. Fernand Auburtin, *La Natalité: La Patrie en danger!* (Paris: G. Crès et Cie, 1921, 4th ed.), p. 61. To Auburtin, one of the most conservative postwar natalists, the revolution represented the absolute triumph of individualism. New laws concerning property inheritance destroyed institutions such as the family and subordinated social structures to individual freedom.

33. See Rageot, *La Natalité*, pp. 137, 139. Rageot offers a full explanation of *capillarité sociale* on pp. 32–33, 135–36, where he describes Dumont's theory as the most adequate and original theory of depopulation. For other examples of the influence of Dumont, see Rageot's "Une grande nation va-t-elle s'éteindre?" *Oeuvre*, 11 September 1920; Bureau, *L'Indiscipline*, p. 65; Victor Giraud, *Le Suicide de France* (Paris: Editions de la *Revue des jeunes*, 1923), p. 28; Jacques Bertillon, "Sous quel auspices notre journal est venu au monde," *La Femme et l'enfant*, 1 November 1918; and Dr. Toulouse, *La Question sexuelle et la femme* (Paris: Bibliothèque-Charpentier, 1918), pp. 142–43.

34. "Aux Educateurs," *Pour la vie*, n.d., Dossier Natalité, BMD. Many of these characterizations were used to describe prostitutes in the nineteenth century. See, for example, A. Parent-Duchâtelet, *De la Prostitution dans la ville de Paris* (1836). On this subject, see also Thérèse Moreau, *Le Sang de l'histoire: Michelet, l'histoire et l'idée de la femme au XIXe siècle* (Paris: Flammarion, 1928); and Joan W. Scott, "L'Ouvrière! Mot impie, sordide . . .": Women Workers in the Discourse of French Political Economy, 1840–1860," in *Gender and Politics of History* (New York: Columbia University Press, 1988).

35. Cattier, *Des Bébés*, p. 9. For the same argument, see Louis Narquet, "La Femme dans la France de demain," *Mercure de France*, 16 July 1917: 263; and Adolphe Pinard, *La Consommation, Le bien-être et le luxe* (Paris: Octave Don et Fils, 1918).

36. See, for example, the way in which the word is used throughout Clément Vautel, *Mademoiselle sans-gêne* (Paris: A. Michel, 1922).

37. Auburtin, *La Natalité*, p. 55. See also "Le Travail," *La Femme et l'enfant*, 15 March 1920; Giraud, *Le Suicide de France*, p. 77; and Moustiers, "Les Conceptions morales."

38. "La Lutte contre la dépopulation." For a similar statement of values, see "Quelques mots d'ordre nécessaire," *Pour la vie*, June 1921, and Andrée d'Alix, "Discipliner et simplifier la vie," *Action sociale de la femme*, May 1922.

39. *Deuxième congrès national de la natalité, Compte rendu* (Rouen: Imprimerie de la Vicomte, 1920), p. 20; Georges Rossignol and Paul Bureau, "Le Sang de France," *Pour la vie*, November 1920; "Pour que les familles soient nombreuses: L'Ambience nécessaire," *Pour la vie*, April 1921; "Comment remoraliser la France," *Pour la vie*, June 1919. See also Fernand Boverat, "La Diminution du nombre des mariages et sa répercussion sur la natalité française," *Bulletin d'Alliance nationale*, March 1922, p. 90; "Lettre à la ligue," *Droit des femmes*, October 1919; "Courage et propagande" and "La Lutte contre la dépopulation." The concept of "devoir" was also stressed by Clemenceau in Bertillon, "*La Femme et l'enfant* chez Clemenceau." For more on this shift in emphasis from "rights" to "duties," see Sylvia Schafer, "Children in 'Moral Danger' and the Politics of Parenthood in Third Republic France, 1870–1914" (Ph.D. diss., University of California at Berkeley, 1992), chap. 2, and Claudia Kselman, "The Modernization of Family Law: The Politics and Ideology of Family Reform in Third Republic France (Ph.D. diss., University of Michigan, 1980).

40. Rageot, *La Natalité*, p. 226. Rageot also argues, pp. 209–10, that such a spiritual regeneration began in the years just preceding the war, after a long era of decadence and moral dissipation. In this sense, his analysis of youth in the period parallels that of Robert Wohl in *The Generation of 1914* (Cambridge: Harvard University Press, 1979).

41. Bureau, *L'Indiscipline*, pp. 1–2.

42. "De Tout un peu," *La Femme et l'enfant*, 1 March 1920. For a similar view, see also Gaston Sauvebois, "La Nouvelle pensée française," *Revue mondiale*, 1 November 1919.

43. See H. B., "Pour le service social des femmes," *La Française*, 9 October 1920; Phédon, "Le Sabotage de la nation," *La Femme et l'enfant*, 1 July 1919, p. 388. For a similar view of modern life, see Abbé L. Rastouil, *La Jeune fille hors du foyer* (Marseille: Imprimerie St. Léon, 1923), p. 13; Gérard Lavergne, *Les Femmes d'après guerre* (Nîmes: Chastenier, 1925). For other instances of the term "frenzy," see *Deuxième congrès*, p. 173; Françoise Vitry, "L'Heure de la femme," *Renaissance politique*, 3 September 1921: 17.

44. Bureau, *L'Indiscipline*, p. 9.

45. Celina Philibert-Blaizac, "La Vague de plaisir," *Mère éducatrice*, August 1920. For a similar argument, see Madeleine Vernet, "Des Ruines," *Mère édu-*

catrice, October 1920. Natalists connected the "mad pleasure" of the postwar world with the rise of new consumer pleasures, such as movies and automobiles, as well as the recent increase in leisure time, marked by the 1919 passage of the eight-hour day. See *Deuxième congrès*, p. 20; Bertillon's reaction to the passing of the eight-hour day, in "L'Alcoolisme et la journée de huit heures," *La Femme et l'enfant*, 15 June 1919, and "Les 'Huit heures' et la natalité," *La Femme et l'enfant*, 1 December 1919. In the secondary literature, see Gary Cross, "Les Trois Huits: Labor Movements, International Reform and the Origins of the Eight Hour Day, 1919–1924," *French Historical Studies* 14 (1985).

46. Bureau, *L'Indiscipline*, pp. 1–2.

47. Paul Bureau, "Le Jour des mères," *Pour la vie*, May 1919; "Courage et Propagande"; and *L'Indiscipline*, p. 162.

48. *Deuxième congrès*, pp. 34–36. Bocquillon wrote several books on pedagogy during the twenties and thirties, and was an avid supporter of *puériculture*, or child-care education. For a similar argument concerning *la femme moderne*, voiced later on in the decade, see C. Jeglot, *La Jeune fille et le plaisir* (Paris: Editions Spès, 1928).

49. L. Narquet, "La Française de demain d'après sa psychologie de guerre," *Revue bleue*, 19–26 October 1918: 629.

50. Paul Bureau, "Honneur aux mères fécondes," *Pour la vie*, May 1920. For other natalist views of woman in the immediate postwar period, see Jean Siane, "La Femme et l'enfant," *La Femme et l'enfant*, 1 January 1919; "Appel aux 20,000 femmes françaises," *La Femme et l'enfant*, 1 November 1919; and Andrée d'Alix, "La Famille, son institution primordiale," excerpted in *Action sociale de la femme*, December 1920. For the history of Mother's Day in France, see Françoise Thébaud, "Maternité et famille," pp. 90–91, and her book, *Quand nos grand-mères*, p. 21.

51. *Deuxième congrès*, p. 173. This is taken from a lecture on "Le Travail professionel de la femme et la natalité" by Mlle. Charrondière.

52. R. Gillet, "Conférence sur la femme de demain et les jeunes filles d'aujourd'hui," *Action sociale de la femme*, March 1919. See also Auburtin, *La Natalité*, p. 326, for similar imagery of cradles and wombs. For another argument concerning France's dependency on women, see Bertillon, "C'est par la femme que la France doit être sauvée" and "Le Salut de la France dépend de la femme."

53. Moustiers, "Les Conceptions morales."

54. Docteur Jules Boudry, *Le Problème de la natalité, envisagé au point de vue morale, économique, et législatif* (Clermont-Ferrand: G. Mont-Louis, 1923), p. 19. Boudry was a medical expert on curative waters and the consulting physician at the spa "La Bourboule" in southwestern France.

55. M. Numa Sadoul, "Une Controverse: L'Emancipation de la jeune fille moderne est-elle un progrès réel?" *Progrès civique*, 13 June 1925, Dossier Féminisme, Vingtième siècle, BMD.

56. Clément Vautel, *Madame ne veut pas d'enfant* (Paris: A. Michel, 1924). The initial *tirage* of the novel was 7,000 copies, a number below average for a popular novel. It is difficult to determine precisely when the phrase came into popular use, but it seems to be almost immediately after the publication of Vautel's novel in 1924. Journalist G. Lhermitte used the phrase in the July–August issue of *Le Droit des femmes* the same year. See also Adolphe Pinard, *"Si vous voulez avoir des enfants": Ainsi parla le professeur Pinard, paroles recueillis par Pierre Bénard,* (Paris: Imprimerie E. Ramlot et Cie, Editions Nilsson, 1930), p. 71 and chap. 4, entitled "Quand Madame veut un enfant." Among secondary sources, see Desanti, *La femme au temps des années folles,* pp. 30, 218.

57. For Vautel's natalism, see his article in *Le Journal,* 23 August 1923, decrying depopulation in the village of Montélimar. For his antifeminist views, see "Le Féminisme en 1958," *Je sais tout,* 15 May 1918, Dossier Anti-féminisme, BMD. Vautel was also called a formidable antisuffragist in *Droit des femmes,* February 1919, p. 31.

58. Gaston Picard, *Renaissance politique,* 21 June 1924.

59. Vautel, *Madame,* pp. 87, 135.

60. Ibid., pp. 82, 135–36.

61. Like many natalists, Vautel also condemns the male *"célibataire,"* or bachelor, as responsible for French depopulation. See, for example, Paul's exchange with Prosper Boisselot, pp. 15–17. Vautel also makes the point on two occasions (pp. 194–5, 306) that the French are intolerant of babies because of the noise they make.

62. Ibid., p. 167.

63. Ibid., p. 255. The novel referred to here is probably Raymonde Marchard's *Tu enfanteras* (Paris: Flammarion, 1919), an unabashed account of maternal love. It is narrated in the first person by a woman experiencing pregnancy and childbirth. See the review of the book by *La Femme et l'enfant,* 15 June 1919.

64. Ibid., pp. 266–67.

65. Ibid., p. 189.

66. Ibid., p. 206.

67. Ibid., p. 191.

68. Ibid., pp. 204, 206.

69. Ibid., pp. 17–18.

70. Ibid., p. 15.

71. Ibid., p. 45.

72. Ibid., pp. 46–48. *"Beefsteaks"* here is a variant for *"bifteck,"* one that is closer to the English derivation of the French word. I have chosen to keep the original word rather than translate it as "steak."

73. Ibid., pp. 26–27. For an illuminating look at the notion of the "real

woman" during the *belle époque,* see Edward Berenson's *The Trial of Madame Caillaux* (Berkeley: University of California Press, 1992), chap.3.

74. Ibid., p. 41. *"Chiqué"* was a popular adjective used in the 1920s to refer to an affected attitude, something pretentious and without real social function.

75. Picard, *Renaissance politique.*

76. Ibid., pp. 65–67.

77. Ibid., p. 121. Vautel also wrote a story for *Le Journal* in 1922 that dealt with this theme of incessantly "going out." It concerned a woman who left her baby with a nurse in order to go to the theater. For some reason, she returned home early only to find no trace of either nurse or child in the house. Frantic, she asked the concierge about their whereabouts. The concierge knew nothing except that the nurse frequently visited a certain popular dancing spot. When the mother arrived there, she found her baby with the *vestiare,* sleeping peacefully with several other "numbered" babies. The implication of the story is that even babysitters cannot resist a night out on the town. Dr. Bizard paraphrases the story in "Syphilis et Domestiques" in *Bulletin de la Société de prophylaxie sanitaire et morale,* March 1922.

78. Ibid., p. 98.

79. Ibid., pp. 162, 208.

80. Ibid., pp. 290, 294.

81. See Picard, *Renaissance politique.*

82. Ibid., p. 314.

83. See Robert A. Nye, "Honor, Impotence and Male Sexuality in Nineteenth-Century French Medicine," *French Historical Studies* 16 (Spring 1989): 70. The citation is from Dr. Louis Huot and Dr. Paul Voivenel, *Le Courage* (1917). These two doctors wrote a number of works on the psychology of the wartime French soldier, including *Le Cafard* (1917) and *La Psychologie du soldat* (1918). Huot also wrote a book on women during the war, *De Quelques manifestations de l'évolution psycho-passionnelle féminine pendant la guerre* (Paris: Mercure de France, 1918). See chap. 1 for a discussion of some of these works. Nye argues that such links between virility and courage had deep roots in nineteenth-century culture and were not unique to the war medical literature.

84. The letter was dated December 1916 and is quoted by Gabriel Perreux, in *La Vie quotidienne des civils en France pendant la grande guerre* (Paris: Hachette, 1966), p. 324.

85. Dr. Huot, *De Quelques manifestations,* p. 9. He noted that sociologists, in particular, were preoccupied with the problem. An alternative way to describe the problem was to refer to a *crise du foyer.* A 1919 article, entitled "La Crise du foyer," offered an analysis of the way that "the home has been sorely afflicted by the war." See Lambert, "La Crise du foyer," pp. 148–49.

86. Duval, "Une Enquête," 5 April 1924. The survey ran from 5 April to 24 May in *La Renaissance politique.*

87. During the war Bordeaux was a captain and then *chef de bataillon* to the deputy chief of staff of the first and second armies. He was also a member of the Légion d'honneur and a recipient of the Croix de guerre.

88. Henry Bordeaux, *Le Mariage, hier et aujourd'hui* (Paris: Flammarion, 1921), Preface, pp. vii-viii.

89. Ibid., pp. 18–19.

90. Ibid., p. 26. See also another letter, p. 67, that Bordeaux uses to make the same point. This analysis of the *crise du mariage* was repeated again and again in the survey on the same subject appearing in *La Renaissance politique* during the spring of 1924. See, for example, the views expressed by the editor Maurice Duval in the 5 April installment, Senator Louis Martin in the 12 April installment, the journalist Yvonne Sarcey in the 19 April installment, and by Henry Bordeaux himself in the 17 May installment.

91. Ibid., p. 28.

92. Ibid. In terms of his own tendency to make generalizations, Bordeaux argues here that "my other correspondents simply repeat the same complaints."

93. Bordeaux devotes a chapter of *Le Mariage* to enumerating the joys of a large family. One social Catholic reviewer of the book praised Bordeaux for his natalist views and called him a "profound moralist." See *Action sociale de la femme*, January 1922.

94. Bordeaux, *Le Mariage*, pp. 33–35. Bordeaux claims that such letters are typical on pp. 25 and 29.

95. Ibid., pp. 44–45, 104. The very same sense of rejection and humiliation is expressed by Paul Abram in his *La Faiblesse de l'homme: Notes d'après-guerre* (Paris: Editions des Amitiés Françaises, 1920), pp. 10–11.

96. Ibid., p. 36, 44.

97. Henry Bordeaux, *Ménages d'après-guerre* (Paris: Librairie Plon, 1921), pp. 89–90, 93.

98. Ibid., pp. 100–101.

99. "Le Foyer de demain: Premier grande enquête de *La Femme et l'enfant*," *La Femme et l'enfant*, 1 April 1920. De Croisset engaged in the war voluntarily and was a recipient of the Croix de guerre.

100. Ibid. A female respondent referred to the wild dancing, high ambitions, bad language, and loose ways of young women. How will they raise children? she wondered. Aurel, a well-known popular writer and another respondent, speculated that the French home would be restored only if and when young women break away from their postwar *"garçonnisme."*

101. Colette Yver, "Le Ménage d'Odette," *Le Femme et l'enfant*, 15 November, 1 December 1918.

102. Edmond Cazal's *La Vie après la guerre: L'Inféconde* (Life after the War: The Sterile Woman) also presents the child as assuring the passage back to traditional femininity, morality and familial stability. Cazal was a veteran and

a writer who penned popular novels during the twenties. His novel opens as a veteran of a prominent bourgeois family, Jacques Rolland, gazes at the black-draped portraits of his brothers, killed during the war. His fiancée, Lucile, is "coquettish and vain," without "awareness of her duties," and preoccupied with "evenings at the theater, dining out, traveling, clothes, jewelry and all vanity's satisfactions." From the first line of the novel, narrative tension builds from the conflict between Lucile's indifference toward her future maternal role and the family's investment in her child-to-be, who is presented as the family's single hope and reason for existence since the death of Jacques's brothers. Lucile's rash desire for adventure leads to an accident, a miscarriage, and terminal sterility. Jacques promptly seeks a divorce, then has a (male) child with another woman, Dinah. In contrast to Lucile, Dinah lives to be a mother; she embodies the honor, sacrifice and devotion of *la mère de famille nombreuse*, even though (as in the case of Vautel's Louise), she is Jacques's mistress, not his wife. The Rolland family is saved, and even Lucile is redeemed through contact with the child, who makes her realize the emptiness and futility of her own life of pleasure.

103. Henry Fèvre, *L'Intellectuelle mariée* (Paris: Albin Michel, 1925).

104. See Ann-Marie Sohn, "*La Garçonne* face à l'opinion publique: Type littéraire ou type social des années 20?" *Mouvement social* 80 (1972). Henry Fèvre (1864–1937) seems to have written in a variety of genres both before and after the war. His first volume of poetry, *La Locomotive* (1883), was published when he was only 19 years old. A few years later, in 1896, he published his first drama, *En Détresse, comédie en un acte*. He also wrote sketches of Parisian and rural life in the years before the war, but turned to novels in the postwar period.

105. Fèvre, *L'Intellectuelle mariée*, p. 105.

106. Ibid., p. 163.

107. Ibid., p. 148.

108. Ibid., pp. 175, 178.

109. Ibid., p. 299.

110. Ibid., pp. 306–7.

111. Ibid., pp. 303–4.

112. Ibid., p. 314.

113. Ibid., p. 316.

114. Ibid., pp. 314–15.

115. Ibid., p. 318, 320.

116. Georges Blet, *L'Avortement. Est-ce un crime?* (Mâcon: Imprimerie J. Buguet-Comptour, 1921), p. 59. See also the tone of the remarks made by Dr. Fouveau de Courmelles, a critic of women's postwar obsession with fashion in "Modes féminines et dépopulation," *Revue mondiale*, 1 November 1919.

Part 3, La Femme Seule: Introduction

1. Henri Robert, "La Femme et la guerre" (Conférence faite à la Ligue de l'enseignement, 26 March 1917), *La Revue*, May 1917: 252. Henri Robert (sometimes Henri-Robert) was president of the Bar between 1913 and 1919.

2. Henri Robert, "La Femme," p. 252. In his response to the lawyer Suzanne Grinberg's *enquête*, "Le Rôle de la femme française après la guerre," *Renaissance politique*, 31 March 1917: 10, Henri Robert used similar language. Louis Narquet's use of "fatale" appeared in "La Femme dans la France de demain," *Mercure de France*, 16 July 1917: 250. For another similar statement made in 1917, see also the journalist Henry Joly, "De l'extension du travail des femmes après la guerre," *Le Correspondent*, 10 January and 10 March 1917.

3. This is from Spont's book, also published in 1917: *La Femme dans la France de demain* (Paris: Jouve et Cie, 1917), p. 3. See also Spont's *La Femme et la guerre* (Paris: Perrin, 1916). For statements similar to Spont's, made during the war, see Paul d'Estournelles de Constant et al., *Les Femmes pendant et après la guerre* (Paris: Charles Delagrave, 1916), p. 9. For similar views expressed after the armistice, see also B. Dangennes, *La Femme moderne: Ce que toute femme moderne doit savoir* (Paris: Editions Nilsson, n.d.), p. 5; "Enquête sur le féminisme de demain," *Revue universitaire* 1 (1919): 277; Yvonne Netter, *L'Indépendance de la femme mariée dans son activité professionnelle* (Paris: Presses Universitaires de France, 1923), p. 7; Georges Renard, "Le Travail féminin dans la France actuelle," *Grand revue*, January 1924: 353; Annette Comin, "Le Niveau de la moralité féminine a-t-il baissé depuis la guerre?" *Le Quotidien*, 17 April 1927; Monseigneur Tissier, *La Femme française. Hier. Aujourd'hui. Demain* (Paris: Pierre Téqui, 1927), p. 53.

4. For other postwar expressions of certainty concerning change in women's lives, see, among almost countless others, Lise Ancelle, *L'Heure de la femme* (Paris: Edward Sansot, 1919), and the review of Ancelle's book in *Droit des femmes*, August 1919); Felix Gaiffe, "Vers quelles carrières diriger nos filles?" *Eve*, 2 March 1920: 4; and Auguste Moll-Weiss, *La Vie domestique d'après-guerre* (Paris: Rousseau et Cie, 1921), p. 7. Louis Narquet, "La Femme dans la France," p. 272. A quite conservative and angry vision of changes in women's lives is given by the anonymous author of "Les conquêtes du féminisme," in *Le Figaro*, 16 March 1924. By contrast, a very radical view is provided by feminist Communist Louise Bodin in "Pour la femme, pour l'enfant," *Humanité*, 27 April 1923. For a more mainstream, bourgeois feminist approach, see Madeleine Vernet, "La Masculinisation de la femme," *Mère éducatrice*, April 1919, and "Qu'appelez-vous une jeune fille bien élévée?" *Fémina*, 1 March 1919: 8.

5. Edouard Herriot, *Créer* (Paris: Payot, 1919), 2:205–6.

6. See Edouard Toulouse, *Comment utiliser la guerre pour faire le monde nouveau* (Paris: Renaissance du Livre, 1919), p. ix. Toulouse's book was re-

viewèd favorably by Pierre Paraf in *Revue mondiale*, 15 September 1919. For other arguments that a "new world" or "new society" was taking shape during the war and postwar periods, see Martin de Torina, *Mère sans être épouse* (Paris: Author, 1918), p. 12; Marcel Barrière, *Essai sur le donjuanisme contemporaine* (Paris: Editions du monde nouveau, 1922), p. 222.

6. There Is Something Else in Life besides Love

1. Suzanne de Callias, "Faut-il importer des maris?" *La Française*, 19 February 1921. Callias refers to the response of the minister of foreign affairs as "a courteous but not encouraging thank-you." In *La Maîtresse légitime: Essai sur le mariage polygamique de demain* (Paris: Vernet et Earin, 1923), p. 38, Anquetil describes it as "a negative thank-you."

2. Ibid. Callias chose to use the English translation of "Nous voilà Lafayette," but I have reinserted the original French of the phrase.

3. In demonstrating support, however, Suzanne de Callias pointed out that under then current regulations, women would lose their nationality on marrying an alien. Unless the law was changed—something that Callias favored—imported American husbands would produce nothing more than "new little citizens for the powerful nation of the Star-Spangled Banner." For Jane Misme's expression of the same opinion, see "Des Maris étrangers." Misme made her own effort as matchmaker in the postwar period. See "Parlons Mariage," *La Française*, 30 September 1922. At one point, it was suggested that the office of *La Française* form a kind of dating service to match up men and women, or create an association of *célibataires* for various amusements and charitable activities.

4. Paul Carnot, "Puisqu'il y a en France un excédent de deux millions de femmes pourquoi ne pas importer des maris?" *Le Matin*, 29 July 1920. A specialist on therapy and the pancreas, Carnot was a member of the Académie de médecine and a professor at the Faculté de médecine in Paris.

5. Paul Carnot, "Enquête sur le problème de la natalité," *Paris médicale*, 36 (Partie médicale), 20 May 1920: 325. Carnot received letters from Americans and Canadians extremely interested in marrying French women.

6. See Ambroise, "Pour les travailleuses: Le Retour à la terre," *Droit des femmes*, April 1924. According to an article in *Soir* (Brussels), extracted in "Au Travers la presse," *Droit des femmes*, October 1921, the *Times* of London had suggested sending single women in England (estimated at 1,900,000) to colonies, where they could give proof of their spirit of adventure.

7. In *Mère sans être épouse* (Paris: Author, 1918), p. 20, Martin de Torina gave the figure of 3.5 million single women. Paul Carnot estimated the number at 2 million in "Puisqu'il y a en France." Other estimates were Georges Anquetil's figure of 3 million in *La Maîtresse légitime*, p. 33, and S. de Callias's count of 1.5 million in "Faut-il importer des maris?" Jane Misme herself varied her estimations of single women. In "Chassé-Croisé de célibataires," *Oeuvre*, 25

September 1919, Fonds speciales de Jane Misme, Album 2, Bibliothèque Marguerite Durand (BMD), she put the number at 2 million. Five years later, in "Des Maris étrangers," *Minerva*, 24 July 1924, she put the number at 4 million.

8. See M. Huber, *La Population de la France pendant la guerre* (Paris: Presses Universitaires de France, 1981), p. 570; Maurice Garden and Hervé Le Bras, "La Population française entre les deux guerres," in *De 1914 à nos jours*, vol. 4 of *Histoire de la population française*, ed. Jacques Dupâquier (Paris: Presses Universitaires de France, 1988), p. 97. Here the authors estimate that in 1921 for every 100 men, there were 120 women.

9. See Colin Dyer, *Population and Society in Twentieth Century France* (New York: Holmes and Meier, 1978), pp. 64–65.

10. Carnot's "Enquête sur le problème de la natalité" ran from March to May 1920. See particularly the first installment, entitled: "Comment sauver la stérilité de deux millions de femmes françaises," 20 March 1920. I am grateful to Dolores Peters for informing me about this inquiry.

11. Carnot, "Enquête," second installment, "Doit-on encourager la maternité chez les inépousées de guerre?" p. 234. Carnot ultimately rejected the polygamy option on practical grounds: a man who was unwilling to have many children with one women would not be willing to do the same with a second. For a somewhat earlier argument against the polygamy option, see Torina, *Mère sans être*, p. 24. For a discussion of the links between the mother and the soldier that Carnot's quote articulates, see chap. 5.

12. Anquetil, *La Maîtresse*, pp. 37–38.

13. Ibid., pp. 27–31. In order to prove that the idea of polygamy was "in the air," Anquetil quotes the scene in *La Garçonne* in which Professor Vignabos acts as a spokesman for Léon Blum. However, despite his belief in the benefit of "free love," Blum was no supporter of state-institutionalized polygamy. Much of the "evidence" that Anquetil uses skips over subtleties of argument such as this! For a more complete analysis of *La Garçonne*, see chap. 2.

14. Jehan d'Ivray, *Revue mondiale*, 15 March 1923.

15. Jane Misme, "Chassé-Croisé de célibataires." Misme also saw another change in courtship regulations: she claimed that many women were no longer waiting to be asked to be married, but were taking more of an initiative in courtship matters. See her "Les Provocatrices," *Oeuvre*, 8 November 1923, Articles de Journaux, Boîte no. 2, Fonds Marie Louise Bouglé.

16. "Dames célibataires," *La Française*, 22 April 1922.

17. Ibid.

18. Doctoresse Madeleine Pelletier, *Le Célibat, état supérieur* (Caen: Imprimerie Caennaise, c.1926), p. 6.

19. Jeanne Perdriel-Vaissière, *La Complainte des jeunes filles qui ne seront pas épousées* (Paris: Edition de Gemeaux, 1918). For this dramatic, hyperbolic kind of writing, see also Berthe Benage, "Entre nous: Pour l'isolée," *Journal des demoiselles*, 1 August 1920.

20. Quoted in Anquetil, *La Maîtresse légitime,* p. 36. For expressions of the same sentiment later on in the decade, see also Maurice de Waleffe, "L'Art de vivre en société: Pitié pour les solitaires!" *Paris-Midi,* 29 April 1927, and Albine Albaran, "Femme seule, ma soeur," periodical unclear, 8 January 1925, both in Dossier La Femme Seule, BMD. For an earlier portrait of a *femme seule* who canot find housing, see "La Femme Seule," *Oeuvre,* 3 January 1919.

21. Paul Carnot, "Enquête." See also Goland, *Féministes françaises,* p. 49; and Anquetil, *La Maîtresse légitime,* who dedicates his book to "the eighteen million European women who are condemned to the physiological and moral miseries of celibacy due to the surplus of women, the massacre of men and the egoism of monogamy."

22 .M. E. Fenouillet, *L'Art de trouver un mari: Etude pratique et lumineuse de la plus grand difficulté sentimentale d'après-guerre* (Paris: Editions Montaigue, 1925). Fenouillet's manual described a kind of frantic competition going on among women for the all-too-scarce husbands and advised women to sharpen their competitive edges.

23. For other historians who have made a similar argument about shifting attitudes toward *la femme seule,* see Marlène Cacouault, "Diplôme et célibat: Les Femmes professeurs de lycée entre les deux guerres"; and Yvonne Knibiehler, "Vocation sans voile, les métiers sociaux," both in *Madame ou mademoiselle: Itinéraires de la solitude féminine, 18–20e siècle,* ed. Arlette Farge and C. Klapisch-Zuber (Paris: Montalba, 1984).

24. André Arnyvelde, "La Femme peut-elle vivre sans le secours de l'homme?" *Eve,* 25 February 1920.

25. Jane Misme, "Controverse sur l'article: "Les Françaises doivent-elles épouser des étrangers?" *La Française,* 17 December 1921. She sums it up pithily with this phrase: "Elles ne le doivent pas, elles le peuvent, c'est bien different."

26. Ibid.

27. Ibid., 2 December 1921. The reader who wrote this letter gave her name only as "M. B." For similar views, see also the 17 December installment of the series, in particular, the remarks of "Le Copiste" and Dr. Yvonne Pouzin.

28. These readers' responses are cited from Fernand Goland, *Les Féministes françaises* (Paris: Francia, 1925). In his analysis of postwar French feminism, Goland leaned heavily on letters written to and printed in *Eve* between June 1923 and November 1924.

29. Ibid., quoted, pp. 42–44.

30. Abbé Louis Muzat, *Les Vieilles filles: Leur caractère, leurs défauts, leurs qualités* (Paris: Librairie des Saints-Pères, 1909), p. 15.

31. "Dames célibataires." For an intriguing analysis of Marcelle Tinayre's novels, see Jennifer Waelti-Walters, *Feminist Novelists of the Belle Epoque* (Bloomington: Indiana University Press, 1990), chap. 3.

32. Goland, *Les Féministes françaises,* quoted, pp. 41–42. For an earlier

but very similar view, see Louise Bodin, "Vieilles dames," *Voix des femmes*, 9 January 1918.

33. In 1913, Brieux wrote a play by the same name, *La Femme seule, Comédie en trois actes*. See below for more details on Brieux and his play.

34. For another attempt to "débaptiser" *la vieille fille* and call her instead a *"demoiselle,"* a *"célibataire,"* or a *"femme seule,"* see Benage, "Entre nous."

35. Maurice Duval, "Une Enquête sur la crise du mariage," *Renaissance politique*, 5 April 1924.

36. Duval, "Enquête," 26 April 1924. For more information on Yver, see Jennifer Waelti-Walters, *Feminist Novelists*. Yver also wrote historical and political essays, and contributed to *Echo de Paris*, *Le Gaulois*, and *Revue des deux mondes*.

37. Goland, *Les Féministes françaises*, p. 49. See also p. 48, where he quotes another *Eve* letter in which *la vieille fille* is described.

38. Ibid., pp. 43–44.

39. Ibid., p. 49. Feminists themselves recognized that many Frenchmen interpreted *la femme seule* in this manner. See Maria Vérone, "L'Amour est-il mort?" *Oeuvre*, 7 August 1924, where she names the novelist Gaston Rageot as a prominent believer that women are now scorning love because they no longer need to be dependent on men financially. Rageot wrote an article on this subject in *Le Temps* in 1924 that was widely commented on in the press.

40. Colette Yver, "Mariage et le travail des femmes," *Le Correspondant*, reprinted in "Les Grandes revues françaises, extrait," *Journal des demoiselles*, 1 July 1920. See also her "Jeunes filles bien élévées, jeunes filles mal élévées," in *Le Correspondant*, 25 December 1919.

41. The surtax was Article 7 of the bill in the Chamber and Article 8 in the Senate.

42. According to James McMillan, *From Dreyfus to DeGaulle* (London: Edward Arnold, 1985), the postwar debt stood at 175 billion francs, five times greater than in 1913 (p. 78). The French government continued to borrow from its citizens in the form of reconstruction bond issues and war bonds renewed at higher interest rates. It had lost its role, at least temporarily, of being one of the major creditor nations. See also chap. 4, note 135, for other references on the interwar French economy.

43. See *Journal Officiel (JO)*, *Débats parlementaires, Chambre*, 13 April 1920, p. 373. Similarly, the *rapporteur-général* of the bill in the Senate, Paul Doumer, referred on 21 May to the "economic crisis" and the "appalling debt" created by the war situation. See *JO, Débats parlementaires, Sénat*, 22 May 1920, p. 595.

44. See Edouard Bonnefous, *L'Après-guerre, 1919–1924*, vol. 3 of *Histoire de la Troisième République* (Paris: Presses Universitaires de France, 1959), p. 104. In his preface, Bonnefous argues that while before the war, the parliament had to deal with mostly ideological issues, afterward, practical, mostly

financial problems preoccupied them. Fiscal issues became "*lancinants,*" whereas before, budget discussions were often simply boring rituals. For a brief discussion on the tax debate, described by Bonnefous as "long and delicate," see pp. 125–26.

45. For a natalist defense of the tax, see Georges Rossignol. "Vous voulez de l'argent: En voici," *Pour la vie,* April 1920.

46. *JO Débats parlementaires, Chambre,* 18 April 1920, p. 1073. In his statement here, Bérard was actually denying that this was so, paraphrasing the words of the critics without counting himself among them. This charge was consistently and repeatedly denied. See also a similar statement by Paul Doumer, in the *JO, Débats parlementaires, Sénat,* 27 May, 1920, p. 688. See also Clément Vautel, "Mon film," *Le Journal,* 19 April 1920, for the way in which the law was perceived as a penalty in the larger press.

47. See, for example, Jean Dupin, deputy from the Loire (L'Entente Républicaine Démocratique), *JO, Débats parlementaires, Chambre,* 18 April 1920, p. 1073: "You want money and we are demanding it from those who do not have dependents and that is all."

48. *JO, Débats parlementaires, Sénat,* 27 May 1920, pp. 687–88. Fernand Merlin was the senator from the Loire from 1920 to 1937. Before this, he had been a deputy in the Chamber for the same region. He was a doctor with a long-time interest in fiscal matters and a member of the Budget Commission during the war. See also, same debate, p. 686, argument of Dominique Delahaye that "to justify placing a surtax on bachelors, we have referred to their selfishness (*égoïsme*)." Dominique Delahaye was a senator from Maine-et-Loire, a fervent Catholic, and a royalist, although not from an aristocratic background. In the Chamber debate, see *JO, Débats parlementaires, Chambre,* 18 April 1920, p. 1072, where Jean Tinguy de Pouët described the surtax as in the "spirit of fiscal justice" because it was directed at taxpayers who were "more or less selfish." De Tinguy de Pouët was a deputy from Vendée, a conservative aristocrat who fought in the war, won the Croix de guerre, and became a member of the Légion d'honneur.

49. For example, thanks to pro-natalist influences, Article 5 of the Chamber bill specified that for every dependent child, the father was able to deduct 1,500 francs from his annual income. After the fifth child, he was able to deduct 2,000 francs for every child. An amendment, introduced by deputy Jean Le Fèvre and sponsored by the Alliance nationale pour l'accroissement de la population française would provide for a 2000 franc deduction after the second child. This last amendment was rejected, but the pro-natalists considered the bill a victory anyway. See Jacques Bertillon, "L'Impôt nouveau charge les célibataires obstinés et exonère les familles nombreuses," *La Femme et l'enfant,* 1 June 1920, for a jubilant evaluation of the final tax bill.

50. The text of the law included the words "*soit veufs.*" What Bérard wanted to do is to remove these words from the text. As we shall see, André Berthon followed Bérard in his plea to remove "*soit divorcés*" from the text of the law.

For reactions to Bérard's speech, see "L'Impôt global sera majoré de 25% pour les célibataires et de 10% pour les ménages sans enfants," *Le Journal*, 18 April 1920; "L'Impôt sur les célibataires," *Le Matin*, 18 April 1920; and "La Chambre: Séance du 17 avril: Les nouveaux impôts," *Le Temps*, 19 April 1920.

51. *JO, Débats parlementaires, Chambre*, 18 April 1920, p. 1074. Bérard was not the only one in postwar France to describe the widow as a helpless object of pity—widows were the object of some of the most negative literature on *la femme seule*. See, for example, Noël Guesdon, in *Aux Veuves: A Celles qui restent seules* (Paris: Imprimerie St. Paul, 1921); and Vice Admiral Besson, "Pitié pour les veuves de guerre," *La Française*, 7 August 1922.

52. *JO, Débats parlementaires, Chambre*, 18 April 1920, p. 1074.

53. Ibid., Charles Dumont was the deputy from Jura from 1898 to 1924 and had always been interested in fiscal matters. For example, he was the minister of finance from 22 March to 9 December 1913 and an active member of the Budget Commission for years. Thus it made sense that he would be *rapporteur-général* of the budget bill.

54. Bérard was deputy from Basses-Pyrénées from 1910 to 1927 and then senator from this region from 1927 to 1944. He was also the minister for public education and fine arts for two brief periods during the postwar years, between November 1919 and January 1920, and then from January 1921 to March 1924. He was known for progressive educational measures taken as minister, in particular, concerning young women and the baccalaureate degree. Throughout his tenure in the Chamber, he was known as a Radical and a strong supporter of Clemenceau. In 1920, he was elected vice-president of the Chamber, and he had a reputation as a brilliant orator. See chap. 4, note 2, for more information on André Berthon.

55. *JO, Débats parlementaires, Chambre*, 18 April 1920, p. 1074.

56. For press reactions to the debate, see L'Oncle Bertrand, "Echos: A mon avis," *Echo de Paris*, 26 May 1920; "Les Nouvelles resources fiscales," *Le Temps*, 29 May 1920; and "Le Sénat vote l'impôt sur les célibataires," *Le Journal*, 28 May 1920. The session quickly collapsed into total disorder because of Senator Dominique Delahaye and his brother's vociferous objections to the article and to various procedural matters. The Delahayes, who were royalists and fervent Catholics, opposed the article on the grounds that it would penalize religious orders. When order could not be restored in the Senate, the session itself was suspended, an event that evoked a great deal of comment in the press. See *Echo de Paris*, 27 May 1920.

57. *JO, Débats parlementaires, Sénat*, 27 May 1920, pp. 684–85. Some of the honorable reasons for male celibacy that Gourju named were: to take care of sick or aging relatives, to do philanthropical work, or to abstain from sexual activity out of fear of transmitting disease. Antonin Gourju was the senator from Rhône between 1900 and 1909 and again from 1920 to 1926. Surprisingly, he was a supporter of several feminist causes, among them, women's

suffrage and various legal reforms giving women more control over their own earnings.

58. Ibid., p. 687. Merlin also submitted an amendment that stressed the situation of the divorcée more than did that of Gourju. It was Merlin's amendment that was ultimately voted on, as Gourju ceded his own in a show of unity. Merlin arrived at the figure of 2.5 million by adding what he saw as the prewar surplus of women (683,245 more women than men), the 1.4 million men dead or missing during the war, and the 450,000 disabled veterans who, he reasoned, would never marry. Gourju was backed by Delahaye, who argued for the case of the religious, and Gaudin de Villaine, the aristocratic senator from Manche, who opposed the law on the grounds of "the old French galantry" (p. 688). Despite Gourju's and Merlin's pleadings, a strong majority rejected the amendment exempting women from the surtax. For the press coverage, see "Le Sénat vote la surtaxe sur les célibataires et les ménages sans enfant," *Le Matin*, 27 May 1920. Because the minority was more vocal than the majority, one can only guess at the reasons why the exemption was voted down, although clearly it was not a simple recognition of female economic autonomy. The senators were certainly aware that many of the wealthiest Frenchwomen did not earn a living by their own means, but instead received an inheritance of some kind. At the same time, *rapporteur-général* Paul Doumer (Course) assured them, first, that no woman earning less than 6,000 francs annually would be taxed and, second, that a woman with an income of 10,000 francs would pay a surtax of only 25 francs. Given the light or nonexistent burden of the surtax on poor women, the senators probably reasoned that it would not be unjust to tax those who were able to afford it, although often by no merit or capability of their own. See also Cécile Brunschvig, "Pourquoi nous acceptons l'impôt sur le célibat féminin," *La Française*, 19 June 1920.

59. Bertillon, "L'Impôt nouveau charge les célibataires obstinés et exonère les familles nombreuses," *La Femme et l'enfant*, 1 June 1920. Clément Vautel made a similar argument in "Mon film," 19 April 1920.

60. See Clément Vautel, "Mon film," *Le Journal*, 31 May 1920. Vautel also accused the senators of believing that "the *célibataire* is like a snail, a being without sex who lives alone, like an egoist, in his shell." The image echoes Vautel's character Prosper Boisselot in *Madame ne veut pas d'enfant*, who reacted to Professor Luminol's condemnation of sexual difference by bellowing "Like snails!" For still another discussion of the tax, see Torina, *Mère sans être*, pp. 36–39, 57.

61. G. Lhermitte, "L'Impôt sur les célibataires," *Droit des femmes*, May 1920. The tax issue became the subject of lead articles in *Droit des femmes* in April and May 1920. In April, Lhermitte argued for the exemption for single women because "all their efforts are futile against two elementary mathematical formulas: 'one plus one equals two' and 'three minus two leaves one.'" Lhermitte's commentary caused an enormous controversy within the Ligue française pour le droit des femmes, of which *Droit des femmes* was the official

publication. For later feminist views of the tax, see Jane Misme, "Opinions contradictoires: Réflexions sur l'impôt," *La Française,* 27 October 1922, and "Célibataires et gens mariées devant l'impôt sur le revenu," *La Francqise,* 10 November 1923.

62. Bérard undermined the natalist justification for the surtax when, in a sarcastic tone, he dared his colleagues to explain to their constituents "that a single man pays fewer indirect taxes [on purchased goods], that is, that he consumes less sugar, coffee, wine and tobacco than do a man and a woman together." Bérard's point—that in fact, single men often consumed many more heavily taxed goods than did families and thus bore more than their share of the indirect tax burden—was supported by a round of "laughs and applause." See *JO, Débats parlementaires, Chambre,* 18 April 1920, p. 1073. For another highly sympathetic view of the bachelor's plight, see George de la Fouchar- dière, "Vae soli," *Oeuvre,* 28 May 1920.

63. See Brunschvig, "Pourquoi nous acceptons." Brunschvig was a promi- nent bourgeois feminist who supported this tax to readers of *La Française.* A *manchette* appeared on the front page of *Eclair,* 31 March, 1920: "The tax on every *célibataire* seems to imply—just ransom—The equal right to vote for the girl as well as the boy." The tax on female *célibataires* was repealed in 1937. Because French women still had not won the vote in 1937, the main argument among feminists for the repeal of the tax was the notion of "no taxation without representation." See "Celles-ci n'auront plus à payer la rançon de la solitude," Dossier La Femme Seule, BMD.

64. J. B., "Encore les célibataires," *Le Temps,* 24 March 1920.

65. Articles were featured in *Le Petit journal, Le Journal, Le Figaro,* and the feminist daily *La Fronde.* See Dossier La Femme Seule, BMD. There are still other articles in the dossier that are from unnamed sources.

66. *Le Figaro,* 22 July 1899, Ibid.

67. *Le Petit journal,* n.d., Ibid.

68. According to historian Stephen Hause, *Le Petit journal* demonstrated "little interest in feminism" in the years before the war, and *Le Temps* was "very cautious, uncommitted" to women's suffrage during this same period. See Stephen Hause with Anne Kenney, *Women's Suffrage and Social Politics in the French Third Republic* (Princeton: Princeton University Press, 1984), p. 153.

69. Benage, "Entre Nous." At the same time, the author saw this mater- nalist role as different, modern, and new: "You are not the laughable and fool- ish old maid [*vieille fille*] of the previous century; you are a woman, a single woman [*femme seule*] who is alone in order to give herself better to others." See Cacouault, "Diplôme et célibat" and Knibiehler, "Vocation sans voile" for two examinations of the way in which the traditional maternal role was pro- jected onto these careers before the war.

70. See Benage, "Entre Nous."

71. See M.-S. Gillet, "Les Oeuvres post-scolaires: Les Veuves de la guerre," *Action Sociale de la femme,* January–February 1919. This Catholic journalist counseled *la femme seule* that "*Le champ d'apostolat* is immense" and that she should occupy herself with the poor, with children, and with workers. See also M.-S. Gillet's article "Les Jeunes filles" in the same issue; the July 1917 article from *Le Grand echo de la Ligue patriotique des françaises* quoted in Yvonne Delatour, *Les Effets de la guerre sur la situation de la française d'après la presse féminine* (Diplôme d'études supérieures d'histoires, Université de Paris, May 1965), pp. 94–95. For the suggestion that single women might help the *mères de famille nombreuse* by serving as domestic servants and by working at infant care centers, see Elisabeth Bénard-Sesboüe, "Questions féministes: Les Femmes au lendemain de la guerre," *Renaissance politique,* 15 September 1923.

72. Geneviève Duhamelet, *Les Inépousées* (Paris: Albin Michel, 1919). The novel was reissued in 1933.

73. E. Jordan, "Toute maternité est-elle sacrée?" *Pour la vie,* December 1919. However, Jordan did believe that "she was not entitled to complete equality with the wife." For words that almost exactly echo these, see la Marquise de Moustiers, "Les conceptions morales de la française," *Action sociale de la femme,* May 1920. For the same view much later in the decade, see also Charles de Rouvre, "Les Filles-mères et la patrie," *La Rumeur,* 1927, Dossier La Mère Célibataire, BMD.

74. In her review of Léon Frapié's *La Virginité* in *Droit des femmes,* November 1923, Maria Vérone remarked: "It is becoming apparent that a movement in favor of illegitimate children is taking shape." One example of this trend was the effort of deputy Réné Richard to correct discrepancies in the military allocations given the families of illegitimate sons. Vérone also discussed the new attitude toward single motherhood several years later in "En faveur des mères non mariées," *Oeuvre,* 19 February 1926, Dossier La Mère Célibataire, BMD. See also Georges de la Fouchardière, "Un vilain oiseau," *La Fronde,* 3 May 1927, for a prominent columnist's support of single motherhood later in the decade. According to Claire Moses, in *French Feminism in the Nineteenth Century* (Albany: State University of New York Press, 1984), p. 230, the demand for paternity suits has a long and complex history in French feminism and was first raised by Olympe de Gouges in her "Déclaration des droits de la femme et de la citoyenne."

75. "Le dernier mot du professeur Pinard," *Le Matin,* 1925.

76. "Honorons et protegeons toutes les mères: L'Opinion du Docteur Jayle," *Le Matin,* 22 August 1925. While Jayle argued that he gave his respect to all mothers, he confessed that he had a special admiration for the single mothers. See also his fascinating *La Gynécologie: L'Anatomie morphologique de la femme* (Paris: Masson, 1918) and the reviews of the volume in *Paris médicale,* 2 August 1919, and *Presse médicale,* 8 May 1919. In this book, Jayle ar-

gued that women's ovaries, not their uteri, were the fundamental determinative factor in their general physiology.

77. See "Honorons et protegeons toutes les mères: L'Opinion du Docteur Tuffier," *Le Matin*, 8 August 1925. He was referring specifically to the 1.5 million *femmes seules* produced by the uneven sex ratio. Tuffier wrote scores of books on topics having to do with pathology and surgery. For a critique of doctors such as Tuffier who argued that all motherhood must be honored and protected, see "Le martyre d'une mère," *Humanité*, 2 August 1926.

78. Carnot, "Enquête sur le problème," 20 March 1920, p. 176.

79. See "Honorons et protegeons toutes les mères: L'opinion du Dr. Devraignes," *Le Matin*, September 9, 1925. Devraignes wrote several books on gynecological and obstetrical topics, and on puériculture. He taught clinical medicine in conjunction with the School of Medicine in Paris. For another doctor who was not as well-respected within the medical community, but nevertheless a prolific author and supporter of *la fille-mère*, see Dr. Edouard Toulouse, *La Question sexuelle de la femme* (Paris: E. Fasquelle, 1918), pp. 190–91. Feminists also showed support for the *fille-mère*. See Maria Vérone, "Respectons les mères," *Oeuvre*, July 6, 1922, Articles de Journaux, Boîte 6, Archives Marie Louise Bouglé (AMLB). She refers to single motherhood as "la materinité triomphante et rédemptrice que la société devrait honorer et respecter." Once again, language facilitated a new attitude toward the *fille-mère*. In "Il n'y a pas de filles-mères," *Oeuvre*, March 16, 1922, Jane Misme complained about the terms *fille-mère* and *vieille fille*. Why do women remain "girls" in the public consciousness until marriage? she asked, preferring the term *mère célibataire*.

80. "L'Opinion du Docteur Jayle."

81. Torina, *Mère sans être*, pp. 10–11.

82. Ibid., p. 25.

83. Carnot, "Enquête," 17 April 1920, p. 235.

84. "L'Opinion du Dr. Tuffier." See also Torina, *Mère sans être*, p. 84, and ibid.

85. For the single working-class woman as a figure of sexual and social disorder, see Alain Corbin, *Les Filles de noce: Misère sexuelle et prostitution, 19e et 20e siècles* (Paris: Aubier Montaigne, 1978), and Jill Harsin, *Policing Prostitution in Nineteenth Century Paris* (Princeton: Princeton University Press 1983).

86. See Françoise Thébaud, *Quand nos grandmères donnaient la vie* (Lyon: Presses Universitaires de Lyon, 1986), p. 222, where she cites the *Le Matin* series, as well as other articles and findings of commissions that supported single motherhood.

87. For this notion of "excess" in representation, I am indebted to Mary Poovey, "Scenes of an Indelicate Character: The Medical Treatment of Victo-

rian Women," in *Uneven Developments: The Ideological Work of Gender in Mid-Victorian England* (Chicago: University of Chicago Press, 1988).

88. Jordan, "Toute Maternité."

89. This commission is described in some detail in Torina, *Mère sans être,* chap. 8. Torina is unclear about the exact period during which the study took place, but it was sometime during the war. Paul Strauss was active in parliament and in other government posts during the prewar years. In these positions, he helped to shape state policy concerning public assistance and social hygiene. Charles Richet was a professor at the School of Medicine in Paris and a winner of the Nobel Prize in 1913. Jacques Doléris was also a professor at the School of Medicine; he would become president of the Académie de médecine in 1924. For biographical information on Adolphe Pinard, see chap. 4, note 22.

90. "Le Dernier mot du Professeur Pinard."

91. Ibid., See also H. Charasson, *Faut-il supprimer le gynécée?* (Paris: Plon, 1924), p. 9, and Torina, *Mère sans être épouse.*

92. Torina, *Mère sans être,* p. 139.

93. "L'Opinion du Professeur Pinard." See also Nast, in "Honorons les mères, toutes les mères," *Le Matin,* 25 August 1925. A typical Catholic view is given by Dr. René Biot in "Ce que la biologie nous apprend de la nature de la femme," *Semaines Sociales de France,* Nancy: XIX Session, 1927 (Lyon: Gabalda, 1927), pp. 134, 141.

94. "L'Opinion du Docteur Tuffier."

95. "L'Opinion du Docteur Jayle."

96. In a survey conducted by the Association française des femmes médecines during the twenties, the question "Is motherhood useful to the female organism?" received only four negative responses out of a possible twenty-eight. See Françoise Thébaud, *Donner la vie: Histoire de la maternité en France entre les deux guerres* (Thèse au troisième cycle, Paris VII, 1982), p. 153. See also her *Quand des grandmères,* p. 23. For further evidence that some of these prejudices were widespread, see J. A. Doléris and Jean Bouscatel, *Hygiène et morale sociales. Néo-malthusianisme, maternité et féminisme, éducation sexuelle* (Paris: Masson, 1918), pp. 79–80, 85.

97. For theories of continence just before the war, see Alain Corbin, "Le Péril vénérien au debut du siècle: Prophylaxie sanitaire et prophylaxie morale" in *L'Haleine des faubourgs,* ed. Lion Murard and Patrich Zulberman (Fontenay-sous-Bois: *Recherches,* 1978), pp. 263–65. According to Corbin, while continence had long been believed medically harmful, at least for men, in the years just before the war, there was a partial reversal of medical opinion. In *L'Instinct sexuel, évolution et dissolution* (1899), Dr. Charles Feré, who was cited frequently by postwar hygienists, argued that the sexual organs maintain health and vibrancy even during long periods of continence. An 1899 medical conference, held in Brussels, also affirmed that continence was not necessarily

harmful to one's health. Debauchery and sexual excess were condemned as injurious to individual health and the capacity for productive work. For French medical views on continence, see also Torina, *Mère sans être*, p. 85. For the causal links believed to exist between the sexual instinct and hysteria, see Jan Goldstein's *Console and Classify: The French Psychiatric Profession in the Nineteenth Century* (Cambridge: Cambridge University Press, 1987), p. 376, note 188. Sexuality did not play an important systemic role in Charcot's theories of hysteria, popularized in France in the early Third Republic.

98. Havelock Ellis's *Etudes de psychologie* were translated and published continuously in France between 1908 and 1935. The first six volumes had been published by 1926. Paul Robinson emphasizes the role of the sexologists, particularly Ellis, in forging a modernist notion of sex. See his *The Modernization of Sex* (New York: Harper and Row, 1976), pp. 27–28. Ellis believed in sex as a good thing and considered abstinence from sex unhealthy. At the same time, however, he believed that energy given to sex was taken away from other kinds of "work" performed by the human organism. On the sexologists, see also Corbin, "Le Péril vénérien." Corbin felt that there was quite a bit of resistance to Krafft-Ebing's views within the French medical body. For example, a majority of the members of the Société française de prophylaxie sanitaire et morale, examined in chap. 7, remained firmly convinced of the health benefits of continence.

99. Maria Vérone, "La Chasteté," *Oeuvre*, 8 July 1925. However, Vérone by no means advocated sexual activity for single women as a result of this. For another radical feminist view, see Madeleine Pelletier's advocacy of female sexuality, in *Le Célibat*, pp. 6–7.

100. This theory was not unique to the postwar period and shows up in Emile Zola's novel, *Fécondité* (1899), as a reason not to use contraception. In this novel, Dr. Boutan warns the hero, Mathieu Froment, that "Every function which is not exercised according to its normal order becomes a permanent source of danger." Cited in Joshua Cole, "The Power of Large Numbers: Population and Politics in Nineteenth-Century France" (Ph.D. diss., University of California at Berkeley, 1991), p. 199.

101. Anquetil, *La Maîtresse légitime*, pp. 46–47. The quote is from the psychologist Dr. Binet-Sanglé's *Le haras humain* (The Human Stud Farm) (Paris: Albin-Michel, 1918), pp. 225–26.

102. See Robinson, *The Modernization of Sex*, p. 15.

103. Biot, "Ce que la biologie apprend," p. 141.

104. For the nineteenth-century medical discourse against masturbation, see Michel Foucault, *An Introduction* to *The History of Sexuality* (New York: Random House, 1980), and Jeffrey Weeks, *Sex, Politics and Society: The Regulation of Sexuality Since 1800* (New York: Longman, 1981), pp. 48–49.

105. See Geneviève Fraisse, "Destins et destinées de la femme seule dans l'oeuvre de Léon Frapié," in *Madame ou mademoiselle*, pp. 283–83. In "Les Filles à marier et la loi Armand Prizeur," *La Française*, 9 May 1925, Misme

called Frapié's obsession with the *femme seule* his new "crusade" and lamented: "So much youth deprived of love, what sadness!"

106. Léon Frapié, *Virginité* (Paris: Flammarion, 1923)

107. Advertisement of *Virginité*, in the form of a small leaflet inside the book itself.

108. Ibid., p. 42.

109. Ibid., p. 40.

110. Ibid., p. 53.

111. Ibid., pp. 199, 203.

112. Léon Frapié, *Les Filles à marier* (Paris: Flammarion, 1925), p. 18. For a description of her improvement in *La Virginité*, see p. 262. Note that Armand commits adultery *outside* the conjugal domicile. In doing so, he protects himself from what could have been an actionable cause of divorce under the provisions of the Civil Code.

113. *La Virginité*, p. 63. He also phrases the choice on p. 64 as "love or nothingness."

114. Ibid., p. 66.

115. Ibid., p. 121. At the end of the scene, Frapié describes Armand and Fanny in this way: "Their hearts beat . . . as after love" (p. 123). Armand justifies his cruel criticism: "And shouldn't we be just as brutal in word as we are in deed, when we approach the mystery of sex?" (p. 116).

116. Ibid., pp. 118, 121.

117. Ibid., p. 181.

118. Ibid., p. 249.

119. Ibid., p. 67.

120. Ibid., pp. 264–65. Specifically what Madame le Guetteux believes is going out of fashion is "this stupid barbarism which bestows the supreme honor on the legitimate wife."

121. For the French reaction to Freud, see Dr. Jean Vinchon, *Hystérie* (Paris: Librairie Stock, 1925). Two works of Freud that Vinchon cited were: *Introduction à la psychoanalyse* (1922) and *Trois essais sur la théorie de la sexualité* (1923). Vinchon argued that Freud's ideas were beginning to penetrate France, and were both passionately defended and attacked (pp. 85–86). Jane Misme complained about the dissemination of Freud's ideas in France in "Maternité: Le plus beau sport," *Oeuvre*, 29 November 1923, Articles de Journaux, Boîte 6, AMLB. She noted that his theories were the subject of great controversy and enjoyed the success of a fashion. Other French works that articulated a notion of female sexual identity or instinct were Dr. Michel Bourgas, *Le Droit à l'amour pour la femme* (Paris: Vigot Frères, 1919), and Dr. Jaf, *L'Art de conserver l'amour dans le mariage* (Paris: Drouin, 1921).

122. Vérone brought up the Frapié book in "Maternité: Le plus beau sport." In her actual review of *Virginité* for *Le Droit des Femmes*, November 1923,

Vérone compared Frapié's solution to polygamy and strongly voiced her opposition to it.

123. See Misme,"Les Filles à marier." She believed that Frapié's theories would destroy marriage as an institution, yet she was for legislation (such as the "Loi Armand Prizeur") that recognized the rights of illegitimate children.

124. Josette Cornec, "Une seule morale pour les deux sexes," *Bulletin des Groupes féministes de l'enseignement laïque*, a supplement of *L'Ecole émancipée*, June 1925. She also claimed that sexual deprivation leads to anemia and several nervous diseases, including hysteria.

125. *Les Filles à marier*, p. 179.

126. Prizeur visits parliament when a heated debate on depopulation is under way. His deputy friend, Gigognot, is sympathetic to the problem but condemns natalists who want to achieve "excessive fertility" at any cost.

127. Brieux was a child of Parisian artisans and was largely self-educated. He wrote plays on aspects of the "Woman Question" before the war. Bernard Shaw called him "the most important dramatist west of Russia" after the death of Ibsen. Because many of his prewar plays dealt with women's right to motherhood and the dangers of the wet-nursing business, he was named to the Extra-Parliamentary Commission on Depopulation in 1902. He became a member of the Académie française in 1910. See Susan Groag Bell and Karen Offen, *Women, the Family and Freedom: The Debate in Documents* (Stanford: Stanford University Press, 1983), 2:130, for a biographical sketch of Brieux.

128. *La Femme seule* (Paris: P. V. Stock, 1913). It was first performed in Paris, Théâtre du Gymnase, 22 December 1912. The aim of the play was to criticize women's education, which Brieux believed woefully prepared them to support themselves if necessary. It concerns an adopted daughter, Thérèse, whose fiancé, René, broke off his engagement to her because she had no dowry. The willful and independent Thérèse rebels against the inherited social wisdom that "our entire existence depends on the man whom we must please" (p. 41). Although her efforts to support herself fail miserably, Thérèse ends the last act on a defiant note, claiming that "a new age has arrived" (p. 240) as she heads off to Paris to find work. The play was considered very radical at the time, as evidenced by the press reaction in *Le Matin*, 26–29 December 1912. The prominent journalist Séverine supported Brieux's arguments in her own editorial in *Le Matin* on 2 January 1913. Finally, on January 8, the daily published all the mail they had received concerning the issue, including one letter that began like this: "The *femme seule* is a monstrosity of the universe." For all these *Le Matin* articles, see Dossier La Femme Seule, BMD. To appreciate how radical Brieux was in this image of the single woman, compare his play to other prewar representations of *la femme seule*, such as Lucie Delarue Mardrus's *Marie, Fille-mère* (Paris, 1908; repr., Flammarion, 1924). In this novel, the pregnant, single woman is a helpless and passive object of pity. After being raped and abandoned by her fiancé, shamed and reviled by her family, she leaves for Paris, where she gives birth in the most pitiful conditions. She ulti-

mately kills her child and dies of a heart attack at the same moment. For a good analysis of the novel, see Waelti-Walters, *Feminist Novelists*, pp. 54–65.

129. Brieux, *Pierette et Galaor (l'enfant)* (Paris: Librairie Stock, 1924). The play was first printed in *La Petite illustration*, a theater publication, on 13 October 1923. In this edition, it is titled *L'Enfant: Pierette et Galaor.* My page numbers refer to the 1924 edition. In his 1924 survey in *Renaissance politique*, Maurice Duval refers to *Pierette et Galaor* as one of the most important contemporaneous studies of the "problem" of *La femme seule.*

130. *Mercure de France*, 15 October 1923.

131. Brieux, *Pierette*, p. 17. He restates the "problem" of *la femme seule* on p. 27. By his count, there was a two-million surplus of women after the war.

132. Ibid., p. 137.

133. Ibid., p. 138.

134. *Renaissance politique*, 15 October 1923.

135. *Mercure de France*, 15 October 1923.

136. Brieux, *Pierette*, pp. 59–60. Brieux highlights the inadequacies of middle-class women's education here through the figure of Caroline Legrand. When the war came, Legrand was compelled to work for a living, but having no profession, she was forced to write pornographic novels for a living.

137. Ibid., p. 140.

138. Ibid., p. 5.

139. Ibid., p. 8.

140. Ibid., p. 82.

141. *Revue des deux mondes*, 15 October 1923.

142. *Pierette*, p. 82. When Brassol calls Henri a hero, the latter remarks: "no big words . . . no words that one no longer even says aloud" (p. 14). Pierette describes Henri: "He has left his soul's youth in the trenches . . . he no longer wants to let himself live" (p. 52). To avoid splitting the family inheritance, Henri had made his home in Brazil before the war. He came back to France in order to fight in the war.

143. Ibid., p. 143.

144. Ibid.

145. Ibid., pp. 27–28.

146. Ibid., pp. 28–29. The emphasis on having a child even becomes a taunt of sorts: "Married or not, the essential thing is to have one!" cries Caroline Legrand, and one woman joins it: "Yes! It's to have one! It's to have one! At least one!"

147. The image of *la mère seule* as a projection of gender anxiety was also found in one of the most popular novels of the era, Victor Margueritte's *La Garçonne* (see chap. 2). Monique Lerbier also tries to have a child on her own to find personal fulfillment apart from male attention; she too limits men to, in the words of one of her lovers, "the job of stud."

148. *Pierette,* pp. 28–29.

149. Ibid., p. 86.

150. Ibid., p. 85.

151. Ibid., p. 118.

152. *Revue des deux mondes,* 15 October 1923.

153. *Pierette,* p. 32.

154. Ibid., p. 35.

155. I use the term "feminism" broadly here, as some of the most prominent feminists of the day disapproved of Brieux's play. See, for example, Jane Misme, "La maternité libre," *Oeuvre,* 27 September 1923, Articles de journaux, Boîte 2, AMLB.

156. *Mercure de France,* 15 October 1923. For a similar view, see the review in *Revue des deux mondes.* For another play on the single woman with a similarly happy ending, see *Le Droit d'être mère,* based on Paul Bru's prewar novel of the same title (Paris: E. Rouff, 1914). Brieux wrote the preface to the novel, praising it for its positive representation of motherhood and *la mère seule.* A young girl is made pregnant by her employer's son, tries to shoot herself in desperation, then gives birth in a *hôtel maternelle,* and ultimately learns to support herself financially. She becomes a nurse and dedicates her own life to maternal assistance at the same time that she singularly devotes herself to her son. In the end she becomes a martyr for the cause, dying of diphtheria in order to save a little child from the same fate. On her deathbed, she marries a doctor whose proposal she had earlier refused. Like Pierette, she does so mostly out of concern for her soon-to-be-orphaned son. According to a review by Maria Vérone in *Droit des femmes,* February 1924, the play was received enthusiastically, with a "veritable ovation" to the author.

157. For more information on Marie Laparcerie, see Actualités, Séries 80, AMLB. The dossier is inconclusive as to whether or not Laparcerie was herself a feminist. Although well-known by feminists such as Maria Vérone and Jane Misme, she was an antisuffragist. She wrote several other popular novels in the late teens and twenties, as well as a book in 1916 called *Comment trouver un mari après la guerre.*

158. Marie Laparcerie, *La Femme d'aujourd'hui* (Paris: Flammarion, 1924), p. 11.

159. Ibid., pp. 9–13.

160. Ibid., pp. 96, 140. At a dinner conversation, recounted on p. 74, a novelist comments that his next book will be about a woman who has a child on her own. Another person responds that a female reader of *Oeuvre* recently wrote to the journalist Gustave Téry declaring her intention to do the same thing.

161. Ibid., p. 138.

162. Ibid., p. 198.

163. Ibid., p. 271.

164. *Renaissance politique,* 25 October 1924.

165. See Thébaud, *Quand nos grandmères,* pp. 219–21. The rate of illegitimate births rose in the immediate postwar years, up to 83,000 per year in 1920, over 65,000 in 1911. However, by 1922, the rate returned to prewar levels. It then declined steadily throughout the interwar years, reaching a low of 41,000 by 1936. Importantly, this pattern repeats that of the overall birth rate, which rose in 1920–21, then declined steadily for the next two decades. This kind of decline occurred throughout Europe. See Garden and Le Bras, "La Population française," pp. 84–85 and 126–27.

166. *Mercure de France,* 15 October 1923. For a similar view, see the review in *Renaissance politique,* 15 October 1923.

7. We Must Facilitate the Transition to the New World

1. Simone de Beauvoir, *Mémoires d'une jeune fille rangée* (Paris: Gallimard, 1958), pp. 145, 243–44. I have relied on the James Kirkup translation, *Memoirs of a Dutiful Daughter* (New York: Harper and Row, 1974) pp. 104, 175–76.

2. According to historians, crisis and change characterized women's education during the postwar period because of a lack of agreement concerning the social role assigned to the French woman. See Françoise Mayeur, *L'Enseignement des jeunes filles sous la Troisième République* (Paris: Presses de la fondation nationale des sciences politiques, 1977), p. 444.

3. The Camille Sée law of 1880, which organized the women's educational system under the Third Republic, based itself on the domestic image of the woman as wife and mother. It established a secondary system of education that did not in any way prepare women for higher education or a career. By 1920, preparation for the boys' baccalaureate had become the chief aim of young bourgeois girls, but the inadequacies of preparation inherent in the curriculum of young girls' lycées forced them to attend the boys' schools or hire special tutors. Parents put pressure on Bérard to reform the girls' system. See Karen Offen, "The Second Sex and the Baccalauréat in Republican France, 1880–1924," *French Historical Studies* 8 (Fall 1983); Mayeur, *L'Enseignement des jeunes filles,* pp. 430–36.

4. The vocational guidance movement, whose prewar roots lay in the research of psychologists such as Alfred Binet, arose from relative obscurity in the years immediately after the war. Alfred Binet was particularly well-known for his methods of testing intelligence. The decree of 26 September 1922 was the first national or state recognition of vocational guidance. It created and funded vocational guidance offices in conjunction with pre-existing employment offices, which were organized on the commune level and administered by local professional committees. The idea was to have someone on location who was trained in vocational guidance. The offices were under the jurisdiction of the Ministry of Public Education. The vocational guidance leader Julien Fontègne administered the system. See M. J. Clément, *Le Mouvement*

d'orientation professionnelle (Aix-en-Provence: P. Roubaud, 1924), pp. 128–29, 145; "Le Décret du 26 septembre 1922 et l'orientation professionnelle," *Orientation professionnelle (OP)*, November 1922: 20–21; Bureau International du Travail, *Les Problèmes de l'orientation professionnelle* (Geneva: Bureau international du travail, 1935), pp. 19–20. For a global perspective of vocational guidance, see Franklin Keller and Morris Viteles, *Vocational Guidance Throughout the World: A Comparative Survey* (New York: W. W. Norton, 1937), and Guy Sinoir, *L'Orientation professionnelle* (Paris: Presses Universitaires de France, 1968), p. 9.

5. The questions were: (1) Should sexual education be instituted in the schools? (2) If so, at what age? (3) What form should it take? (4) Should it be given to girls as well as boys? (5) Should it be taught in the context of natural science courses? See M. L. Chevrel, "Germaine Montreuil-Straus educatrice et novatrice, Histoire du Comité d'éducation féminine," *Femmes médecins* 6 (October 1970). Response to the Bérard questionnaire was large (15,000 returns) but negative, so sex education was not instituted by the ministry. Despite much effort, I was not able to locate the responses to the questionnaire.

6. Much of this debate was reprinted and published in Marc Semenoff, ed., *L'Education sexuelle: Les Ecrits pour et contre* (Paris: André Delpeuch, 1924). The debate was also excerpted in Madeleine Vernet, "L'Education sexuelle," *Mère éducatrice*, June 1925. Vernet apologizes in this article for her own journal's silence on the issue, something about which her readers had complained. For examples of the debate in the bourgeois press, see a series of articles in *Oeuvre*: "Ce que l'on appelle l'éducation sexuelle," 5 February 1922; "Doit-on le dire?" 3 August 1922; B. de la Fouchardière, "Hommage à la vielle morale bourgeoise," 4 August 1922. See also "Faut-il les initier," 26 January 1922 (periodical unclear), and R. Archambault, "Doit-on à l'école faire l'éducation sexuelle des enfants?" with response by Yvonne Netter, *Paris-soir*, 4 August 1927, all in Dossier Education sexuelle, Bibliothèque Marguerite Durand (BMD). For the medical press, see Georges Vitoux, "La Vie sexuelle et ses dangers," *Presse médicale*, 29 October 1921. For the feminist press, see A. Aubriot, "L'Education sexuelle," *Droit des femmes*, February 1922; Dr. Montreuil-Straus, "La Question de l'enseignement sexuel à l'école," *La Française*, 11 March 1922; Marceline Hecquet, "L'Education sexuelle de la jeune fille et la protection de la mère," *Mère éducatrice*, February 1923. In *Un Scandale jésuite. L'Initiation sexuelle, d'après une brochure de l'Action populaire: Faut-il parler? Que dire? Comment le dire?* (Paris: Librairie Moderne, 1924), I. de Recalde cites articles about sexual education in the more conservative press published during these years, among them, "Billet de Junius," in *Echo de Paris*, 16 January 1922, and M. François Albert, "Le Père initiateur," *Dépêche de Toulouse*, 30 April 1923.

7. The condemnation was made in a statement by the General Assembly of Cardinals and Archbishops in France on 28 February 1923. See James McMillan, *Housewife or Harlot: The Place of Women in French Society, 1870–1940*

(New York: St. Martin's Press, 1980), p. 168. See Recalde, *Un Scandale jésuite,* pp. 5–6, for the original statement. It is also reprinted in the Association du mariage chrétien, *Les Initiations nécessaires, Deux discours by R. P. de Ganay, S. J., and Dr. H. Abrand* (Paris: Association du mariage chrétien, 1922). Both Ganay and Abrand remarked that there was "much discussion" about sexual education in their day.

8. In the "Rapport moral de l'année 1922" for the Société française de prophylaxie sanitaire et morale, Dr. H. Gougerot, a dermatologist and important social hygienist, proclaimed that "the most important question studied this year has been the sexual education of young men and women." See the *Bulletin de la Société française de prophylaxie sanitaire et morale (BSFPSM),* March 1923. For natalist support of sexual education, see the *BSFPSM,* March 1922.

9. The Ministry of Hygiene funded the CEF's efforts from its inception. In 1925, it received 60,000FF; in 1926, 25,000FF; in 1927, 10,000FF; in 1928, 10,000FF; in 1929, 15,000FF; and so on until 1934. See "L'Oeuvre accomplie par le CEF," Rapport présenté à l'Assemblée générale du 14 mars 1935 de la Société française de prophylaxie sanitaire et morale, 1935. Fonds Germaine Montreuil-Straus (GMS), Archives Marie-Louise Bouglé (AMLB). (Montreuil-Straus also appears as Montreuil-Strauss in some sources.)

10. The SFPSM was founded by Dr. Alfred Fournier in 1901. For an analysis of the activities of this organization before the war, see Jacques Donzelot, *The Policing of Families* (New York: Pantheon Books, 1979), pp. 180, 186. For the reaction of the SFPSM to the 1922 survey on sexual education, see "Education sexuelle des jeunes gens. Discussion des propositions de M. le Dr. Péraire. Rapport de M. Bobin. Séance du 22 février, 1922," *BSFPSM,* January 1922, and Justin Sicard de Plauzoles, "L'Education sexuelle de la jeunesse," *BSFPSM,* March 1923.

11. Montreuil-Straus gave her first series of lectures on women's anatomy and physiology at the Ecole pratique du service social du Pasteur Doumergue in 1920; these lectures were published in her classic work, *Avant la maternité,* in 1922. An address at an international hygiene conference the following year brought her recognition and supporting funds from the Ministry of Hygiene. See Chevrel, "Educatrice," p. 244. Montreuil-Straus was unanimously elected to the SFPSM on 7 December 1922, when she was already a doctor. See *BSFPSM,* December 1922. She asked for permission to begin the Comité on 6 November 1924. For an account of the formation of the CEF within the SFPSM, see the *BSFPSM,* November–December 1924: 93–94.

12. An interesting comparison with Montreuil-Straus is provided by Marie Stopes in England. Her *Married Love,* published in 1918, became the most popular and influential sex manual of its time. On Stopes, see Samuel Hynes, *A War Imagined: The First World War and English Culture* (New York: Atheneum, 1991), pp. 366–67.

13. For a turn-of-the-century view of *la vraie jeune fille,* see Leopold Lacour, "Incapables d'aimer," n.t., 1889, Dossier La Jeune fille—psychologie, BMD. For the twenties, see Paul Gaulot, "La Jeune fille moderne," *Le Figaro,*

11 June 1924; Felix Gaiffe, "Vers quelles carrières diriger nos filles?" *Eve*, 24 February 1920. For a fascinating examination of the relations among *la jeune fille*, innocence, and flowers, see Alain Corbin, *Le Miasme et la jonquille. L'Odorat et l'imagination sociale, XVIII–XXe siècle* (Paris: Aubier-Montagne, 1982).

14. Marcel Prévost, *Nouvelles lettres à Françoise, ou la jeune fille d'après guerre* (Paris: Flammarion, 1924), p. 7.

15. Edith Wharton, *French Ways and Their Meaning* (New York: D. Appleton, 1919, 1930), p. 116. A journalist for *Comoedia* wrote that while before the war "the task of educators consisted solely in keeping the garden of young women closed up tight," in the postwar period "the fearful novitiate of love, that up until now has been women's education, seemed like a highly absurd luxury." See "Jeunes filles," *Comoedia*, 26 January 1926.

16. For an expression of such fears, see Clément Vautel's novel, *Les Folies bourgeoises* (Paris: Albin Michel, 1921); "L'Emancipation de la jeune fille moderne," *Progrès civique*, 20 June 1925; and "A Quoi rêvent nos jeunes filles?" *Journal des instituteurs*, 14 March 1924, all in Dossier Jeune Fille, BMD; Suzanne Babled, "La Jeune fille idéal," *La Française*, 18 August 1923, "La Tenue des jeunes filles," *La Française*, 6 May 1922. For anxiety concerning women's tendency to venture out alone, see Gonzague Truc, "Enquête sur la condition et les aspirations des jeunes filles d'aujourd'hui," *Grande revue*, September 1925: 439, 447, and *Fémina*, August 1919. Finally, for the expression of fear concerning more male-female contact, see Truc, "Enquête," *Grande revue*, September: 439; Berthe Dangennes, *La Jeune fille et l'émancipation* (Paris, Editions Nilsson, 1919), pp. 90–92; Dr. Edouard Toulouse, *La Question sexuelle de la femme* (Paris: Bibliothèque-Charpentier, 1918).

17. Paul Reboux in Semenoff, *L'Education sexuelle*, p. 9. See also Avril de Sainte-Croix, *L'Education sexuelle* (Paris: Librairie Félix Alcan, 1918), p. 12; Truc, "Enquête," *Grande revue*, June 1925: 562; August: 269–71; October: 631–32, 636. See also the *Fémina* survey, comments of A. Nahmias and Dangennes, *La Jeune fille*, pp. 90–92.

18. Prévost, *Nouvelles*, p. 42. Prévost's book was reissued in new editions in 1928 and 1932. Nicolas Ségur, literary critic for *Revue mondiale*, praised Prévost for "discerning the spirit of the times. So much so that his book is also a precious historical document." See his review, 15 October 1924. For other similar statements concerning the loss of ignorance among young girls, see Yvonne Sarcey, "Jeunesse—La Jeune fille," *Les Annales*, 11 December 1921; Gérard Lavergne, *Les Femmes d'après-guerre* (Nîmes: Chastenier, 1925), p. 14, and Toulouse, *La Question sexuelle*, p. 14.

19. Truc, "Enquête," *Grande revue*, June 1925: 557. See also June: p. 556; July: 60–61; August: 268, 273; October: 618. For an earlier expression of the fear of celibacy in relation to careers, see the survey in *Fémina*, particularly the remarks of Madame Cestre, and Gaiffe, "Vers quelles carrières."

20. *Les Carrières féminines* (Paris: Rue de Mt. Thabor, n.d.), p. ii. Many

other natalists argued that women's work had become a necessity in this way. See also Mgr. Tissier, *La Femme française. Hier. Aujourd'hui. Demain* (Paris: Pierre Téqui, 1927), p. 68, and Gaulot, "La Jeune fille moderne." For other statements of the "new" necessity of women's work among others of diverse political views, see the comments of Paul Margueritte, Léon Brunschwicg, and Madame Avril de Sainte-Croix in Suzanne Grinberg, "Le Rôle de la femme française après la guerre," *Renaissance politique*, 31 March 1917; Léontine Zanta, *L'Activité féminine de demain*, Conférence de la *Revue des jeunes*, 18 February 1919 (Paris: *Revue des jeunes*, 1919), p. 178; Léon Abensour, "Le Problème de la démobilisation féminine," *Grande revue*, January 1919: 494.

21. For a view of the "disciplines" or "professions" on which this analysis is based, see Foucault, *Discipline and Punishment* (New York: Random House, 1979); Jan Goldstein, "Foucault among the Sociologists: The Disciplines and the History of the Professions," *History and Theory* 23 (1984).

22. Jean-Jacques Becker and Serge Berstein, *Victoire et frustrations, 1914–1929*, vol. 12 of *Nouvelle histoire de la France contemporaine* (Paris: Seuil, 1990), pp. 390–91.

23. Frederick Taylor's *Principles of Scientific Management* first appeared in France in 1911. For Taylorism in France, see Margorie Beale, "Advertising and the Politics of Public Persuasion in France, 1900–1939," (Ph.D. diss., University of California at Berkeley, 1991), chap. 3; Richard Kuisel, *Capitalism and the State in Modern France: Renovation and Economic Management in the Twentieth Century* (Cambridge: Cambridge University Press, 1981); Charles Maier, "Between Taylorism and Technocracy," *Journal of Contemporary History* 5 (1970); *In Search of Stability: Explorations in Historical Political Economy* (Cambridge: Cambridge University Press, 1987); James McMillan, *From Dreyfus to DeGaulle: Politics and Society in France, 1898–1969* (London: E. Arnold, 1985), p. 98; and Judith Merkle, *Management and Ideology: The Legacy of the International Scientific Management Movement* (Berkeley: University of California Press, 1980). For the connection between vocational guidance and "le système Taylor," see Jules Amar, *L'Orientation professionnelle* (Paris: Dunod, 1920), Conclusion.

24. Charles Maier, *Recasting Bourgeois Europe: Stabilization in France, Germany and Italy in the Decade after World War I* (Princeton: Princeton University Press, 1975). Maier's study also includes the postwar economies of Germany and Italy, and he acknowledges that his argument concerning the "recasting" of economic relations in rationalist, corporatist terms works better for Germany than for France. Indeed, his work has been criticized on this basis. See, for example, Gary Cross, "The Quest of Leisure: Reassessing the Eight Hour Day in France," *Journal of Social History* 18 (Winter 1984). For still more information about rationalization trends, see also Barnett Singer, *Modern France: Mind, Politics, Society* (Seattle: University of Washington Press, 1980), p. 77; P. Bernard and H. Dubief, *The Decline of the Third Republic, 1914–1938* (Cambridge: Cambridge University Press), pp. 132–33;

Thomas Grabau, "Visions of the Future: Wartime Perceptions of the Goals of Postwar Reconstruction in France, 1914–1919," *Proceedings of the Annual Meeting of the Western Society for French History* 7 (1979); and Paul A. Gagnon, "La Vie Future: Some French Responses to the Technological Society," *Journal of European Studies* 6 (1976).

25. The efforts of Montreuil-Straus's CEF and the social hygiene movement generally resemble rationalization trends in Germany during the same period. In Atina Grossman's words, the attempt "to rationalize, discipline, channel and control changes in sexual mores and behavior" marked interwar Germany. See Atina Grossman, "Crisis, Reaction and Resistance: Women in Germany in the 1920s and 1930s," in *Class, Race and Sex: The Dynamics of Control*, ed. A. Swerdlow and J. Lessinger (Boston: G. K. Hall, 1982), p. 67; "The New Woman and the Rationalization of Sexuality in Weimar Germany," in *The Powers of Desire*, ed. Ann Snitow, Christine Stansell, and Sharon Thompson (New York: Monthly Review Press, 1983); "Girlkultur or Thoroughly Rationalized Female: A New Woman in Weimar Germany?" in *Women in Culture and Politics: A Century of Change*, ed. Judith Friedlander et al. (Bloomington: Indiana University Press, 1986). The German sex reformers, who were funded by local governments and who aimed their efforts strictly at the working classes, dealt with a much wider variety of issues, including legalized abortion, contraception, eugenic health, and even women's right to sexual satisfaction—a spectrum that makes Montreuil-Straus's agenda appear conservative by comparison.

26. The career manuals included the following: Suzanne Grinberg and Alice Lamazière, *Carrières féminines, nouvelles écoles* (Paris: Larousse, 1917); Maurice Facy, *Quelles sont les meilleures carrières* (Paris: Payot, 1919); Hélène Bureau, *Guide pour le choix des carrières féminines* (Paris: Librairie Armand Colin, 1921); and Jean Bordeaux, *Les Carrières féminines intellectuelles* (Paris: France Edition, 1923). The perception that the war had been a turning point for women's work lasted throughout the decade. See Colette Yver, *Femmes d'aujourd'hui: Enquête sur les nouvelles carrières féminines* (Paris: Calmann-Lévy, 1929); and R. Lagorce, *Carrières et métiers de femmes* (Paris: Editions de Centaure, 1929).

27. In 1917, Senator Charles Chenu described the "ancient delimitations according to which occupations and professions had until now been classified by sex" and argued that the war's "experience demonstrated the artificial, prejudicial nature of this traditional classification." See Grinberg, "Le Rôle de la femme," *Renaissance politique*, 17 March 1917: 6; Dr. Toulouse, *La Question sexuelle*, p. 17; Toulouse, *La Question sociale* (Paris: Editions du Progrès Civique, 1921), p. 201; L. Narquet, "La Femme dans la France de demain," *Mercure de France*, 16 July 1917, p. 258; Louise Weiss, "Carrières féminines d'aujourd'hui et de demain," *Europe nouvelle*, 26 January 1918, p. 129; B. Dangennes, *La Femme moderne: Ce que toute femme moderne doit savoir* (Paris: Editions Nilsson, n.d.), p. 6; and her *Mariée ou non, la femme doit être*

indépendante (Paris: Editions Nilsson, 1923), p. 62; "Pour l'égalité," *Âme gauloise,* June 1926, Dossier Féminisme, BMD.

28. Bureau, *Guide,* p. vii, Introduction. Bureau was a teacher who also wrote for the weekly journal *L'Ecole et la vie.*

29. Bordeaux, *Carrières féminines,* Preface. See also Grinberg and Lamazière, *Carrières féminines,* p. 4; Facy, *Quelles sont les meilleures carrières,* pp. 19, 47–48; Bureau, *Guide,* Introduction, p. v.

30. See Bureau, *Guide,* p. 45. According to Grinberg and Lamazière, *Carrières féminines,* p. 9, the schools of law, medicine, physics, and chemistry were not only allowing but sometimes even urging young female students to enter. For secondary literature, see McMillan, *Housewife,* pp. 117–18.

31. Grinberg, *Carrières féminines,* p. 5. See also her "Le Rôle de la Femme," 3 March 1917; Manolui, *Le Choix et l'exercice d'une profession pour la femme mariée* (Paris: Jouve et Cie, 1922), and Dr. Toulouse, *La Question sociale,* p. 201. In the *Truc* survey, see *Grande revue,* June 1925: 559, words of Mlle. Estelle Maurin.

32. Census figures show that more women were active in the working population (39 percent) in 1921 than at any other time this century. But this figure is deceptive in that it largely reflects the massive participation of women in agriculture in the years immediately after the war. In fact, analysis of similar census figures excluding agricultural professions, demonstrates that, contrary to popular perception, there was no significant increase in the number of women working in the postwar years, and in fact this number was lower in 1926 than it had been in 1911. Colin Dyer supplies the 39 percent figure in *Population and Society in Twentieth Century France* (New York: Holmes and Meier, 1978), p. 67. Françoise Thébaud also refers to it in *Donner la vie: Histoire de la maternité en France entre les deux guerres* (Thèse du troisième cycle, Université de Paris VII, 1982), p. 167. Other historians to dismiss quantitative "gains" in women's work are Stephen Hause in "More Minerva than Mars: The French Women's Rights Campaign and the First World War," in *Behind the Lines: Gender and the Two World Wars,* ed. Higonnet et al. (New Haven: Yale University Press, 1987), p. 106, and his book, *Women's Suffrage and Social Politics in the French Third Republic* (Princeton: Princeton University Press, 1984), p. 198; James McMillan, *Housewife or Harlot,* p. 120; Jean-Louis Robert, "Women and Work in France during the First World War," in *The Upheaval of War: Family, Work and Welfare in Europe, 1914–1918,* ed. Richard Wall and Jay Winter (Cambridge: Cambridge University Press, 1988); Jean Daric, *L'Activité professionnelle des femmes en France* (Paris: Presses Universitaires de France, 1947), pp. 15–21. But as Daric puts it: "Although the external boundaries of the nonagricultural working female population did not change significantly from the turn of the century, profound transformations did occur in the internal structure of this population" (p. 29).

33. In *Housewife,* pp. 117–20, McMillan compares women employed in commercial jobs in 1906 as 779,000 and in 1921 as 1,008,000. In liberal profes-

sions and public services, the figure jumped from 293,000 to 491,000, and in civil service, from 100,000 to 200,000 in the same years. McMillan argues that the rise in female labor in the tertiary sector can be attributed primarily to young, single girls. To prove this, he compares the slow rise of married women in the commercial professions—from 4.8 percent in 1906 to 6.4 percent in 1936.

34. Marcel Prévost, *Les Don Juanes* (Paris: Renaissance du Livre, 1922); Victor Margueritte, *Le Compagnon* (Paris: Flammarion, 1923); M. Brieux, *Pierette et Galaor (l'enfant)* (Paris: Stock, 1924). See also, as a sampling, Geneviève Duhamelet, *Les Inépousées* (Paris: Albin Michel, 1919); J. H. Rosny, jeune, *Claire Tercel, avocate à la cour* (Paris: Grasset, 1924); Henry Fèvre, *L'Intellectuelle mariée* (Paris: Albin Michel, 1925).

35. See McMillan, *Housewife*, p. 120. Even by 1929, there were only one hundred female members of the bar in Paris, and three in Lyons. As for medicine, McMillan argues that women doctors were still regarded with suspicion, which made it difficult for them to set up a practice. Women were more numerous in dentistry and pharmacy. For the same argument about women's entry into the professions at the turn of the century, see Debora Silverman, "The 'New Woman,' Feminism and the Decorative Arts in Fin-de-Siècle France," in *Eroticism and the Body Politic*, ed. Lynn Hunt (Baltimore: Johns Hopkins University Press, 1990).

36. See Joan Scott and Louise Tilly, *Women, Work and Family* (New York: Holt, Rinehart, and Winston, 1978), pp. 152–54 and 161. Sylvie Zerner, "De la couture aux presses: L'Emploi féminine entre les deux guerres" *Le Mouvement social* 140 (July–September 1987); Martine Martin, "Femmes et société: Le Travail ménager (1919–1939)" (Thèse du troisième cycle, Université de Paris VII, 1984). Between 1906 and 1936, women in the tertiary sector increased from 44 percent to 56 percent. Those employed in industry declined from 57.1 percent to 42.3 percent. McMillan also provides statistics on the decline of women in the textile industry. See his *Housewife*, p. 157. He argues that as women's participation in the textile industry declined, they entered other industries, such as·chemicals, electricity, and light engineering. He also provides statistics on the rise of female participation in the tertiary sector of the economy. See also Jean Rabaut, *Histoire des féminismes français* (Paris: Stock, 1978), p. 276, and Daric, *L'Activité*, for two other explanations of these types of changes in women's work.

37. According to Tilly and Scott, *Women, Work*, the percentage of nonagricultural working women in domestic service fell between 1896 and 1936 from 19 percent to 16.4 percent. The number of live-in female domestics declined from 688,000 in 1906 to 422,000 by 1936. In addition, the live-in servant population was aging, that is, domestic service was no longer the province of young single girls, but increasingly was performed by older, married women who did not live within the household itself. Although these trends in working-class women's labor toward white-collar and commercial occupations can largely be

understood in structural terms, there were personal reasons for them as well, mainly the refusal on the part of working-class girls to submit to the restrictions imposed on their freedom and leisure time as domestic servants. For the *crise des domestiques*, see also Desanti, *La Femme au temps des années folles* (Paris: Stock, 1985), pp. 42–45; Robert L. Frost, "Machine Liberation: Inventing Housewives and Home Appliances in Interwar France" (manuscript), pp. 4–5; Martine Martin, "Femmes et société." For a contemporary view, see Auguste Moll-Weiss's survey on *domestiques*, *Les gens de maison* (Paris: G. Doin, 1927). In this book, Moll-Weiss even gives a sweeping history of the profession from the days of the Greeks and Romans. See also her *La Vie domestique d'après guerre* (Paris: Rousseau, 1921), in which she urges the rationalization of household duties as a remedy for the crisis. In *L'Activité*, p. 44, Daric argues that isolated workers, classifiable in the census as "petites patronnes et travailleuses isolées" accounted for 35.9 percent of all working women in 1906, 26.7 percent in 1921, and only 19.0 percent in 1936. McMillan draws on these figures to make the same point, in *Housewife*, p. 157. But McMillan sees this decline in domestic piecework particularly among married women, a fact that, according to him, proves that women became more, not less, domestic after the war.

38. Several commentators in the Truc "Enquête," *(La Grande revue),* particularly in June 1925, remark on how movies have become the favored leisure activity of working-class women.

39. Mary Louise Néron, "Doit-on donner un métier aux jeunes filles? *La Fronde*, 30 September 1926. The Congrès international d'orientation professionnelle féminine was held 23–26 September 1926, in Bordeaux. Mauvezin was secretary-general of the congress, which brought people to France from all over Europe, including Italy, Spain, and Switzerland. See *Congrès international d'orientation professionnelle féminine, Bordeaux, 23–26 Septembre 1926* (Bordeaux: Secretariat, 57 rue de Trois Conils, 1926). Documents on the congress reveal links between Mauvezin's women's vocational guidance movement and the bourgeois feminist movement. *La Fronde*, which was undergoing a brief revival at that time, covered the congress at the request of Louise Mauvezin, who wrote a personal letter to Marguerite Durand, who was then editor. See this letter, dated 9 September 1926, in Dossier Orientation professionnelle, BMD. See also Maria Vérone, "L'Orientation professionnelle de la femme," *Oeuvre*, 22 September 1926. In this article, Vérone, another bourgeois feminist, credited Mauvezin with recognizing the plight of bourgeois women, and their need to work.

40. Louise Mauvezin, *Congrès*, p. 19.

41. An example of a female association that set up a vocational guidance office for working class women was the Association féminine pour l'étude et l'action sociale. See the brochure *Une Véritable chambre d'apprentissage féminin* (Bar-le-Duc: Imprimerie Brodard et Cie, 1923), and *OP*, August–September 1923. For an example of an office that catered to middle-class

women, see Dossier Orientation professionnelle, BMD, and the offices set up by La Société des amis de l'étudiante, and L'Union des françaises diplômées d'universités in the 1930s. Many of the women in these associations were doctors, lawyers, engineers, and pharmacists. They claimed to follow the "scientific investigatory procedures" laid down by the Institut national d'orientation professionnelle at the Sorbonne.

42. This commitment was also expressed at the congress by Madame Deysson. See *Congrès,* p. 38, and the range of traditionally bourgeois professions studied and discussed at the congress, among them medicine, law, dentistry, pharmacy, radiology, journalism, industrial design, banking, and administration. There was even a presentation of a monograph for *"la maîtresse de maison."* For discussion of other occupations that were performed by middle-class as well as working-class girls, see Maugeis DeBourguesdon, "La Stenographie," *OP,* May 1920, and "Les Emplois féminins dans l'administration des P.T.T.," *OP,* March 1923.

43. This institutional context imprinted vocational guidance with a distinctly working-class, industrial, and artisanal orientation. Vocational guidance arose out of a concern with technical education, the creation of a "perfect" labor force, already addressed by the Astier Law of 1919. This law reorganized technical education in France and aimed both to revive respect in the *métiers* and to raise the general level of technical competence in the French artisanry. For more information on the law, see "Pour la formation professionnelle: Au Congrès des Syndicats féminins du Boulevard des Capucines," *Vie catholique,* Dossier Orientation Professionnelle, 1924–38, BMD.

44. Julien Fontègne, "Orientation professionnelle, psychologie et professions," *Bulletin de l'Association française pour la lutte contre le chômage et l'organization du marché du travail* (Paris), no. 38–39 (June–July 1920): 3.

45. F. Mauvezin, *Rose des métiers. Traité d'orientation professionnelle* (Paris: Editions Littéraires et Politiques, 1922), p. 5.

46. In French: *taille, force, santé, agilité, sang-froid, attention, ténacité, observation, mémoire, sens artistique, tenue, manières.*

47. See Jules Amar, *L'Orientation professionnelle* (Paris: Dunod, 1920), p. 2. See also Amar, "Méthode scientifique d'orientation professionnelle," *OP,* November 1919: 1–2; Clément, *Mouvement,* p. 8; Edouard Gauthier, "L'Orientation professionnelle," *Revue internationale du travail,* May 1922: 769. The scientific credibility of vocational guidance was buttressed by the fact that its leaders were associated with prestigious research institutions such as the Académie des sciences, the Conservatoire national des arts et métiers, and the Institut Jean-Jacques Rousseau in Geneva. Vocational guidance leaders leaned heavily on the authority of medical science, demanding that each male adolescent be examined by a physician in order to determine his general state of health, with particular attention given to such "counterindications" as would prevent entrance into any one profession. The results, which were recorded on a *fiche sanitaire individuelle,* constituted "a primary scientific base, solid

data on which one can lean" in guiding the child's choice of career. See Clément, *Mouvement*, pp. 29–30, 100; Julien Fontègne, "Le Cabinet d'orientation professionnelle de l'Institut J. J. Rousseau, à Genève," *OP*, March 1920: 38–39.

48. Edouard Claparède, *L'Orientation professionnelle, ses problèmes et ses méthodes* (Geneva: Bureau International du Travail, Etudes et Documents, October 1922, Série J. Enseignement #1), p. 29.

49. Redressement français was formed in 1925 by Ernest Mercier, who had been dismayed by the inefficiency of France's industry during the war. The organization was allied with the right-wing political and military elite, including marshals Foch and Pétain, and premiers Tardieu, Flandin, and Laval, all of whom were Mercier's friends. Mercier was a member of the Croix de Feu and a fomenter of the antiparliamentary riots of February 1934. He believed that the small shopkeeper was crippling the French economy and sought a streamlined marketing system by which individual shopowners would either become branch distributors or disappear. As a Redressement handbook stated, "Individualism is very nice; it's very pleasant. But it's obsolete." For contemporary works, see Ernest Mercier, "Les Conséquences sociales de la rationalisation en France," in *L'Aspect social de la rationalisation, Redressement français* (Paris: SAPE, 1927); Lucien Romier, *Qui sera le maître? Europe ou Amérique?* (Paris: Hachette, 1927). In the secondary literature, see Richard Kuisel's "Technocrats and Public Economic Policy," *Journal of Economic History* 2 (1970), and Kuisel's biography, *Ernest Mercier, French Technocrat* (Berkeley: University of California Press, 1967).

50. "In the Right Place," *Le Temps*, 25 December 1919. The need for a new level of productive efficiency was usually justified in terms of the war's economic and demographic destruction. See also Julien Fontègne, *L'Orientation professionnelle et la détermination des aptitudes* (Paris: Editions Delachaux et Niestlé, S.A., 1921), pp. 10–11.

51. For an argument concerning vocational guidance and economic regeneration, see: Fontègne, *L'Orientation*, p. 10; Fontègne, *Avant d'entrer en apprentissage* (Paris: Librairie de l'Enseignement Technique, 1924), p. 7; Edouard Gauthier, *L'Orientation professionnelle. Sa nécessité. Ses difficultés. Etat de la question dans divers pays* (Paris: Revue international du travail, 1922), p. 2; Mauvezin, *Rose des métiers*, pp. 77, 79; Mauvezin, *Avant de choisir son métier ou sa profession* (Paris: Editions Littéraires et Politiques, 1921), pp. 37, 84; Claparède, *L'Orientation*, p. 18; "Projet de modèle-type d'office d'orientation professionnelle présenté par M. le sous-sécretaire d'état à l'enseignement technique," *OP*, October 1921: 25. For arguments concerning moral regeneration, see: Gauthier, "L'Orientation"; Fernand Mauvezin and Julien Fontègne, "L'Orientation professionnelle," *La Formation*, no. 25 (1920): 27; Fontègne, "L'Orientation," p. 1.

52. *Congrès*, p. 19. Reporting on the 1926 congress, *La Fronde* noted that "everyone's preoccupation was the material and moral well-being of the child." See Néron, "Doit-on donner?"

53. See *Congrès*. Fernand Philippart was also president of the Bordeaux Caisse pour allocations familiales, an administrative organ that provided wage subsidies or allowances to mothers with small children.

54. *Une Véritable chambre*, p. 5.

55. *Congrès*, p. 117.

56. Ibid., p. 180.

57. Support for the *allocations familiales* became one of the major resolutions of the congress.

58. In her *Rose des activités féminines pour l'orientation professionnelle des jeunes filles* (Bordeaux: Editions "des Roses," 1925) p. 18, Mauvezin described domestic work as "a marvellous panacea" to the "problem" of women's work. See also same volume, pp. 35, 419. See also *Congrès*, where domestic work was favored in many sessions. For feminists' views of domestic work at this time, see Marcelle Richard, "Une Exploitation trop méconnue de la femme: Le Travail à domicile," *Bulletin des groupes féministes de l'enseignement laïque*, November–December 1925, and Maria Vérone, "Le Travail à domicile," *Oeuvre*, 2 September 1925, articles de Journaux, Boîte no. 6, Sa–Ve, AMLB. Both Richard and Vérone saw domestic work as highly exploitative.

59. See Fontègne, *Avant d'entrer*, p. 173; Louise Mauvezin, *Rose des activités féminines*, p. 22, and F. Mauvezin, *Rose des métiers*, p. 69.

60. See, for example, Joan Wallach Scott, "'L'Ouvrière! Mot impie, sordide . . .'": Women Workers in the Discourse of French Political Economy," in *Gender and the Politics of History* (New York: Columbia University Press, 1988), and Mary Lynn Stewart, *Women, Work and the French State: Labour Protection and Social Patriarchy, 1879–1919* (Kingston, Ont.: McGill-Queen's University Press, 1989).

61. Joan Wallach Scott, "The Woman Worker in the Nineteenth Century," in *Storia della Donna*, ed. Georges Duby and Michelle Perrot (Rome: Laterza, 1991), vol. 4.

62. Fontègne, *L'Orientation professionnelle*, p. 17.

63. Louise Mauvezin, *Rose des activités*, p. 22. See also *Congrès*, p. 19. For the emphasis on *la femme seule* among other vocational leaders, see Julien Fontègne, "Orientation professionnelle," p. 6, and Fontègne, *L'Orientation professionnelle*, pp. 15–16. Vocational guidance counselors particularly targeted three other groups besides women: the unemployed, the elderly, and the disabled veterans.

64. F. Mauvezin, *Rose des métiers*. There were 21 "métiers speciaux à la femme," approximately 107 "métiers disponible à la femme," and several hundred "métiers speciaux à l'homme."

65. The twenty-one professions listed as "exclusive" to women were: trouser-maker, children's seamstress *(costume d'enfant)*, dressmaker *(couturière, costume flou)*, tailoress *(couturière, façon tailleur)*, corset-maker, linen-maid *(lingère)*, embroiderer (2 kinds, one for embroidery in gold and white,

the other for embroidery in color), lace-maker, milliner, worker with flowers and feathers, invisible mender *(stoppeuse),* ironer-finisher *(repasseuse-apprêteuse),* furrier, mechanical embroiderer, mechanical hosier *(bonnetière mécanique),* colorist, stamper *(timbreuse),* knitter, worker with hair *(ouvrière en cheveux),* maid. Many of these translations are imprecise because of both lack of exact English translations, and my own lack of expertise concerning women's professions in the early twentieth century. In these cases, I have also provided the French.

66. My aim here was to determine if those occupations determined by Mauvezin as specifically "male" or "female" were based on assumptions concerning different physical and intellectual capacities between the sexes. My procedure for this comparative analysis was to choose 100 professions considered "exclusive" to men and 100 exclusive or accessible to women. Because Mauvezin listed only 21 professions as "exclusive to women," I also chose 79 métiers that he considered open to women without qualifications, or with very few reservations. For each category or aptitude, I determined a numerical scale of values. For example, in the case of "health," an "indifférent" merited a score of 1 and a "très bonne" merited a score of 9. In this, I was following a method of "quantifying" the monographs that was also chosen by Julien Fontègne in "L'Orientation professionnelle et les professions supérieures," *OP,* January 1921. It was impossible to determine the same numerical value scale for all different aptitudes and therefore to compare the relative strengths of each category with each other. But the same scale was applied equally within each aptitude across gender boundaries. After arriving at a numerical scale of values for each aptitude, I determined the numerical score of each aptitude in each of the 200 *métiers.* Then I added up all these scores, arriving at a total score for each aptitude in the case of both male and female professions. I transformed these scores into percentages, dividing them by the number of total possible points. I then compared these percentages across gender.

67. Jules Amar, *L'Orientation,* p. 65. Amar's research on women was well-known. His image of woman recalled that of Jules Simon or Jules Michelet; woman was a being incapable of prolonged work or concentration of any kind, plagued by nervous disorders brought about by, among other things, the menstrual cycle. See his "Réflexions d'un physiologiste sur la femme et le 'féminisme,'" *Revue bleue,* 16–23 February 1918. See also "Les Lois du travail féminin et de l'activité cérébrale," 14 October, and "La Fonction mentale dans le travail féminin," 25 November, both in *Compte rendus hebdomaires de l'Académie des sciences,* 167 (1918); "Origines et conséquences de l'émotivité féminine," January 6, *Compte rendus hebdomaires de l'Académie des sciences* 168 (1919). For an analysis of Amar's research on the woman worker, see Mathilde Dubesset, Françoise Thébaud, and Catherine Vincent, "Les Munitionnettes de la Seine," in *1914–1918: L'Autre front,* ed. Patrice Fridenson (Paris: Editions Ouvrières, 1977). For a contemporary feminist response to Amar, see "Sexe Faible," *Lutte féministe,* 3 April 1919.

68. Julien Fontègne, "L'Orientation professionnelle féminine," *OP*, January 1922.

69. In fact, vocational guidance theory took a conservative attitude concerning rising above one's own class level as well. See Mauvezin and Fontègne, "L'Orientation"; F. Mauvezin, *Rose*, pp. 15, 62; Fontègne, *Avant*, p. 34.

70. Néron, "Doit-on?"

71. Alfred Siredy, Preface, pp. xii–xiii, in Germaine Montreuil-Straus, *Avant la maternité: Précis des connaissances indispensables aux futures mères* (Paris: Stock, 1922). A member of the Légion d'Honneur, Dr. Siredy helped to develop the CEF and was at one time called *"notre maître"* by Montreuil-Straus.

72. Germaine Montreuil-Straus, "L'Amour: Son rôle dans la vie individuelle, familiale et sociale," *Comité national d'études sociales et politiques*, Imprimerie d'études sociales et politiques no. 385, Dossier Germaine Montreuil-Straus, BMD, p. 30; "L'Oeuvre éducative accomplie par le Comité d'éducation féminine de la SFPSM," *Bulletin de l'Académie de médecine*, Séance du 30 avril 1929, Fonds GMS, AMLB, p. 1.

73. On the social hygiene movement, see Schneider, *Quality and Quantity: The Quest for Biological Regeneration in Twentieth-Century France* (Cambridge: Cambridge University Press, 1990), p. 46, and Corbin, *Les Filles de noce: Misère sexuelle et prostitution* (Paris: Flammarion, 1978), pp. 386–87.

74. Dr. Fournier was the director of the St. Louis Hospital in Paris and on the faculty at the School of Medicine at the University of Paris. He was an expert on syphilis who published extensively. For an analysis of Fournier's work in the late nineteenth century, see Jill Harsen, "Syphilis, Wives and Physicians: Medical Ethics and the Family in Late Nineteenth-Century France," *French Historical Studies* 16 (Spring 1989), and Alain Corbin, "Le Péril vénérien au début du siècle: Prophylaxie sanitaire et prophylaxie morale," in *L'Haleine des faubourgs*, ed. Lion Murard and Patrick Zulberman (Fontenay-sous-Bois: Recherches, 1978). According to Corbin, the SFPSM was formed in 1899 as part of an international conference in Brussels. See his *Les Filles de noce*, p. 390. See also William Schneider, *Quality and Quantity*, p. 50; Jean-Alexis Néret, *Documents pour une histoire de l'éducation sexuelle en France* (Paris: Néret, 1957), chap. 5, and Harsin, "Medical Ethics."

75. For the social composition of the SFPSM, see Corbin, *Les Filles de noce*, pp. 391–92; Schneider, *Quality not Quantity*, p. 51. In "Le Péril vénérien," Corbin describes the SFPSM as the birthplace of sexual education in France. On 10 May 1901, Fournier put the question of antivenereal education to a meeting of the Société, and they decided to support it for boys who were at least sixteen and who had received parental authorization. See Dr. Carle, *Le Prophylaxie des maladies vénériennes* (Paris: Librairie Octave Doin, 1921), pp. 20–21. Also in 1901, Eugène Brieux wrote a play called *Les Avaries* about venereal disease, in which he advocated sexual education for boys. The play,

which Brieux dedicated to Fournier, was first censored, then ultimately performed to great notoriety and effect.

76. From Prévost, *Nouvelles lettres de femmes*, retold in Anne Martin-Fugier, *La Bourgeoise: Femme au temps de Paul Bourget* (Paris: Bernard Grasset, 1983), p. 56. Historians of sexual education argue that there was generally more openness in dealing with sexual matters during the eighteenth century and that Rousseau was a major force in the creation of the modern "silence" concerning sexuality in the nineteenth century. See Jean-Alexis Néret, *Documents*, and Maria-José Garcia Werebe, *L'Education sexuelle à l'école* (Paris: Presses Universitaires de France, 1976). For a completely different view on this "silence" surrounding sexuality, see Michel Foucault, *An Introduction* to *The History of Sexuality* (New York: Random House, 1980), and Peter Gay, *The Bourgeois Experience: Victoria to Freud* (New York: Oxford University Press, 1984).

77. Montreuil-Straus, "Les Préjugés auxquels se heurte la lutte antivénérienne," *Paris médicale*, 2 March 1929, Fonds GMS, AMLB, p. 208.

78. Ibid.

79. Montreuil-Straus, *L'Enseignement se rapportant à l'hygiène sexuelle et aux maladies vénériennes est-il actuellement réalisable dans nos écoles normales d'institutrices?* (Paris: R. Tancrède, 1926).

80. Montreuil-Straus, *Avant*, p. xiii. See also Dr. J. Doléris and Jean Bouscatel, *Hygiène et morale sociales. Néomalthusianisme, maternité, et féminisme, éducation sexuelle* (Paris: Masson et Cie, 1918), p. 143, and the remarks of Pierre Paraf in Semenoff, ed., *L'Education*, p. 124.

81. Germaine Montreuil-Straus, *Avant*, pp. xix–xx. See also Montreuil-Straus, "Exposé de Mme. Montreuil-Straus sur l'enseignement de l'hygiène sexuelle à l'école," 26 January 1922, Dossier GMS, AMLB, p. 12; "Activité du Comité d'éducation féminine depuis sa fondation," *BSFPSM*, November–December 1925: 109; "La Fonction maternelle," Conférence faite à la Ligue des sociétés de la croix rouge, March 1926, Dossier GMS, BMD; Comité d'éducation féminine, untitled pamphlet (Paris: Imprimerie de Tancrède, n.d.), p. 15; "La Question," *La Française*, March 1922. The belief that innocence was not equated with ignorance was widely expressed among participants in the sex education debate and was therefore neither new nor unique to Montreuil-Straus alone. In 1903, for example, Dr. Georges Surbled argued in his *La Vie de jeune fille* (Paris: A. Maloine et fils, 1925), p. ix, that "ignorance is not a virtue, but rather sometimes its downfall." For the postwar period, see also Dangennes, *La Jeune fille et l'émancipation;* DeWitt Schlumberger, "Instruction morale et biologique de la jeunesse," in Semenoff, ed., *L'Education*, p. 88; *Manuel d'éducation prophylactique contre les maladies vénériennes à l'usage des éducateurs et des éducatrices de la jeunesse* (Paris: Librairie Maloine, 1922), p. 9; André Lorulot, *Morale et éducation sexuelles basées sur la physiologie et sur l'experience* (Paris: Editions du Fauconnier, 1922), p. 6; *Les Initiations nécessaires*, p. 3.

82. See also *Avant*, p. 50. The slogan of the CEF was "Ignorance is not synonymous with purity."

83. See Montreuil-Straus, *Tu seras mère. La Fonction maternelle* (Paris: Société française de prophylaxie sanitaire et morale, 1928), p. 4; "Exposé sur l'enseignement de l'hygiène," p. 11.

84. *Avant*, p. 37. On the sexual instinct, see also *De l'Enfance à l'adolescence: La Crise de la puberté* (Paris: Imprimerie de Tancrède, n.d.), Dossier GMS, AMLB; *Avant*, p. 57; "Rapport sur l'éducation sexuelle," *Deuxième congrès quinquennal de l'Association internationale des femmes médecins, Paris, 10–15 April 1929* (Paris: Imprimerie Tancrède, 1929), Fonds GMS, AMLB, p. 38. For similar notions of the female sexual instinct, see Dr. Denise Blanchier, *Faut-il parler aux enfants? Quand et comment?* (Paris: Imprimerie Tancrède, n.d.), Dossier GMS, Archives MLB, p. 6; Dr. Siredy, *Du Rôle prépondérant de la mère dans l'éducation sexuelle de ses enfants* (Paris: Comité d'éducation féminine, n.d.), p. 3; Doléris and Bouscatel, *Hygiène*, pp. 131, 177; Professor A. Calmette, *Simple causerie pour l'éducation sexuelle des jeunes garçons de quinze ans* (Paris: Masson et Cie, 1920), pp. 3–4; and Sicard de Plauzoles, "L'Education sexuelle de la jeunesse." For a somewhat more radical notion of sexual instinct, particularly for women, see André Lorulot, *Morale et éducation sexuelles*, p. 6.

85. See chap. 6, notes 98 and 121, for the introduction of Havelock Ellis's and Sigmund Freud's work into France.

86. In 1925 Adolphe Pinard described the sexual instinct as "the most powerful of all, and the most novel . . . because it is the safeguard of the species, whose conservation is its mission to assure." See Adolphe Pinard's pamphlet, *A la Jeunesse pour l'avenir de la race française* (Paris: L.P.V., 1925), p. 8.

87. Cited in Chevrel, "Educatrice," p. 246.

88. *Avant*, pp. 130, 134–35.

89. Semenoff, "La Pureté: Point de vue catholique," in *Education*, p. 37. See same volume, remarks by Abbé Jean Viollet. See also Association, *Les Initiations nécessaires*, Discours de Ganay, p. 3, and Discours d'Abrand, pp. 7, 11; Dr. H. Abrand, *Aux Parents et aux éducateurs: Education de la pureté et préparation au mariage* (Paris: Association du mariage chrétien, 1922), pp. 1–2, and Abbé Jean Viollet, *Education de la pureté et du sentiment* (Paris: Association du mariage chrétien, 1925), p. 7; l'Abbé and André Lorulot, *Morale sexuelle chrétienne ou morale sexuelle libertaire? Controverse publique entre MM. l'Abbé Viollet et André Lorulot* (Conflans-Honorine: A. Lorulot, 1922). Abbé Fonssagrives began this movement in the early twentieth century with his book *Conseils aux parents et aux maîtres sur l'éducation de la pureté* (Paris: Librairie C. Poussielgue, 1903). In the secondary literature, see Corbin, "Le Péril vénérien," p. 261; Donzelot, *The Policing of Families*, p. 185. For a critique of the more liberal Jesuit position on sexual education, see Recalde, *Scandale*. As late as 1929, sexual education was the subject of the Seventh

Congress of the Association du mariage chrétien. See *L'Eglise et l'éducation sexuelle* (Paris: Association du mariage chrétien, 1929).

90. Association, *Les Initiations nécessaires*, pp. 2, 5–6, 10. See also Viollet, *Education*, pp. 53, 63–64, 74–75, where he talks about the increasing activity of both the bourgeois and the working-class girl outside the home; Abrand, *Aux parents*, pp. 28–29; Recalde, *Scandale*, pp. 39–40, 70, who objected to all forms of sexual education in books on the grounds that it was too "total and abrupt" and risked "wounding" a child's modesty; the opinion of "Junius" of *Echo de Paris* and M. François Albert of *Dépêche de Toulouse*, cited in Recalde, pp. 59–60.

91. See Avril de Sainte Croix, *L'Education sexuelle* (Paris: Librairie Félix Alcan, 1918), p. 39; Corbin, "Le Péril vénérien," p. 261.

92. Both the CEF and the SFPSM argued for the teaching of sex education within the natural science curriculum of the state-run schools. Again by contrast, Catholic opinion, including that of the General Assembly of Cardinals and Archbishops, held that state-sponsored sexual education "would be collective, neutral from the point of view of religious morality and exclusively anatomical and physiological in kind, which is to say that this education would be disastrous." Association, *Les Initiations nécessaires*, Ganay, p. 3. See also the critique, same volume by Dr. H. Abrand, p. 10.

93. Montreuil-Straus, "Exposé sur l'enseignement de l'hygiène," p. 14. Montreuil-Straus believed that the moral element of sexual education should be undertaken by the family rather than the school. See "L'Education sexuelle de nos enfants," *Nouvelle éducation*, November 1927, Dossier GMS, BMD, p. 163. See also Dr. Siredy, *Du rôle*, p. 10; "A Propos de l'éducation sexuelle," *BSFPSM*, July 1922.

94. Association, *Les Initiations*, Ganay, p. 4.

95. See *Avant*, p. 61. In *Hygiène*, p. 120, Doléris and Bouscatel also try to distance themselves from what they call the "Christian moralists" and do so by emphasizing the importance of science in sexual education.

96. Montreuil-Straus, "Exposé sur l'enseignement," p. 15. The popular educator was Professor Félix Thomas. When, in 1919, Thomas reissued his popular educational manual for boys, originally published in 1908, he decided to write another new book, this time for girls. In the foreword of the new book, he explained that "the role that a woman is asked to play outside the family . . . has grown considerably. It is for this new role that the instruction and education given to our daughters must prepare her." See P. F. Thomas, *L'Education dans la famille: Les Péchés des parents—nos filles* (Paris: Librairie Félix Alcan, 1919), p. xvi. See also Doléris and Bouscatel, *Hygiène*, pp. 130–31; Montreuil-Straus, "Rapport sur l'éducation sexuelle," p. 37; and Madame Leroy-Allais, *Comment j'ai instruit mes filles des choses de la maternité* (Paris: Mabine, 1930), p. 5; *Manuel d'éducation*, p. 22; Dr. Gougerot, "La Lutte antivénérienne à l'école primaire," *BSFPSM*, June 1920.

97. See Corbin's "Le Péril vénérien," pp. 269, 280.

98. Paul Good, *Lettre aux marins: Hygiène et morale* (Paris: Cercle d'études et d'action sociale, 1922), p. 8.

99. Sicard de Plauzoles, "L'Education sexuelle de la jeunesse." Sicard de Plauzoles was a leading hygienist, a member of the SFPSM, and vice-president (one of five) of Montreuil-Straus's CEF. In 1925, Adolphe Pinard warned his male readers that beginning in puberty, "special appetites and needs until then unknown to you are going to awaken little by little." See Pinard, *Jeunesse*, p. 7. See also Dr. L. Jullien, *La Vie sexuelle et ses dangers* (Seine-et-Oise: Ligue nationale française contre le péril vénérien, 1925); Calmette, *Simple causerie*, p. 5.

100. See Sicard de Plauzoles, "L'Education sexuelle de la jeunesse," p. 46. For an example of how this fear was discussed among members of the BSFPSM itself, see "Discussion du rapport de M. le Dr. Rulot sur la lutte antivénérienne en Belgique," Séance du 22 février 1922, *BSFPSM*, January 1922.

101. Rapport de M. Charles Fouquet, "Abstinence sexuelle chez la femme, d'après le congrès allemande de Dresde (1911) sur la prophylaxie des maladies vénériennes," *BSFPSM*, February 1912.

102. Harsin, "Medical Ethics."

103. For *la femme isolée* as a symbol of social disorder, see Scott, "L'Ouvrière," p. 147. An examination of the minutes of the society from 1910 to 1919 demonstrate that the subject came up on only a few occasions in 1912, but not at all in any other year until 1919. In "Le péril vénérien," pp. 259–60, Corbin argues that the notion of women's sexual education was greeted with a hostile reception both inside and outside the SFPSM. See also René Martial on his failed attempts at women's sexual education before the war in "A Propos de la discussion du rapport de M. Bobin: L'Education sexuelle," *BSFPSM*, May 1922: 72–73.

104. See Mme. Leroy-Allais, "La Protection de la jeune fille, ouvrière et domestique," *BSFPSM*, November 1912. For another example of a prewar view of the working-class woman, see Fouquet, "Abstinence sexuelle"; Dr. Charles Burlureaux, *Le Péril vénérien, Conseil aux jeunes filles* (Paris: Librairie Delagrave, 1904); Dr. Mathé, *L'Enseignement de l'hygiène sexuelle à l'école* (Paris: Vigot Frères, 1912), p. 109.

105. A few times in her writings from the 1920s, Montreuil-Straus presented the world outside the "domestic greenhouse" as potentially dangerous and immoral. Even at these times, however, she seemed to redefine the dangers involved in two ways: first, they applied as much to the bourgeois woman as they did to the *femme isolée,* and second, they sprang from twentieth-century forms of mass culture and communication as much as nineteenth-century forms of urban disorder. Montreuil-Straus feared most that the young girl would discover the facts of sexual life in unhealthy ways because of her exposure to the mass press, advertisements, and movies. See, for example, her "Devons-nous donner un enseignement sexuel à nos filles?" *Rapport au Con-*

grès *international de propagande d'hygiène sociale, 23–27 mai 1923* (Paris: Comité nationale de propagande d'hygiène sociale, n.d.), pp. 383, 385. See also Dr. Aimé Gauthier's "La Femme contre le péril vénérien," *Vers la santé* 6 (November 1925), Fonds GMS, Achives MLB; and Baudry de Saunier's description of the young girl in *Education sexuelle* (Paris: Flammarion, 1930).

106. As Montreuil-Straus explained it in 1925 to the SFPSM, "the goal pursued is the creation of anti-venereal prophylactic education and the preparation for marriage for young girls of popular as well as bourgeois backgrounds." See "Minutes, réunion de 5 février 1925," *BSFPSM*, February–March 1925: 5. She announced at the same meeting that she had made her first lecture at the Ecole normale de Lille. See also *Avant la maternité*, p. xix; Comité d'éducation féminine, untitled brochure (no publisher or date), Fonds GMS, AMLB; "L'Oeuvre éducative," p. 1; the comments of Siredy in "Rapport de M. Bobin," p. 21; and Burlureaux, "Indications à donner," p. 78. Several years later, in 1928, Montreuil-Straus claimed that her aim to reach all classes had been fulfilled. See "L'Education antivénérienne des femmes et des jeunes filles," *Rapport présenté à la Conférence internationale de défense sociale contre la syphilis, Nancy, May 1928* (Nancy-Paris-Strasbourg: Imprimerie Berger-Levrault, n.d.), Fonds GMS, AMLB.

107. To some extent, Montreuil-Straus's abandonment of the dual image of female sexuality was true of the SFPSM generally after the war. For example, in 1930, Madame Leroy-Allais, the same SFPSM member who promoted the image of the highly sexualized, working-class girl in 1912, made another plea for sexual education. Here, her argument presents a completely different image of the young girl, one who was apt to forget about her sex altogether. See *Comment j'ai instruit*, p. 5, and *Manuel d'éducation*, p. 207. There were, however, still portrayals of working-class women in traditionally sexualized terms. For example, see Dr. Gougerot, *Conférence antivénérienne faite à des ouvrières* (Melun: Imprimerie Administrative, 1919), particularly pp. 22–23, and Martial, "A Propos de la discussion," pp. 79–80. Another tendency was to turn the young bourgeois girl into a sort of *femme isolée*. For example, another SFPSM member argued that middle-class women were now frequently subject to the same sexual temptations and disillusions as working-class women had been before the war. See "Communication de M. Bobin à propos de la discussion du rapport de M. Péraire dans la séance du premier juin 1922," *BSFPSM*, June 1922, and A. Siredy's Preface to Montreuil-Straus's *Avant la maternité*, pp. xi–xii.

108. Rather than focus strictly on antivenereal protection, as had the SFPSM, Montreuil-Straus and her colleagues were determined to give young girls a general education in female physiology and anatomy. See *Tu seras mère*, pp. 4–5; "L'Education sexuelle de nos enfants," p. 163.

109. *Avant la maternité*, p. 58. See the same volume, p. 61, for a similar argument and a good articulation of her attempt to mediate "science" and "morality."

110. Cited in Chevrel, "Educatrice," pp. 245–46.

111. "Devons-nous donner un enseignement?" p. 383. See also Montreuil-Straus, "L'Education sexuelle de nos enfants," pp. 163, 166; CEF untitled pamphlet (see above, n. 81).

112. *Avant la maternité*, pp. 21, 26.

113. Ibid., 58–59. See also the CEF pamphlet *Amour et mariage* (Alençon: Imprimerie Corbière et Jugain, n.d.), Dossier CEF, Boîte No. 5: Divers, AMLB. Love outside marriage led to "abandonment, abortion, infanticide, prostitution, despair and suicide, tragedies and crimes"; in short, it was "an inexhaustible source of complications, distress and grief." See also *Tu seras mère*, pp. 17–18. Postwar social hygiene literature concerning boys' sexual education also discussed male sexuality in terms of reproduction and fatherhood. See Paul Good, *Lettre aux marins*, pp. 3–4; Calmette, *Simple causerie*, p. 2; Pinard, *A la jeunesse*, p. 8. But these hygienists also produced a notion of male sexual desire outside of a reproductive context simply by cautioning young boys to guard against it before they were married.

114. "Devons-nous donner un enseignement?" p. 282.

115. See Montreuil-Straus, *Tu seras mère*, p. 4; CEF. untitled brochure (see above, n. 106).

116. For notions of female sexual identity in Great Britain during the 1920s, see Susan Kent, "The Politics of Sexual Difference: World War I and the Demise of British Feminism," *Journal of British Studies* 27 (July 1988); Ellen Holtzman, "The Pursuit of Married Love: Women's Attitudes Toward Sexuality and Marriage in Great Britain, 1918–1939," *Journal of Social History* 16 (Winter 1982); Ruth Hall, ed., *Dear Dr. Stopes: Sex in the 1920's* (New York: Penguin, 1981); Sheila Jeffreys, *The Spinster and Her Enemies: Feminism and Sexuality, 1880–1930* (London: Pandora, 1985). For Germany, see the citations in note 25 above. For the United States, see Paula Fass, *The Beautiful and the Damned* (New York: Oxford University Press, 1977), and Elaine Showalter, *These Modern Women: Autobiographical Essays from the 20s* (Old Westbury, N.Y.: Feminist Press, 1978). For a precursor to Montreuil-Straus in France, see Madeleine Pelletier, *L'Emancipation sexuelle de la femme* (Paris: Giard et Brière, 1911).

117. In "Le Péril vénérien," p. 262, Corbin argues that in their drive to control venereal disease before the war, the SFPSM created a highly negative view of sexual activity.

118. *Tu seras mère*, p. 4.

119. *L'Enseignement se rapportant*, p. 7. Another young woman noted that she felt better prepared to face a life alone after having listened to Montreuil-Straus.

120. See Harsin, "Medical Ethics," pp. 73–74.

121. See "Les Préjugés," p. 211: "In this desire to confine the woman in ignorance concerning venereal diseases out of fear of disturbing contaminated

homes, there is an inexcusable lack of scientific and social courage among persons [*personnalités*] aware of the gravity of these infections . . . one asks oneself how certain doctors can still advocate silence in order to attenuate the consequences of contagion within the family." See also *Avant la maternité*, pp. 88–89, 98–99, and 119–20; "L'Oeuvre éducative," p. 1.; *Tu seras mère*, p. 18, and "Devons-nous donner?" p. 382. Finally, see *BSFPSM*, February and March–April 1924, when Montreuil-Straus confronted other members concerning this issue. Many other members of the SFPSM joined Montreuil-Straus in her battle against female contamination. See, for example, H. Gougerot, "Lutte antivénérienne dans les milieux sportifs et post-scolaires," *BSFPSM*, May 1920: 82–83.

122. Radical feminist Louise Bodin made much the same critique of medical practices in her article "La Syphilis" for the socialist-feminist review *Voix des femmes*, 19 June 1919. The "feminist" nature of Montreuil-Straus's efforts can perhaps be demonstrated by the support she received from well-known feminist groups in France. See "Une Oeuvre qu'il faut connaître: La Comité d'éducation féminine de la Société française de prophylaxie sanitaire et morale," *Droit des femmes*, February 1926; A. Montégudet, "L'Education sexuelle," *Bulletin des groupes féministes de l'enseignement laïque*, March 1925. Furthermore, bourgeois feminists had long used a strategy for social change similar to that employed by Montreuil-Straus. They, too, concealed the radical nature of their demands for civic identity by couching them in their demand for "social motherhood," the opportunity (through the right to vote) to "mother" the social house, clean up public health, and reaffirm family life.

123. Maier, *Recasting Bourgeois Europe*.

124. The role of the guidance counselor, as it was defined at the first Women's Vocational Guidance Congress, was "not to make a decision or settle on a choice, but simply to establish a link between the profession, the school and the family." See *Congrès*, p. 199. Delegates to the congress discussed the "corporatist nature" of vocational guidance and the need for "a perfect collaboration" between family, state, and vocational education counselor (pp. 38–39). Similarly, the CEF sought a cooperative relation between "expert," school, family, and individual child. See Montreuil-Straus, "Exposé," p. 14.

125. Justin Sicard de Plauzoles described social hygiene in this way: "Social hygiene is an economic science that has human capital or material as its object, the latter's production or reproduction (eugenics and puériculture), its conservation (hygiene, medicine and preventive assistance), its utilization (physical and vocational education), and its output (scientific organization of labor). Social hygiene is a normative sociology: let us think of man as an industrial material, or more precisely, as an animal machine. The hygienist, then, is the engineer of the human machine." Quoted in Donzelot, *Policing*, pp. 185–86.

126. See Yvonne Knibiehler and Catherine Fouquet, *La Femme et les médecins: Analyse historique* (Paris: Hachette, 1983), p. 236. For contemporary sources, see Justin Sicard de Plauzoles, "L'Education physique et l'éducation

prophylactique," *BSFPSM*, May 1920, and his "La Lutte contre les maladies sociales et pour la preservation de la race," *Principes d'hygiène sociale: Cours libre professé à la Sorbonne* (Paris: Editions Médicales, 1927). The social hygiene movement was international. See the speeches of the Swiss physician Robert Chable, and the Uruguayan physician Pauline Luisi at the Congrès international de propagande d'hygiène sociale et d'éducation prophylactique sanitaire and morale, Paris, 24–27 May 1923, *Compte rendu* (Paris: Comité national de propagande d'hygiène sociale et d'éducation prophylactique sanitaire et morale, n.d.).

127. The ministry was first headed by leading natalist Jules-Louis Bréton, who created a permanent Conseil supérieur de la natalité and a Comité nationale de propagande d'hygiène sociale et d'éducation prophylactique. According to William Schneider, although the latter was hampered by lack of funds until 1924, it "was a direct forerunner of the much more important National Social Hygiene Office." See *Quality and Quantity*, pp. 120–21.

128. See Knibiehler and Fouquet, *La Femme*, pp. 237–38, and Stewart, *Women, Work and the French State*, pp. 181–82. With the help of American funds, Adolphe Pinard created the Institut de puériculture in 1920 and the Ecole de puériculture in 1926 at the Faculté de médecine in Paris. For SFPSM support of *puériculture*, see "Communication de M. Péraire sur l'éducation prophylactique de la jeunesse, séance du premier juin," *BSFPSM*, June 1922: 112.

129. The natalist movement was a strong supporter of sexual education for both young men and women. See, for example, the "Troisième congrès de la natalité: Voeux sur la proposition de la section de l'enseignement," *Bulletin de l'Alliance nationale pour l'accroissement de la population française*, November 1921.

130. Thébaud, *Donner la vie*, p. 240. See also Knibiehler and Fouquet, *La Femme et les médecins*, pp. 240–41. Knibiehler also refers to a 1939 medical thesis by Suzanne Barot-Herding describing Baudelocque as a prime example of "masculine science dominating and rationally making use of feminine nature." This maternity clinic was imitated throughout Paris and the provinces.

131. See Corbin's addendum to *Les Filles de noce* in the English version, *Women for Hire: Prostitution and Sexuality in France after 1850* (Cambridge: Harvard University Press, 1990), pp. 338, 340. This new prophylactic, hygienized form of prostitution may explain the relative absence of the disorderly *femme isolée* in Montreuil-Straus's ideology of sexual education.

132. Moll-Weiss's postwar writings include: *La Pratique ménagère* (Paris: Colin, 1919); *La Vie domestique d'après guerre* (Paris: Rousseau et Cie, 1921); "La Taylorisation du travail domestique et ses consequences sociales," *Grande revue* 114 (1924): 635–48; and "Le Rôle de l'enseignement ménager dans la vie contemporaine," Institut de France, Academie des sciences morales et pol-

itiques, Séances et travaux, *Compte rendu,* November–December 1930: 478–89.

133. Depopulation was another big concern motivating interest in sexual education. See Germaine Montreuil-Straus, "Devons-nous donner," p. 381; Werebe, *L'Education sexuelle,* pp. 52–56.

134. *Une véritable chambre,* p. 5. Montreuil-Straus called depopulation "one of the most agonizing problems in contemporary France." See her *La Lutte contre la mortalité infantile: Hygiène social de l'enfance* (Paris: A. Poinat, 1926).

135. Henry Joly, "De l'extension du travail des femmes après la guerre," *Le Correspondant,* 10 January 1917, and 10 March 1917, p. 24. Joly was a major contributor to *Revue mondiale, Journal des débats,* and the conservative and nationalist *Libre parole* after the war. For other classic statements of this antinomy, see Doléris and Bouscatel, *Hygiène,* p. 22; Auguste Moll-Weiss, *La Vie domestique,* p. 140; Françoise Vitry, "L'Heure de la femme," *Renaissance politique,* 13 August–18 September 1921.

136. The social hygienist's vision of a perfectly engineered society, based on the normative intervention of the state and medical profession, had deep roots in French culture and can be traced back as far as Saint Simon and the early utopian socialists. Many of the members of *Redressement français* were called "neo-saintsimonians." See Maier, "Between Technocracy," and Kuisel, *Ernest Mercier,* pp. viii–ix.

137. Henri Gabelle, "La Place de la femme française après la guerre," *Renaissance politique,* 17 February 1917: 7. Gabelle wrote books on technical education in connection with the Conservatoire national des arts et métiers.

138. See Beale, "Advertising and the Politics of Public Persuasion," pp. 115–88, 125.

139. According to Charles Maier, Romier was the second-in-command at Redressement français, behind Ernest Mercier. See "Between Taylorism and Technocracy," pp. 57–58. Born in 1885, Romier was also a political editor of *Le Figaro* until 1927. Romier's books in this period included *Explication de notre temps* (Paris: B. Grasset, 1925), which was well-known among students of political science, and *La Promotion de la femme* (Paris: Hachette, 1930). An historian by training, Romier also wrote several works of religious history during the twenties. For more biographical information on Romier, see *Anthologie des essayistes français contemporaines* (Paris: Editions Kra, 1929); and Kuisel, *Mercier,* pp. 64–65, 144. On Romier as a social Catholic, see Beale, "Advertising and the Politics of Public Persuasion," pp. 229–36.

140. For my translations, I have relied on the 1928 English translation *Who Will Be Master? Europe or America?* (New York: Macaulay Company, 1928), p. 127. Romier wrote this book after a voyage to America in the mid-twenties.

141. Ibid., pp. 32, 38. According to Romier, postwar rationalizing trends resulted from the adoption of American technology, applied science, and

methods and values such as standardization, efficiency, and productivity. According to Beale, "Advertising," pp. 229–35, Romier made many of the same points at two speeches delivered at the eighteenth and nineteenth sessions of the Social Catholic *semaines sociales,* in 1926 and 1927. In 1927, the topic of the *semaine sociale* was "La Femme dans la société." On the anti-American response to technocratic reform, see Gagnon, "La Vie future."

142. Ibid., pp. 106–7.

143. Ibid., pp. 106–22. Romier felt that women had been slowly moving outside the home since the end of the nineteenth century, but that this process had been accelerated during the war. These changes in women's behavior were particularly acute among the younger generation, who "neither understand nor respect the old ways that seem only too absurd to them." With nostalgia, Romier described what he saw as women's old need for protection in the home: "Within this double frame, familial and social, woman was severely protected. . . . She found within these domestic and social limits, everything she was supposed to be in need of. . . . She lived in and for the home, guardian of the hearth."

144. Ibid., p. 117.

145. Beale, "Advertising," p. 125. See also Beale's statement that "Modernity was palatable only if it could be presented as a renovation of time-honored customs" (p. 118).

.146. For an excellent treatment of the way in which gender inequities organized the civil code, see Claire Moses, *French Feminism in the Nineteenth Century* (Albany: State University of New York Press, 1984), chap. 2. For a contemporary examination of the subject, see the feminist and lawyer Maria Vérone's *La Femme et la loi* (Paris: Larousse, 1920). See also Mary Poovey, "Covered but Not Bound: Caroline Norton and the 1857 Matrimonial Causes Act," *Uneven Developments: The Ideological Work of Gender in Mid-Victorian England* (Chicago: University of Chicago Press, 1988), for a thorough exploration of how the domestic ideal sustained property relations in nineteenth-century Victorian Britain.

Conclusion

1. Maurice Duval, "Une enquête sur la crise du mariage," *Renaissance politique,* 5 April 1924.

2. Jean-Jacques Becker and Serge Berstein, *Victoire et frustrations, 1914–1929,* vol. 12 of *Nouvelle histoire de la France contemporaine* (Paris: Seuil, 1990), p. 178.

3. Ibid., p. 411.

4. Richard Kuisel, *Ernest Mercier, French Technocrat* (Berkeley: University of California Press, 1967), pp. 64–65, 144.

5. On Vichy, see Robert Paxton, *Vichy France: Old Guard and New Order, 1940–1944* (New York: Columbia University Press, 1972), pp. 165–68; 352–57.

INDEX